African Ethics and Personal Names

Jonathan Musere

Christopher Odhiambo
Department of Literature, Moi University, Eldoret, Kenya

Ariko Publications
Los Angeles

Musere, Jonathan.
    African ethnics and personal names / Jonathan
Musere, Christopher Odhiambo. -- 1st ed.
    p. cm.
    Includes bibliographical references.
    LCCN: 98-94806
    ISBN: 0-9645969-1-1
                    T   89033
    1. Names, Personal--African--Dictionaries--English.
    2. Names, Personal--Africa--Dictionaries--English.
    3. African languages--Etymology--Names.
    I. Odhiambo, Christopher   II. Title.

    CS3080.A35M87 1999   929.4'096
                    QBI98-1771

Copyright © 1999
Ariko Publications

Ariko Publications
12335 Santa Monica Blvd., Suite 155
Los Angeles, CA 90025
United States of America

To
George William Bakibinga

Acknowledgments

Several sources have been involved in assembling this volume. My colleague Christopher Odhiambo of Moi University did a fine job at ferreting out names of the Embu, Kikuyu, Luo, Luyia, and the Maasai of Kenya. Peter J. Ibembe provided a lot of the names of the Soga of Uganda. Stephen B. Isabirye (Northern Arizona University) provided a large amount of pertinent information on the ethnic groups of Uganda. My communication with Edward Callary (American Name Society/ Northern Illinois University), Jan Daeleman (Filos. & Theol. College, Belgium), Adrian Koopman (University of Natal, South Africa), and Willy van Langendonck (International Council of Onomastic Sciences, Belgium) has variously profited this names' venture. Permission for use of the *Luganda-English Dictionary* by John D. Murphy and *Luganda Proverbs* by Ferdinand Walser was acquired from the publishers Catholic University of America Press and Dietrich Reimer Verlag respectively. Many thanks to all that each of the mentioned has done toward the construction of this title. Special and tremendous thanks to our father George William Bakibinga for the widespread assistance and committed positive influence, beyond words, that he has rendered the numerous people, much besides his family. This book is indeed dedicated to him.

Jonathan Musere
Culver City, California
November/ December 1998

*"Amagezi gandi ku mwoyo" ng'omufuuwi
w'engombe.*
"The idea lies on my mind" is like the (unplayed) tune
on the mind of the hornblower.
--A proverb of Ganda--

Ijambo rya mukuru litorwa mo igufa.
A whole bone gets extracted from just a word that is
of the elder.
--A proverb of the Hutu, Tutsi, and Twa--

Ab'oluganda bye bita; bikoonagana, ne bitayatika.
Kindred are the beer calabashes; they knock against
each other, but they do not crack.
--A proverb of Ganda--

Contents

Contents (cont.)

Introduction

This work dwells on examining over 4000 personal names used in the southern and equatorial African countries Angola, Botswana, Burundi, Central African Republic, Congo (Zaire), Republic of the Congo, Kenya, Lesotho, Malawi, Mozambique, Namibia, Rwanda, South Africa, Sudan, Swaziland, Tanzania, Uganda, Zambia, and Zimbabwe. Historical and cultural legacy backgrounds of ethnic groups involved and their countries of habitation are provided. Issues of language, history, culture, and ethnicity are part and parcel of the study and understanding of African names. With this premise in mind, concerted effort is involved here in the detail of cross referencing, and in the direct translation from oral and written ethnic sources. More names together with further onomastics data dwelling on central, eastern, and southern Africa are furnished elsewhere (Musere and Byakutaga 1998).

Many of the names appear for the first time in translated form. But the names presented do not necessarily originate from, nor are they necessarily exclusively confined to use by the ethnic groups to which they are assigned in the main listing. And to list and give background information to all the ethnic groups in the circumscribed African region would be an overambitious, endless, and burdensome task. Further, an ethnic group is a fluid other than static entity whose delimitation can be arbitrary. Many ethnic groups have even simply adapted their vision of themselves from what the agents of colonialism demarcated them as, or as these agents psychologically pictured the ethnics as. The idea of European nationhood that was employed, did not fit in the reality of African ethnicity. Ethnic groups also vary in their degree of conservativeness, but all have undergone transformation through their precolonial, colonial, and postcolonial histories. Some of the African names, as will be implied throughout this text, may not therefore have the significance they had in the past.

A name may function to associate one with the prevailing occupation and implements in one's home environment. A name can establish one as a member of, an associate of, or relation of a family or occupational class. A personal name can be a reference to the name of the locality one lives in or to names of prevailing geographical phenomena in the area. Names depict past and present modes of production and living in an area. They also commemorate major occurrences or traditions at the time of the birth of the children that are given the names. It is common for the names to serve as descriptions of either the physical, or the physiological, or the behavioral characteristics of the newborns that are named. Many names allude to the mode of birth (such as whether smooth or difficult) of those named, the number of children in the family, and the progeny sequence of birth. Naming also involves corroborating the spiritual or religious backdrop of either the newborn or its family.

1

Many of the names even involve opinion of negative or positive bearing either directed to neighbors, or to kin including to the mother orto the father, or to enemies, or to the newborn itself, or even to ancestral spirits and Gods. Though by and large, one of or both of the parents have precedence in the naming, in many societies the extended family has tremendous influence in this process that can involve a lot of discussion. There are cases for example where the combination of the mother, the traditional midwife (during and after the pregnancy and delivery of the child) and the child's paternal grandmother has exclusive powers in the naming. So one can imagine why in many African societies, there is a wealth of names that openly involve negative and even derogatory remarks about one or both of the parents. The form a name takes will then significantly depend on the relation in the family system that gives the newborn the name.

Given that several African societies did not have written works prior to the nineteenth and twentieth centuries, names have served as cultural history maps that depict milestone events in a family's history, as well as depict the needs, values, and concerns of Africans in the past and the present. In a non-literate society devoid of records in writing, event names serve as a recording system, and it is common among such people to refer to an event whenever one asks for their dates of birth, the names functioning as birth certificates (Mohome 1972: 173). And in a technologically backward society, as is represented in African traditional settings, peoples' livelihood is directly affected by the fluctuations in nature which in turn affect peoples' emotional states. Several names hence reflect births that coincide with earthquakes, thunderstorms, hailstorms, locust invasions, epidemics, floods, and famines. Names, on the other hand, can reflect welcome circumstances like rainfall, bountiful harvests, and cattle proliferation.

That African societies are predominantly communalistic and exogamous, calls forth for social harmony between neighbors, kin, spouses, and in-laws. A multitude of African names are seen to express social harmony, social disharmony, concern and wonder over such relationships, pleas or hope for reconciliation, and resignation or regret over the social progress. Examples include names that translate to "they (i.e. neighbors or in-laws) are killers," "they hate me," "bring back the bride dowry," "they despise me," "they are stupid," "they conspire against me," "they love me," "they are ungrateful," "of words," "I laugh with them," "peace," "love," "hope," "she (i.e. the mother of this child) is a queen," "joy," "gratitude," "help me," "welcome me," "accept me," "console me," "I am neglected," "court case," "I am ridiculed," "the hated one," and "gossip."

Africans are quite cautious in what they say and how they deal with others, such that the messages (more so the negative ones) in such names tend to be conveyed in a roundabout fashion. The commonplace "they" (and "them") in African names exemplifies this indirectness, but it can imply suspicion. In the literary sense of "they," nobody in particular is being pinpointed as the agent, so the name translates to a generalization which offers the neighbors or kin something to think about, or offers them the realization that the namer is aware of the malice and ill will directed to his family. Most of the African names that refer to neighbors as killers are in reference to killing in remote ways such as witchcraft or suspected poisoning, other than to the physical act itself. Despite the use of "they," the ones to whom the namer is directing the message almost always know.

It may be surprising that a sizable number of African names are either derogatory, "non-human," or depict pessimism. Such names tend to be given to children that are critically sick, that are born to a family that has had many deaths, that are not pleasing in appearance, or whose birth coincides with an occurrence of disaster or evil. They include such names as "hyena," "pig," "large head," "large stomach," "skunk," "he (or they) will die tomorrow," "dog," "grass," "hornbill," "the dead one," "in the death hut," and "one more night." Fundamentally, children born after their preceding siblings died are given death-related names in memory of the deceased. Such names can also portray indignation on the part of the parents. However, by and large, there is a "protective" rationale (laden with superstition) behind the names that is intended to be for the good of the child given such a name.

Africans are traditionally very religious in character, believing in the invisible and remote interplay of the forces of good and evil. In giving a child a derogatory name, there is the belief that the forces of evil, fate, or death that are hitting on and causing the child to be so, will be tricked into backing off through believing that the family does not want the child and actually wishes evil on it. The belief then is that if the family gives the child a derogatory or pessimism laden name, the negating forces will become convinced that the family of the child will itself easily carry out the malice that these satanic forces would have done. John Middleton's explanation on the Lugbara is different, but the rationale behind it is similar (1957: 41).

The giving of names associated with death reflects a pessimism rather than any morbid fear of death, but in addition provides an assurance and protection against death. Death comes from God. There is the feeling that by drawing attention to the number of deaths that have occurred in a particular family God may be persuaded to spare the family in the future and to turn his attentions to other families. By bringing the fear into the open, it is dissipated or at least lessened.

And T.O. Beidelman (1974: 289) puts forward an explanation on the Kaguru, as he contrasts African with European philosophy.

Some names reveal valued personal attributes, either attained or hoped for, but what is striking, when contrasted with our own society, is the large number of names associated with negative qualities and experiences. To many of us, it may seem strange that one would bear a name which constantly recalled unpleasant happenings that one would have thought were best put out of mind. Kaguru, however, see one of the best protections against adversity in an emphasis of it. Conversely, speaking of good fortune may lead one to lose it. Thus, it is much more likely to find Kaguru disparaging their children (especially to strangers) and emphasizing their own poverty and difficulties. Kaguru say that if the dead were to hear children praised, they would strive all the more to draw them back into the land of the dead. Similarly, boasting of one's children or wealth is likely to prompt a witch or sorcerer to harm them out of envy. There is an onomastic emphasis upon negative qualities and events by Kaguru because Kaguru want to outwit misfortune and secure the best for themselves. If one is to strive to be well, one must do so un-obtrusively; the person who boasts with his name must be strong indeed to avert possible danger.

The traditional reasoning of the *Sotho* is along similar lines (Ashton 1952: 32-33).

There are...cases in which special names are given to children. ...after a stillborn child or the death of a child before weaning. The death of these children is believed to be due to sorcery, so that apart from the usual anti-sorcery precautions, an attempt is made to safeguard the next child born by making a show of neglecting it in the hope of lulling the sorcerer's vigilance. It is kept dirty and unkempt, its head is incompletely shaved, leaving a small tuft of hair (hlotho) at the back, which is not removed until initiation, and, as a final of indifference, it is given an unpleasant name, such as *Ntja* (dog), *Moselantja* (dog's tail), *Tsoene* (monkey), *Makhokolotsa* (rubbish) or *Masepa* (human excrement).

Many that were originally given names depicting negativism have in-deed grown up to be very productive and remarkable people. There is the connected belief that the child given a negatively laden name will struggle hard, as it grows, to correct it's negative image portrayed in the name. Names therefore can serve to "help a person grow" and many African societies encourage children to retain their birth names, negative or otherwise, throughout their lives. In some African societies, however, pessimism-protective names are bestowed on children only temporarily. Further, names denoting pessimism appear to have been more common in the past when infection and infantile rates were high. A lot of such names may have emanated from the prevalence of a relatively high mortality rate which called forth for a system of triage in which the healthy and strong are blatantly differentiated from the weak and ailing. Several African names reflecting alarmingly sick children, pessimism, and high mortality in the family, have words like "death," "soil," "clay," or "ground" attached to them.

In some instances a name taken from a neighboring ethnic group can have derogatory or pessimism connotations, more so if the relations with that ethnic group are unfavorable. However, in most cases when parents name their child names like *Mutwa* or *Mututsi*, the implication is that the child either looks like those ethnics, or that the parents admire those ethnics, or that the family is getting on well with those ethnics, or that the family has recently been involved in friendly negotiation with such ethnics, or that the family wishes to be assimilated into the ethnic group. In theory, names of an ethnic group are not given to children of the same group since that would be superfluous. In reality, however, there are many instances whereby people take on the name of their very own ethnic identity. That can be because many ethnic titles have more than one meaning attached to them. Furthermore, an external ethnic group can nickname one by his or her ethnic identity. In essence, therefore, a person carrying an ethnic identity title as his or her name may or may not belong to the same ethnic group, although the name prevailingly implies some association with the same group. It is also important to bear in mind that many of the names of ethnic groups developed out of associating a category of people with a named occupation or a trade. The categories that grew in population and became powerful would still maintain such names as they assimilated neighboring groups.

Names with the same basic meaning, can still have varying interpretations. Hence a personal name that translates to "alligator" or "crocodile" may be a derogatory name in one society, but one of virtue and strength in another. Among the Sotho, the name *Polo* (=alligator) is a derogatory name given to infants whose previously born siblings died or were still born. Among the Baganda, the name *Kigoonya* (=crocodile/ in the manner of a crocodile) does not appear to be related to derogation, and crocodiles have been associated with immense, and even supernatural power. Indeed animals are commonly used in Africa as totems for clan family identification. So whereas in parts of Africa, animals like the dog, the jackal, and the hyena may symbolize evil, misfortune or death, in other parts of the continent they serve as highly respected family identity emblems and people are named after them.

Both the place and mode of birth are common threads in African names. A child's name may describe it as having been the product of a pregnancy that was smooth, that was difficult, that was lengthy, that was long awaited, that cemented relations, that was premature, or that came as a surprise. Though the preferred place of delivery was the mother's home or her parent's home, more so in the traditional past, it was not unusual for women to give birth while on a journey, at a stranger's home, or while in the field. The children of such births are given such names as translate to "the traveler," "in the bush," "on the road," "journey," and "in the plain."

Several categories of African births are followed by ritual, fear, or suspicion. Twins prevailingly treated as special beings, though for

Introduction

whom it is "a must" to carry out cleansing rituals in the proper way. The birth of twins is hence a magnificent happening surrounded with a mix of joy, suspicion, and sacredness. Particular names, depending on which gender they are for, are given to twins as well as to those that precede or follow twins. Those whose birth follows that of twin siblings generally symbolize a cleansing and detachment from the sacredness and rigor of ritual attached to the twins that were previously born. The category of children born feet first and those born with visible teeth is another one to consider. These, depending on which society, are associated with wonderment, with conveying of evil, or with witchcraft. In the past, some societies such as the Kikuyu and the Ganda executed by burning or strangling, those born feet first. The Ganda believed that if a child born feet fast was left to grow, it would eventually become a thief. After strangulation, the child was buried at the crossroads. Many societies consider those born with visible teeth as having supernatural powers and such children are treated with special care. Among the Nandi, children who cried while in their mother's womb, those born feet first, and those born with teeth were buried alive in cow-dung (Hollis 1969: 68). Even those born blind, born badly deformed, or born out of wedlock, were done away with (Hollis 1969: 68).

The names given to youth subjected to initiation (such as circumcision, graduation to womanhood or manhood, and entry into a higher level age-group), tend to be temporary. It is commonly the elders who conduct the rituals and ceremonies that become known by names associated with initiation duties. Youth initiation names can reflect an attribute or quality of some kind such as speed, shooting accuracy, knowledge, and agility. They can also reflect the numerical order in which one is initiated, and it is prestigious to be the first in line.

An ideal African family is recognized as the one in which the ratio of male to female children is about equal. There is concern when this balance is not met. Most African societies are patrilineal, and if the female children far outnumber the male ones, there will be concern about inheritance and the perpetration of the father's descent and the family name. Many African names reflect the sequence of birth, as well as pinpoint those whose older siblings are either all male or all female. Since human numbers were important in precapitalist African societies (given the high infection and mortality rates, the labor intensive economies, as well as high labor intensive defense and conquest that involved low-level technology). Many names, such as those that translate to "I surpassed" and "surplus," serve to celebrate the large family.

Theoretically, there would not be differentiation between what is a female and what is a male name. There are instances when the same name (or one with the same content or meaning), is regarded as female in one ethnic group and male in another, and bestowed on both genders in another group. Many names of Goddesses are also used, as personal names, by males (though the other way round is less common). However, many African words (or names) are prefixed so as to specify gender allocation. Names allotted prefixes "Mma-," "Nyina-," "Nyinawa-," "Nyira-," and "Ina-" which theoretically translate to "mother of" or the "the mother," (and "Muka-" translating to "the spouse of" or "the spouse") also have the function of specifying the gender, associating a female with something (such as an occupation, an activity, or a residence) or someone (usually a male relation or ancestor), as well as serving as honorific gestures to females regardless of how old the female is. This stems from African society traditionally measuring the worth of a female in terms of becoming married, having many children, and establishing a commendable home. Prefixes like "No-" and "Na-" found in countless female names of the Bantu groups appear to be versions (or corrupted versions of) "mother of" or "the mother."

Similarly, names with male identification prefixes such as "Ishe-," "Ise-," and "Isa-," (translating to "father of" or "the father") allude to the traditionally recognized worth of a male. Names with such prefixes are also commonly given to children whose status is relatively high up in the extended family hierarchy, and children of (or affiliated with) a privileged and powered social group. This system of naming may have partly emanated from the African tradition of holding people, more so the elders, in high esteem. It is prevailingly taboo and a gesture of disrespect to refer to someone higher in the social hierarchy by his or her name. Many (parents) are hence referred to as "the father or mother of so and so" in normal speech, and many are hardly known by their birth names. It should be borne in mind that approximately 50% composition of the African nation populations south of the Sahara is less than 20 years of age.

Such prefixes (or pre-prefixes) as "Sse-" and "Se-" (connoting magnitude, power, or numerical strength) serve to reinforce the esteem given to a name. These prefixes may even be corrupted versions of "Ishe-," "Ise-," and "Isa-" mentioned above. A child can also simply be named after an ancestor or relation of high prestige with such a name. There are countless other signifying prefixes in African names and such are determined by the culture and language of the ethnic group.

Some names are derived from proverbs, words of wisdom, or other forms of expression. These offer succinct lessons and opinions such as on culture and tradition, courage, friendship, marriage, morality and ethics, religion, family, giving birth and offspring, discipline, thrift, industriousness, judiciousness, resourcefulness, appreciation, humility, respect, anger, pain, remorse, patience, malice, hope, strategy, protection, responsibility to children and the elderly, response to and advice for those in both the higher and the lower social hierarchy, possessiveness, playing and having fun, wit, sarcasm, and satire. The parents may then give a child a name that has an aphoristic meaning relating to the birth of the child or other circumstances during that period of time. Although several African names have aphoristic meanings, this issue has not been adequately examined in the academic circles, so warrants more vigorous investigation. It is hoped that other works (Musere and Byakutaga 1998; Musere 1998: 73-79; Musere 1997: 89-97) will further stimulate exploration into this vastly neglected field. The main listing in this text details several proverbial names.

Primary Country Residences of the Ethnics Mentioned

Angola: *Kongo, Luba, Ovimbundu, Yaka.*
Botswana: *Shona.*
Burundi: *Hutu, Tutsi, Twa.*
Central African Republic: *Gombe (Ngombe), Kongo, Ngbandi.*
Congo (Zaire): *Bolia, Bushong, Gombe (Ngombe), Hemba, Hindo, Hutu, Kakwa, Kanyok, Kongo, Luba, Lugbara, Luwa, Madi, Mongo, Ngbandi, Ngwi, Ntomba, Nuer, Sanga, Songye, Tabwa, Tetela, Topoke, Tutsi, Twa, Yaka, Yombe.*
Congo Republic: *Gombe (Ngombe), Kongo.*
Kenya: *Elgeyo, Embu, Hanga, Isukha, Iteso, Kikuyu, Luo, Maasai, Nandi, Luyia, Suk, Swahili, Syan, Taturu, Taveta, Tsotso, Tuken, Turkana.*
Lesotho: *Sotho, Zulu.*
Mozambique: *Shona.*
Rwanda: *Hutu, Kiga, Tutsi, Twa.*
South Africa: *Shona, Sotho, Zulu.*
Sudan: *Jie, Kakwa, Karamojong, Madi, Nuer.*
Tanzania: *Hutu, Luo, Maasai, Ndali, Nyakyusa, Nyamwezi, Pare, Swahili, Tutsi, Zaramo.*
Uganda: *Acholi, Ganda, Gisu, Hutu, Iteso, Jie, Jopadhola, Kakwa, Karamojong, Kiga, Konjo, Langi, Lugbara, Luo, Luyia, Madi, Nuer, Nyankore, Nyole, Nyoro, Samia, Soga, Toro, Tutsi, Twa.*
Zambia: *Hemba, Luba, Sanga, Shona, Tabwa.*
Zimbabwe: *Shona, Zezuru (Wazezuru).*

The Ethnics

Acholi

The *Acholi/ Acoli* (sing./ pl.) ethnics are an amalgamation of several ethnic and clan lineages and their area of habitation in a large and sparsely populated expanse of northern Uganda (and into southern Sudan) is also referred to as Acholi. These agropastoralists are bordered by the *Langi* and *Nyoro* to the south, the *Karamojong* to the east, and the *Madi, Alur,* and *Lugbara* to the west. The Acholi comprise 4.4% (0.88 million people) of Uganda's population, some live in Sudan, and the language spoken (*Acholi*) is of Sudanic Luo structure. Some assert that the Acholi group is a product of intermarriages between the *Luo* (River-Lake Nilotes) and the *Madi.* Like other Sudanic-Luo ethnics, the Acholi origins are traced to Rumbek in southern Sudan which renders them related to the *Nuer* and *Dinka.* Acholi legend asserts that their furthest ancestor was named *Luo,* he had no human parents so it is presumed that *Jok* (God) was his father and his mother was Earth. Luo's son *Jipiti* had a daughter named *Kilak.* There is an instance when Kilak got lost in the bush, after which she emerged with a son *Labongo* who was believed to be fathered by the devil *Lubanga* (or *Lubaya*). Labongo was said to be endowed with supernatural and magical powers, he was born with feathers in his hair and bells around his ankles and wrists, and he was fond of dancing around with his jingling bells. Labongo drove his ax into the ground and out emerged those that would be the chiefs of the many Luo groups.

The Acholi economy of mixed farming includes the keeping of cattle, goats, sheep, and fowls; and the cultivating of sorghum, millet, sesame, and beans. In addition, the Acholi are skilled hunters and trappers. Except for a few minor differences, the Acholi social set up is the same as that of the Langi, and includes an age group system, and a patrilineal clan system that is exogamous. A lot of Acholi personal names are used by the Langi. The Acholi age-set system differed from that of related Sudanic-Luo and Sudanic-Hamitic ethnics in that it involved the mobilization of youth between the ages of 15 and 20 for war. An Acholi chief (*rwot*) was often a hereditary leader, a kind of mini-king to whom a number of villages owed allegiance. Acholi villages were relatively large, most of them were located on hilltops or elevated ground, and they were often surrounded by stockades. Just like those of the Langi, Acholi villages were created to also serve as defense mechanisms. Though the Acholiland village was important and econo-, mically self sufficient, it did not have the significance it had in the Langi sociopolitical set up.

That many villages were increasingly coming under the same *rwot*, would indicate that a centralized political system similar to southward states such as of the *Ganda,* the *Nyankore,* the *Nyoro,* and the *Toro* was evolving. Some even assert that the Acholi already had a centralized system, even though the colonial machinery preferred to rank this society as stateless. Acholi society possessed regalia such as drums and spears. Larger chiefdoms such as *Payera* and *Padibe* were larger and better organized that some of the smaller precolonial Bantu kingdoms to the south. The second half nineteenth century episode of colonial penetration into Acholiland, coupled with an intense huntdown for slaves and ivory by Sudanese, Arabs and Europeans, may have brought an end to the evolving of Acholi states towards full centralization. Two major agents of Anglo-Egyptian imperialist aggression, Samuel Baker and Emin Pasha, testify to the devastation that involved decimation of a well populated cattle and the human population, the disruption of a friendly and peaceful people, the opportunistic disease ravages (such as sleeping sickness), and the regression of the land into a wilderness. The impact was profound even though the East African Slave Trade was short-lived compared to that of West Africa. It cropped up, paradoxically, at the time the trade in West Africa was dying down. Many of the East African enslaved were shipped to islands in the Indian Ocean to work on plantations.

The Acholi traditionally believed in a goodly Supreme Being (Jok) and the devil, evil or death (Lubanga). Jok had a shrine (*abila*), but Lubanga was degraded in various ways with everything bad attributed to him. But when white missionaries came, they (paradoxically) forced the people to take on the concept of Lubanga as the Supreme Being. Children were named when three or four days old at the mother's house, following the mother's confinement in the hut during which time she and her newborn are fed on special food for recuperating purposes and for protection against evil influences. On the naming day, a delegation of maternal and paternal relatives led by an old woman who acted as a midwife came to the house. The old woman would suggest a name for the child. There was no fixed criteria for the old woman deciding which name to pick, but if the child was born under circumstances considered atypical or unfavorable (such as during famine, or a child whose older siblings had died, or a birth during a time of friction in the family, or a baby born with more than five fingers), the mother's choice of name was given preference and it depicted some such circumstance. Twin births were considered the most atypical, and all abnormal births were said to be under the powerful influence of *Jok*. However, a mother who became convinced that her child's deformity was too severe for her child to lead a healthy and productive life, would drop the child in a river as if accidentally. The severely deformed who got to grow up were not killed or abused later in life, for fear of *Jok's* wrath. All ceremonies concerning normal births were not directed to *Jok*. The mother would thereafter the naming ceremonies of her first child be referred to as "the mother of..." other than by her birth name, now that she was fully accepted in her husband's clan. The mother of a child called Olanya would henceforth be referred to as *min Olanya* (mother *Olanya*). Indeed in most African societies it is a form of dis-respect as well as taboo to refer to an elder or one of a higher age and social class by his or her birth names. It is then common in many African societies for the name of one in reference to his or her child to take precedence when one becomes a mother or father.

Alur

The Alur (sing./ pl.) ethnics are like the Acholi, an amalgamation of several ethnic and clan lineages. Their area of habitation along the northeastern banks of Lake Mobutu (also known as Lake Muttanzige and Lake Albert) includes a part of northwestern Uganda, and includes a portion of Eastern Zaire across the border with Uganda. These Sudanic-Luo agropastoralists are bordered by the related *Jonam* ("lakeside people") and the Langi to the east, the Nyoro to the south, and the *Lugbara* to the north. The Alur number approximately 1 million people. Their numbers seem to have grown faster than those of their neighbors, this attributed to their high birth rate, to their system of family ownership alongside communal policy, to the migration of many non-Alur neighbors into neighboring Congo (Zaire) that allows Alur to expand more easily, and to deliberate ventures on the part of the Alur to assimilate neighboring ethnics as well as expand into neighboring territory. Among others, the Alur intermarried with the Sudanic Madi, the *Lendu*, the *Okebu*, the *Nyai*, the *Bendi*, and the *Bira*. Legend traces Alur origins from the direct descendent of God--King *Atira*. Atira was succeeded by his son *Otira* who was later succeeded by his son *Opobo*. When Opobo died, three sons *Tiful*, *Nyapir*, and *Labongo* vied for power. One day Nyapir borrowed Labongo's spear for the intention of spearing an elephant. Nyapir speared an elephant in the hunting process, but the injured elephant got away with the spear lodged in its skin. Upon hearing about the inadvertent loss of his spear, Labongo annoyingly insisted that he get his spear back, and he refused Nyapir's offers of a substitute spear. Nyapir decided to attempt to track down the elephant, and in the process found himself in a cool and beautiful land after having crossed a large river. While wandering into this land he encountered an elderly woman who took him to a place where among other spears, Nyapir recognized his brother's spear. Nyapir retrieved the spear, and along with a wondrous bead that the old woman gave him, he headed for home. There he gathered his brothers and some other kin together, and he presented the spear. All were amazed at Nyapir's story, especially regarding the bead. But while it was being passed around, one of Labongo's infant children accidentally swallowed the spear. Nyapir sought to exact revenge by demanding that he get his bead back from Labongo, and he refused any possible substitutes. Labongo handed the infant over to Nyapir to open and take out the bead. In the process, Nyapir killed the child and retrieved the bead. The brothers got annoyed at the act so they decided to separate.

Nyapir's accounts of a wonderful land beyond the river had so impressed Tiful that he moved his followers that included the Lendu and the Okebu to the highlands to the west and into Congo (Zaire). Nyapir followed Tiful, and in the process established his son *Dosha* as the ruler of Pakwach. Nyapir settled permanently in the West Nile highlands where the environment was better suited for cattle. This Alur legend of the spear is said to be a manifestation of the struggle between two brothers over royal power. Following the brothers separating they became intermingled with a variety of groups.

Alur food production activity includes the cultivation of millet, sorghum, cassava, sesame, potatoes, and beans; and the keeping of goats, chicken, cattle, and sheep. Cash crops include cotton and coffee. The Alur village consisted of a dozen huts and was the most important social and political unit. Additional huts served as food grain stores and shelters in which household chores were performed. The village was often inhabited by one extended patrilineal family. Should the family grow bigger, the original village was not extended, and instead some of the members were encouraged to start another settlement nearby. Like the related Acholi, a given number of villages were entrusted to the care of one chief. The chief organized hunting trips, ensured that village taboos and customs were adhered to, and acted as mediator when complex matters or disputes arose. The quest by a stranger wanting to acquire land had to meet with his permission. Though acquisition of land was hereditary, the son able to succeed his father upon death, there was an overlapping system of communalism. A family could acquire as much available land as possible as long as the land was kept in use. Should the land be abandoned or become underutilized, it would revert back to the chief who would then redistribute it to demanding families.

The Supreme Being is *Rubanga*, and other Gods include *Rukidi, Rateng, Riba (Kakonda)*, and *Rut*. The names Rubanga, Kakonda and Rukidi were borrowed from the Nyoro neighbors. Religious rituals were mediated by a diviner (*Ajoga, Julam Bira*, or *Jolam Wara*) whenever misfortune struck. The misfortunes and diseases were believed to be caused by spiritual entities and dead ancestors that were not being honored enough with beer, food, meat, or other forms of sacrifice. Not recognizing and attending to their needs would cause the afflictions to spread in the population. Misfortune was also said to emanate from evil spirits, and from evil, sorcery manipulating persons. The most important ceremony among the Alur was rainmaking and it involved goat sacrifices and the singing of songs to a God.

Bolia and Ntomba

These are ethnics of Bantu ethnolinguistic background that primarily reside in Western Congo (Zaire) east of the Republic of the Congo. Their cultures and languages are in the class of those of the *Mongo* who occupy the forests of the Congo Basin. *Bolia* migration from *Mandombe* (*Bondombe*) to their present river and forest habitat in the fifteenth century appears to have been prompted by either over-population or pressures from their neighbors. The Bolia are presumed to have originally been patrilineal, but the influence of the *Nsese* mat-rilineal people in what became the new Bolia environment caused them to shift to a system of dual descent. The *Ntomba* living in the vicinities of Lake *Tumba* lying north of Lake *Mai Ndombe*, and in the Lake Mai Ndombe environs, were renowned for their skilled special-ization in fishing, and they served as related allies of the Bolia.

The Bolia people, characterized as warriors, were by the late nine-teenth the domineering and most famed group in the vicinity of Lake Mai Ndombe in the Congo River Central Basin. The Bolia kingdom was surrounded by chiefdoms such as of the Nsese and Ntomba. The Bolia in turn founded their chiefdoms by conquest and assimilation. The king or chief was referred to as *nkum/ nkumu* and the royalty involved a sp-ecial place of residence, specific privileges and taboos, a string of sy-mbols and emblems, and the ascription of honorific titles to dig-nitaries of his household (Vansina 1990: 120). The close association of political structure with divine kingship and the emblems of it is a sin-gular characteristic of the Bolia amongst Central African kingdoms. As-cension to kingship was not a simple matter of automatic succession derived from a limited number of candidates, but a result of a complex series of ritual examinations, cleansing rituals, and dream revelations. Spirits were hence recognized as the major players in the choice of king. Contrariwise, territorial and court offices were basically attained along patrilineal descent lines (Vansina 1968: 99-102).

Bushong

The name *Bushong* (*Bushongo*) means "People of the Throwing Knife." They are of Bantu ethnolinguistic background, and they are related to the *Mongo* and the *Tetela*. They live in south central Congo (Zaire), part of which territory is known as *Kasai*. One unique char-acteristic of the Bushong was their practice of monogamy, though at times this was not strictly adhered to. Three centuries ago they sub-jugated older settlements in Central Congo (Zaire) and established *nkumu* institutional chiefdoms similar to those of the Bolia and Ntomba, and expanded the *Kuba* Kingdom. The Bushong and the *Lele* (*Leele*) trace their origin to an ancestor named *Woot*.

When the Kuba settled in their present day territory around 1600, they already embraced a centralized political system. The villages were either built around one section of a matrilineage, or groupings of several sections of several different clan. The chiefdom embraced one to several villages whose leader was a chief chosen from the royal clan by a group of councilors themselves elected by a group of specified "founding clans." The founding clan council wielded most of the authority and the chief could be deposed. The Bushong altered the residing political structure including diminishing the powers of the council of the founding clans. In granting the Bushong chief (king) powers over life and death, it was declared that he could not be removed and that the junior branch of the royal clan was excluded from succession (Vansina 1968: 119).

The Bushong are believed to have initially gained their wealth from fishing, but in the seventeenth century they took on corn and tobacco growing which added to their wealth. The healthy economy allowed for the Kuba kingdom to expand and involve a growing number of artisans and aristocrats. The Kuba began to control major trade routes through sections of Central Africa as they exported luxury cloth and ivory, and imported salt, copper, beads, and slaves. The kingdom reached its pinnacle in the eighteenth century, and the burgeoning trade went on until well into the colonial times.

But the friction in the Kuba kingdom that involved other groups competing for dominance rendered the Bushong system vulnerable. Around 1630 the *Pyang* attacked and almost destroyed the Kuba kingdom. The innovations instituted, involved alteration of Bushong culture and political structure. The period of quietude and opulence followed soon after, until the nineteenth century invasions by *Lulua* neighbors and revolts from the eastern chiefdoms, culminating in civil war by 1900. The later traditional political structure of the Bushong is characterized by a proliferation of titles and number of councils, and a unique set of courts that helps control excessive royal authority (Vansina 1968: 119).

Most of the Kuba languages are of the Bushong group. The Kuba traditional way of living involves agriculture, fishing, and hunting. Towards the end of the seventeenth century, cassava had replaced yam as the major staple. Cassava has higher yield and storage longevity properties. Crops still grown include corn, tobacco, peanuts, beans, and millet. Kuba art and culture is one of the oldest and most impressive in Africa. This includes wooden sculpture (including statues of the kings), initiation masks, effigy cup (such as depicting revered ancestors), and finely embroidered raffia cloth. The Kuba were renowned iron forgers, and it is from their throwing knife (the *shongo*) that the ruling group, the Bushong, derived its name.

Embu (See Kikuyu)

Ganda

The *Ganda* (sing./ pl.) ethnics are commonly referred to as *Baganda* (pl.), and a single one of them referred to as a *Muganda*. The predominantly agricultural territory of the Baganda (referred to as Buganda) lies on the north and northwestern shores of Lake Victoria and occupies a quarter of Uganda's land mass. The Baganda comprise

16.2% (3.24 million people) of Uganda's population, and the language used (*Luganda*) is mostly of Bantu structure. A singular feature of Luganda is the numerous geminate consonants in the words.

Various accounts of foreign arrivals into Buganda during the nineteenth and early twentieth century singled out this domineering kingdom-state as excellently organized and more impressive than the others they had seen (Churchill 1908: 86-87; Mamdani 1976: 33). The national name Uganda is adapted from the territorial name Buganda, and prior to the establishment of the British protectorate territory of Uganda in 1894, the names Uganda and Buganda were synonymous partly as a result of foreigners either mispronouncing or inadequately adapting to the word "Buganda." Compared to many other parts of Africa, there is an abundance of literature on Buganda that continues to grow given the fascination for this entity. Clan and royal court historians meticulously preserved their traditions and historical accounts. Though the kingdoms and kings of Uganda such as Ankole, Buganda, Bunyoro, Busoga, Toro were re-established in 1993 following having been dissolved twenty five years earlier for the sake of national unity, they are now more of a ceremonial token of honor and custom to feed the nostalgia.

The Buganda (or *Kiganda*) system had the king (*Kabaka*) at the top of the political hierarchy and beneath him were powerful hereditary clan chiefs (*bataka*). From the eighteenth century, so as to counter the burgeoning power of the *bataka*, the *Kabaka* began to appoint territorial chiefs (*bakungu*) basing them on merit more than societal status. There was conflict with the *bataka*, but the result was a decline of the aristocratic hereditary clan model, and the emergence of a civil servant controlled system tending toward a classless society. Even those that were war captives would now take up high office. To further strengthen his civil power, the Kabaka appointed personal stewards (*batongole*), a military commander (*Mujaasi*), and an admiral (*Gabunga*). Since the seventeenth century, military service had been mandatory for all Baganda, and they would be drummed up when needed.

Anglo militarists like Henry Stanley, display amazement at the speed, order and efficiency by which Baganda commanders would mobilize their military and naval forces at short notice. The canoe builders were highly experienced, the intelligence system quite discerning, and the military campaigns carried out with extreme caution such as prior knowledge of the seasons and the availability of food supplies before setting out for war (Kiwanuka 1972: 14). Buganda's power became feared even beyond the African Great Lakes area. The Baganda, for the most part, eventually became collaborators with the victorious British during the era of colonialism. This followed a bloody and macabre drama between 1880 and 1900 in which Baganda variably allied to French Catholics, British Protestants, Arab Muslims, and indigenous Traditionalists engaged in intense religious and political conflict.

Buganda was a kingdom for centuries. The factors that favored Buganda's rise to prominence include her remote location in interior Africa encouraged by her being surrounded by monumental landforms such as high mountains and East African Rift Valley faults (to the east and west), lengthy rivers, massive lakes, dense equatorial forest (to the west), formidable resistors (such as the Karamojong, Masai, and Nandi) to colonial entry and establishment (to the east), and swampy environment (to the north). This allowed for uninterrupted development and peaceful coexistence. The consistent equatorial rainfall and sunshine (65-75 degrees fahrenheit) all year round on a fertile soil profile allowed for ample crop, livestock, forestry, and fish supplies to nourish a healthy population. Fruitful trading with less privileged neighbors became enhanced and commonplace in an atmosphere of organized and peaceful coexistence.

The laws governing customary and civic duties were consistently upheld by a regal and civil system that would crush any semblance of breaching at a whim. The massive Lake Victoria served not only as a military buffer zone and grounds for establishing an efficient naval fleet, but also one that halted movements of migrants moving south. Buganda then became a conglomerating place for a diversity of ethnics whose talents would be exploited here. A growing Buganda population translated to a numerical advantage over neighbors, an advantage so critical to political and military power in the past. Further, Buganda has an impressive array of hills such as in Kampala that have served for military strategy.

And during the nineteenth century, Anglo-Egyptian, Arab-Islam, and Sudanese colonialist and commercialist forces increased their quest for slaves and ivory in parts of East and Central Africa. Though the slavery and slave trade came late to East Africa and did not take on the dimensions of that of West Africa, it served to disrupt many of Buganda's powerful neighbors to the north and west, this further allowing for Buganda to develop peacefully and also further encroach on weakened neighbors. The (Nyoro) rulers of Bunyoro to which Buganda had been tributary to, even took on competing with the foreign commercialists for the control of ivory resources following the intensified demand in Europe, and in view of the abundance of elephants in present day northern Uganda. The Ganda made frequent raids on the Soga living to the immediate east of Buganda and even ruled portions of the territory. Some of the dialects of Busoga are close to the language of Buganda (i.e. Luganda), and also for reasons of proximity and influence, a lot of the same personal names are used by both ethnic entities.

The basing of the Ganda political system on royal absolutism astride the parceling out of magnanimous civil and chiefship responsibilities and powers to designated clans and clan heads, is of significance to the naming system of Buganda. With time, clan names of Buganda have denoted specialization, royal affiliation, civil occupation, civil and clan power, civil or royal privilege. The significance of a clan hence went far beyond that of functioning as family identification in an exogamous and polygynous social system. Clan names have been brought down that relate to such groups or dignitaries as were traditionally military or naval commanders, hunters, canoe builders, executioners, weapon forgers, fishermen and divers, midwives, rainmakers, raiders, cattle keepers, and seers. The Baganda displayed tremendous skill in aspects like reed house construction, canoe building, and basket making. Many personal names reflect the specialists that worked these trades, as well as the names of the materials and devices involved. The Baganda have special words for every part of the canoe.

On account of the dreaded powers of the royal class and the powerful clans, it became safer as happened many times, for people of less privileged clans to forge their way into membership in the powerful classes by getting assimilated into them through blood brotherhood tie ceremonies, through merely claiming familial association with them, through sending their children (later assimilated) to perform voluntary services at the royal palaces, or through dwelling (and later getting assimilated) with the privileged, through exceptional performance that would guarantee upward mobility into the high classes, or through assimilation of youthful captives following war. There are also instances of a small clan merging with a large clan, those of the lesser clan then taking on the full identity of the powerful clan. The royals also maintained family contact with the commoners through marrying women from lesser clans. The king who took many wives, was also traditionally furnished with wives from designated clans, and a lot of the titles given women from such clans have become personal names. The feeling of family connection and common descent among the Baganda allowed for their kingdom-state to prosper peacefully. The Baganda have an elaborate array of personal names including lineage (clan) names, names of Gods and Goddesses, and proverbial names.

Gisu

The *Gisu/ Gishu/ Masaaba* (sing./ pl.) ethnics are commonly referred to as *Bagisu/ Bagesu/ Masaaba* (pl.), and a single one of them referred to as a *Mugisu/ Mugishu*. The fertile soiled territory of the Bagisu (referred to as *Bugisu/ Bugishu*) lies on the slopes of Mount *Elgon* (or *Masaaba*) in eastern Uganda, and spill over into neighboring Kenya. The mountain slopes provide an area capable of harboring a large population. The expanse contains numerous all-the-year-round streams and waterfalls, as well as forests full of game and wood construction materials. Periodic attacks on the Gisu by the *Maasai*, *Kalenjin* and the *Nandi* to the east, prompted them to settle on the southwestern slopes of Mount Elgon. The era of British colonialism allowed for the Gisu to descend and settle on the lower slopes. The caves in the upper elevations, where the Gisu hid their cattle during raids, can still be seen. Rolling boulders would be let on the enemy hordes. The Bagisu comprise 5.1% (1.02 million people) of Uganda's population, and the language used (*Lugisu/ Lumasaaba*) is mostly of Bantu structure.

Oral tradition traces Gishu origins to their male and female ancestors *Mungu* and *Sera* respectively. Very little is known about the early history the Gishu, though they are related to the *Luyia* subgroup of Kenya known as the *Bukusu*. There is belief that the Gishu broke away from the Bukusu during the 19th century. The earliest Gishu immigrants into their present Mount Elgon habitat are believed to have arrived there during the 16th century, having migrated westwards from Kenya. The Gishu appear to be the product of a mixing of ethnics of varying origins and cultures.

The practices of agriculture and pastoralism in Bugisu, unlike amongst other Lakes area peoples have been on a limited basis. The goats reared were more prized than the sheep, since the goats were better suited to the environment and grew fatter and bred better. Chickens were kept in cages at night to protect them from bush cats. Cattle keeping was limited, and cattle were mainly used to pay dowry for brides, and for the butter to smear the body. Donkeys for transportation of luggage or produce have recently been introduced. The most common food among the Gisu has been mashed plantain. Sweet potatoes, peas, plantains, corn, beans, tomatoes, and marrows are also grown. Milled millet is used for porridge, and fermented millet for beer. Pottery was practiced by both men and women, and the blacksmiths imported the iron from the *Soga* to the west. Spear blades, knives, and some ornaments would be forged from these. The clans owned the land which was parceled out to individuals by the clan and village heads. These heads were voluntarily given gifts, this a marked contrast to many African lacustrine states where it was obligatory to offer gifts to leaders. Youth were normally allocated land upon getting married.

A clanship system requiring exogamy, as well as mandatory ritualized and public circumcision for adolescent males, existed. The initiation ceremony involves spirit possession, animal sacrifices to God conducted by a priest, and dancing. Unless circumcised, one would not be considered a man, would not be allowed to get married, would not be allowed into council meetings and beer drinking sessions, and would forfeit confirmation into the clan.

Those who refuse to be circumcised can be hunted down and forcibly and scornfully subjected to the ritual. The ceremony takes place bi-annually during leap years. Prior to the day of circumcision, the initiates are attuned by walking and dancing around the villages for three days. There is much drumming and singing, and relatives of the initiates dance with them. The origin of the Gishu circumcision ceremony remains a mystery with several traditional theories therein proposed (Nzita 1995: 82-83). Marriage was traditionally arranged by the parent, and naming was delayed until the baby cried continuously such as throughout the day or throughout the night. Children tended to be named after ancestors.

Gisu beliefs and involvement in magic and witchcraft are very strong. The witchdoctor or sorcerer (*umulosi*) was the most feared agent in this domain, and there was no remedy against his powerful and often harmful influence. He cast spells, and was a direct medium of communication between Gods and the people. The position of the umulosi was hereditary and he lived alone in the forest. The *umufumu* was the next agent in line, and he had the powers to detect the sources or the perpetrators of witchcraft, and to assist in fashioning the appropriate remedial measures. The umulosi would at times combine his functions with those of the umufumu. The umufumu wielded so much power in the judicial system that even when he identified one who may be innocent as the perpetrator, this person would be killed or be required to commit suicide. The medicine man came next in the hierarchy and he provided the medicines to avert witchcraft and snake bites. He supplied charms for use in war, including those to debilitate the enemy forces. Other things he did included prophesying, and averting creditors from coming to demand from the debtors (Nzita 1995: 81-82).

Each clan had a chief who was chosen on the basis of age and wealth. The chief was charged with maintaining law and order, warranting the unity and the continuity of the clan, maintaining the cultural values of the clan, and making sacrifices to ancestral spirits. Though stronger chiefs often extended their influence to lesser clans, none of the chiefs managed to unite all the clans into one political entity by conquest (Nzita 1995: 81). The Creator is referred to as *Weri*, *Mweri*, *Kumbamba*, or *Kibumba*. *Gibini* is the God associated with the plague, and *Enundu* the God associated with smallpox.

Gombe

Gombe (*Ngombe*) is essentially a colonially created and poorly representative term for "bushmen" that was applied to groups of people living around the Congo (Zaire) River in Western and Northwestern Congo (Zaire) towards the border with Republic of the Congo and Central African Republic. The Ngombe are of Bantu ethnolinguistic background, and their habitat that is mostly rainforest has restricted their ability to live in large groups.

Hemba, Mongo, Tetela

These are related groups of Bantu ethnolinguistic background and they occupy the forested inner basin of the Congo (Zaire) River Bend, west of Lake *Tanganyika*. Their descendants migrated here in massive waves and intermarried and assimilated with the original inhabitants.

The elaborate network of the massive river, over at least five centuries, advantaged these groups with rare mounds that were elevated enough for village settlement. The trade along the river allowed for the sharing of cultural elements. The varied environment also allowed for populations in these groups to specialize in fishing, farming, and hunter gathering.

The dreaded *Tetela* (*Tetel Otetela*) had a reputation for ferocious warriorhood. In their migration westward from the Atlantic Ocean Coast they were disposed to marching in groups with *Bokoko* warriors in the forefront, then the leaders, women, and dependents in the middle, then the Tete warriors in the rear. Some of the military advantages this grouping had was the employment of massed spearmen whose first lines were protected by large shields and cuirasses, and their mode of fighting until the enemy surrendered unconditionally so that the conquerors would destroy enemy settlements and disperse the inhabitants. The iron-tipped and iron knives which the Tete had, may have been an early advantage over the wooden javelins of their opponents. Their warrior numbers were also massive (Vansina 1990: 142). Some *Hemba* groups are linguistically and culturally associated with the *Luba* people.

The *Mongo* who speak the *Lomongo* language are said to have been descended from a man named *Mongo* and his wife *Numbandele* who bore a son named *Membele*. Despite the recognition of a single ancestor, the histories of specific Mongo groups suggest some diversity of origin. Lomongo constitutes a mix of dialects and related languages. The Mongo were famed for their hunting skills. The Mongo are sometimes taken to collectively include the smaller groups such as the *Mbole, Ntomba, Metoko, Lengola,* and *Tetela.* In 1959 the renowned Congo Premier Patrice Lumumba (Lomomba) attempted to unify the Mongo, Tetela, and other related groups but met with little success. For one, there were concrete differences between the forest and savanna people that had over time evolved between the related groups. And over the past century before Lumumba's attempt, Swahili commercialism and culture, and Belgian colonialism and catholicism, further created variegated divides between the groups.

The traditional setting of the Hemba, Mongo, and Tetela groups is one of a village in which the chief of a dominant lineage by birthright is also the chief of the client lineages. This dominant patriarch in the very decentralized patriarchate exercised the functions of high priest of the ancestral religion and of land owning appropriator. Kinship association would even emanate from common acceptance of a spiritual ancestor. the dominant chief is sometimes referred to as the big man of the House. The emergence of a dominant House to which the inhabitants of the locale identified, would happen when the choice of Houses became more limited, and if a number of villages were settled in a general spot for a long time. Disintegration would be avoided if competition for leadership in the founding House upon the death of its big man was adequately channeled to avoid a disruption. Scarcity of suitable land for settlement would also restrict the mobility of Houses and villages. Village populations dependent on fishing other than farming, given that only rare headlands were suitable for settlement and farming, would afford to stay on the site for a long time.

The Mongo are still involved in their hunter-gatherer way of life, and they collect a wide variety of products from the rainforest that include fruits, vegetables, palm kernels, mushrooms, and snails. A variety of roots and vegetation is used as herbs, spices, and beverages. Shifting cultivation is still common and it involves the growing of crops like cassava, oil palms, fruits, bananas, coffee, rubber, cotton, sugar, tea, and cocoa. A lot of the cash crops are grown on plantations. Hunting and trapping is done by men, while most of the farming and gathering is done by women. Over the centuries, as more and more of their land was cleared of the dense vegetation, many became involved in pottery making, ironworking, and dugout canoe construction. They Mongo then tended towards agriculture as it became integrated with fishing, hunting, gathering, and trapping. High ivory demand in Europe during the nineteenth century, stimulated Mongo traders to engage in the trade, and specialized elephant hunters like the *Twa* provided it to the traders. In exchange for the products such as cassava, tobacco, corn, raffia crafts, pottery, basketry, knives, iron, salt, canoes that the Mongo provided, they received from neighboring peoples other regionally manufactured crafts, and pieces of copper and brass. The Mongo also exchanged their products with Europeans for a variety of European manufactured goods. The Mongo social and political life evolves around the household of twenty to forty members that is headed by a senior male called the *tata* (father). Several households of 100 to 400 people form a village under the authority of a village chief (the *bokulaka*) and a council of elders. High status was in the past either hereditary, or based on demonstration of good leadership skills, or based on the level of one's family's economic power and influence. When the wide community was threatened by war, villages banded together. The decisions were then made by a collection of village chiefs, elders, and religious leaders.

Many Mongo traditions have persisted, despite the encroachment of Christianity and foreign culture. Veneration of and respect for ancestors is still practiced, and belief in witchcraft is still strong. Oral tradition is very rich and centers around proverbs, folk tales, poems, and songs that promote mutual obligation, importance of the family, wisdom, respect for authority, hunting and trapping, and rituals and ceremonies. Mongo crafts that include masks, figurines statues, weapons, jewelry, knives, and hats are very impressive masterpieces.

Hutu, Tutsi, and Twa

The Bantu ethnolinguistic terms Hutu, Tutsi, and Twa serve for both singular and plural forms. The singular forms *Muhutu, Mututsi,* and *Mutwa,* as well as the plural forms *Bahutu, Batutsi,* and *Batwa* are also used as personal names. A good number of African names are in reference to an ethnic group or a clan, and these names directly or indirectly associate an individual with such. The Hutu, Tutsi and Twa are of Bantu ethnolinguistic background, and they primarily live in Rwanda and Burundi. However, because of history, political surges, or population pressures, there are populations of these groups in other parts of East and Central Africa.

Naming is traditionally a ritual treated with importance amongst Hutu, Tutsi and Twa societies (Kimenyi 1989: 12-13). Prior to the naming ceremonies which take place in the evening of the seventh day after the child is born, both the child and its recuperating mother are to stay indoors in part to protect them from contagion and to treat them. In this period called *ikiriri* (large bed), relatives bring food to the mother in her bed or around the big fire which keeps her warm. The day the child is seven days old is called *gusohora* ("bringing out" i.e. the child into the open). Food and drinks are prepared by relatives and all the three to ten year olds of the village are invited to the naming ceremony. A ceremonial piece of land is given to the children to temporarily cultivate using sticks shaped like hoes. In throwing water at the children after a few minutes, an elder brings to an end the cultivating activity. The children immediately run home since the water symbolizes that it is raining. When they get home they eat in a ceremony known as *kurya ubunnyano* during which the adults are watching them.

After the eating, they are requested to give two names to the baby. This is only ceremonial since none of these names is considered in the final name choice. After everybody leaves, the mother also gives names to the baby though these too will not be official. The father ultimately names the child, and this is done soon after the mother's action or early the next morning. There are, traditionally, no family lineage names among the Hutu, Tutsi, and Twa. Each member of the family has his or her own name, and the wife does not change her name when she gets married.

Like many traditionally cattle keeping and cattle passionate African groups, personal names of the *Nyarwanda* (Rwandans/ Rwandese) and the *Barundi* (Burundians) are prevailingly related to raiding activity, to war, to mobility and mobilization, to pastures and rains, to cattle classifications, to various cattle phenomena including cattle names and cattle complexions, to seasonality and other weather conditions, to bravery and cowardice, to captives, to hunting, to cattle ownership and royalty, and to the demeaning of those of cultivating (other than cattle owning) class.

A striking aspect of the Hutu, Tutsi, and Twa peoples who primarily reside in Rwanda and Burundi, is that though the population is dense (one of the highest in Africa) and is linguistically and culturally homogeneous (Bantu), it is still divided into these three groups. The three groups have lived side by side, often intermarried, and there is not a designated "Hutuland" or a "Tutsiland." Kinyarwanda, the language spoken in Rwanda is considered a dialect of Kirundi the language spoken in Burundi.

There is a significant refugee and labor migrant population (including their descendants) spillover from landlocked Rwanda and Burundi into neighboring East and Central African countries Congo (Zaire), Kenya, Uganda, and Tanzania. The dense population pressures on two small colonially demarcated and landlocked African countries would be an expected major impetus to the continuous and significant outmigration to neighboring countries. When the migrant population is taken into account, Rwandan and Burundian people number approximately 20 million. In Uganda, the migrant population (generically referred to as Banyarwanda) numbers over one million, and it has been so influential in the socio-economics and politics of Uganda that it is enumerated as an ethnic group. The Banyarwanda who have for centuries inhabited a small portion of Uganda bordering Rwanda are sometimes referred to as *Bafumbira* (and *Bufumbira* is the land they inhabit). And the *Banyamulenge* who consider themselves Tutsi, have lived in the southern part of Eastern Congo (Zaire) around the city of Uvira for centuries. The Banyamulenge and other Tutsi groups and sympathizers in the African Great Lakes Region were instrumental in the ousting of the Zairean (Congolese) dictator Mobutu Sese-Seko and the installation of Laurent Kabila in 1997. However dealings with Kabila have not been smooth and have involved Tutsi rebelling against the Kabila government which has not satisfied their expectations and those of many other Congolese. In 1998 the conflict moved towards a regional affair as Kabila enlisted the military assistance of Angola, Namibia, and Zimbabwe as Tutsi rebels attempted to gain a stronghold in western Congo where the capital Kinshasa lies. Kabila also turned to the Tutsi's traditional opponents the Hutu, as Uganda and Rwanda were accused of aiding the rebels who had gained control of such major cities in eastern Congo as Bukavu and Kisangani. Peace talks were fortunately taking place over a conflict that had come to involve not only east, central, and southern Africa, but also the western powers. The people of resource wealthy Congo have remained impoverished and disgruntled following more than three decades of unconcern and exploitation by Mobutu's military regime.

Given that Rwandan and Burundian refugees and migrant labor have periodically been subjected to massacres at home, as well as to prejudice, pogroms, deportation, and other forms of harassment in the neighboring countries, many have attempted to assimilate themselves into neighboring country populations of similar ethnolinguistic background. Those born in the African countries where the internationally spoken language is English have had a difficult time re-establishing their home country roots since most are not culturally well grounded and they have a scanty knowledge of French, Kinyarwanda, and Kirundi.

The pygmoid Twa at 1% of the population are the most marginalized of the three groups, they are traditionally the pariahs of society and aside from their occupation of hunting and gathering in the forested areas, have served as professional soldiers, as entertainers at the royal court or at households of the wealthy, and as potters. But despite their small size, there are instances in history when the Twa were very much dreaded as they ruthlessly raided their Hutu, Kiga, and Tutsi neighbors. The Twa have been valued as good soldiers. They are considered the original inhabitants of the region, but their numbers have declined as a result of their low birth rates, as well as conquest and assimilation by their domineering neighbors. Much of the original language and traditions of the Twa have either disappeared or become part and parcel of Tutsi-Hutu culture. The Twa were known to be environmentally attached to the land and to live a basic existence in which they dressed simply. They did not bother to own land or anything much in terms of material possessions. They did not cultivate and instead exchanged their hunting tools (bows and arrows) and gains (animal skins and trophies) with the Hutu and Tutsi for grains and beer. They sometimes begged from the Hutu and Tutsi or were servants to them.

There is a load of interesting racist myths about the virtues and anatomical features of the traditionally cattle herding "Semite looking" Tutsi as in sharp contrast to those of the "Negroid Bantu looking" Hutu and Twa. Needless to say, racist theories have for so long tended to associate anatomical and skin complexion features with level of human development and civilization, other than with physiological adaptation. Preoccupation with such notions manifested itself in European anthropology excusing some blacks resident on the African continent from being Africans, while pinpointing others as being typically negroid. Such romanticized and exaggerated colonial inferences have, as happened with many other African groups, served to forment needless and sometimes bloody hostilities between the Hutu and Tutsi, indeed partly serving as a "divide and rule" strategy. The estimate of the Tutsi as numbering 17% of the Rwandan population, is in itself racist insofar as it basically defined the category as families of men that owned twenty or more cows whereby the men were at least six feet tall. The United Nations has estimated the percentage at 30%, whereas national estimates have been between 10% and 15%.

African nomads (as would be generally applied to the Tutsi who originally settled in the area) are generally taller, and more slender and athletic than settled cultivators (as generally applied to the original Hutu residents in the area whom the migrating Tutsi subjugated earlier on). And much of the precolonial history of the African Great Lakes area is about cattle herders establishing monarchic rule over Bantu cultivators. Since the subjugated were more numerous than the conquering invaders and given the precolonial African situation whose power depended greatly on human numerical strength, it was more resourceful to assimilate into the ways of the conquered peoples other than to annihilate or overly antagonize them.

The origin of the Tutsi is still heavily debated. Though the Tutsi, like the Maasai, may be believed to have a Cushitic origin, the centuries of intermingling with the more numerous original residents would render it virtually impossible to anthropologically distinguish a Tutsi from a Hutu. An Ethiopian Cushitic origin ascribed to the Tutsi would have involved a very long trek from the the northeast through present-day Kenya, Sudan, and Uganda over the typically forested, mountainous, waterway and swamp ubiquitous environment of the African Great Lakes region, as well as traversing the domain of well established and imposing ethnic groups. This would be quite an accomplishment by a small group managing to keep itself so intact over thousands of miles of semi-inhabited and imposing environment. Nevertheless, several semitic ethnic groups are known to have migrated eastwards, westwards, and northwards along the guiding network of numerous rivers and lakes of East and Central Africa. The Semitic or Cushitic origin concerning the Tutsi therefore still merits consideration. The ascription of the Tutsi to a Semitic (or Hamitic) origin is sometimes extended to Somalia and Egypt, sometimes with the application that the Tutsi "resemble" Somalis, the *Galla*, or the *Oromo*. One theory traces Tutsi origins to the nearby territory of Karagwe in northern Tanzania. Over the centuries, when placed side by side, the Tutsi and Hutu categories appear to have evolved into more of class (or caste) than ethnic categories.

Many personal names of the Rwandans and Burundians relate to the system of clientage called *ubuhake*. This system has aroused a great amount of interest and controversy within and outside Rwanda and Burundi, and needless to say is involved in the friction between the Tutsi and the Hutu. In the ubuhake system, the *shebuja* (traditionally a Tutsi patron) and the *mugaragu* (traditionally a Hutu client) entered an unequal clientship contract in which the Tutsi lord gave a cow to his Hutu client partly in exchange for labor services. The Hutu were theoretically not allowed to own cattle (the symbol of wealth and power), so this cattle transfer served as goodwill, an "economic" gift, and a form of upward mobility for the Hutu client. Should the cow which the Hutu looked after reproduce, the cows would be shared between the patron lord and the client. Depending on the humaneness of the patron, once the Hutu became endowed with cattle, he alongside his family lineage became capable of climbing into the Tutsi class.

Similarly, a Tutsi who happened to lose all his cattle and took onto the despised Hutu domain of tilling the soil could become "Hutuised." Children of impoverished Tutsi would sociologically be lured into marrying into Hutu lineages, while the upwardly mobile Hutu could be accorded the privilege of marrying into a Tutsi lineage. Hutu families were capable of taking on the clan identity of their patron overlord. That Hutu and Twa were frequently mobilized by the Tutsi masters to defend against external enemies and raid neighbors for cattle, also propagated conditions of goodwill and assimilation between the three categories. In recent times there have been Hutu dissidents that have joined up with Tutsi. Yet the Tutsi-Hutu relationship remains a mystery subject to vigorous debate.

There is the theory the Tutsi and the Hutu have been ethnically the same people for centuries, and that the Tutsi evolved as a higher social class that gradually came to be defined along the lines of an ethnic group. There is also the theory that the original invading Tutsi, despite their subjugating the resident Hutu, were so numerically inferior to the residents that they resourcefully took on the clan identities of the Hutu in the locales (such as hills) that they established as their territories. The Tutsi cattle based economy demanded large amounts of pasture land, and as cattle herds expanded, Tutsi lords wound up competing for land with other Tutsi lords. The variety of conflicts and subjugations that followed, are hypothesized to have created a class of Tutsi cattle and landowner overlordship as contrasted with the subjugated Tutsi lords and their Hutu clients that were forced into an inferior position of Hutu "cultivators." The Tutsi-Hutu situation would then be defined as a continuing class struggle whose primordial backdrop may have been ethnic.

Debate will continue as to whether the ubuhake system is a form of quasi slavery that has enabled Tutsi lords to exploit the poor Hutu, or a social system linking lineages into a friendly symbiotic contract. The violence in Rwanda forced many Tutsi into exile between 1959 and 1964, and in more limited quantities from 1972-73. In the 1990's it is estimated that the Tutsi-Hutu conflict has involved the massacres, starvation to death, incapacitation, and fatalities associated with epidemics of hundreds of thousands of Rwandans and Burundians. The mass exoduses have involved millions of people.

Iteso

The *Iteso* (pl.) ethnics are also referred to as *Itesyo/ Tesiol/ Teso*, a single one of them referred to as an Itesot, and the language is *Ateso*. They are fundamentally a Sudanic-Hamitic people with ethnic ties to the *Kumam*, the *Karamojong*, the *Jie*, and the *Dodoth*. The prevailingly cattle keeping and millet growing territory of the Iteso (also referred to as Teso) occupies north-central Uganda, southeastern Uganda into a small portion of neighboring Kenya. The approximately 10% of the Iteso that strayed away from the main group have their descendants in

Kenya across the border, some in the nearby Tororo area of Uganda, where they are mostly known as the Itesyo. The Iteso collectively comprise 2.5 million people. Milled millet porridge is a staple in Teso society. Millet is also fermented into beer which is collectively drunk through long reed straws placed in one large beer pot surrounded by the seated drinkers. Both genders drink beer, though separately. Maize and sesame, marrows, sweet potatoes, peas, cassava, peanuts, and beans are also grown. Cultivation is done by both genders though the men do the laborious work of clearing the bush and breaking new ground. Most of the families have cattle. The homesteads are generally scattered and each usually lies adjacent to its own agricultural land. The Iteso way of life has greatly been influenced by such neighbors as the *Soga* to the south.

A pervading characteristic of Teso society is the age-set system which places people in their prescribed roles according to their age and what is expected of them. One of the age-set systems traditionally involved elders (belonging to senior sets) initiating young men into the learning of indigenous songs and dance, as well as learning to cater to the elderly. The inter-set competitions that were occasionally held involved, for example, a variety of contests between a group comprised of 12 to 18 year-olds and departing members of this age-set. The situation would at times become violent. Such initiations were also a means to encouraging people to improve on their crop yields. The age groups called *aturio* were the basis of the military organization, the war leaders were known as *Aruwok*, and the army was called *Ojore*. A fortune teller (*Amurwok*) would be consulted and if he predicted success, then war would be declared following the consultation and approval of the elders.

Another renowned system mainly involved two initiation ceremonies. The first involved transition to adulthood involving a youth having to live and carry out menial duties at home. He had to have a sponsor who would then recommend him for the final stage of transition. Crowning initiation into the next stage was accompanied by beer festivities. The next phase ceremony involved initiation of males between the ages of 15 and 20. The ceremony described as "handing over power," confirmed attainment of adult responsibility and involved a great feast. British colonial agents under the Ganda collaborator Semei Kakungulu discouraged and destroyed the age-set system. Yet the system, prior to the pacification of the Iteso, had fostered resourcefulness, including stimulating agricultural growth in Teso.

The most important sociopolitical unit amongst the Iteso was the settlement known as the *etem*, and it is here that discussion of ritual, judicial, and social matters took place. The *etem* unit took precedence over the *ateker* (clan) unit. The Iteso do not appear to have had the pantheon of Gods so characteristic of the Bantu groups like the Ganda, and their most important ceremony was rainmaking. The few Gods honored in Teso society include *Apap* (or *Akuj*) the God of the Sky, *Edeke* the God associated with disaster (and supplicated during times of sickness, cattle disease, and persistent drought). The emuron, the most prominent person in Teso society, possesses magical powers that are used for good purposes. He undoes the evil of sorcerers, foretells the future, cures the sick, performs rainmaking rituals, and sells charms and love portions.

Like many African groups, the Iteso name their children according to the circumstances under which the child was born, or the condition of the mother during the pregnancy or delivery, or the season (or weather conditions) during which the child was born, or the day of the week the child is born. Children are often named after ancestors. The naming ceremony involves a lot of eating and drinking amongst mostly same clan members. The newborn was initiated into the clan through a ceremony (*etale*). The restrictions on non-clan members attending is to prevent evil influences from affecting the vulnerable newborn.

Jopadhola

The *Jopadhola/ Adhola*, a Sudanic Luo people, live in east-central Uganda on the southern end of Lake Kyoga, their area running like a strip into the frontier with Kenya. They consist of about 20 clans, and they are bordered by the *Iteso* and *Bagwere* to the north, the *Samia* and *Bagwe* to the south, *Luyia* (*Nyole*) and *Soga* to the west. Adhola territory is known as *Padhola*, and the language known as *Dhopadhola*. Despite their location amidst a variety of ethnics, the Adhola have persistently held on to a lot of their traditions that are similar to those of such peoples as the *Luo* (*Joluo*), the *Alur*, and the *Acholi*. Nevertheless, the Adhola have evidently not been immune from the cultural influences of neighboring *Bantu* and Hamitic groups. The Adhola were frequently invaded by the Iteso and the Nyole, while they in turn raided the Samia. The Adhola number close to 0.5 million, and they are ethnically related to the Acholi, the Alur, and the Lango. They practice fishing, crop cultivation, and cattle herding. *Jamalo* is the Supreme Being and sky God; *Were* is the God responsible for human fertility; *Were Thim* (*Were Othin*) is the God of the wilderness, of fighting, and of safe journeying; and *Were Madiodipo* is the God that protects the home and family. Each home had a shrine established for Were, and each morning and whenever one of the household was going to travel, the owner of the house would approach the shrine and pray.

British gun equipped colonial forces under the leadership of the *Ganda* collaborator Semei Kakungulu, invaded Padhola in 1903 and overthrew the priest-king Majanga. Their efforts to christianize and "educate" the "heathen" Adhola using *Luganda* (language) as the medium of instruction, achieved little success. There were better results when Fr. J. Willemen founded a Catholic mission in Padhola and used Dhopadhola. Majanga is said to have universalized the cult of *Bura* which originated from the neighboring *Bagwere* ethnics. Besides the concept of Were, this is the other religion that the Adhola embraced. It is claimed that the Bura cult was introduced by Akure of *Bugwere* territory, who was the uncle of Majanga. In universalizing the Bura cult, Majanga simultaneously consolidated the Adhola clans and this unification allowed for the resistance to the Ganda-British imperialism.

A traditional procedure towards marriage was the parents of a boy identifying a suitable girl from another clan then carrying on negotiations with the parents of the girl. If negotiations were successful the girl became engaged and became identified so by wearing a traditional ring on her finger or a necklace around her neck. The other method towards marriage involved boys of the same age group acting in collaboration and identifying a suitable girl. She was then ambushed and forcefully carried to the home of the male candidate, and then would in effect become the wife before further negotiations were made between the parents of the boy and the girl. Bride dowry payments involved at least five cows, six goats, a cock, a knife, barkcloth, salt and meat. Polygamy was allowed in Adhola society, and a man's ability to have more than one wife mostly depended on his family wealth and therefore ability to meet bride dowry obligations. One could only marry those from outside his or her clan. Ritual observations surrounded pregnancy and birth. During pregnancy the woman was restricted to particular foods and was not to use some types of wood for cooking. The names of snakes and the dead were not to be mentioned in her presence, and only her husband was to pass behind her when she was seated. These measures were believed to help prevent miscarriage or other pregnancy or birth misfortunes. As with many Sudanic-Luo and Sudanic-Hamitic peoples, a mother was to remain confined in her house for three days if she had given birth to a boy, and four days if she had given birth to a girl. Naming ceremonies for the newborns were held following confinement and names were mostly given by grandparents. A lot of the children are named after their ancestors (Nzita 1995: 102-104).

Kaguru

The *Kaguru* are of the Bantu ethnolinguistic group, they number approximately 0.35 million and they live in eastern Tanzania in a territory referred to as *Ukaguru*. The Kaguru are surrounded by several ethnics that principally include the *Maasai* to the north, the *Nguu* to the east and northeast, the *Luguru* to the southeast, the *Sagara* to the south, and the *Gogo* to the west. Aside from the Maasai who are Sudanic Hamites, all of Ukaguru's neighbors are of Bantu ethnolinguistic descent. One fifth of Ukaguru is plainland that includes scrub land and somewhat heavier vegetation in the river valleys. A third of the land is a spectacular mountain area lying 4500 feet above sea level. Half of Ukaguru is high plateau of 2000-4500 feet above sea level, and it is where most of the population lives.

Most of Ukaguru receives adequate amounts of rainfall (80 centi-
meters, 30 inches), and it allows for a variety of agricultural activity.
The Kaguru cultivate vegetables, bananas and plantains, maize, citrus
fruits, sugar-cane, and coffee. The Kaguru have an elaborate system
of agriculture, in which there is assignment of cash and food crops to
specific areas and types of land, some of which is rotated and is laid
fallow for years. Specific crops are assigned to valley gardens, to the
well watered highland fields, to home gardens, and to cleared bush.
Cattle, goats, and some sheep are also kept. Domestic animals are
mostly slaughtered at ceremonial feasts.

Kaguru society consists of about one hundred matrilineal clans. Bride
dowry is traditionally given by the bridegroom's maternal kin to the
bride's maternal kin. Both polygamy and sacrifices to ancestral spirits
are still tolerated despite the profound influence of Anglican Protestantism.

Kakwa

The *Kakwa* who number 0.1 million, primarily live in the extreme
northwestern Uganda (in *Koboko* county of *Arua* district) and over the
national borders into Congo (Zaire) and Sudan. They live to the immediate northwest of the Lugbara ethnics. The Kakwa are a Sudanic-
Hamitic people of Kushitic-Ethiopian origin, so are related to such ethnics as the *Bari*, the *Iteso*, the *Karimojong*, and the *Langi*.

Two traditions on Kakwa origins prevail. One of the traditions traces
the origins to a man named *Yeki* who migrated from *Karobe* Hill in
Southern Sudan and settled on Mount *Liru* in Koboko. Yeki fathered
seven sons here, and the one who was characteristically fond of biting
his brothers became nicknamed *Kakwan-jj* which means "bitter." Yeki's
descendants then took on the plural form *Kakwa* for ethnic identity.
The second tradition asserts that the Kakwa were originally known as
Kui. The Kui are alleged to have been fierce fighters who frequently
subjugated their enemies. Their ferocious attacks were likened to the
bite of a tooth and so the Kui went on to call themselves the Kakwa.
The linguistics heavily link the Kakwa to the Bari of Southern Sudan
although it is not certain as to where and when the Kakwa split from
the Bari (Nzita 1995: 133).

Kakwa sociopolitics evolved around the clan in a segmentary and
matrilineal system. Each clan was politically independent and was
headed by a chief (*Matterh*, *Ba-Ambogo*, or *Buratyo*) entrusted with
political, judicial, and rainmaking authority. In the rare cases of clans
that did not have rainmakers, these would be borrowed temporarily
from other clans for a fee. But it was only in the clans with leaders with
a rainmaking function that the chiefship position was hereditary. The
chief had the duty of protecting the hunting grounds of his clan against
other clans, and of ensuring that his people's cattle did not graze

outside the clan jurisdiction. He negotiated for peace with neighbors and shifted his people away in times of danger. The clan disputes were settled by clan elders, but they were referred to the chief if they were serious. Though the clans did not have standing armies, there was a military leader (*Jokwe*) who mobilized the people in times of war. Those caught committing murder, adultery, or theft were often killed. When such acts were committed within the same clan, the punishments tended to be less severe. So both murder and adultery within the clan often lead to fining the perpetrator a cow (or a reasonable number of goats instead) or two (equated to compensation or ransom). The murder of a person from another clan would bring about warfare involving striving for sufficient revenge. The mobilization for war was preceded by discussion between the chief, the Jokwe, and the elders that was accompanied by war related rituals. In a limited number of cases, women would accompany men to war. It was taboo to assail such women, and their duties were to urge on their husbands such as by yelling, and also to take away the injured and the dead (Nzita 1995: 133-135).

Though Kakwa society did not have distinct classes of people, there still existed those of the upper and lower classes. There was also a clientship system in which an upper class person looked after persons of the lower classes that would include house servants, cattle herders, and young children. But a client could easily leave a master if he was mistreated or despised. But a client on good terms would have his bride dowry paid by his master and could even be assimilated into the clan. The economy of the Kakwa traditionally involves subsistence agriculture alongside some elements of mixed farming. The principal food crops are millet, sorghum, and beans (*burusu*). Pawpaws, cassava, potatoes, and maize are also grown. The domestic animals include cattle, goats, and sheep. The men cleared and dug the fields, sowed the seeds, looked after the animals, and built and repaired the houses. The women mainly removed the trash from the tilled fields, weeded and harvested the crops, and cleaned and stored the crops away in granaries. In addition the women weaved baskets, processed salt from the *morobu* and *bukuli* plants, and molded pots. The *Nyangila* clan had the specialists in smelting iron, and forging spears, knives, hoes, and a variety of other iron instruments. The yardstick for wealth was the numbers of food filled granaries and the numbers of livestock one had. In times of famine, it was common for people to migrate to other areas where there was a plenitude of food (Nzita 1995: 134-136).

Kanyok

The *Kanyok* (*Kaniok*) are of the Bantu ethnolinguistic groups, and they primarily inhabit an area west of Lake Tanganyika in southcentral Congo (Zaire) where they are surrounded by the *Luba*, *Lunda*, *Chokwe*, and *Songye*. The early history of the Kanyok remains obscure, though they claim to have migrated from the north. However, during the eighteenth and nineteenth centuries, fighting between the Kanyok and their neighbors was frequent. The Kanyok resisted Luba encroachment, and they also launched several attacks on neighbors. In addition the Kanyok had to contend with the ivory and slave raiding in the area by East African Coastal Arabs and their local allies. Chief among these organized slaving and ivory raiding commercialists who operated over an extensive area was the Afro-Arab (Swahili) nick-named Tippu Tib (Tip).

Karamojong/ Jie

The *Karamojong* (*Karimojong*) are fundamentally a Sudanic-Hamitic people with ethnic affiliation to such peoples as the the *Iteso*, the *Kipsigis*, the *Langi*, the *Nandi*, the *Pokot*, the *Suk*, and the *Turkana*. The cattle loving Karamojong belong to the large group of ethnics known as *Kalenjin*. Similar to these groups, they are elegant and athletic nomadic pastoralists that thrive on a diet of goat and cattle meat, milk, and blood supplemented by millet, sorghum, maize, and beans. They live in a semi-arid portion of northeastern Uganda into neighboring northwestern Kenya, and some are in southern Sudan. The Karamojong constitute 2% of the Uganda population i.e. 0.4 million people. The Karamojong have for at least the past 300 years suffered from a number of severe droughts.

The age-set system among the Karamojong rigorously demands that those in junior age-set rungs respect the older in the senior age-set. The clan system is also very important, with each clan having its characteristics such as ritual ceremonies and cattle brand. The Karamojong, an independent minded and proud people, frequently raided for cattle. They thoroughly resisted all efforts to be colonized and in Uganda were branded as "warlike and a security risk" and "isolated" by colonial law from the rest of the country until independence in 1962. In precolonial times the Karamojong controlled a large portion of land, including several water holes, to their northeast past the rift valley wall inhabited by the Turkana. This land was later officially ceded to the Turkana when the Kenya-Uganda/ Turkana-Karamojong boundary was settled along the rift wall. Nevertheless, even as recent as the 1970's and 1980's, the Karamojong have crossed the border to raid Turkana for cattle.

The Karamojong, like many pastoralists in equatorial and southern Africa, suffered the cattle decimation brought on by the Great Rinderpest of the 1890's. Other human and animal diseases, crop failures, and locust invasions occurred simultaneously, worsening the situation that involved starvation. All these contributed to the present widespread scattering of the Karamojong. Even during the past few decades, the Karamojong who happen to live in the most arid part of heavily vegetated Uganda, have suffered bouts of starvation, alongside scuffles with the national government over their cattle raiding practices. Thousands of Karamojong were massacred during the Idi Amin regime (1971-1979) on account of their "primitivity." Following Amin's fall, they armed themselves with the abundance of modern weapons from abandoned barracks. The cattle raid and crime rate escalated. Armed scuffles with the new Uganda government administration followed. In recent times groups of Karamojong elders have attempted to brutally curb the lawlessness, and there have also been peaceful negotiations with the national government and attempts at local police training, community policing, and vigilantism.

It is around the nineteenth century time of the cattle epidemics that the Swahili traders entered the area and begun bartering cattle for the high quality East African ivory abundant in the area. The Swahili established a trading center and this trade was active up to 1920. This helped the cattle dependent Karamojong recoup their herds, but the Swahili were not generally popular owing to unfair trade practices, and disruption of the traditional way of life including attempts to take rough control of the natives. In some cases, the situation degenerated into guerrilla warfare between the Karamojong and the traders. The British colonial administration was only a trifling with a small post on Mount Moroto, but it attempted with government soldiers to consolidate Karamoja into fewer chiefdoms under chosen leaders.

The chief traditional requirements of the Karamojong were metal goods and spears, and these were obtained from the neighboring *Labwor, Langi,* and *Acholi*. During prosperous times this century, they even exported cattle. Other animals now herded include sheep and goats. The cultivating, almost entirely done and decided by women, involved millet and to a much lesser extent maize, peanuts, eleusine, gourds, and marrows. Later on ploughs were introduced and men became increasingly involved. A lot of men have personal names associated with cattle, whereas the women's names are associated with grains.

The Karamojong as children, as related to their order of birth, are named after their ancestors. The eldest tends to be given a name of the grandfather, the next born given a name of the grandmother, the third given a name of a great aunt or uncle, and so forth. The majority of Karamojong names are not gender specific although some name associations vary with gender. At birth the infants could be given names by assisting midwives, these names associated with significant circumstances at birth such as the time of birth. Such names were often only tentatively conferred, and their acceptance or refusal depended on the baby either breast sucking the mother contentedly or crying. The substitute of goat's milk administered to the baby from a small gourd shaped like a feeding bottle would serve in case of inadequate mother's breast milk. Though twin births are traditionally considered strokes of luck, it is believed that if both of them get to grow up, either their mother or father will sicken and die as a result (Nzita 1995: 118-119).

Among the *Jie Karamojong*, oxen are traditionally an integral part of the process of naming (Gulliver 1952: 72-75). Though there are herds of ordinary cattle that are owned by groups of brothers, every male has up to five or more cattle of his own. A boy is given cattle at the age of three or four, normally by his father or brother. In later life he can beg cattle from other men, and this is considered a part of the friendship and socialization process in the society. He returns the compliment later when the giver demands an ox from him. Jie adults can also beg cattle from others when in need of assembling a bride dowry payment. In the past bride dowry payments could consist of as many as fifty to one hundred cattle. The high demand for cattle was one of the reasons for the Karimojong tradition of frequent cattle raiding. And the high cost of marriage limited the numbers of polygamous households

Jie bell-oxen are castrated and bell adorned cows that start off as specially selected calves on account of their quality appearance. As they grow their horns are worked so as to curve in particular ways. Examples include horns curved over the head, in front of the head, and downwards near the eyes. Males are often named according to the shape of horns, the color of its hide and other features of the bell-ox or ordinary ox the owner is associated with. However, one can also be na-med after a dead ox that was a great favorite. Women are occasionally given cattle names, though most commonly, female names are in reference to some agricultural activity. While cattle herding is chiefly confined to men, cultivating is mostly the work of women. Examples of female names are *Apa-loputh* i.e. greyish grain and *Apa-longwa* i.e. white sorghum. Examples of male names are *Apa-longor* i.e. greyish-brown hide and *Apa-lokodo* i.e. horns curve and meet over the head (Gulliver 1952: 73-75). Karimojong men are known to value their ritual related cattle more than their parents, wives, children, and other possessions

Religion in traditional Karimojong society involves clan family gather-ing and prayers to ancestors in times of misfortune, sickness, or trouble. Family generations would congregate around an ancestor's grave and here would milk the cows, bring out the tobacco, and kill an ox. The contents of the ox's stomach were smeared on the people and on the burial stones as prayers were chanted. The failure of rains to arrive would prompt three elders to approach the medicine man (*emurron*) with the present of a calabash of milk and a request to cause rain to fall. The emurron would instruct the elders to present a (usually) black bull, as well as appoint a day for the *akirriket* (rainma-king ceremony). The ceremony involved elders gathering at an ap-pointed spot, slaughtering, roasting and eating of the bull, and the emurron calling upon the rain to come (Nzita 1995: 121).

The Karamojong tradition of cattle raiding in part stems from the exorbitant bride dowry requirements which have ranged from 50 to 100 head of cattle in addition to many goats. Because of the dowry requirements, it is usual for couples to be engaged for up to five years. The demands also limit the amount of women one can marry, although polygamy is allowed in the society. Marriages between those of the same clan or any extended family relative are not allowed. Each of the clans has its own cattle brand.

Kiga

The *Kiga/ Chiga* "mountain inhabitants" (sing./ pl.) ethnics are commonly referred to as *Bakiga* (pl.), and a single one of them referred to as a *Mukiga*. The predominantly agricultural territory of the Bakiga (referred to as *Kigezi*) lies amongst the African Great Lakes in the extreme southwestern Uganda corner, bordering Rwanda and Zaire and bordering with the Nyankore to the north. The Bakiga comprise 7.1% (1.42 million people) of Uganda's population, there are pockets of them in Rwanda and Tanzania, and the language used (*Lukiga/ Rukiga*) is mostly of Bantu structure and is close to the language of the *Nyankore* (*Lunyankore*). The Kiga environment is composed of mountainous terrain of 6000-7000 feet that extends seventy miles from north to south and thirty miles from west to east. The mountainous region is generally unsuitable for the cattle breeding and keeping which all the neighboring ethnics practice, and the Kiga grow millet, maize, sorghum, beans and peas, alongside keeping goats and sheep. Though the Kiga are primarily agriculturists, there are cattle keepers that live on the lower slopes of the mountains. The Kiga are skilled at pottery, carpentry, and basketry and they produce a wide assortment of such products. They were also excellent at ironsmithing and produced hoes, knives, and spears. The Kiga dwelled communally, and they worked communally in such activities as grazing animals, clearing bush, cultivating, harvesting, and hut construction. These activities were confined to men, while the women tilled the land.

The Kiga live in the most fertile and most densely populated area of Uganda. This may partly explain the intense competition for resources that relates to accounts of the Kiga having been fiercely independent minded and martial. Little is known about the Kiga prior to colonialism. One theory claims that they migrated southward to *Karagwe* in northern Tanzania from nearby Bunyoro to the north following pressure from southward moving Luo invaders. Thereafter they moved northwards to their present locale. Another theory is that the Kiga migrated from neighboring Rwanda to the north as they searched for fertile land, fled internal political squabbles, and fled natural disasters. After a series of movements through Congo (Zaire), the Kiga finally settled in Kigezi in Uganda. The Kiga were often harassed by *Twa* (pygmies) to the northwest, the *Mpororo* to the north, and the Rwandan *Hutu* and *Tutsi* to the south. They were virtually placed in a tight corner in which they were surrounded by adversaries on all sides. The steep ravines of Kigezi strategically enabled the Kiga to ambush parties of enemy raiders. The Kiga were often armed even as they harnessed their gardens, and there was friction between clans and even those of the same clan affiliation. Kiga resistance to all forms of subjugation by neighboring ethnics and by colonialists could be compared to that of the Nyoro and the Karamojong. Though the Kiga were a politically segmented society and did not have a standing army, they had warlords who mobilized and lead the people in the case of an invasion. The position of warlord could be acquired by leading warriors that had annihilated a large number of enemies in war without losing any of their men or weapons. Every able-bodied man was required to defend Kiga territory when necessary.

The Kiga precapitalist societal organization is one of clans comprising several villages clustered together. The Kiga have lived in beehive shaped round grass-thatched huts in circular compounds within enclosures of living trees and thick thorny shrubs. The typical Kiga village or compound is organized around patrilineal familism, the head is the oldest male, the eldest of a group of brothers (Knappert 1987: 209-210). The lineage leader tended to have excellent oratory and military skills. He was charged with the duty of administering justice impartially. The village head (*mukungu*) would rent out inherited land on an annual basis. Unlike other African Great Lakes states, the Kiga system did not have overlords. However, the religious leaders had immense political powers to the equivalent of that of kings and, they were held in high esteem. The *basubi* were endowed with mystical skills that allowed them to serve in leadership roles. The rainmakers, as well as the mediums (*bagwira*) of the *Nyabingi* cult, also assumed leadership roles. Like many ethnics in the western African Great Lakes area, the Kiga recognized *Ruhanga* the Creator as the Supreme Being.

The Kiga are traditionally a polygamous society. The number of wives one had were mainly limited by the availability of bride dowry. Dowry involved cows, goats, and hoes although the amounts requested varied from group to group, and varied from family to family. Divorce was common among the Kiga, and commonly emanated from barrenness or laziness on the part of the wife or the husband, or from misunderstanding between a husband and a wife (Nzita 1995: 57). In many cases, elders from both sides of the family would prevent a divorce following negotiation. The Kiga were highly disciplinarian when it came to enforcement of communal social norms. Heavy punishment was meted on those who stole, murdered, or performed sorcery. A murderer could be buried alive in the same grave as his victim. The most lenient punishment on an unmarried girl who became pregnant was cursing and ostracization by her people. Otherwise she would either be bound feet and arms and thrown over a cliff, or she would be tied to a tree in a forest so that wild animals would devour her (Nzita 1995: 60).

Kikuyu

The *Akikuyu* (*Kikuyu/ Gikuyu*) belong to the Bantu ethnolinguistic group, and are a large amalgamation of several related groups that number approximately 6 million. This is the largest ethnic group in Kenya and its major categories are the Akikuyu proper, the *Embu*, the *Meru*, and the *Chuka*. Those of the group that originally called themselves Kikuyu, live west and north of the capital Nairobi on thickly populated farmland lying along the slopes of rising elevation as one moves westward, the *Aberdare* Range in the west and Mount Kenya in the north. The Akikuyu claim ancestry from *Kikuyu* (*Gekoyo*) whose nine daughters gave birth to the ancestors of the nine Akikuyu subdivisions or clans (*mihiriga*). The mihiriga are traditionally subdivided into *mbari* lineages, each of which communally owns a piece of land (*githaka*) composed of grazing area, cultivated fields, and bush. Several *nyumba* (houses) are contained in the mbari, and each is owned by its establisher who is the head of his family. The whole family lineage is administered by an elected chief (*muramati*) who presides over the clan council composed of heads of households. The Supreme Being and Creator is referred to as *Ngai, Engai*, or *Murungu*. He has powers of allocation to humans, and controls the rain, the lightning, and the thunder which phenomena he can amplify so as to punish evildoers. The Supreme Being is placated by animal sacrifices.

The Akikuyu habitat is very fertile, although much drier than when it was heavily forested generations ago when the first Akikuyu settled here. The Akikuyu traditionally cultivated sweet potatoes, beans, and millet, but cassava, maize, bananas, yams, peas, and irish potatoes, coffee, tea, tobacco, rice, and castor oil have been added to the picture. The Akikuyu have a preference for vegetables, and traditionally rarely ate beef, fish, or game. Goat and mutton were the main meat dishes. In precolonial times Akikuyu huts were round and conical roofed and constructed out of poles, wattle and clay. The blacksmiths forged, from locally mined iron ore, iron tipped digging sticks, knives and axes, spears, swords, and arrows.

The Akikuyu had an elaborate military system that involved age set regiments and systems of ambush. Prior to a battle, scouts (*athigani*) would be sent out to reconnoiter the enemy's standing. These would be followed by an advance guard (*ngerewani* or *mbutu*) who would move into enemy territory and raid and bring back cattle. When the enemy (usually the *Maasai* to the west) counterattacked and followed the advance regiment, they would be ambushed by the main body of the Kikuyu army (*gitungati*) positioned in hiding. This afforded the advance guard the opportunity to more easily drive the raided cattle toward the *murima* (the rear guard) where the war council conducted the main battle. The Maasai, however, often won in the battles against the Akikuyu.

When in 1895 the present-day Kenya became the colonized British East Africa, the British set up a town and railroad center at Nairobi.

The construction of the Uganda railway that stretched from the coast into neighboring Uganda was in progress. The British began to settle in fertile Kikuyuland, they took over much of the land while they confined the Kikuyu to a small reserve. The reserve was too inadequate to farm on, though the Kikuyu had previously been accustomed to having an abundance of land whereby parts were abandoned whenever the soil became exhausted. The limited land forced many Kikuyu into working for the settlers and laboring in the factories that sprang up in Nairobi. The Kikuyu were treated as third class citizens as they were discriminated against and allocated menial jobs. Some became potters and cooks for the settlers, and those that served in World War II against the Germans were inadequately compensated and regarded. The Kikuyu began to rally with other ethnic groups and their anti-colonialist actions reached their climax in the Mau Mau rebellion some of whose leaders was the future Kenya president Jomo Kenyatta. 13000 Africans were killed in this rebellion that ended in 1956.

Kongo and Yoombe

The *Kongo* (sing./ pl.) ethnics are of Bantu ethnolinguistic background, speak the *Kikongo* language, and they are commonly referred to as *Bakongo* (pl.) while a single one of them referred to as a *Mukongo*. The same terms are also generally applied to the people of the two Congo (one of them formerly Zaire) nations which derive their names from the fascinating and renowned ancient kingdom of Kongo. Kikongo comprises more than fifty dialects. The *Yoombe* (*Yombe*) are northern Kongo people (living north of River Congo). The Kongo number approximately 5 million.

During both the fifteenth and sixteenth centuries, the Congo kingdom encompassing a large western part of Congo (Zaire) and traversing into Republic of the Congo and Angola up to the Atlantic Ocean coast was a fully sovereign state that even made independent attempts at incorporating Christianity and elements of Europeanism into its own structure. The arrival of the Portuguese and the emergence of Kongo in the late fifteenth century as unquestionable leader among all the Central African coastal states made this possible. However, the influence of the Portuguese colonialists led to stiff and destructive warfare encroachment on Kongo by *Tyo* (*Tio*), *Ndongo* (*Mbundu*), and *Jaga* neighbors. Portuguese troops saved the now helpless Kongo from total destruction by the Jaga. But the Angola colony that was around the time founded by the Portuguese, would a century later lead to the destruction of Kongolese political power (Vansina 1968: 37). Portuguese interest in Kongo was dependent on their reliance on the kingdom for slaves. The enslaved were shipped to Brazil and other parts of the Americas to work the plantations. Interest of the Portuguese wavered following the invasions by neighbors. Kongo in the seventeenth century attempted to break away from the Portuguese and join up with the Dutch, but the Portuguese prevailed in the Battle of Ambuila in 1665. Epidemics, many imported by the Portuguese, had set in as slavery decimated the population. Inflation as a result of the importation of vast amounts of seashell (*nzimbu*) currency had cheapened the economy. There was also significant vying for power among the princes. The kingdom deteriorated as colonial rule moved in. The Portuguese ruled Angola, the French ruled (Republic of the) Congo, and Congo (Zaire) came under the domain of the Belgians.

The basic Kongo political unit in the sixteenth century was the village, and it had a localized matrilineage at the core. This grouping encompassed the children of the lineage head who was oftentimes hereditary, as well as of the client lineages. There appears to have existed enslaved captives, enslaved criminals, and free captives. Above the village level were districts headed by either king appointed or provincial governor appointed officials. The king could remove the district officials at his discretion. The officials were invested with judicial and administrative power. While some districts were directly under kingly governance, some were integrated into one of six provinces. The provinces were headed by governors appointed by the king who could again remove them at his discretion. The functions of the governors were almost the same as those of the district chiefs although they appear to have often functioned as the king's councilors. The military structure composed of a permanent bodyguard of mostly captive foreigners such as *Tyo* (*Teke*). There was not a standing army and, in the case of war as among the Ganda, every able bodied man was summoned by territorial officials and village headman to assemble at a convenient place. Kongo neither had military technicians though there were military title holders, nor elaborated war schemes. Again without logistics, war could not be prolonged (Vansina 1968: 41-44).

The poorly organized military structure was a strength insofar as casualties in the case of war would likely be small, whereas it was a weakness in the case of stalwart attacks by adversaries. Kongo's political structure was strong in that, as compared to other Central African polities, it was highly centralized. The weaknesses that would again prove tragic were the overdependence on the personality and discretion of the king, and the lack of clear rules of ascendancy to the throne that frequently lead to the formation of opposing factions.

The Kongo are today a highly urbanized population within whose territory the nation capitals Brazzaville and Kinshasa are located. The local headmen do not wield much authority. The economy the Bakongo engage in includes mining, engineering, and construction. The rural areas have villages of up to 300 dwellers. The crops include cassava, rice, peppers, peas, peanuts, corn, beans, eggplants, and oil palms. The men do most of the clearing of the land for cultivation, while the women do the tilling and the rest of the farm work. Hunting and fishing is carried out, but much of the herding is commercial ranch based. It is women that mostly carry out the marketing of the produce. Following the influence of the Portuguese and the Vatican over the centuries, most of the Kongo are Christians--mostly Roman Catholics. But indigenous practices still exist including the practices of medicine men or herbalists (*banganga*), prophets or spirit mediums (*bangunza*). As in many African groups, the Kongo revere and appease dead ancestors since their spirits protect the descendants. The Supreme Being is *Nzambi Mpungu*. Contact with him is through spirit mediums and ancestral spirits. Nzambi was generally regarded as a Goddess until the introduction of Christianity whereby a lot of churches regard him as the Almighty. There are also lesser traditional Gods that the Kongo appeal to. Shrines, sacred objects (*minkisi*), and medicines are dedicated to these Gods. Minkisi take various forms including pouches filled with special herbs or medicines, and statuettes. The minkisi are concentrated on during prayers. During such special ceremonies, the minkisi are to be arranged in a special way, and the appropriate songs are sung. Improper observance of rituals can cause Nzambi or the spirits to get angry and rain misfortune on the people. Kongo artists are renowned for their beautifully carved and polished sculptures. A lot of the carvings portray a mother holding her child, with an emphasis on the face of the mother. The sculptures celebrate fertility, beauty, and dignity of the Kongo mother. Minkisi figures are often ones of powerful and frightful expression, some riding on animals while holding spears or knives.

Family descent is matrilineal. The males start having a close association with, and some even start living with, their maternal uncles at puberty. The property of a man is inherited by his sister's children. The father still has an important role to play in the lives of his children, although the matrilineal system essentially renders additional protection to a mother and her children. When a man rises to a position of importance, his children tend to develop a closer relationship with him than with their maternal uncle. The father also receives part of the dowry for her daughter, and he is recognized as having great spiritual power over his children. In the case of his child getting ill, the father can be consulted to get rid of a curse or to provide a medicament.

Langi

The *Langi* (singular: *Lango*, though a lot of the literature treats this as plural form too or as a mega class of ethnics) like related Sudanic-Luo ethnics like the *Acholi*, *Alur*, *Lugbara* and *Madi*, still have the basic characteristics of Sudanic Hamites like the *Iteso*, *Turkana*, *Jie* (*Lango-Olok*) and *Karimojong* (*Lango-Dyong*) which include the nomadic pastoralist and and the age-set system. The area of habitation of the Langi is referred to as *Lango*. A singular characteristic of the Langi is that while their language affinity is with the Acholi, their cultural way of life bears resemblance to that of the Iteso. The Langi comprise 5.6% (1.12

million people) of Uganda's population, and they occupy a center part of Uganda north of Lake Kyoga, with the Nyoro to the west, the Acholi to the north, the Ganda and Soga to the south, and the Iteso to the east. It is noteworthy that this text deals with the Langi of Uganda as opposed to the Langi of northeastern Tanzania (who are also known as *Rangi* and *Irangi*) further to the south. The two groups are not closely related in ethnolinguistic characteristics, and the Ugandan Langi are three to four times larger in population.

Tradition states that the Ugandan Langi originated from Mt. *Otukei* (*Awil*) in an environment of abundant rainfall. This land is sometimes equated with *Kaffa* in Abyssinia (Ethiopia). The Langi are said to have separated from the Karamojong and the Jie. The Langi were tradition-ally known for heavily adorning, tattooing, and piercing themselves. They wore large quantities of beads and bracelets, wore metallic objects in their noses and upper lips, pierced their ears and tongues, and plastered themselves.

The Langi exhibit a patrilineal, polygynous, and exogamous way of life that involves two levels of ancestral descent. They are the lineage (*doggola*) and the clan (*atekere*) levels. Since oftentimes the chief func-tioned as the head of the lineage, it could become difficult to differ-entiate the clan from the lineage system. The clan comprised of two or more lineages, and the lineage enlarged proportionate to the ex-pansion of the clan. Identification with lineage superseded that with the clan, partly because clans would expand and migrate, but still cling to their lineage as family identity. But the prevalence of migration that would lead to a group becoming absorbed into the lineage group al-ready living at the new place, renders the lineage model more theo-retical than realistic. Intra-clan and intra-lineage marriages, though ta-boo, were therefore at times difficult to avoid. Despite the pervading importance of lineage identity, the clan evolved into the system th-rough which kinship was associated, and the clan did command the respect and loyalty of everyone. Cattle were often branded with clan symbols. The manifestation of supernaturalism among the Lango was *Jok*. *Jok-Lango* was approached concerning diseases that had little or nothing to do with demon possession. Demon possession issues were addressed to *Jok-Man*. Other Jok manifestations included *Jok-Atida* and *Jok-Orogo*. The concept of Jok involved flexibility given that he was still regarded as an individual entity that would sometimes be equated to the devil. Each Langi family had a shrine (*abila*) to which sacrifices were offered to avert evil and to ensure food abundance.

The agricultural aspect of Lango society involved work groups called *wang tic* that were allied to twenty to forty households of each village. This group, headed by elders, controlled the allocation of new and abandoned land, and carried out the heaviest tasks such as clearing the land for sowing. The man whose land was cleared was obligated, at the end of the day, to provide beer to the work team as a token of

appreciation to them. The Langi harvest a large variety of food products. They cultivate sweet potatoes, cassava, eleusine and sorghum,
and millet. Bananas, yams, and maize are grown in much smaller quantities. The vegetables include beans, gourds, marrows, pumpkins, and
peas. Grapes, figs, plums, and cherries grow in the wilderness. Cattle,
sheep, and goats are kept and, like several African semi-nomadics, the
Langi have a special fondness for cattle. The riverine and lacustrine
environment provides for the harvesting of fish. Birds are shot with arrows, and like many African Lakes ethnics, the Langi catch and fry
edible flying ants during the season. The Langi were originally a pastoral people that fed on meat and milk mixed with blood. But as some
of their numbers moved southward into the river and swamp environment of Lake Kyoga, and also came in increasing contact with cultivating peoples, their economy became one of a mixed nature.

At the micro level, the village was the most important sociopolitical
unit. It would consist of between 10 and 150 huts congested together in
linear and circular form as a defense mechanism against raids from
other villages. Granaries belonging to individual families were built in
front of the huts, while there were communal cattle kraals in the distance. "Bachelor/ single" huts (*etogo*) as well as girls' dormitories formed segments of these villages. The youth and guest huts had narrow
doorways enough for one to crawl in, this intended to lower the like-
lihood of enemies successfully aiming and shooting their spears at the
people sleeping inside during the night. The village also functioned as
a communally owned and managed self sufficient mechanism carrying
out activities like fishing, cattle grazing, and water collection. A means
similar to the *wang tic* is the *jo dwi dyang* that reared cattle on a communal basis. Conflict related to competition for resources would at times accompany clan and village expansion. Most of such clashes became sparked off by either a leader or a lesser individual having a dispute with a member of another village. It was in times of significant
danger, such as from a large-scale raids from a neighboring group, that
the Langi would ally themselves under a strong leader referred to as
the *Jago* ("paramount chief"). A war successful Jago would bring together a group of Jagos (to form the *Odonge-Ateker*), and as their overlord would be referred to as the *Rwot* (*Awitong*) which is equated to
"king," or "chief," but more specifically "war lord," since the status of
Rwots which in precolonial times consistently changed, depended on
their success in battle and on the breadth of territory under their
jurisdiction. Following battle, the Rwot arranged a feast during which
military ranks (*moo/ moi*) were conferred upon the gallant. The Rwot
was assisted by a council of elders and the leading elders of the clans.
The council of elders was charged with general administration and maintaining law and order within the clans. The council ensured and arranged the payments of debts, fines and restitution, and bride dowry.
The council also arranged for the disposing and distribution of the pro-

perty of the deceased.

A unique characteristic of the Langi was an "arms control" enforcement on society. The customary law disallowed the involvement of clubs, spears, and shields in any Langi intra-ethnic dispute, regardless of which village the disputants were from. At times when a dispute became difficult to arbitrate, warriors from the two villages would fell a tree that would separate the two parties. The two disputants on either side would be provided with whips. They would lash these at each other until the referee became satisfied that justice had been meted out to each other through this process. The Langi judicial system contained elements of harshness for such offenses as theft, adultery, murder, and wizardry (Nzita 1995: 113-114). Execution of the perpetrator could easily be the consequence.

Just as in the related Sudanic-Luo and Sudanic-Hamitic groups, the age-set system was very important in aspects such as organizing hunting groups and funeral ceremonies, resolving inter-clan conflicts, and the overseeing of moral and social conduct in society. Unlike such ethnics as the Karamojong, the Langi system was not organized to determine who, based on age, would fight in wars, or who would found new settlements as was the case with the Iteso.

A growing Langi population spurred on the quest for additional resources, and the Langi periodically raided neighboring ethnics. They carried out raids on the *Nyoro* and *Ganda*, often taking livestock, and also women and children. Subsequent intermarriage, adoption, and initiation of the captured resulted in the emergence of Langi leaders that were not originally Langi and those that were born of non-Langi mothers. The Langi always fought courageously, but their spear and bow technology was no match for the formidable gun equipped force of Arabs, Europeans, Sudanese and Acholi looking for slaves and ivory from the mid-1850's to late in the century. The Langi acted as mercenaries for or against the Nyoro, and were often involved in royal dynastic strife in Bunyoro and Buganda in the latter part of the nineteenth century.

The onslaught of all these forces coupled with disease outbreaks (such as of human and livestock sleeping sickness) proved to be so overwhelming. The previously enforced system of "arms control" became ignored and for the first time, a Lango would spear or knife another Lango in the event of inter-clan and inter-village conflict. The barter trade system between the Langi and the Nyoro, which had involved millet, simsim, goats and poultry in exchange for salt and ironware from the Nyoro and the Labwor, broke down. The Langi, given their limited skill in iron forging, had consistently imported lots of ironware including hoes from surrounding neighbors. Langi and Nyoro traders had, under full legal protection, often passed through each other's territory.

Luba

The *Luba* (sing./ pl.) ethnics are of Bantu ethnolinguistic background and they speak *Kiluba (Tshiluba)*. The three sub-categories of the Luba are the Luba of *Shaba* province (formerly known as *Katanga*), the *Luba Hemba* (or Eastern Luba) that live in northern Shana and southern Kivu provinces, and the *Luba Bambo* (or Western Luba) of Kasai province. The Luba all number approximately 2 million people. Luba descent lines are either matrilineal or patrilineal, depending on which group. Families form villages which generally compose of from one hundred to several thousand people. The chiefs still maintain some control, although the central government influence is there. Polygamy is not as common as it was in the past, bride dowry is still provided, and male initiation ceremonies that involve circumcision are still practiced. Traditional religion is still practiced alongside Christianity. Luba religion, like many African religions believes in a supreme being, in the existence of evil spirits that harass and even kill the living, and in the existence of ancestral spirits that protect the living. Elders and dead ancestors are venerated. Herbalists and medicine men combat diseases and evil spells, and serve as medical advisors.

Luba origins are traced to sixteenth century invaders (*balopwe*) in the area west of the upper Lualaba River and north of Katanga Lake in Congo (Zaire). They founded the early Luba empire and later on moved on to Lunda land where they established a kingdom. Luba emigrants would for more than century move in the eastern, western, and southern direction. Their impact was so profound that by 1750 Luba-Lunda culture and political influence was felt between the Kwango River in the west to Lake Tanganyika to the east. This encompasses a large area of Congo, Angola, and Zambia. Before the balopwe first established themselves, the area between Lake Tanganyika and the upper Kasai River in Southeastern Congo was mainly inhabited by small chiefdoms. The only two kingdoms in the area were those of the *Kanyok* and the *Bena Kalundwe* (Vansina 1968: 70-71).

The traditional Luba political unit was mostly that of a corporate or segmentary patrilineage. Each of the lineages consisted of clients affiliated by contract with the lineage and affiliated by domestic slaves. The village consisted of one to several lineages under the charge of a headman selected from the main lineage in the village by a superior chief if not the king himself. A council of all the heads of the lineages of the village assisted the headman with the governing. A chiefdom headed by a territorial chief consisted of several villages grouped together. A grouping of several chiefdoms made up a province headed by a provincial chief, and the provinces together made up the kingdom. There were however cases whereby chiefdoms came directly under the charge of the king, some whereby chiefship was hereditary, and some whereby the chiefs were appointed by their immediate superiors and then confirmed by the king. Some chiefdoms were parceled out for life while with others it was for a term of four years. The king could, at his discretion, still depose any chief. The king ruled at his capital, and a new king would found a new one (Vansina 1968: 72-73).

The central government consisted of the king and his title holders. Chief among the title holders was the war leader and head of an officer police corps (the *Twite*), the senior provincial chief and custodian of the sacred emblems (the *Inabanza*), a lesser senior chief (the *Sungu*), and a chiefdom ruler during an interregnum (the *Nsikala*). The majority of such titles were held by relatives of the king, more so those of his mother's patrilineage. Title holders resigned upon the king's death but could be reappointed or replaced. A new title holder was required to pay tribute to the king in the form of presents so as to secure his nomination, and in many cases titles were actually bought. Many of the titles were not hereditary, but close kinsmen often succeeded in such positions. The act of ascension to kingship and chiefship was believed to be transmitted through a (royal) bloodline by supernatural agencies (*bulopwe*). The king was therefore invested with divine and absolute authority. The checks on his power would mainly stem from opposing half-brothers and patrilineal relatives who would garner the support of the court and the populace in such cases as when the king was an overbearing tyrant (Vansina 1968: 73-74).

The Luba environment is one of savanna and tropical rainforest. The Luba are traditionally hunters and farmers that practice slash-and-burn agriculture. Slash-and-burn agriculture involves the clearing of portions of the forest for agriculture by cutting and burning the vegetation. These are abandoned upon the soil becoming exhausted, after which the farmers move on to another patch while allowing for the used soil to recuperate. The main crops are cassava, corn, millet, sorghum, vegetables, bananas, mangoes, and tobacco. The river and lake network in the area allows for extensive inland fishing. Goats, pigs, poultry, and sheep are raised, and hunting dogs are bred. Local industries include pottery, woodworking, basket making, blacksmithing, and net making. Salt is extracted from the marshland waters. The Luba, like the Mongo, employed fleets of caravans in their trading in the past. The rural markets of the present are recognized as the ones that replaced the outmoded trading practices. the Luba are artists of expertise and their products include wood figures that are completed carefully and thoroughly polished, masks for ceremonial use, jewelry, and an established core of oral literature.

Lugbara

The *Lugbara* (sing./ pl.) ethnics are a Sudanic people, shifting agriculturists primarily living in northwestern Uganda (of which they are 3.6% [0.72 million people] of Uganda's population). Offshoots of the Lugbara live in Sudan and Zaire. The Lugbara collectively number slightly over 1 million people. The Lugbara were originally known as

Madi, and the term Lugbara seems to have gained currency following the intrusion of Khartoum Arab slavers in the second half of the nineteenth century. The Lugbara are believed to have migrated southward from the Juba or Bari regions in Sudan. According to oral tradition, the Lugbara trace their origins to two male and female superhumans i.e. *Gboro-Gboro* and *Meme* respectively. God had filled Meme's womb with living things, but a gazelle happened to rapture the womb with its hoof. All the worldly creatures flowed out, with mankind last to emerge. Meme died immediately after giving birth to the male and female twins *Arube* and *Addu* respectively. These two married each other later in life and gave birth to future Lugbara generations. The Lugbara in the northwestern section claim to be descendants of *Jaki* (see below) whose sons migrated from Mt. Liru in Sudan towards the beginning of the 18th century. A group called the *Rubu* also claims to have come from Mt. Liru, but descended from *Aroba*.

The basic Lugbara traditional arrangement is the family cluster system of huts within a village divided into the clusters, with village membership consisting of between ten and twenty people, and headed by an old and venerable sage entrusted to the charge of complex ritual ceremonies. The Lugbara traditionally permit polygyny, though the majority of married men are monogynous. A single political unit called the *jo* is occupied by one wife and her small children, whereas the compound called the *aku* is the home of a married man.

Lugbara descent is patrilineal, such that the family cluster typically consists of men that are related to each other by descent from one grandfather or great-grandfather, of wives, and unmarried daughters. This lineage is a corporate group that owns its livestock and land jointly. The customary law of exogamy precludes anyone from marrying from his or her lineage, and marriage involves lengthy negotiation between the two lineages involved. Marriages were usually initially arranged by the parents, and the negligible numbers of divorces that took place usually resulted from a wife failing to bear children or a wife found in possession of poisonous and witchcraft charms.

Lugbara justice is administered by lineage heads who settle the minor offenses, and by clan heads who settle the serious offenses. Serious offenses included witchcraft and sorcery, unpaid loans, killing, and adultery. A lineage court consisted of family heads whereas the higher clan court consisted of lineage heads in collaboration with selected wealthy villagers and other notables. Court proceedings tended to take place under a big tree in the compound, and trials were conducted in privacy. The standard was for a murderer or an adulterer to be fined a cow or a bull. A male youth guilty of incest was fined a sheep which was consequently slaughtered and eaten for ritual cleansing purposes. Inter-clan offenses had more serious consequences than inter-clan ones. one caught committing adultery was killed or subjected to the lesser punishment of having his sexual organs maimed. In the case of fornication, the boy was held at ransom until he agreed to marry the girl or paid an appropriate fine. Noncompliance would result in the maiming of the boy's organs (Nzita 1995: 141-142).

The social classes of Lugbara society are the *Uruleba* (high people) and the *Andraleba* (low people) who claim descent from the brothers *Jaki* and *Dribidu* who migrated from the north in Sudan. Their numerous sons became the ancestors of the Lugbara clans that are more than fifty in number. Most disputes among the Lugbara arise over land ownership and allocation, as well as over inadequate payment of bride dowry. The Lugbara clientage system was called *Amadingo* and in this system the rich would protect and be influential in the lives of the poor in exchange for services such as manual labor. The clients could be assimilated into the upper class family, and they could be allotted land and their bride dowry could be paid by their masters.

Because the Lugbara shifted from place to place in search of fertile land, following rotating the crops and exhausting the soil, a non-static clan system arose. A clan was normally headed by a leader (*Opi*). Clan dispersal and members seceding from their clusters and forming new lineages would take place, and this would reduce the impact of the frequently congested village arrangements. It became more important to trace family lineage from a sub-clan other than the major clan. There is a differentiation in Lugbara society between names that depict descent and those that depict circumstance. Naming that depicts circumstance is the prerogative of the newborn's mother in collaborative discussion with the married women of the family cluster and the mother of her husband. This mother in law can give the child a second name. But upon the birth of the child, the first thing done was the cutting off of the umbilical cord. The midwife was required to cut the cord into three if the child was a boy, and into four if the child was a boy. The numbers three and four symbolize males and females respectively. This also corresponds with the number of days a woman that has given birth is required to stay in home confinement i.e. three for a male newborn, and four for a female newborn. During this time, the mother was to abstain from eating certain foods and she was to accept only a handful of visitors. These birth rituals were meant to cleanse and protect the fragile newborn and recuperating mother from evil and sickness. Festivities followed the ritual of confinement. Lugbara initiation for both genders took place during puberty. These involved the very painful practices of tattooing and extracting the six frontal teeth of the lower jaw. One who had not undergone these was despised and called a child and was not allowed to get married.

Lugbara land is fundamentally treeless open plateau surrounded by three mountain masses that effectively isolate the land. This isolation advantaged the Lugbara away from the horrendous slave raids in the late nineteenth century that negatively impacted neighboring southern Sudan and northern territories of Uganda such as Lango and Acholi.

Even the Anglo-Egyptian administrative posts set up along the River Nile section in the vicinity did not affect the Lugbara. The Belgian post set up at Ofude in 1900 (when most of Lugbara land was under Belgian Congo [Zaire/ Congo]) was the first colonial center in the land. After Leopold II died, Lugbara land came under the jurisdiction of Anglo-Egyptian Sudan, and the lawless ivory poaching in the area took precedence. In 1914, a large section of Lugbara were transferred to Uganda. Despite the transformations in the Lugbara society that involved missionary instruction and colonial agents exploiting Lugbara as military and production labor, the Lugbara have tended to be a proud people that regard the outside world as hostile and their own way of life as the most fitting.

Animals kept include cattle, goats, sheep, and fowl. The crops grown include eleusine, sorghum, sesame, peas, beans, sweet potatoes, groundnuts, pumpkins, maize bananas, sugar cane, and cassava. The game population has been reduced, but fish is caught in streams with the use of nets. Hunting buffaloes, bushbucks, antelopes, rabbits, squirrels and several other animals used to be commonplace. Edible flying ants are captured at the beginning of the rainy season. Seasonal and local grasshoppers are eaten. The shea-butter nut is the most important herb collected, and the roots and fruits of some wild plants were commonly collected. Though the Lugbara are essentially agriculturists, they owned large numbers of cattle before rinderpest epidemics decimated the herds. Lugbara women make various handicraft items including baskets and pots.

Luo

The *Luo/ Lwoo* as a collective group of related ethnics, comprise the group here referred to as Sudanic-Luo group that includes such groups as the *Alur*, the *Acholi*, and the *Jopadhola*. On a more restricted basis, the Luo or *Joluo* ("the people of the swamp") are often recognized as the Sudanic-Luo group that inhabits the environment east of Lake Victoria (mostly in Kenya) where they live adjacent to the *Luyia*, the *Suba*, and the *Kuria* (who are of the Bantu mega-group). The Luo therefore live in an environment in the surrounding where the Kenya, Uganda, and Tanzania borders together cross. These Luo number approximately 4 million, and are one of the largest East African groups. In Kenya, only the population numbers of the *Kikuyu* and the *Luyia* are larger than those of the Luo who number 13% of the population. They are known for their ability to adapt and take to imported aspects like the English language, western academics, and technical skills. The Luo are essentially an agricultural people and they grow millet, maize, sweet potatoes, beans, and sesame. They also keep cattle, sheep, goats and fowl. The Supreme Being is *Nyasi*, and he lives in the forest and bestows good health on the people.

Luwa (See Yaka and Luwa)

Luyia

The *Luyia/ Luhya/ Abaluyia/ Waluya* are a large collection of approximately seventeen ethnic groups with related Bantu ethnolinguistic
characteristics. They live in the vicinity of the southeastern and eastern
shores of Lake Victoria in an area that traverses southeastern Uganda
into southwestern Kenya, and is south of Mount Elgon. The area is
largely hilly, and is traversed by several rivers. The Luyia number
approximately 4 million and include such groups as the *Vukusu*, the
Tsotsu, the *Isukha*, the *Ragoli*, the *Hanga*, the *Nyole*, the *Samia*, and
the *Nyala*. Some in Kenya are referred to as the Bantu of Kavirondo
(i.e. in reference to the area and to the gulf of Lake Victoria called by
the name). The area serves as a confluence between his- torically
unrelated groups (i.e. Bantu, Sudanic Hamites, and Sudanic Luo), such
that the process of interethnic assimilation is still taking place. Ethnics
such as the *Iteso*, the *Nandi*, the *Gisu*, and the *Masai* are in the
surrounding. Many personal names used by the Luyia are of
Sudanic-Luo and *Sudanic-Hamite* origin. In Kenya, the Luyia (next to
the *Kikuyu*) are the second largest ethnic group, and they comprise
about 15% of the population.

Agriculture is the mainstay of the Luyia economy, though cattle may
have previously been the major source of food. Crops grown include
maize, millet, eleusine, beans, sweet potatoes, bananas, and tobacco.
Alongside cattle and dogs, chickens, goats, and sheep are kept. Fish
consumption is popular. The precolonial Luyia hunted with bows and
arrows, spears, clubs, dogs, and with the use of fire. They also used
wooden hoes in cultivating. Clubs, leather shields, and spears were
used in the warfare against raids by neighboring ethnics. The sus-
pension bridges across the numerous rivers were skillfully constructed,
even though they required constant maintenance. Baskets and mats
are made from hardy grass and palm tree leaves and midribs. Pots are
made by specialized potters that employ the spiral-coil method. Spear
blades and bill hooks are made by iron smiths. Some of the names of
God in Luyia society are *Nasaye* and *Liuva*. Like most African societies, the Luyia believe in respect for and sacrifice to ancestors, and
the prevalence of forces of evil in sickness and other misfortunes.

Maasai

The *Masai/ Maasai*, a *Sudanic-Hamitic* people, originally lived in
Ethiopia. Most of the nineteenth century involved the Masai trekking in
swarms southward into present day Kenya. The migration explosion
took place so suddenly, and was so aggressively successful, the reasons for which are still debated. They expanded as far southward as
far southward as Mountains Kenya and Kilimanjaro, covering vicinities
of Lake Turkana and the Rift Valley. Masailand covers one of the sin-

gle largest ethnic territories in East Africa, and the Masai number approximately 1 million.

Masai inclination to high mobility was a result of their exclusive dependence on animals for their livelihood, as well as their system of age-set initiation. The age-set system propelled bands of young men to wander about, do battle with other ethnics, raid cattle, and forcibly acquire land for their grazing cattle. The relatively high population of the Masai, coupled with the existence of numerous herds of intensely foraging Masai cattle, necessitated frequent abandonment and acquisition of land. A lot of the land that the Masai lived in or traversed was semi-arid, and this only intensified their hunger for new pastures. Though the Masai were sometimes beaten off by other groups, they generally expanded so successfully that entire ethnic groups were dislodged from their homelands. The displaced would in turn drive away other groups as the displaced ones retreated and searched for new territory.

Though the mobility and heavy dependence on cattle contributed to territorial expansion of Masailand, this would emerge as a weakness. During the late nineteenth century, rinderpest, trypanosomiasis and pleuro-pneumonia of the cattle decimated the herds and resulted in widespread starvation. There are numerous accounts of the "Great Rinderpest" that decimated as much as 90% of cattle owned by some ethnic groups of eastern and southern Africa. To worsen the situation, locust invasions and smallpox epidemics took their toll. The Masai also became disadvantaged when the British colonial administration effectively outlawed raiding and warfare, and assigned fixed territory to a lot of the ethnic groups. The constant need for new land by a culture that spurned agriculture, could not be adequately met. Though the Masai have always been known to be a very proud people resistant to change, a lot of the population has over the years had to relinquish the traditional way of living and even migrate to urban areas and assimilate with others. The Masai now occupy 41000 square miles lying in Kenya through to a portion of northern Tanzania. Alongside the cattle, the Masai have the pressure of having to feed their sheep and goats, and also compete for vegetation resources with game.

The Masai traditional setting involves a village kraal of many households built a few miles from the well. Elders build the kraal known as the *enkang* that houses the elder's wives and children. The *manyata* is the kraal for the bachelors (*moran*), but also houses post-childhood sisters, and some mothers that are grown out of the child-rearing phase. Though the Masai are traditionally polygamous and a man can have as many wives as he can pay cattle dowry for, households with more than one wife are now rare, and even a unit with more than two wives was not common in the precolonial past. The bachelors were the warrior age-set that raided cattle from neighboring groups, and also functioned as frontier guards. Boys functioned as shepherds until their teens when they were circumcised and became warriors (*ol-murrani/ morani*). Later at the age of about 25, a ceremony confirmed them into elderliness, they could marry, and they became known as *ol-moruo* (elders).

The Masai traditionally despised occupations like fishing, cultivating, hunting, and blacksmithing. The blacksmiths forged the swords and the spear blades for fighting, constituted a low caste of the Masai group, and the members could only marry other blacksmiths' daughters. Only buffalo and eland which the Masai consider close in biological relationship to cattle, were seen to be worthy of consumption. They did not eat eggs, fish, or fowl. Elephant was hunted for ivory to sell to the Swahili traders for copper wire to be made into ornaments. Trading with other groups was confined to women who even in time of war continued with their commercial traveling since they were not molested by warriors. Masai, unlike other groups, have managed to maintain a lot of their traditional ways.

Mongo (See **Hamba, Mongo, Tetela**)

Nandi

The *Nandi* are part of the *Sudanic Hamite* ethnic family referred to as the *Kalenjin* that also includes the *Kipsigis*, the *Marakwet, Tugen,* and the *Suk.* They live in western Kenya and they number approximately 0.6 million. The Nandi have traditionally been nomadic pastoralists with a special fondness for their numerous cattle which symbolize wealth, pride, and prestige. The Nandi are very conservative, and take to cultivation quite reluctantly though their land is quite fertile. The Nandi like to wander, and they have preferred to herd and water cattle, and take the cattle to salt licks. Cultivation tended to be left to women who would grow minimal amounts of millet to make into porridge for their children, and to ferment into beer for the men. However, some ox-ploughing now takes place, and eleusine, maize, sweet potatoes, pumpkins, tobacco, and bananas are grown. Women perform the domestic work that includes making clothing and moulding pots, while the men clear the field of trees and stumps, forge iron, and make wooden objects. Both men and women are today engaged in milking, herding, breeding the cattle, and planting and harvesting the crops.

The ethnic group was given the name *Nandi* (derived from the Swahili word in singular: *mnandi*) by Swahili travelers and traders from the East African coast, that likens them in manner and looks to the voracious cormorant. The Nandi originally called themselves *Chemwal* i.e. cattle raiders. Nandi are world renowned for their stamina, especially as connected to their record breaking endurance in middle and long distance running. The most distinguished of such runners has been Kipchoge "Kip" Keino with a gold medal in the 1500 meter run at the 1968 Olympic Games in Mexico City, and a gold in the 3000 meter steeplechase and silver in 1500 meters run at the 1972 Olympics in Munich, Germany. More recently, Wilson Kipketer broke the decades old world record for the 800 meter run in 1997.

Nandi homesteads are mostly grouped together in a *koret* (parish) containing 30-90 units scattered in the neighborhood. The *kokwet* (parish council) under a chairman called "elder of the council" administers the koret and convenes a meeting when necessary to discuss important issues on a communal basis. Such issues can include crimes, debt settlement, taxation, environmental catastrophes (such as locust invasions, droughts, and cattle sicknesses), and inheritance of estates. In the precolonial, the warriors of a given district would be organized into an independent local conscription unit (the *bororiet*) under an officer (the *kiptaiyat*). Every parish was required to provide a company of 50 (the siret) under a lieutenant (the *kirkit*). A bororiet went out and fought independently during a raid.

The Nandi comprise about seventeen clans (*oret*), each of which has a totemic animal. They are patrilineal and exogamous. Approximately one third of all the Nandi households are today polygamous, with each wife presiding over her own household. Each man belongs to an age-set (*ipinda*), the set consisting of age-mates that undergo circumcision collectively. Circumcision, carried out on males between the ages of seven and fifteen, confirms men into warriorhood, as well as allowance to marry and construct a homestead in which the family will be raised. The circumcision ceremonies take place every fifteen years, and those of each group are required to respect members of the older age groups. Parents and elders are involved in initiation decisions that include choosing two respected married elders that are well versed in Nandi folklore to maintain a special mentorship relationship with the initiates throughout life. Initiation involves shaving of heads, singing, dancing, hunting, bathing in the river, seclusion, feasting, taking an oath involving swearing to secrecy, and gift presentation. The more rigorous aspects involve immersion of the young men into approximately five feet of water, and tightening of the tiny finger with a thong during the swearing to secrecy.

Ngbandi

These Congo (Zaire) people of *Adamawa-Eastern* ethnolinguistic backdrop were a domineering group in the seventeenth and eighteenth centuries. They were feared for their large numbers, aggressive migratory movements that involved subjugation and displacement of other groups, their valiant warriorhood, and their slave raiding. The *Ngbandi* expansion mainly took place southward and westward along the upper stretches of the Congo (Zaire) River in the inner basin. They trained with throwing knives, and the riverine people referred to them as "warriors." The Ngbandi even waged pitched battles with relatively powerful groups like the *Mongo* from whom they had acquired a large territory by the late 1880's. Groups like the *Doko* and the *Ngombe* responded to the Ngbandi threat by reinforcing their strong and large villages as well as reinforcing the level of social and political cohesion. Sometimes the overwhelming force of the Ngbandi would still prove too strong for the countering united and reinforced villages whose inhabitants were adamant about retreating and getting assimilated.

The Ngbandi founded dynastic chiefdoms in which their culture that stressed seniority of rank was emphasized. Their domineering stance is borne out by the fact that their language and culture became the most prestigious over a wide area of Congo.

Ntomba (See **Bolia and Ntomba**)

Nyankore

The *Nyankore/ Nyankole* (sing./pl.) ethnics are commonly referred to as *Banyankore/ Banyankole* (pl.), and a single one of them referred to as a *Munyankore* (or *Munyankole*). The predominantly cattle keeping territory of the Banyankore (referred to as *Nkore/ Ankole*) lies amongst the African Great Lakes in southwestern Uganda. Ankole is now recognized as the colonially created district that encompasses the original Nkore plus the formerly independent kingdoms of *Igara*, *Sheema*, *Buhweju*, and sections of *Mpororo*. Throughout most of its precolonial existence, Nkore was on the defensive against persistent attacks from the *Nyoro* (to the north) as well as from ethnics living in present-day Rwanda and northwestern Tanzania. However, the nineteenth century decline in strength of the attacking neighboring kingdoms of Bunyoro and Mpororo gave Nkore the opportunity to expand. The Banyankore comprise 8% (1.6 million people) of Uganda's population, there are pockets of them in Rwanda and Tanzania, and the language used (*Lunyankore*) is mostly of Bantu structure and is close to the language of the Kiga (*Lukiga*).

Similar to Bunyoro, political power was in Nkore entrusted to the king (i.e. *Mugabe*) and the *Bahima* ruling class, this aristocratic power largely based on wealth by cattle ownership in a fertile territory flourishing with livestock. The cattle attached Bahima class despised agriculture and on the bottom rung were the *Bairu* peasantry (the original inhabitants) associated with tilling. The Bahima were traditionally responsible for milking and herding cattle, whereas the Bairu did the bush clearing, worked the gardens, repaired the huts, and brewed the beer. The Nyankore had a more rigid caste system than their Nyoro kinship enemies, whereby the Bairu in Nkore were denied the right to own high quality cattle and to hold high office. Not all the Bahima were from the ruling clan, and the Mugabe frequently appointed ministers and chiefs to rule over the Bairu as well as Hima non-ruling producers. To assist him, the Mugabe had below him a Prime minister (*Enganzi*), the provincial chiefs next in line, then the lesser chiefs who were in charge of local affairs at the parish and sub-parish levels.

The staple food of the pastoralist Bahima was milk and it was surrounded with numerous taboos. Butter was smeared on the body, rubbed into leather to soften it, and also bartered for weapons and tools. The cow was standard currency. Both the Bahima and Bairu classes owed allegiance to the Mugabe and paid taxes and tribute (a lot in form of cattle, beer, and millet) that would subsequently be redistributed to the people according to their sociopolitical status. There was a reasonable level of friction between the Bahima and the Bairu even during the colonial era (from the late 19th Century to 1962) and after, and during the European scramble the Bairu "underdogs" took to the side of Catholicism while the Bahima "pro-colonialists" embraced Anglican Protestantism. Intermarriage, assimilation, and upward sociopolitical mobility still took place despite the rigid caste system in Nkore.

The Nyankore barely had priests, and it is medicine men that usually performed as priests. Offerings and sacrifices (mostly in form of cows and milk) were made to Gods and to ancestral spirits. Oral tradition ranks *Ruhanga* as the Supreme Being who lives in the sky and who created the first man and woman, *Rugabe* and *Nyamata*, respectively. It is believed that evil persons can employ sorcery to interfere with the good wishes of Ruhanga, and cause disease, drought, death, barrenness of land, and human infertility. Lesser Gods include *Isimbwe*, *Kagoro*, *Kazoba*, *Kyomya*, *Omusisi* (also known as *Nyabinge*), and *Wamara*. There were lesser Gods associated with particular families, and for which Gods shrines were erected and frequented for worship. Names of Gods also function as personal names.

Nyoro

The *Nyoro* (sing./ pl.) ethnics are commonly referred to as *Banyoro* (pl.), and a single one of them referred to as a *Munyoro*. The predominantly cattle keeping territory of the Banyoro (referred to as Bunyoro) lies amongst the African Great Lakes, and was originally a vast empire called *Bunyoro-Kitara* that ruled and exacted tribute from virtually all of what is now southwestern Uganda (i.e. the territory of the *Bakonjo*, *Kiga*, *Nyankore*, *Toro*, and part of *Buganda*), southward into Tanzania and Zaire, and even Rwanda (where some *Hutu*, *Tutsi*, and *Twa* reside), and eastward into the territories of the Acholi, the Ateso, and the Soga. The Nyoro comprise 2.9% (0.58 million people) of Uganda's population, many with Nyoro roots are found in Zaire, and the language used (*Lunyoro*) is mostly of Bantu structure and is close to the language of the Toro (*Lutooro*).

Nyoro food staples include millet, potatoes, cassava, beans, meat, and bananas. The Nyoro lived in scattered settlements found in the populated parts of the country, with the homesteads lying very close to one another. Each homestead had a family head (*nyineeka*) who in the event of death was succeeded by his eldest son. The village consisted of several homesteads under the charge of a specially recognized elder (*mukuru w'omugongo*) selected from among the village elders.

He was an intermediary between elders and the chiefs and headed an informal court with the assistance of a few elders. This court village settled village disputes. The level of cooperation and politics within the village was much more significant than outside it (Nzita 1995: 30-31). Prior to the colonial entree during the mid-late nineteenth century Bunyoro was a renowned center of trade. The major exports from Bunyoro included salt, iron ore, and ironsmith products such as red-hoes.

Prior to the twentieth century, political power was entrusted to the king (*Mukama*) and the *Babito* ruling class, the counties into which Bunyoro was divided, ruled by chiefs. This aristocratic power was largely based on wealth by cattle ownership in a fertile territory of grasslands flourishing with hundreds upon thousands of cattle. The *Bahima* cattle owning class beneath the Babito, similarly despised agri-culture but, did not constitute a ruling aristocracy. The *Bairu* peasantry (the original inhabitants) at the bottom rung did the cultivating and provided much of the surplus production and free labor services to the aristocrats. However, the marriages that gradually took place between these classes and the allowance for sociopolitical upward mobility lessened the importance of clan and ethnic differentiation. The obs-curing of class significance was, in the late nineteenth century, hastened by Mukama Kabarega's nationalistic military organization of mass levies (*abarusura*) of peasants whereby leadership was open to successful soldiers of any class (Steinhart 1977: 21). Military contin-gents were also secured from amongst the *Alur* and the *Acholi* to aid in countering the crumbling of Bunyoro, including resisting Arab and European militarism and commercialism.

Like the Ganda, the Nyoro have had an elaborate system of traditional religion involving priests and set rituals. Amongst the most important deities, and whose names function as personal names, are *Kaikara* who is the Goddess of harvest, and *Mulindwa* the Goddess of war. The Gods include *Muhingo* associated with war, *Ndaula* ass-ociated with pestilence, *Mugizi* associated with Lake *Muttanzige* (also known as Lake Mobutu/ Albert), *Kigare* associated with cattle, *Lubanga* associated with health, *Munume* associated with weather, and *Wamala* associated with human, animal, and crop fertility and abundance.

Male children are traditionally named three months after they are born, whereas with females it is four months. A simple naming ceremony takes place in which a parent, a grandparent, or some other relative gives the child a personal name as well as a traditional *mpaako* (pet) name. The father of the child, if known and present, has the final say in the naming. *Mpaako* names include *Abwoli*, *Adyeri*, *Araali*, *Akiiki*, *Atwoki*, *Abooki*, *Apuuli*, *Bala*, *Achaali*, *Ateenyi*, and *Amooti*. These *mpaako* names are of Sudanic Luo origin. Some of the Nyoro personal names are clan specific, while some portray significant circumstances during the birth or circumstances involved in the actual birth. But it is significant that most Nyoro names are real words derived from everyday speech and portray the state of mind of the namer. These names revolve around circumstances of disappointment, misfortune (such as death and poverty), and spite. Examples of such names translate to "they (i.e. the neighbors) do not remember (i.e. the good I did for them)"--*Tibaijuka*, "I eat with those (who are in reality enemies)"--*Ndyanabo*, "the little one arrives right in the midst of it (i.e. is born during an epidemic, or is born into a family that has had several deaths)"--*Kabwijamu*.

Polygamy is traditionally permitted among the Nyoro, and because bride dowry is not always a prerequisite as in most societies of Uganda, having more than one wife was not as difficult. Most cases allowed for bride dowry to be paid later i.e. after years of marriage. Marriages in Bunyoro are said to have been unstable, and divorce was frequent. The payment of dowry therefore required demonstration of some level of marriage stability within a family unit. Marriage potentiality began with mutual attraction between a girl and a boy (usually of the same locality). This was followed by formal acceptance and recognition on the part of the boy's family and the girl's father. But there are many informal unions in Nyoro society (Nzita 1995: 25).

Ovimbundu

The *Ovimbundu* (*Umbundu*) ethnics number approximately 3 million, are the largest group in Angola, and they primarily live in and around the Benguela Highlands of central Angola, an area stretching from the Atlantic Ocean coast to the *Kuanza* (*Cuanza, Kwanza*) River. The language is also *Umbundu* and it is of Bantu ethnolinguistic structure. The Ovimbundu group is the result of intermingling between the *Jaga* people and the resident indigenous populations. The Jaga are of the *Lunda* group of ethnics of Central Africa, and they came from northeast Angola as they invaded west and central Angola. The Ovimbundu became established as a distinct group in the sixteenth and seventeenth centuries. The Jaga tradition of warriorhood that the Ovimbundu embraced, gradually became diluted as they basically became a trading population. The Ovimbundu are frequently associated with and also confused with the *Mbundu* ethnics who live in northwestern Angola.

The Ovimbundu political system became well established during the eighteenth century, whereby royal families served as both political and ritual leaders through the king and his counselors. Before Portuguese colonization of the Benguela highlands i.e. prior to 1880, the political units were seven chiefships which though they had some minor civil wars among themselves, were in alliance. The beginning of the seventeenth century up until the early twentieth century involves violent encroachment on and exploitation of the Ovimbundu by Portuguese colonists. During this time, the slave trade was a major part of the economy, and it is estimated that during this time, up to 3 million enslaved were exported to Brazil.

The Ovimbundu are renowned for their traveling, and they are distinct in all the cities of Angola. Many have traveled to neighboring countries such as the Congo (Zaire) and South Africa to trade and to work. The Ovimbundu kingdoms strategically located between the coast and the interior served as trading crossroads whereby the Ovimbundu served as middlemen. Their economy became distinctly enriched in the nineteenth century, with Ovimbundu caravans traveling across the continent dealing in rubber, ivory tusks, wax, and slaves. The caravans sometimes involved thousands of people, and some of the Ovimbundu personal names are in reference to such caravans. But though high grade rubber became almost the single export of the Ovimbundu economy in the last quarter of the nineteenth century, increased competition with rubber from West Africa, Asia, and South America led to a large fall in price of Angolan rubber, whose value became declassified in relation to the rubber from competing countries. The horrific oppression of the Ovimbundu by the Portuguese that involved forced labor, discrimination, and heavy taxation made the plight of the Ovimbundu worse. All this triggered the *Bailundo* War during 1902-1903, the collapse of Ovimbundu caravan trading, and large-scale famine. The Angolan war of liberation began in 1966, and the civil wars have greatly disrupted the Ovimbundu way of life.

Ovimbundu farming is a mix of cattle rearing plus food and cash crops. The food and cash cash crops include cassava, corn, palm oil, palm kernels, cotton, coffee, bananas, and sisal. The highlands of the Ovimbundu are advantaged in that they are relatively free from the tsetse fly (that transmits sleeping sickness in cattle) which prevents animal husbandry in much of Angola. Ovimbundu family structure is both matrilineal and patrilineal, although the patrilineal mechanism has taken precedence over the years. Patrilineal connection gives an individual claims to land and residence rights, while matrilineal connection allows one to inherit movable property. The matrilineal system allowed a woman to belong to her birth family following marriage; for her children to belong to this family and to look to their maternal uncle as their highest authority. Primarily in the past, matrilineal kin provided an individual with financial resources for engaging in trading ventures, and was therefore an important aspect of the Ovimbundu economy. The prevailing custom is now for the father to arrange the marriages of his daughters and to receive the bride dowry (*ilombo*). It is common among the Ovimbundu, as is the case with many Bantu groups, for the first born male to be named after his paternal grandfather, and for the first born female to be named after her paternal grandmother.

Pare

The *Pare* (*Wapare*) ethnics are of Bantu ethnolinguistic background and they primarily live in northeastern Tanzania amidst the northern highlands that include the mountain ranges *Kilimanjaro* and *Usambara*. The Pare number 0.45 million, they speak the *Kipare* language, and family affiliation is based on clan. Pare society traditionally consisted of chiefdoms that contained villages. There were however political reforms in the nineteenth century that further centralized Pare society. The reforms included installation of district administrators. It was through the chief minister that one could get to the chief. The minister for agriculture was entrusted with encouraging and leading people to cultivate their fields. He also collected tribute. There was also a minister in charge of military and foreign affairs, and one in charge of health matters.

The Pare environment is one of perplexing variety that in addition to mountains incudes valleys, plateau, winding roads, broken hills, arid plains, and steep descent. Habitation, rainfall, and soil structure also varies from region to region. The name Pare may have originated from a name of one of the smaller mountain ranges--*Mpare*. Prior to the nineteenth century, the Pare were known as the *Asu*.

The variegated environment of Pare land translated to varying economic and subsistence activity from area to area, as well as differing languages and dialects. Before the nineteenth century, there was one centralized kingdom in northern Pare and no more than seven smaller units in the middle and southern parts. The coming of capitalist trading system that stretched from the coast to the hinterland of East Africa was a major instrument in the changes that took place in Pare land. Caravans manned by Swahili and Arab traders were frequent in the Pare area by 1861. A trading base became established in the Kilimanjaro area where elephant ivory was in abundance. The western and eastern plains offered a natural convenience for the caravans. Local supplies of sheep, sugar cane, chickens, goats, beans, peas, sweet potatoes, yams, cassava, pumpkins, baskets, groundnuts, corn, and bananas were exchanged for calico and beads. The impressive road network allowed for the Pare to trade with local peoples such as the *Chaga*, the *Samburu*, the *Taita*, the *Galla*, and the *Maasai*. The Pare also had iron smithing centers.

Initiation of boys and girls involved confinement of camp groups in the forest. The rites could involve up to six months, and they entailed loyal citizenship training. The initiates were taught obedience, perseverance, and morality. The boys were given physical and military training. All the training was to be kept secret under oath, including the learning of a secret language constructed by coining words (Kimambo 1969: 52). The numerous details included use of drums and other musical instruments, sometimes used to frighten away evil spirits from the camps. Boys were divided into age groups and among some Pare societies, they were circumcised during initiation.

Samia

The *Samia/ Samya* (sing./ pl.) ethnics are commonly referred to as *Basamia* (pl.), and a single one of them referred to as a *Musamia*. The Basamia are frequently grouped together with the *Bagwe* who they have intermingled with, the group collectively known as the *Basamia-Bagwe*. The Basamia-Bagwe live on the northern shores of Lake Victoria in a small area that traverses the Kenya-Uganda border. While the Samia are ethnically related to the *Luo* (*Joluo*), the Bagwe are related to the *Luyia*. The Basamia-Bagwe traditionally embraced a loose and segmentary sociopolitical system that did not even have chiefships. The village was the central unit, and it was under the charge of an elder (*Nalundiho*) who administered law and order, settled disputes, and served as rainmaker. The economy was based on subsistence agriculture involving millet, sorghum, cassava, and beans. Cattle, goats, sheep, and chicken have for long been reared. Land was communally owned on a clanship basis. In the past, the little trade the Basamia-Bagwe did with their neighbors was mainly the barter type.

The Supreme Being is referred to as *Were* or *Nasaye*. The ancestral spirits are the spirits of dead ancestors. They protect and advise their children and descendants, but when not appeased through ritual observance, they can cause harm, death, or misfortune. Ancestral spirits also act as a link between the the living and Nasaye. Children, as they approach puberty, traditionally stop sleeping in the same house as their parents. And it is not proper for sons-in-law and to have close contact with their parents-in-law so they would not sleep in the same hut. Women are traditionally forbidden from eating chicken, pork, or lung fish, but this rule is now hardly abided by. These religious and cultural expressions exist among several Bantu ethnolinguistic groups.

When it came to marriage, it was rare for parents of two households that were friendly to arrange for marriage between their children. The more common practice was for the boy to seduce the girl. If the girl's response appeared positive, the boy would plant a spear in front of the hut of the girl's mother. A consenting girl would take the spear inside the house, and thereafter negotiations would take place. There was no fixed bride dowry, and the demand tended to depend on the status and wealth of the boy's family, so that the rich were charged more than the poor. Bride dowry could range from four to eight cows and a wide assortment of goats (Nzita 1995: 74). Upon giving birth, the mother was to confine herself in the house for four days in the case of a female child, and for three days in the case of a male child. The mother and father were required to shave their hair upon the birth of a child. The child was named immediately after it was born. The name was given by the mother and it depended on the circumstances surrounding the birth. Many Basamia-Bagwe names are a depiction of children born during such circumstances as daytime, night, afternoon, and harvesting. As in many African societies, the twins among the Basamia-Bagwe are associated with both good and evil. Upon their birth, a sheep is slain and those that are present participate in treading on it. This was one of the rituals meant to wash away the taboos that accompany such births, and to also cleanse the twins.

Shona

The *Shona* (*Vashona*) are the dominant ethnic group in Zimbabwe, but there are Shona populations in the neighboring countries Botswana, Mozambique, South Africa, and Zambia. The Shona together number approximately 9 million. They are a people of Bantu ethnolinguistic background, and like many pastoralist oriented African people, they traditionally attach great importance to cattle which are of higher social than economic significance. The people known as the *Zezuru* (*Wazezuru*) live in Central Shonaland and other of the Shona groups include the *Karanga*, the *Ndebele*, and the *Vabudja*. The Shona are renowned for their impressive constructions of dry-wall enclosures (*zimbabwe*) that took place from the 1100's into the 1300's. The enclosures served as palaces, all numbering about 200, and the Great Zimbabwe which was the large of them displays excellence of this building system. European colonialists long held that Great Zimbabwe was built by Arab and Phoenician traders, on the grounds that blacks could not have been capable of such stone craft. The Great Zimbabwe became the commercial, political, and religious center of a prosperous economy whose basis was trade, mining, and agriculture. Iron, copper, and gold was mined. Cattle were herded and raised. The Shona controlled between the African interior and the Arab and Swahili coastal ports in present-day Mozambique. Ivory copper, and gold were exported, while a variety of fine products were imported from Europe and Asia. Clay, metal, and soapstone artifacts illustrate the skill and variety of Shona craftsmanship.

A major characteristic of the Shona despite the transformations in Africa over the decades including a lengthy European presence in Zimbabwean (Rhodesian) sociopolitics, is their continued close attachment to their traditional practices in such matters as religion, diet, marriage, nurturing, herbal medicine, and farming. The traditions and the background philosophies only differ slightly among the Shona groups. The Shona system comprises several independent chiefdoms built from several migrations and assimilations over the last few centuries. A common language and culture, as well as geographical propinquity unites these chiefdoms. Shona society also comprises a number of dispersed exogamous patrilineal clans and subclans. The village evolves around patrilineages that are four or five generations in depth.

Many Shona are employed in the mining involving a wide variety of mineral products. The important of these are gold, nickel, coal, copper, and iron. However, for the most part, Shona economy is agriculture based. The food crops include corn, barley, sorghum, millet, wheat,

vegetables, fruit, cassava, and soybeans. The cash crops include tobacco, sugar, and cotton. In addition to the cattle, the Shona raise
poultry, pigs, sheep, and goats.

Numbers of cattle owned in Shona society signify status and wealth,
and owners carefully herd and check on the count. Cattle are an integral source of bride dowry which can number in the tens of cattle. But
bride dowry can now be in the form of cash or an alternative service.
The payment of bride dowry (*roora/ lobola*) is a symbol of commitment,
a safeguard against groundless divorce, and symbolizes a covenant
between two families. Polygamy is accepted in Shona society although
it is now not as common as in the past. Cattle slaughtering is of ritual
importance in birth ceremonies, weddings, and ceremonies. Fertility
rites are carried out when crops are about to ripen, whereby young
heifers are slaughtered to enhance the productivity of the crops. Cattle
are involved in the rainmaking ceremonies that are at the beginning of
summer each year. In the case where a young couple fails to have
children, a heifer is slaughtered and the meat from which is mixed with
herbs and given to the couple to eat is believed to make them more
fertile.

Cattle are a source of milk which the Shona prefer to drink sour.
They are also used to plough the fields and they are an important
source of fertilizing manure. Cattle are also sold to fulfill financial obligations such as paying for the education of children. In some cases,
cattle serve as compensation for grievous offenses. Boys and young
men traditionally herd the family cattle. Parents without boys old
enough to herd cattle can negotiate to borrow a herding child from
another family. The borrowed boy herds the cattle for one or two years,
after which his family is rewarded a cow for each year of his services.
The cow and its offspring can in part serve as his bride dowry when he
reaches marriageable age. More so in the past, girls could similarly be
recruited to baby sit for families for an indeterminate period of time
and were rewarded meals and clothing for their services.

As with peoples like the *Nyakyusa*, the herding phase is one of the
most rigorous ones of a boy's life. Boys eat breakfast and leave for the
pastures early in the morning. Unless he carries food along with him,
he can spend the whole day without food other than wild fruit. Herding
boys also spend the time when the animals are resting trapping and
shooting at birds, shooting at lizards, playing hide-and-seek, swim-
ming, boxing and fighting with one another, and hunting with dogs.
These activities, including the fighting, are considered an integral part
of socialization including bonding with peers, growing up, and maturing
into a man.

This phase generally tends to go on from early childhood up to the
age of 14. Herding boys form groups and the squabbles and fights involve each boy striving to be a leader of his group. A leader or bull
emerges and there is a hierarchy with vested authority and duties

beneath him. But the bull is ever vulnerable since challenge to his authority is frequent. A challenge can begin with a defying boy starting an argument with the bull. This degenerates into a third boy erecting two mounds of sand that represent the breasts of the bull's mother. The challenger then kicks one of the mounds, this representing the spiteful form of insult to the bull. Should the challenger win in the fight that erupts, he becomes the leader. Sometimes the bull arranges fights in a series style that can start with two challengers, then the winner progressing to the next stage of fighting someone else. These fighting contests for dominance which sometimes involve sticks can take days and the fights are usually broken up when one of the boys starts to bleed or is obviously losing in the battle. Fighting can also involve one village (or extended family) group fighting another village group of boy herders.

Yet as a rule the fighting is treated as a socialization and moulding game, the tensions are short term, and the disharmony is not carried into later life. The parents are not told about the fights and they do not get directly involved even when their sons appear to be injured. And such fighting games are not carried out at school. On the other hand, the girls of this stage of growth usually stay in the village assisting their mothers. They now and then have quarrels and fights and their mothers can become involved and take sides in strife between their daughters and other girls.

In addition to the parents, the extended family is involved in the social and moral teaching of young Shona and this teaching continues throughout life. The grandmothers, the paternal aunts, and the wives of the uncles are important in giving customary and etiquette instruction to a girl. The boys are trained by their grandfathers and their maternal uncles. At the formal level this training is conducted in the house (*imba*) and the council place (*dare*). Such matters as use of clean language, marriage conduct, work ethics, bringing up children, learning traditions and folklore are taught to and discussed with the Shona youngsters.

The Shona mother, even during pregnancy, is treated as a crucial part of the well being and bringing up of her child. When pregnant the mother is encouraged to focus on people of admirable quality since it is believed that these can be transmitted to the unborn baby whose psyche, character, and physical appearance is then influenced. Simultaneously, the pregnant mother is to fill her mind with pleasant thoughts, and avoid looking at sights that are unpleasant or grotesque, and avoid looking at people with deformities. Special herbs and other medicines are often administered to pregnant women. Newborn babies are treated as fragile beings vulnerable to sickness and evil and are kept indoors during the first five or six days following birth. During this time only the mother, the midwife, and sometimes the grandmother take care of the baby. The midwife carefully buries the fallen off umbilical cord after it is treated with preventative medicine to combat possible evil action by witches against the baby. The midwife's looking out for the welfare of the newborn can continue right into late childhood. It is after the umbilical cord falls off that the child is taken outside the hut for the first time. After she is bathed, she is given a name by the midwife, but the naming does not have a specific time and can be done weeks after birth. The name that the midwife gives the child is done in collaboration with the father.

A child is commonly given a name of a grandparent, and (or) a name that relates to significant circumstances in the family or the country at the time the child is born. However there are slight differences in naming practice from one Shona regional population to another. It is now forbidden by law to kill a twin, or to leave unfed or to die babies with deformities. However, the Shona traditionally treat twins as unwelcome evil omens whereby one of the infants is exposed and left to die. Similarly, those with deformities would be subjected to conditions that would lead to their deaths.

The Shona, like most African societies, believe in a Supreme Being (*Mwari*) and ancestral spirits (or the living dead, *wadzimu*). A function of the spirits of dead elders is to protect their immediate descendants. Elders are then to be highly respected and appeased when they are alive and after they die. Upon death the rituals in their honor are to be properly carried out, they are to be accorded proper burial, children are to be named after them, and their names are not to be uttered carelessly or in a defamatory style. Many African peoples believed that the ancestral spirits would punish their ancestors with illness or death if their needs are neglected.

Soga

The *Soga* (sing./ pl.) ethnics are commonly referred to as *Basoga* (pl.), and a single one of them referred to as a *Musoga*. The highly fertile region of the Basoga (referred to as *Busoga*) embraces both pastoralism and crop cultivation in roughly equal proportions and lies amongst the African Great Lakes between the northern shores of Lake Victoria and southern shores of Lake *Kyoga* (*Kioga*), to the immediate east of *Buganda* (i.e. east of the River Nile) and to the immediate west of Bukedi. The River Nile starts flowing from Lake Victoria at the border between Buganda and Busoga. The Basoga comprise 7.7% (1.54 million people) of Uganda's population, and the language used (*Lusoga*) is a generalization of several dialects in the area that embrace Bantu, Sudanic-Hamitic, and Sudanic-Luo structure, the degree to which they embrace these depending on which part of Busoga in relation to historical association with neighboring ethnics. The history of Busoga is complex in part because movements of people and intermingling within this region took place at a very rapid, continuous, and liberal rate. But this sociopolitical fluidity that little encouraged large-scale unity and centralization, rendered the inhabitants vulnerable to influence by the powerful neighboring kingdom states *Bunyoro* and *Buganda*.

It is believed that the earliest inhabitants in Busoga were *Langi*, *Iteso*, and *Gisu*. The region later became flooded by Ganda immigrants whose primary origin, like others of Bantu ethnolinguistic descent is traced to Katanga in Congo (Zaire). The erroneous grouping of Soga and their domineering Ganda neighbors as the same people has negatively overshadowed the importance and devotion to study of Soga tradition and language. But given the existence of several Soga dialects alongside the varying cultures, the better standardized Ganda language (*Luganda*) has for a long term still served as an important lingua franca in Busoga.

Busoga has a checkered history, and originally did not have the centralized political structure that its powerful westside neighbor Buganda had evolved. Busoga was organized in small principalities estimated to number from forty five to seventy, and an overriding clan system in a social system of polygyny and exogamy served for family identity. Northern Busoga was originally part of the *Nyoro* kingdom, and southern Busoga during the nineteenth century was at times tributary to the Ganda kingdom. Frequent Ganda raids on the area, as well as Ganda migrations and political influences resulted in the entity known as Busoga that had previously not had a common name. Each area had tended to be named after its ruler. Ganda conquistadors applied the name Busoga, named after Chief Kasoga's area in the neighborhood of Buganda, to the rest of the region. The Basoga do not appear to have been a martial people, although they had their scuffles with the Ganda, as well as with British colonial armies (heavily composed of Ganda and Sudanic Nubian soldiers) in the late nineteenth century. Busoga for a long time had the advantage of limited access since it is heavily forested.

The Busoga population did not suffer the periodic decimation experienced in some other parts of Uganda, and was often a peaceful refuge for neighboring ethnics searching for greener pastures, as well as a retreat for neighbors fleeing violence and persecution. Busoga also had the advantage of being relatively self contained. It is a very fertile land, with well watered agricultural land on which is grown plantains, millet, sweet potatoes, sugar cane, maize, and coffee. Cattle, goats, and sheep are also reared, and blacksmiths traded iron with neighboring groups. The large diversity of cultural practices and dialects among the Basoga reflects the territory's historical prominence as one of in-migration and assimilation.

The deities of Busoga include *Lubaale* the Supreme Being. Others are *Nawandyo* the Goddess that protected the family against sicknesses and other problems in the unit, *Nakiwulo* the Goddess who assisted people detect thieves and recover lost property, *Nnaalongo* the healer of all illnesses, *Bijungo* (*Bilungo*) the God associated with plague, *Gasani* the God associated with human fertility, health and the sky; *Kitaka* the God associated with earthquakes, *Kumbya* the God associated with freshness of well and stream water, *Kibumba* the mediator God, *Jingo* (*Jjingo*) the public God, and *Mpologoma* ("the lion") the God associated with the river called by his name. *Mukama* is the Creator, and a child born with visible teeth is believed to have supernatural powers, and is named after him. *Ssemaganda* was, paradoxically, associated with death as well as wealth and fertility. The several fetishes have included *Gomba* the fetish believed to instruct women on how to go about becoming mothers, *Nambaga* the fetish who at night told men how to become wealthy, and *Nnakalondo* whose function was to announce the slayer of one that had recently died under mysterious circumstances. The Basoga believe in the existence of a spirit world. Spirit mediums, magicians, and fetish custodians are called *baswezi*.

The Gods *Gasani*, *Kibumba*, and *Mpologoma* were very important in the lives of the *Kene* (*Kenyi*) living in the environment of Lake Mpologoma (Salisbury), the eastern extreme section of Lake Kyoga in east central Uganda. Perhaps the *Bakene* (also plural for *Kene*) are best renowned for their remarkable adaptation to the marshy riverine environment containing little arable land. Their dwellings are constructed from papyrus stalks, and the homes float on root systems of papyrus plants. There is very little cultivation and the main occupation is fishing with use of large fish traps, and with rod and line from canoes. Fish composes the main diet, and a lot is harvested and smoked for trade. The Bakene have traditionally been the ferrymen of Uganda, and get paid for ferrying people and their cattle across the waters.

The *Bakene* have never collectively been known to be a belligerent people, but their unique adaptation to an aquatic setting, as well as their ability to move swiftly, served as defense. Most accounts equate the word *Bakene/ Bakenyi* to "the fish people." Michael Nsimbi's definition of the term as having been adapted from the Ganda word "bagenyi" which means "visitors," as the Bakenyi are said to have been referred to in the areas they settled in Buganda, is questionable but likely contains elements of truth. The Bakenyi did not maintain a large population, partly because families migrated frequently and became assimilated into other groups.

Sotho

The *Sotho* (sing./ pl.) ethnics of southern Africa are commonly referred to as *Basotho/ Basuto* (pl.), and a single one of them referred to as a *Mosotho/ Mosuto*. The Sotho are of Bantu ethnolinguistic background and they number 5 million. The Northern Sotho live in the northern and eastern Transvaal province of South Africa, while the Southern Sotho live in Orange Free State (in South Africa) and in the nation *Lesotho* (formerly *Basutoland*). The language of the Northern Sotho is known as *Sesotho sa Leboa*, while the closely related one of the Southern Sotho is known as *Sesotho*.

The Sotho are believed to have migrated from west and central Africa where they had developed a mode of life based on ironworking and farming. From around the year 1000, they gradually absorbed the resident *Khoisan* population as they adapted several aspects of Khoisan culture including language and musical instruments. By about 1400, the Sotho had established their main clans that were symbolized by animal totems. Groups of these clans merged to form the Southern Sotho, the Northern Sotho, and the Western Sotho (*Tswana*). The Tswana are now frequently regarded as an ethnic group separate from the others. During the seventeenth century, the *Pedi* category of clans became dominant among the Northern Sotho, establishing the Bapedi empire that lasted more than 200 years. During the time, the Southern Sotho were living in an era of relative peace and prosperity. The internal intrigues, the cattle raids, and punitive expeditions were infrequent among the scattered and mostly independent Southern Sotho groups.

Then came the 1820's when Sotho society became disrupted by the *Mfecane/ Difaqane* that involved mass migrations prompted by upheavals east of the *Drakensberg* Mountains, as many groups fled the devastating *Zulu* invasions. Many ethnic groups fled the pursuing and plundering impi regiments of Shaka Zulu. These included the *Ngwane*, *Ngoni*, and *Khumalo* groups, and they attacked and dispossessed neighboring groups as they fled. Clans were disrupted, fields destroyed or abandoned, and famines set in. This circle of events lasted for nearly 20 years. Following the Mfecane, the Bapedi area became colonized by *Boers* (*Afrikaners*), and the region (*Transvaal*) became part of the Republic of South Africa. Under the imposed apartheid policy of 1948, the Northern Sotho became third class citizens. The 1959 establishment of *Bantustans* (homelands) in which the black population was forced to live, was a further attempt by the South African government to separate the white from the black population. The Northern Sotho were allotted a number of separate regions together known as *Lebowa*.

Among the Southern Sotho, the only category that successfully resisted the Mfecane were members of the *Kwena/ Koena* (crocodile) clan led by *Moshoeshoe* (*Moshesh*) I. He managed to unify southern Sotho clans and establish the Basuto Kingdom. Moshoeshoe's strategic advantage of high and flat-topped mountain location encouraged refugees and many local chiefdoms to ally themselves with him. The Europeans who moved into the kingdom, did so gradually as missionaries, hunters, and traders, initially coming sporadically in tented wagons. They were even granted rights of temporary cultivation and grazing. But their intentions to settle soon became apparent, and their superior strength in gun munitions worked against Moshesh. Upon losing roughly two-thirds of the kingdom's arable land to the Boers' newly established Orange Free State, Moshoeshoe asked for British protection as he fought hard against Boer invasion. More setbacks included the withdrawing of British support in 1854 that had been granted in 1848. Moshesh was even forced into manufacturing his own gunpowder. But encouraged by the support of French migrants, Basutoland became a British protectorate in 1868, and remained so until it became the independent Lesotho in 1966.

The traditional political unit of the Sotho is the village averaging between thirty and fifty families. Sotho families belong to clans that are affiliated with a common ancestor, a totem, and sometimes cultural characteristics. People generally do not marry those of their clan. Up to well into the nineteenth century, Sotho economy was strongly cultivation and cattle based. The Sotho had large herds of cattle, and they exported grain to other regions of southern Africa. But since that time, a large proportion of the men have taken to the migrant laboring in the coal, diamond, gold, and other industries of South Africa. The raising of the children, and the tending of farms is mostly done by the women. The crops grown include sorghum, corn, wheat, and vegetables. The animals raised include pigs, goats, sheep, and cattle.

Many Sotho still follow traditional religion. The souls of the dead (*badimo*) are believed to influence, so offerings to portray thankfulness are periodically made to them. There are also traditional herbalists and ritualists. These function to help combat disease, misfortune, and evil. These practitioners also help enhance crop and human fertility, and they convey good luck and prosperity. Sotho oral tradition is very strong and it includes praise poems (*lithoko*), songs that describe the lives of migrant workers (*lifela*), and groups of people singing together in harmony (*tumellano*).

Suk

The *Suk* (also known as *Pokot*) are *Sudanic-Hamites* that belong to the *Kalenjin* family of ethnics, whereby they are related to the *Nandi* and the *Karamojong*. They live in western Kenya and a small portion of eastern Uganda and they number approximately 0.25 million. Like the Nandi, the Suk are largely nomadic and have a fondness for their numerous herds. The precolonial Suk were frequently raided by the Turkana to the northeast, and by the Masai. There were also ceaseless disputes with the Karamojong over grazing land along what became the Kenya-Uganda frontier north of Mount Elgon.

A large part of Suk land does not get adequate amounts of rainfall, and the Suk adapted to eating herbivorous game, and even some omnivorous game that is trapped and speared. During famines, the Suk even ate roots and berries. Irrigation, under strict water rationing rules, takes place in the land, and the crops cultivated include millet, eleusine, and tobacco. The Suk also consume milk along with raw blood let out from the jugular vein of cattle that is opened by a special arrow (*terema*). The boys take cattle to the pastures at sunrise, and after the new moon is sighted, the cattle are driven to the salt lick.

The Suk are divided into twenty clans which are again divided into two to twenty sub-clans. Clan names are commonly animal, bird, or insect names, and such phenomena as sun, rain, or thunder. After the boys are, in small groups, circumcised upon reaching the age of ten, they take on confirmation into warriorhood and take on the name prefix "son of" ("*Arap*"). The Suk traditionally did not have chiefs or any form of elected leadership, though a council of elders empowered by communal agreement would take on such duties. A group of homesteads would form a council of elders chaired by a highly respected senior householder. Thieves were heavily fined, and executed if the behavior reached an extreme habitual level. One who committed manslaughter was required to pay up to fifty herd of cattle to the family of the victim. The ritual leader predicted war and provided the warriors with magical power. Priests conduct the religious ceremonies, including cleansing and chasing away evil spirits. The Supreme Heavenly God is *Tororut*, the wife is *Seta* (the Pleiades), and their sons include *Ilat* (the rain God), *Arawa* (the moon), and *Topoh* (the evening star). *Asis*, the Sun God, is the brother of Tororut.

Swahili

The *Swahili* ("coastal dwellers") are mainly recognized as people of the African-Arab ethnolinguistic tradition that mainly developed along the East African (Indian Ocean) coast and adjacent islands as a result of commercial and religious contacts from the second century between Arabs and indigenous (mostly Bantu and Cushitic) peoples. Slaves, ivory, iron, gold, timber, cloth, porcelain, and pottery were involved in the trade over the past centuries. Some of the items were supplied by Chinese and East Indian merchants. Evolution into a Swahili language (*Kiswahili*) also involved incorporation of Persian, Hindi, Portuguese, Urdu, Gujarati, and English elements that have been integrated on the coast over the centuries. The first Arabs and Persians came from southwest Asia. The trade in skins, ivory, and slaves attracted them, though some were fleeing political or religious persecution. Arabs established settlements in Mogadishu, Lamu, Malindi, Zanzibar, and Kilwa (in Somalia, Kenya, and Tanzania) during the tenth and eleventh centuries. Some of the settlements were governed by Arabs, while others were governed by indigenous Africans. The trade and marriages between the indigenous people and the Asians created the Swahili who by the eleventh century had emerged as a distinct group. But the Swahili are still not regarded as a truly distinct group, given their ethnic admixture and politico-cultural history that varies from group to group, and given that they have lived alongside a variety of indigenous ethnic groups. The status of "true Swahili" tends to be given to families claiming descent from the early Arab settlers. Such older and respected families were in the past distinctive in that they lived in the sections of affluence, were dressed in Arabic fashion, they were proficient at Arab-Islam verse, and they had control over life in the towns. The Swahili are approximated to number 0.5 million.

The Swahili golden age came to an abrupt end with the arrival of Portuguese adventurers on the coast during the late fifteenth and early sixteenth century. Swahili independence fell to the Portuguese until the seventeenth century when the in-migrating Omani Arab traders drove out the Portuguese. Between 1822 and 1837, the coast was ruled as part of the Oman empire, during which time the Omani sultan Seyyid Said moved his capital from Muscat in Oman to Zanzibar Island. This was so as to gain control of the trade routes. Zanzibar's prominence as East African trade capital and international trading depot, mainly depended on the slave trade. The development of French sugar plantations on Indian Ocean islands, and of Arab plantations of cloves and coconuts on the coast and islands, demanded labor. Arab and Swahili traders made fortunes from their caravans going into the interior to as far away as Malawi to capture people that would be sold at the Zanzibar slave market. The abolition of the slave trade, and the arrival of the German and British colonists in the late nineteenth and early twentieth century effected Zanzibar's decline.

Kiswahili involves several dialects and pidgins, but is largely recognized as a language of Bantu groups, but one containing a large Arabic vocabulary incorporated over the last several centuries. Arab and Swahili commercialists carried the Swahili language on their trade routes through East Africa and to as far west as Burundi, Rwanda, and Congo (Zaire). Kiswahili developed as a common mother tongue along the Indian Ocean coast and in Zanzibar by the thirteenth century and it is associated with Islamic tradition. Apart from commercial convenience, Kiswahili served as a tool of communication between colonialists and the indigenous populations, and the language became commonly used amongst local labor pools and troops in East and Central Africa. Kiswahili is spoken by 30 million people, it is the official language of Tanzania, and it is one of the national languages of Kenya and Uganda. It is spoken by some in Madagascar, Mozambique, Somalia, and Djibouti. A dialect of Swahili is the main language of the Comoros Island off the coast of East Africa.

In the past when their standard of living was very high, the Swahili were recognized as town dwellers, and their houses were built of stone and coral, and they had plumbing, elaborate furniture, and several imported luxury goods. Most town houses are now made of *wattle-and-daub* with palm leaves that thatch them. The dwellers include various tradesmen such as builders, carpenters, and leatherworkers. The Swahili do not dominate trade in East Africa anymore, and they tend to look down upon the retailing occupation. Some families own land, and the crops farmed include coconuts, millet, sorghum, rice, fruits, and vegetables. Fishing is done by women who wade into the shallow waters of the ocean with capturing nets, and by men who sail further to the grounds where the fish are in abundance.

The many mosques dramatize the importance of Islam in Swahili culture and religion. There are also impressive written works that chronicle Swahili life and history on the coast of East Africa, which illustrate the importance of literacy and literature in this society. Poetry and written verse chronicles are in abundance.

Tetela (See **Hamba, Mongo, Tetela**)

Toro

The *Toro/ Tooro* (sing./ pl.) ethnics are commonly referred to as *Batoro/ Batooro* (pl.), and a single one of them referred to as a *Mutoro/ Mutooro*. The predominantly cattle keeping territory of the Batoro (referred to as Toro) lies amongst the African Great Lakes in southwestern Uganda to the north of Nkore, to the south of Bunyoro, and to the west/ northwest of Buganda. The Batoro comprise 3.2% (0.64 million people) of Uganda's population, there are pockets of them in Zaire, and the language used (*Lutooro/ Rutooro*) is mostly of Bantu structure and is close to the language of the Nyoro (*Lunyoro*). There is a diversity of migrants from the neighboring environment of western Uganda that have settled in Toro, and chief among them are the Kiga.

Toro was for a long time a very important part of Bunyoro, and despite its efforts to secede (with Prince Kaboyo declaring Toro an independent kingdom state in 1830), Toro never managed to fully break away from Bunyoro until the British in the late nineteenth century moved in to crush the Nyoro under Mukama Kabarega. Toro's secession was enhanced by the weakening of Bunyoro's power emerging from internal squabbles and the task of governing such a large state. In the middle of the squabbles and Kabarega's attempt to hold on to Toro, the British forces consisting of heavily armed Sudanic-Nubian and Ganda soldiery moved in to crush the heavily armed Kabarega forces. The devastation of Toro, once the most prosperous pastoral heartland of Bunyoro, is staggering to the mind. Bunyoro declined alongside as British commanders allowed their Nubian soldiers to live off the land by plundering.

Toro was traditionally a cattle province with political power parceled out as that of Bunyoro i.e. a ruling cattle intimate aristocracy on top, followed by a nonruling class of cattle keepers (*bahuma*), and at the bottom a *bairu* peasantry of original inhabitants. The sociopolitical and economic relationship between the bahuma-bairu caste system was mainly one of symbiosis. The bahuma obtained beer and cultivated crops from the bairu, whereas the bairu got meat, milk, hides, and other cattle products from the bahuma. Both groups valued cattle as a symbol of wealth. The crops cultivated included millet, sorghum, bananas, peas, and various green vegetables. The local industries produced barkcloth and salt, iron implements such as spears, hoes, knives, and arrowheads. Potters molded water pots, beer pots, and sauce pots. The women were skilled at basketry and items produced included winnowing trays, harvesting baskets, and bags. The men communally did the hunting, the clearing of bushes, and the constructing of houses.

Turkana

The *Turkana* number 0.35 million, and are *Sudanic Hamites* that primarily live in northwestern Kenya, west of Lake Turkana, and east of the Escarpment which delineates the Kenya border with Uganda. They are ethnolinguistically related to the *Karamojong*, the *Iteso*, and the *Jie*. Though most Turkana live within their political boundaries, this geographical insulation accentuated by significant differences in height with surrounding country, the Turkana have even in recent times suffered cattle raiding incursions from their Karamojong cousins in Uganda to the west. Turkanaland is semi-arid and its vulnerability to drought is a factor in the low birth rate of the Turkana.

The Turkana are traditionally nomadic pastoralists with the special attachment to cattle so common amongst African cattle herding economies. They are said to easily recognize their own cattle and their neighbors' cattle on sight. The men carry out the herding, and even sing and dance to the cattle. Taking cattle to pastures and to water is an arduous task that can involve long treks. The women carry out the milking, and give a name to each of the cows. Turkana drink both cattle milk and blood, and slaughtering is done for ritual and feasting purposes. The cattle hides are processed into sleeping mats, into covering for huts during the rains, and as foot sandals. Cattle raiding was much more common in the pre-colonial times. Turkana are born into a patrilineal clan (*ateger*) whose ritual they abide by together with the rule of exogamy. The cattle are branded by male and female clan marks. Upon marriage, a woman adopts the clan of her husband.

The Turkana traditionally have a characteristic fondness for wood carving and decoration. These carvings include large water troughs, water containers of varying sizes, walking sticks ornamented with poker-work, and neck bands. Most Turkana homesteads are of the semi-permanent type made of thorn boughs and brushwood.

Tutsi (See **Hutu, Tutsi, and Twa**)

Twa (See **Hutu, Tutsi, and Twa**)

Yaka and Luwa

The *Yaka* primarily live in Western Congo (Zaire) around and over the border (demarcated by the *Kwango* River) with Angola. The terms

Luwa and Yaka are frequently used interchangeably. The Yaka state was founded either by a skilled militaristic group called the Jaga who nearly destroyed the renowned Kongo kingdom, or by the Luba-Lunda ethnics. Two to three centuries ago recall the Yaka peoples who speak the Bantu Kiyaka language as associated with the rise of Yaka as a dreaded slave trading state. The pressure of Yaka raids in the Kwango River area had by 1800 caused many to migrate away towards the east and the north and this in turn put some pressure on the already settled peoples around the Kasai River.

Yoombe (See Kongo and Yoombe)

Zezuru (See Shona)

Zulu

The Zulu are of Bantu ethnolinguistic background, and emerged from the Nguni grouping that includes such peoples as the Swazi and Xhosa whom the Zulu are culturally and linguistically closely related to. Several groups scattered over Zululand and numbering approximately 7 million refer to themselves as Zulu. Most of Zululand is the province of KwaZulu/ Natal on the east coast of South Africa. The Zulu language is called Zulu/ Isizulu, and it has grown to incorporate many Dutch and English words as a result of significant European presence in South Africa.

Prior to the conquest and reign of Shaka (Chaka) Zulu (1816-28), the Zulu were one of hundreds of clans living along the southeastern belt of Africa in chiefdoms. Shaka belonged to the Mthethwa clans, but neighboring peoples that became incorporated into the Zulu grouping include the Khumalo, Ngwane, Cele, and Ndwandwe. Though the ethnic name Zulu originally referred to those descended from Shaka's clan, the name later came to refer to a broader population following the wars and migrations (Mfecane/ Difaqane) triggered by Shaka. A major backdrop to the Mfecane was the unprecedented decade long drought in the region at the beginning of the nineteenth century, the scramble for limited resources resulting in bloody struggles between the major kingdoms in the region--the Mthethwa, Ngwane, and Ndwandwe. Shaka's successful conquest involved reform and rigorous training of his age regiments initially gathered from the pubescent youth of his clan and then housed in barracks. The army reforms included the use of the short stabbing assagai at close quarters in place of the long assagai hurled from a long distance. Shaka had an intelligence network of spies that would reconnoiter an area and ensure that Shaka's troops could attack by surprise. The short stabbing method advantaged Shaka in that the adversaries were not familiar with it and were not familiar with fighting at such close quarters. One who lost his one spear during battle would suffer death.

The "chest and horns" battle formation in which two rings of the Zulu army surround the enemy while the center attacks and the reserves follow the center formation, was effectively employed. Shaka emphasized discipline and commitment among his soldiers. Some in his army were even prohibited from marrying. The mobility of these dreaded soldiers was increased with Shaka having them go barefoot while relieved of the responsibilities of carrying their own baggage. The Zulu soldiers were also required to conquer the enemy or face death if they returned to Shaka as a vanquished army. It was hence instilled in them to fight ruthlessly to death if necessary, to conquer or die. Assimilation was involved in the conquests including the incorporation of captured women and children. However Shaka sometimes broke with African tradition in ordering his men to kill any who resisted including women, children, and the elderly.

The customs among the Zulu groups are basically similar, despite some differences. Despite the spread of Christianity in Zululand, ancestors are still believed to influence the lives of their living descendants, so the ancestors are venerated. Herbalists and diviners function to alleviate diseases or psychological problems some of which are believed to be the result of supernatural influences or defective social relationships. Polygamy is accepted though not as common in practice as it was before. Marriages are however not recognized as legitimate until a bride dowry arrangement, usually involving cattle, is made between the families of the betrothed. Marriages between those of the same clan are not encouraged. Families are built along the extended family descent line spanning three or more generations. Traditionally, the patrilineal family with many wives would live around three large kraals, one for each of the premier wives of the progenitor. A mother looked after and lived with her parturition children. The imzi head is an elder and members of his extended family occupy an imzi. Imzi of the same ward are usually occupied by related families. The homestead (*imzi*) is now generally one of a group of circular thatched or brick houses enclosed by a fence. A group of imzi spaced half a mile to a mile from each other, make up a village or ward. There are also clan and district heads, as well as a customary and ceremonial Zulu king. Agriculture is still the backbone of the Zulu economy, despite the many males that have left Zululand to work as laborers in the mines and industries of South Africa. Though the soil is generally poor and vulnerable to erosion, the Zulu still manage to grow a good variety of crops and to raise animals. Some of the crops are sweet potatoes, corn, millet, and vegetables. The animals include cattle, sheep, and goats. The Zulu share with many other southern African groups the tradition of skilled metalworking. The variety of tools and weapons that have been manufactured included axes, hoes, and spears. The Zulu are also skilled at ceramics, woodworking, basketry, and beadwork.

Abaga (f) *[ah-bah-gah]* That has been fermented [*Luo*].

Abakhwana (f) *[ah-bah-kwah-nah]* Twins: a nickname given to one who gave birth to twins [*Luyia*] (Wako 1985: 37).

Abanji (f/m) *[ah-bahn-jih]* A name given to a child whose twin sibling dies [*Luyia*] (Wako 1985: 38).

Abiero (f) *[ah-bjeh-roh]* Placenta [*Luo*].

Abila (f) *[ah-bih-lah]* "The house of the man" [*Luo*].

Aboyo (f) *[ah-boh-yoh]* The one who saunters [*Luo*].

Abungu (f) *[ah-buh-ndgh-uuh]* Of the forest [*Luo*].

Abura (f) *[ah-buh-rah]* One who sits in judgment [*Luo*].

Abuto (f) *[ah-buh-toh]* "I have hidden" [*Luo*].

Achar (f) *[ah-tch-arh]* "White"; "despise" [*Luo*].

Achayo (f) *[ah-tch-ah-yoh]* "I despise" [*Luo*].

Achiel (f) *[ah-tch-yehl]* One; "I try"; "I shot" [*Luo*].

Achieng (f) *[ah-tch-yeh-ndgh]* The one of the sun [*Luo*].

Achoka (f) *[ah-tch-oh-kah]* To deliver; midwife; "the dark one" [*Luo*].

Achoki (f) *[ah-tch-oh-kih]* "I gather"; "I collect" [*Luo*].

Achol (f) *[ah-tch-ohl]* Dark [*Luo*].

Achola (f) *[ah-tch-oh-lah]* Name given to the child born first following the mother remarrying [*Luyia* and several other ethnics of East and Central Africa] (Wako 1985: 36).

Achungo (f) *[ah-tch-uh-ndgh-oh]* "I have raised" [*Luo*].

Adala (f) *[ah-dah-lah]* Of home [*Luo*].

Adar (f) *[ah-dahr]* "I have shifted" [*Luo*].

Adede (f) *[ah-deh-deh]* Grasshopper [*Luo*].

Adek (f) *[ah-dehk]* Three; main meal: one born at a time there is an abundance of food, or when a rich variety of food is being served [The *Luo*].

Adero (f) *[ah-deh-roh]* Granary [*Luo*].

Adeya (f) *[ah-deh-yah]* The one who strangles: a name given to one born with the umbilical cord twisted around her neck [*Luo*].

Adhoch (f) *[ah-tdh-oh-tch]* A name given to a child born feet first (as opposed to the conventional head first) [*Luo*].

Adhola (f/m) *[ah-tdh-oh-lah]* Wound [*Luo*].

Adika (f) *[ah-dih-kah]* "Hitting" [*Luo*].

Adit (f) *[ah-diht]* Basket [*Luo*].

Adiyo (f) *[ah-dih-yoh]* "I squeezed" [*Luo*].

Adok (f/m) *[ah-dohk]* "I have returned"; labor pains [*Luo*].

Adongo (f) *[ah-doh-ndgh-oh]* A name given to the second born of a pair of twins [*Luo*].

Adoyo (f) *[ah-doh-yoh]* "I am weeding" [*Luo*].

Aduda (f) *[ah-duh-dah]* Basket [*Luo*].

Adundo (f) *[ah-duhn-doh]* "The short one" [*Luo*].

Aduol (f) *[ah-dwohl]* A name given to one born in a place animals are kept [*Luo*].

Aduor (f) *[ah-dwohr]* A name given to one born at dawn [*Luo*].

Adwar (f) *[ah-dwahr]* "Hunt"; "search for"; "look for" [*Luo*].

Agak (f) *[ah-gahk]* Hawk [*Luo*].

Agali (f/m) *[ah-gah-lih]* "Men prevent": a name such as given to one whose mother had been married to other men before her present husband, and the previous men are all said to have been infertile [The *Lugbara*] (Middleton 1961: 36).

Agalo (f) *[ah-gah-loh]* "I have mesmerized"; "I thought" [*Luo*].

Agbaku (f/m) *[ahg-bah-kuuh]* "I do not beat": a name such as given to one whose father claims he has never beaten his wife [The *Lugbara*] (Middleton 1961: 36).

Agengo (f/m) *[ah-geh-ndgh-oh]* "I have blocked (or stopped, or closed, or shut)"; "close the door (temporarily)" [*Luo*].

Agifya (m) *[ah-gih-fjah]* God [*Karamojong*] (Huntingford 1930: 102).

Agipi (m) *[ah-gih-pih]* God [*Karamojong*] (Huntingford 1930: 102).

Agola (f) *[ah-goh-lah]* Verandah; outside [*Luo*].

Agot (f) *[ah-goht]* Mountain [*Luo*].

Agunga (f) *[ah-guh-ndgh-ah]* A homestead deserted (following deaths in the family) [*Luo*].

Agwang (f) *[ahg-wah-ndgh]* Wolf [*Acholi, Langi, Luo*].

Ahero (f) *[ah-yeh-roh]* "I love" [*Luo*].

Aila (f) *[ah-yih-lah]* That which itches [*Luo*].

Ajambo (f) *[ahdj-yahm-boh]* A name given to one born in the evening [*Luo*].

Ajara (f) *[ah-jah-rah]* A name given to a child born with more than the normal number of fingers [*Acholi*] (Nzita 1995: 92).

Ajiambo (f) *[ah-djih-yahm-boh]* A name given to a child born in the afternoon [*Samia*] (Nzita 1995: 73).

Ajuoga (f) *[ahj-woh-gah]* Doctor; witchdoctor [*Luo*].

Akado (f) *[ah-kah-doh]* Soup; stew [*Luo*].

Akani (m) *[ah-kah-nih]* "You build": a name such as implying that this desiringly welcome second boy born is regarded as reinforcement grounds for building on, as well as for the continuity of, the family name [*Zulu*] (Herbert 1995: 3).

Akayesu (m) *[ah-kah-yeh-suuh]* The little one of *Yesu* (=Jesus) [*Hutu, Tutsi, Twa*].

Akello (f) *[ah-kehl-loh]* "I bring" a name given to one whose birth follows that of her twin siblings [*Luo*].

Aketch (f) *[ah-keh-tch]* A name given to one born during a famine [*Luo*].

Akeyo (f) *[ah-keh-yoh]* Scatter; harvest: a name given to one born during the season of harvest [*Luo*].

Akich (f) *[ah-kih-tch]* Bee; orphan [*Luo*].

Akinyi (f) *[ah-kih-ndjh-ih]* A name given to one born in the morning [*Luo*].

Akoko (f) *[ah-koh-koh]* The noise maker [*Luo*].

Akoth (f) *[ah-koh-sth]* A name given to one born at a time it is raining [*Luo*].

Akoto (f) *[ah-koh-toh]* "I have rolled" [*Luo*].

Akumu (f) *[ah-kuh-muuh]* "Bent": name given to a child born with her head between the legs [*Luo*].

Akumu (f) *[ah-kuh-muuh]* "Punished" [*Luo*].

Akune (f) *[ah-kuh-neh]* "I have rejected"; "I have saved" [*Luo*].

Akunno (f) *[ah-kuhn-noh]* "I have saved" [*Luo*].

Alal (f) *[ah-lahl]* "I am lost" [*Luo*].

Alala (f) *[ah-lah-lah]* The lost one [*Luo*].

Alando (f) *[ah-lahn-doh]* The brown complexioned one [*Luo*].

Alego (f) *[ah-leh-goh]* A name given to one associated with the locale *Alego* [*Luo*].

Alifaijo (m) *[ah-lih-fahy-joh]/* **Arifaijo** (m) *[ah-rih-fahy-joh]* "He will die tomorrow": a name such as given to an alarmingly sick child not expected to survive [*Nyoro*] (Beattie 1957: 101).

Aligaweesa (m) *[ah-lih-gah-weh-eh-sah]* "The one who will do the sharpening (or forging) of them (i.e. spears/ weapons)"; this name is commonly associated with the war related proverb "the one who will do the sharpening (or forging) of the spears/ weapons, does not (or would not) use his hand in eating" implying that one ought to take extra care of things that are essential such as to one's livelihood; this name is also commonly associated with the proverb "the one who will do the sharpening (or forging) of the spears, will suffer when those spears turn on him" implying that one ought to be fully aware of the dire consequences that may accrue from one's engaging in unwholesome ventures, and not be overly confident that they are immune from directly suffering the consequences of their actions [The *Ganda, Soga*].

Alijunaki (m) *[ah-lih-juuh-nah-kih]* "Of what use will he be (should he grow)?": a name such as given to an alarmingly sick child not expected to survive, the name implying that even if he gets to survive, he will be a very delicate being [*Nyoro*] (Beattie 1957: 101).

Alingo (f) *[ah-lih-ndgh-oh]* "I have slotted" [*Luo*].

Alobo (f) *[ah-loh-boh]* "Of the soil": a name given to a child whose previously born siblings died--the named child's umbilical cord and placenta are traditionally both buried in the house under a cooking pot previously used for keeping water, and this is so as to keep them out of reach of wizards and other ill wishers that would use them to downgrade the health of the child and the fertility of the mother [*Iteso, Langi*] (Nzita 1995: 132).

Alogo (f) *[ah-loh-goh]* "I have washed off my hands" [*Luo*].

Alonjeru (f/m) *[ah-lohn-jeh-ruuh]* "Cattle-stake taken away": a name such as given to one whose father gave away all his cattle to his father-in-law as bridewealth and grudgingly complains about the avarice of his wife's kin [*Lugbara*] (Middleton 1961: 36).

Alot (f) *[ah-loht]* Plant vegetable [*Luo*].

Aluma (f/m) *[ah-luh-mah]* "Curse": a name such as given to one whose father has been cursed [*Lugbara*] (Middleton 1961: 36).

Aluoch (f) *[ah-lwoh-tch]* A name given to one born during extreme cold weather conditions [*Luo*].

Aluru (f) *[ah-luh-ruuh]* A species of bird called *quillea* [*Luo*].

Amayo (f) *[ah-mah-yoh]* "I have snatched"; "I have forcefully taken" [*Luo*].

Amazingazengungumbane (m) *[ah-mah-zihn-gah-zehn-guhn-guhmb-ah-neh]* "Porcupine quills": a name such as given to metaphorically imply that this child is a "thorn" in the side given that the family was already, before this child was born, satisfied with the number of children it had and did not expect or want more children [*Zulu*] (Suzman 1994: 258).

Amba (f) *[ahm-baah]* A name given to a parent of twins [*Bolia, Mongo, Ntomba*] (Daeleman 1977: 194).

Ambala (f) *[ahm-bah-lah]* Scar [*Luo*].

Amenya (f) *[ah-meh-ndjh-ah]* One who lights [*Luo*].

Amoke (f) *[ah-moh-keh]* To slurp [*Luo*].

Amol (f) *[ah-mohl]* "I have crawled" [*Luo*].

Amondi (f) *[ah-mohn-dih]* "I wake up early": the early riser [*Luo*].

Amor (f) *[ah-mohr]* "I am happy"; "I have thundered" [*Luo*].

Amoyo (f) *[ah-moh-yoh]* To air [*Luo*].

Anditi (f/m) *[ahn-dih-tih]* "Confusion in giving birth": a name such as given to a child alleged to be the product of an act of adultery [The *Lugbara*] (Middleton 1961: 36).

Angiela (f) *[ah-ndgh-yeh-lah]* Role [*Luo*].

Angima (f) *[ah-ndgh-ih-mah]* "I am well"; "I am alive" [*Luo*].

Anglawa (f) *[ah-ndgh-lah-wah]* One that is hanged [*Luo*].

Anindo (f) *[ah-nihn-doh]* "I am sleeping" [*Luo*].

Ankeanker (f/m) *[ahn-keh-eh-ahn-keh-eh-rh]* The owners of the graves : a name given to a parent of twins [*Ngwi*] (Daeleman 1977: 194).

Anyal (f) *[ah-ndjh-ahl]* "I can manage" [*Luo*].

Anyang (f) *[ah-ndjh-ah-ndgh]* Crocodile [*Luo*].

Anyango (f) *[ah-ndjh-ahn-goh]* A name given to one born early in the morning when it is still chilly with the sunshine not intense; dawn [The *Luo*].

Anyim (f) *[ah-ndjh-ihm]* Sesame [*Luo*].

Anyona (f) *[ah-ndjh-oh-nah]* "The one who tramples on"; "the one who steps on" [*Luo*].

Aod (f) *[ah-ohd]* "I am tired" [*Luo*].

Aooko (f) *[ah-woh-oh-koh]* Outside [*Luo*].

Aot (f) *[ah-woht]* Of the house [*Luo*].

Apa-Barua (m) *[ah-pah-bah-ruh-wah]* Of the ox whose hide markings are like writing--the name is adapted from the Kiswahili word *barua* which means "letter" [*Jie/ Karamojong*] (Gulliver 1952: 74).

Apa-Bilikwanga (f) *[ah-pah-bih-lih-kwah-ndgh-ah]* Of one whose hoe broke as she cultivated [*Jie/ Karamojong*] (Gulliver 1952: 75).

Apa-Emaler (m) *[ah-pah-eh-mah-lerh]* Of the ox with a red colored hide [*Jie/ Karamojong*] (Gulliver 1952: 74).

Apa-Epuri (m) *[ah-pah-eh-puh-rih]* Of the ox which bellows a lot [*Jie/ Karamojong*] (Gulliver 1952: 74).

Apa-Erothe (m) *[ah-pah-eroh-sth-eh]* Of the ox with a hide whose color is like that of a shrike [*Jie/ Karamojong*] (Gulliver 1952: 74).

Apa-Imudan (m) *[ah-pah-ih-muh-dahn]* Of the ox with ears that are slit [*Jie/ Karamojong*] (Gulliver 1952: 74).

Apa-Kitabu (m) *[ah-pah-kih-tah-buh]* Of the ox whose hide markings are like writing--the name is adapted from the Kiswahili word *kitabu* which means "book" [*Jie/ Karamojong*] (Gulliver 1952: 74).

Apa-Loboi (m) *[ah-pah-loh-bohy]* Of the ox whose owner did not decorate it with a collar or bell [*Jie/ Karamojong*] (Gulliver 1952: 74).

Apa-Lochulul (m) *[ah-pah-loh-tch-uh-luhl]* Of the ox which is very fat [*Jie/ Karamojong*] (Gulliver 1952: 74).

Apa-Lochulut (m) *[ah-pah-loh-tch-uh-luht]* Of the ox with one horn curving forward, the other backward [*Jie/ Karamojong*] (Gulliver 1952: 74).

Apa-Lokodo (m) *[ah-pah-loh-koh-doh]* Of the ox whose horns curve and meet over the head [*Jie/ Karamojong*] (Gulliver 1952: 74).

Apa-Lokomar (m) *[ah-pah-loh-koh-mahr]* Of the ox with one horn curving forward, the other curving overhead [The *Jie/ Karamojong*] (Gulliver 1952: 74).

Apa-Lokori (m) *[ah-pah-loh-koh-rih]* Of the ox with the blotched hide [*Jie/ Karamojong*] (Gulliver 1952: 73).

Apa-Lomerimug (m) *[ah-pah-loh-meh-rih-muhg]* Of the ox with the brown spotted hide [*Jie/ Karamojong*] (Gulliver 1952: 73).

Apa-Lomugerukwen (f) *[ah-pah-loh-muh-geh-ruh-kwehn]* Of grain color like a brown leather strap [*Jie/ Karamojong*] (Gulliver 1952: 75).

Apa-Longor (m) *[ah-pah-loh-ndgh-ohr]* Of the ox with the greyish-brown hide [*Jie/ Karamojong*] (Gulliver 1952: 73).

Apa-Longwa (f) *[ah-pah-loh-ndgh-wah]* Of white sorghum [The *Jie/ Karamojong*] (Gulliver 1952: 75).

Apa-Lopeot (m) *[ah-pah-loh-peh-yoht]* Of the ox with a hide that resembles the color of that of a wild dog [*Jie/ Karamojong*] (Gulliver 1952: 74).

Apa-Lopetangama (f) *[ah-pah-loh-peh-tah-ndgh-ah-mah]* Of wide opening ears of sorghum [*Jie/ Karamojong*] (Gulliver 1952: 75).

Apa-Lopua (m) *[ah-pah-loh-pwah]* Of the ox with a dust colored hide

[*Jie/ Karamojong*] (Gulliver 1952: 74).

Apa-Loputh (f) *[ah-pah-loh-puh-sth]* Of greyish grain [The *Jie/ Karamojong*] (Gulliver 1952: 75).

Apa-Loputh (m) *[ah-pah-loh-puh-sth]* Of the ox with the grey hide [*Jie/ Karamojong*] (Gulliver 1952: 73).

Apa-Lorionkimiat (f) *[ah-pah-loh-rjohn-kih-mjaht]* Of black eleusine [*Jie/ Karamojong*] (Gulliver 1952: 75).

Apa-Lotheroi (m) *[ah-pah-loh-sth-eh-rohy]* Of the ox with a hide with the color of that of a dik-dik [*Jie/ Karamojong*] (Gulliver 1952: 74).

Apa-Loyetan (m) *[ah-pah-loh-yeh-tahn]* Of the ox whose horns are so spread out that they get stuck in the bushes as the ox walks through [*Jie/ Karamojong*] (Gulliver 1952: 74).

Apamo (f) *[ah-pah-moh]* "I have clapped"; "I have slapped"; "I clap"; "I slap" [*Luo*].

Apa-Namuru (f) *[ah-pah-nah-muh-ruh]* Of stony cultivating ground [*Jie/ Karamojong*] (Gulliver 1952: 75).

Apa-Tulia (m) *[ah-pah-tuh-ljah]* Of the ox with a hide as black as a scorched and soot covered pot [*Jie/ Karamojong*] (Gulliver 1952: 74).

Apengela (f) *[ah-pehn-geh-lah]* "One who does not intend": this name is commonly associated with the saying "The one who does not intend to complete the journey" [*Ovimbundu*] (Ennis 1945: 5).

Apingo (f) *[ah-pihn-goh]* "I oppose" [*Luo*].

Apiyo/ Apio (f) *[ah-pih-yoh]* A name given to the first born of a pair of twins [*Luo*].

Apondi (f) *[ah-pohn-dih]* "I am hiding": name given to one who is the product of a long and overdue pregnancy [*Luo*].

Apudo (f) *[ah-puh-doh]* The fat one [*Luo*].

Apunda (f) *[ah-puhn-dah]* Donkey [*Luo*].

Arap (m) *[ah-rahp]* "Son of" [*Nandi, Turkana*].

Arapkipet (m) *[ah-rahp-kih-peht]* "the son of *Kipet*"; "the son of one born in the morning" [*Nandi*] (Hollis 1969: 68).

Arapkoko (m) *[ah-rahp-koh-koh]* "The son of the old woman" [*Nandi*] (Hollis 1969: 68).

Arapmoi (m) *[ah-rahp-mohy]* "The son of *Moi*"; "the son of war" [*Nandi, Turkana*].

Aria (m) *[ah-rih-yah]* "At the drum": child who it is said would sound the drum at its parents' death dances [*Lugbara*] (Middleton 1961: 35).

Arieyo (f) *[ah-rjeh-yoh]* Two [*Luo*].

Arijole (f/m) *[ah-rih-joh-leh]* "The remaining blood": a name such as given to one whose mother, it is thought, will never conceive again [*Lugbara*] (Middleton 1961: 35).

Arinaitwe (m) *[ah-rih-nahy-tweh]* "He has a large head": a degradation laden name given to either an alarmingly sickly newborn or to one whose previously born siblings died, and implies an attempt to "mislead" the forces of death into thinking the child is unwanted, to therefore "trick" these forces into turning their backs from, and hence into sparing the life of the child [*Kiga, Nyankore, Nyoro, Toro*].

Arogo (f) *[ah-roh-goh]* "Shout" [*Luo*].

Aroko (f) *[ah-roh-koh]* "I have pierced"; kidneys [*Luo*].

Arua (f) *[ah-ruh-wah]* That dawns; "stayed long" [*Luo*].

Asiko (f) *[ah-tsih-koh]* "I am permanent" [*Luo*].

Asin (f) *[ah-tsihn]* "I am tired"; annoyed; bitter [*Luo*].

Asiro (f) *[ah-tsih-roh]* "I support" [*Luo*].

Asis (f/m) *[ah-tsihs]* God; the sun; sunlight; daylight; day [The *Nandi, Tuken*] (Huntingford 1930: 102-103).

Asita (m) *[ah-tsih-tah]* God; the sun [*Taturu*] (Huntingford 1930: 102-103).

Asiyo (f) *[ah-tsih-yoh]* To graft [*Luo*].

Asol (f) *[ah-tsohl]* "I collect" [*Luo*].

Ataro (f) *[ah-tah-roh]* Upside down; puzzle [*Luo*].

Atich (f) *[ah-tih-tch]* Hard worker; the one who works [*Luo*].

Atieno (f) *[ah-tjeh-noh]* Name given to one born during the night [The *Luo*].

Atigo (f/m) *[ah-tih-goh]* Beads [*Acholi, Langi, Luo*].

Atingo (f/m) *[ah-tih-ndgh-oh]* "I have carried"; "I have lifted" [*Luo*].

Atumwa (f/m) *[aah-tuh-mwah]* "That is ordered/ sent/ commissioned": a name given to the last born of triplets [*Hemba*] (Daeleman 1977: 193).

Auderu (f/m) *[ah-wuh-deh-ruuh]* "Chicken finishing": a name such as given to one born to a mother who had recently killed off and fed on several of her husband's fowls [*Lugbara*] (Middleton 1961: 35).

Audi (f) *[ahw-dih]* Houses [*Luo*].

Auma (f) *[ah-wuh-mah]* Covered [*Luo*].

Awich (f/m) *[ah-wih-tch]* "Big head" [*Luo*].

Awino (f) *[ah-wih-noh]* A name given to one born at the time the whisks on the maize harvest are visibly emerging from the cobs; fishing hook [*Luo*].

Awiti (f) *[ah-wih-tiih]* The one that is thrown [*Luo*].

Awubwa (m) *[ah-wuh-bwah]* One that goes astray (or is mistaken); "he makes a mistake (or fails)"; this name is commonly associated with the war related proverb "even a very intelligent one can be confounded, for even the ears cannot sense smell" [*Ganda, Soga*].

Awuor (f) *[ahw-wohr]* The greedy one [*Luo*].

Ayah (f) *[ah-yah]* "I am leaving" [*Luo*].

Ayako (f) *[ah-yah-koh]* "I have looted"; grabbed; plundered [*Luo*].

Ayal (f) *[ah-yahl]* "I open" [*Luo*].

Ayieko (f) *[ahy-yeh-koh]* A sieve used as a special tray; shaking [*Luo*].

Ayira (f) *[ahy-yeh-rah]* The chosen one [*Luo*].

Ayodo (f) *[ah-yoh-doh]* "Hit"; "hammer" [*Luo*].

Ayoki (f) *[ah-yoh-kih]* To shake [*Luo*].

Ayondela (f) *[ah-yohn-deh-lah]* "We bend towards": this name is co-mmonly associated with the proverb "The little tree bends and bends, and all of us bend towards death" and is given to a child some of whose previously born siblings died, or name given to one born into a family that has recently had deaths, or name given to one who is alarmingly sick [*Ovimbundu*] (Ennis 1945: 3).

Ayoo (f) *[ah-yoh-oh]* A name given to one born along the path (or road) [*Luo*].

Ayot (f) *[ah-yoht]* "I am light"; "I am fast" [*Luo*].

Ayugi (f) *[ah-yuh-giih]* Sweepings [*Luo*].

Ayuka (f) *[ah-yuh-kah]* Shaker; one who shakes; hurry; haste; dis-organized [*Luo*].

-B-

Baagala (f/m) *[baah-gah-lah]* "They (i.e. the people) like (or love)"; this name is commonly associated with the proverbs "they (i.e. the peo-ple) like (or love) the one who has a place" and "they (i.e. the people) like (or love) the one who has accumulated lots" which image the ten-dency for those who are materially well endowed to be better regard-ed than those who have little [*Ganda*].

Baagala-Aliwawe (f/m) *[baah-gah-laah-lih-wah-weh]* "It is the one who has a place that is liked (or loved)": this proverbial name images the tendency for those who are materially well endowed to be better regarded than those who have little [*Ganda*].

Baagala-Ayaze (f/m) *[baah-gah-laah-yah-zeh]* "It is the one who has accumulated lots that is liked (or loved)": this proverbial name im-ages the tendency for those who are materially well endowed to be better regarded than those who have little [*Ganda*].

Baagala-Azimbye (f/m) *[baah-gah-laah-zihm-bjeh]* "They (i.e. people) like (or love) the one that has built himself/ herself a house": this proverbial name images the tendency for those who are materially well endowed to be better regarded than those who have little [The *Ganda*].

Baagalakyabwe (f/m) *[baah-gah-lah-tch-aah-bweh]* "They (i.e. people) have a liking (or preference) for that which is theirs" [*Ganda*].

Baagalamugagga (f/m) *[baah-gah-lah-muh-gahg-gah]* "It is the one who is wealthy that is liked (or loved)": this proverbial name images the tendency for those who are materially well endowed to be better regarded than those who have little [*Ganda*].

Baagalawaabwe (f/m) *[baah-gah-lah-waah-bweh]* "They (i.e. people) have a liking (or preference) for their own niche" [*Ganda*].

Baagalayazimba (f/m) *[baah-gah-lah-yah-zihm-bah]* "It is the one who has built himself/ herself up that is liked (or loved)": this proverbial

name images the tendency for those who are materially well endowed to be better regarded than those who have little [*Ganda*].

Baamutta (m) *[baah-muht-tah]* "They killed him"; this name is commonly associated with the proverb "'they killed him' is preferable to
hear (or deserves more praise) than, 'He died (of sickness at home)'"
which was intended to encourage warriorhood [*Ganda*].

Baanabakintu (m) *[baah-nah-baah-tch-ihn-tuuh]* "The children of *Kintu*
(the originating ancestor of the *Ganda*)"; this name is commonly
associated with the proverb "the children of *Kintu* will never die out"
implying that the human species (or more specifically 'the children of
Kintu' i.e. the *Ganda* ethnics) will (seemingly) always be sustained
despite the effects of gross depopulating factors such as wars and
epidemics [*Ganda*].

Baba (m) *[bah-bah]* "Father" [*Zulu* and several other ethnic groups of
East, Central, and Southern Africa] (Koopman 1979: 154).

Babi (m) *[bah-bih]* The bad ones; "they (i.e. the people) are bad"; this
name is sometimes associated with the proverb "a mass of people
(or a crowd) looks bad when it comes to sharing and eating food, but
looks good when it comes to allotting work" meaning that practically
in either situation, the food or the work gets finished quickly, and
though with the food there will likely be friction over sharing, in the
case of the work the synonym "many hands make light work" will
likely apply--human relations hence depend on circumstances that
are rarely or never unconditional [*Ganda, Soga*].

Babiri (f) *[bah-bih-rih]* Two people; "they are two people"; this name
is commonly associated with the proverb "two partners that travel (or
pass) together, remind each other" which is synonymous with "two
heads are better than one" and contains the message of meriting and
fostering a spirit of human cooperation and togetherness; this name
is also sometimes associated with the proverb "one that is helpless is
like two paupers that walk together" [*Ganda*].

Baboola (f) *[bah-boh-oh-lah]* "They ostracize (or discriminate against)"; "they disown"; this name is commonly associated with the proverb "people ostracize (or discriminate against) the poor one" which
mirrors the tendency for those who are materially well endowed to be
better regarded than those who have little [*Ganda*].

Baboolamwavu (f/m) *[bah-boh-oh-lah-mwaah-vvuh]* "People ostracize
(or discriminate against) the poor one": this proverbial name images
the tendency for those who are materially well endowed to be better
regarded than those who have little [*Ganda*].

Babyenda (m) *[bah-bjehn-dah]* "They (i.e. people) like them (i.e. things like property or riches)": a name given to child born into a family
that is poor, the name implying that wealth is desired but is so
difficult (for the family) to obtain [*Nyoro*] (Beattie 1957: 103).

Bacia/ Bachia (m) *[bah-tch-ih-yah]* A child born to a family enduring
tragedy such as deaths [*Lugbara*] (McKinzie 1980: 30).

Bafanini (m) *[bah-fah-nih-nih]* "When did they die?" [*Zulu*] (Koopman 1979: 161).

Bafanyana (m) *[bah-fah-ndjh-ah-nah]* "Small boys" [*Zulu*] (Koopman 1979: 154).

Bafiirawala (m) *[bah-fiih-rah-wah-lah]* "They (i.e. men) die in places afar": this is a war related expression [*Ganda*].

Bafikile (f) *[bah-fih-kih-leh]* "They have arrived" [The *Zulu*] (Koopman 1979: 162).

Bafunani (m) *[bah-fuh-naah-nih]* "What do they want?" [The *Zulu*] (Koopman 1979: 79).

Bafuuwa (m) *[bah-fuuh-wah]* "They (i.e. people) blow"; this name is commonly associated with the proverb "the horn blowers blow their instruments in harmony" which urges the spirit of community and co-operation as exemplified by horn blowers who are of different background and character, yet they work together to produce a fine tune [*Ganda*].

Bagaanira (f) *[bah-gaah-nih-rah]* "They (i.e. people) defend"; this name is commonly associated with the proverb "they (i.e. people) defend the person they like (or love)" [*Ganda*].

Bagaaniragwebaagala (f) *[bah-gaah-nih-rah-gweh-baah-gah-laah]* "They (i.e. people) defend the person they like (or love)" [*Ganda*].

Bagamba (m) *[bah-gahm-bah]* "They (i.e. neighbors or people) say/ talk": the name implies that most of what neighbors harp about the family of the child named so, are untruths that it is best to ignore [*Nyoro*] (Beattie 1957: 103).

Baganda (f/m) *[bah-gahn-dah]* Ganda ethnics; blood (or kinship) re-latives; this name is sometimes associated with the proverb "the Ganda ethnics are (like) the stinging nettle: they get stung on it while seeing it with their open eyes" implying that the Ganda (or people in general) will ridiculously carry out acts that they fully know are de-trimental to themselves such as befriending bad elements and being hospitable to thieves; this name is also sometimes associated with the proverb "the Ganda ethnics detest the very thing that they eat" implying that the Ganda (or people in general) practically carry out acts that it is seemingly only in theory or words that they gravitate against--such as violating cultural taboos [*Ganda*].

Bagandamuliro (f/m) *[bah-gahn-dah-muh-lih-roh]* "Blood or kinship relations are (like) fire"; this name is commonly associated with the proverb "blood (or kinship) relations are (like) fire: although the fire dwells in the house, it hates the house and sometimes burns it down" [*Ganda*].

Bagandanswa (f/m) *[bah-gahn-dahn-swah]* "The Ganda ethnics are (like) edible flying ants"; this name is commonly associated with the proverb "the Ganda are (like) edible flying ants: the ants cover their backs with fragile wings, whilst their stomachs hang out bare)" implying that the *Ganda* (or people in general/ or relations) harbor a false sense of protection, or that they superficially look harmless and kind with the soft wing covering though inwardly they are coarse and stingy; this name is also commonly associated with the proverb "the *Ganda* ethnics are (like) edible flying ants: they throw their shields onto their backs" which is a humorous statement that the *Ganda*, in carrying shields on their backs (which was more commonplace with men in the past), have the appearance of the edible flying ants with their wings folded [*Ganda*].

Bagendanarwo (m) *[bah-gehn-dah-nah-rwoh]* "They go (around) with it (i.e. death)": the name implies that wherever they are, death is inescapably involved in peoples' lives, and the name given to a child either born during a period of bereavement or one that is alarmingly sick and is not expected to survive [*Nyoro*] (Beattie 1957: 102).

Bageya (m) *[bah-geh-yah]* "They make slanderous statements"; this name is commonly associated with the proverb "those who make slanderous statements are (like) birds, with the (quietly listening) wagtail on the (rooftop openings of the) house" meaning that backbiters are always in danger of their talk getting heard by listening sources they are not aware of [*Ganda*].

Baggala (m) *[bahg-gah-lah]* "Those (i.e. people) who close"; this name is commonly associated with the proverb "those who close the doors forget that there are still spaces between the door and the wall" implying that there is a tendency for people to dwell on one source of trouble and evil, though they ought to consider the multiple sources; this name is also commonly associated with the proverb "those that block (or close off) the path must be very powerful, just as are those that open up the path" which refers to pioneers, revolutionaries, stubborn persons, and decisive persons [*Ganda*].

Baggala-Miryango (m) *[bahg-gah-lah-mih-rjaahn-goh]* "Those (i.e. people) who close the doors"; this name is commonly associated with the proverb "those who close the doors forget that there are still spaces between the door and the wall" implying that there is a tendency for people to dwell on one source of trouble and evil, though they ought to consider the multiple sources [*Ganda*].

Bagonzenku (m) *[bah-gohn-zehn-kuuh]* "Those who like the firewood, (despise the one who gathers it)": a name given to a child whose mother was deserted by the child's father [*Nyoro*] (Beattie 1957: 100).

Baisi (m) *[bahy-sih]* "They are killers"; killers; this name is commonly associated with the expression "we eat with killers" implying a situation in which neighbors, kin or friends are seemingly close to one, but in truth harbor malicious intent--the name can then appropriately be given to a newborn whose parent is sending a message to the forces of enmity to display cognizance and unappreciation of the insincerity [*Soga*].

Bajula (f) *[bah-juh-lah]* "They (i.e. the people) wish for (or yearn for, or desire, or miss)"; this name is commonly associated with the proverb "they (i.e. the people) wish for (or yearn for, or desire, or miss) the one that is no longer around" which is synonymous with "absence makes the heart grow fonder" [*Ganda*].

Bajula-Avuddewo (f) *[bah-juh-laah-vuhd-deh-woh]* "They (i.e. the people) wish for (or yearn for, or desire, or miss) the one that is no longer around": this proverbial name is synonymous with "absence makes the heart grow fonder."

Bakamempisi (f/m) *[bah-kah-mehm-pih-sih]* "Those that milk a hyena"; this name is commonly associated with the proverb "those who (attempt to) milk a hyena have to exertingly persevere and concentrate" which implies that those who are to succeed in what is considered almost impossible (such as getting money from a stonehard miser) have to put into it a lot of effort and dedication [*Ganda*].

Bakebwa (m) *[bah-keh-bwah]* "They (i.e. the neighbors) forget": the name implies that though the neighbors may forget or shift aside the malicious things they did or said about the parents of the child named so, how the neighbors acted is very much remembered by the parents [*Nyoro*] (Beattie 1957: 103).

Bakidambya (m) *[bah-tch-ih-dahm-bjah]* "The slovenly and despised woman"; this name is commonly associated with the proverbs "the good-for-nothing slut gives birth to the fine and strapping lad" and "it is the unsightly and despised woman gives birth to a splendid boy or heir" implying that the unexpected can happen, good can come out of things or people that are looked down upon, so nothing or no one should easily be dismissed as being of no use [*Ganda*].

Bakondeere (m) *[bah-kohn-deh-eh-reh]* Trumpeters; horn blowers; this name is commonly associated with the proverb "the horn blowers blow their instruments in harmony" which urges the spirit of community and cooperation as exemplified by horn blowers who are of different background and character, yet they work together to produce a fine tune [*Ganda*].

Bakubanja (f/m) *[bah-kuh-bahn-jah]* "They demand debt payments from you"; this name is commonly associated with the proverb "it is better to be in debt than to steal" implying that it is more virtuous to borrow and be in debt than to steal [*Ganda*].

Bakulu (m) *[bah-kuh-luh]* Elders; adults; seniors; chiefs; leaders; this name is commonly associated with the proverbs "two masters (or elders) of the same village, that are jealous of each other, will not guarantee peace in the village" and "masters (or elders) are like pillars: once they are removed from the clan, the power of the group crumbles" [*Ganda*].

Bakulumpagi (m) *[bah-kuh-luhm-pah-jih]* "Elders (or leaders) are pillars"; this name is commonly associated with the proverb "masters (or elders) are like pillars: once they are removed from the clan, the power of the group crumbles" [*Ganda*].

Bakumba (f/m) *[bah-kuhm-bah]* "They march"; this name is sometimes associated with the proverb "they (i.e. people) march (or show off) only with those that are alive" which is synonymous with "out of sight, out of mind" [*Ganda*].

Bakumbanamulamu (f/m) *[bah-kuhm-bah-nah-muh-lah-muuh]* "They (i.e. people) march (or show off) only with those that are alive": this proverbial name is synonymous with "out of sight, out of mind" [The *Ganda*].

Bakusaggira (m) *[bah-kuh-sahg-gih-rah]* "Driving the hunted animal into your net"; this name is commonly associated with the proverb "when the animal pursuers are at the final stage of driving the animal into your net you cough at the risk of alarming the animal and hence forfeiting what would have been your great catch" which is advising one to pay close attention to important issues, otherwise he will likely spoil his chances and suffer loss [*Ganda*].

Bakuseera (m) *[bah-kuh-seh-eh-rah]* "You are being overcharged"; this name is commonly associated with the proverb "(the one who suggests) 'you are being overcharged' would not lend you anything)" which exemplifies the sarcasm involved in day-to-day living (such as a rich one giving sarcasm laden advice to a poor man) [*Ganda*].

Balaba (m) *[bah-lah-bah]* Those that see (or perceive) or get; "they are conscious (or are alert)"; "they are awake"; "they are perceptive"; this name is sometimes associated with the proverb "people with sound minds and healthy bodies still get stung by the nettle while they see it" implying that people will still run into the trouble they have clearly envisioned; this name is also sometimes associated with the proverb "the *Ganda* ethnics are (like) the stinging nettle: they get stung on it while seeing it with their open eyes" implying that the *Ganda* (or people in general) will ridiculously carry out acts that they fully know are detrimental to themselves such as befriending bad elements and being hospitable to thieves [*Ganda*].

Balikuddembe (m) *[bah-lih-kuhd-dehm-beh]* "Those that are at peace"; this name is commonly associated with the proverb "those that are at peace are inattentive to potential danger (or do not realize what is coming)" which mirrors the tendency for those that are experienced a lengthy period of peace and prosperity, to drop their guard and not be attentive to the potential threat to their well being that always lurks around; this name is also commonly associated with the proverb "those who are at peace (or are well off) make fun of the one in a state of squalor" [*Ganda*].

Balimuttajjo (m) *[bah-lih-muht-tahj-joh]* "They will kill him tomorrow"; this name is commonly associated with the proverb "(being told) 'they will kill him (i.e. the chief) tomorrow' does not prevent you from becoming his tenant" implying that one need not take on seriously neighborhood matters that would not endanger him or her [*Ganda*].

Balintuma (f/m) *[bah-lihn-tuh-mah]* One that will be assigned a mission; "I will be assigned a mission"; this name is commonly associated with the proverb "(one who patiently thinks) 'when my turn comes they will send me on an errand (or give me a job)' ends up with nothing" implying that one should take advantage of available opportunities which may well not be available in the greater abundance that one may think they will be later on, i.e. as synonymous with "make hay while the sun shines" [*Ganda*].

Baliokwabwe (m) *[bah-ljoh-kwaah-bweh]* Those living in their homestead (or family neighborhood) [*Ganda*].

Balizza (m) *[bah-lihz-zah]* "They (i.e. my comrades) will come back with (the whistling)": this name is a contraction of *Balizzakiwa* and relates to bravery in a war situation, whereby one is willing to fight until death.

Balizzakiwa (m) *[bah-lihz-zah-tch-ih-wah]* "They (i.e. my comrades) will come back (from the war) with (just) the whistling (about my death)"; "when they (i.e. my comrades) return while just whistling in surprise (it will mean I met my death there)": this name relates to bravery in a war situation, whereby one is willing to fight until death [*Ganda*].

Balizzalinnya (m) *[bah-lihz-zah-lihn-ndjh-aah]* "They (i.e. my comrades) will return with just my name (and not me)": this name relates to bravery in a war situation, whereby one is willing to fight until death [*Ganda*].

Balogonzaki (f/m) *[bah-lih-gohn-zah-kiih]* "What will they (i.e. the neighbors) like?": neighbors have been so annoying or malicious to the family to which the child so named is born, that the bewildered parents imply in the name that little else would soften the hearts of the neighbors if the birth of this beautiful infant does not [The *Nyoro*] (Beattie 1957: 103).

Balongo (f) *[bah-lohn-goh]* Twins: nickname given to one who gives birth to twins [*Luyia*] (Wako 1985: 37).

Balubuuliza (m) *[bah-luh-buuh-lih-zah]* "They demand for (or inquire about) it (i.e. the cow)"; this name is commonly associated with the proverb "they demand a butchering ax for it (i.e. the cow), while it continues to munch on the grass (in the field)" which exemplifies a situation in which one in danger does not heed a warning [*Ganda*].

Balungi (f) *[bah-luhn-jiih]* "They are beautiful"; "they are good/ or virtuous/ or right"; "they are desirable"; the good (or virtuous) people; the beautiful people; this name is sometimes associated with the proverb "the beautiful are like the dog with big, beautiful, and startling eyes: it will turn out to either be a thieving dog or a good hunter" which depicts that there is a general tendency to believe that those of exceptional esthetic appearance will exploit the advantage to effect good or evil in either extreme; this name is also sometimes associated with the proverb "the beautiful (or the good) are like fresh banana leaves: new ones always sprout out and never cease to exist in the banana plantation" implying that there will always be beautiful people, and that however ugly or bad the circumstances get, there are elements of beauty and good that always emerge; this name is also sometimes associated with the proverb "a mass of people (or a crowd) looks bad when it comes to sharing and eating food, but looks good when it comes to allotting work" meaning that practically in either situation, the food or the work gets finished quickly, and though with the food there will likely be friction over sharing, in the case of the work the synonym "many hands make light work" will likely apply --human relations hence depend on circumstances that are rarely or never unconditional [*Ganda*].

Balyeesiima (m) *[bah-ljeh-eh-siih-mah]* "They (i.e. the neighbors/ people) will be pleased with themselves": the name implies that the neighbors have so much spite towards one or both of the parents of the child named so, that the neighbors would be delighted at the death of this newborn [*Nyoro*] (Beattie 1957: 103).

Bamunoba (m) *[bah-muh-noh-bah]* "They (i.e. neighbors or people) hate him" [*Nyoro*].

Bananuka (m) *[bah-nah-nuh-kah]* "They trust" [*Nyoro*].

Banata (f/m) *[baah-nah-tah]* "Carry them (i.e. the twins)": name given to one whose birth precedes that of his or her twin siblings [The *Yaka*] (Daeleman 1977: 193).

Bangi (f/m) *[bahn-jih]* "Many (people)"; this name is sometimes associated with the proverb "if many congratulate you for your work, then your day's cultivation is at it's end (or it has reached a very commendable level)"; this name is also sometimes associated with the proverb "the involvement of many people results in a killing catch of the tiny mud-fishes" which is synonymous with "many hands make light work"; this name is also sometimes associated with the proverb "a mass of people (or a crowd) looks bad when it comes to sharing and eating food, but looks good when it comes to allotting work" meaning that practically in either situation, the food or the work gets finished quickly, and though with the food there will likely be friction over sharing, in the case of the work the synonym "many hands make light work" will likely apply--human relations hence depend on circumstances that are rarely or never unconditional [*Ganda*].

Bangifa (m) *[bahn-gih-fah]* "He fights over the inheritance"; "fight over the inheritance" [*Zulu*] (Koopman 1979: 160).

Bangisibanno (f) *[bahn-jih-sih-bahn-noh]* "The presence of many people does not imply there are friends among them"; "'many people' are not (necessarily) friends" [*Ganda*].

Bangu (m) *[bahn-guuh]* "Bang": a name given to a child who often falls to the ground and his head makes the "bang" sound [The *Shona*] (Jackson 1957: 120).

Bangubukhosi (m) *[bahn-guh-buhk-hoh-sih]* "Fight over the chieftainship": name such as given to a child born during family disputes [The

Zulu] (Koopman 1979: 68).

Banja/ Bbanja (f/m) *[bbahn-jah]* Debt; this name is sometimes ass-ociated with the proverb "a visitor puts you in debt" meaning that with the arrival of a visitor, one often goes to borrow from a neighbor so as to be able to give the visitor a proper treat; this name is also so-metimes associated with the proverb "poverty is not the same as (or is not as bad as) a debt (or indebtedness)" implying that what belongs to one without a debt is truly his and he can not be charged for being poor, whereas a rich one in debt can face serious charges and even confiscation [*Ganda*].

Banoba (m) *[bah-noh-bah]* "They (i.e. neighbors or people) hate": the name implies that the parents of the child named so, are cognizant of the hatred some people (such as neighbors) harbor towards them [*Nyoro*] (Beattie 1957: 103).

Bantu (m) *[bahn-tuuh]* People [*Zulu* and several other ethnics of east-ern, central, and southern Africa] (Koopman 1979: 69).

Banya (m) *[bah-ndjh-ah]* Debt: a name such as given to one born to a father still owing on the dowry [*Acholi*].

Bapoto (m) *[bah-poh-toh]* Noise: a name such as given to a child born amidst quarreling and noise [*Zezuru*] (Marapara 1954: 8).

Barasa (m) *[bah-rah-sah]* Name given to one born on Saturday [*Luyia*].

Baruzalire (m) *[bah-ruh-zah-lih-reh]* "They (that is the parents) have borne (a child) for it (i.e. death)": a name such as given to an alarm-ingly sick child not expected to survive [*Nyoro*] (Beattie 1957: 102).

Barwogeza (m) *[bah-rwoh-geh-zah]* "They wash (the child) for it (i.e. death)": the name implies that though the parents spend so much time cherishingly tending to the needs and problems of this alarm-ingly sick child (i.e. "cleansing and beautifying their child"), their ef-forts would eventually be for the benefit of the phenomenon of death [*Nyoro*] (Beattie 1957: 102).

Basajja (m) *[bah-sahj-jah]* Men; this name is sometimes associated with the proverb "men are like iroko timber trees: they shed (or lose) their leaves, but they do regrow their thick foliage" implying that peo-ple experience both good and bad days and times; this name is also sometimes associated with the proverb "men are like iroko timber trees: they shatter but they also make firm" implying that men can be remarkably good and of great use, but on the other hand they can be so malicious and damaging [*Ganda*].

Basajjakambwe (m) *[bah-sahj-jah-kahm-bweh]*/ **Basajjankambwe** (m) *[bah-sahj-jahn-kahm-bweh]* "Men are (like) a fierce animal": in this war related proverbial name, it is implied that men are ferocious and do not easily give in without a fight [*Ganda*].

Basajjansolo (m) *[bah-sahj-jahn-soh-loh]* "Men are (like) wild an-imals"; this war related name is commonly associated with the pro-verbs "men are (like) wild animals: when you pursuingly follow into the bush after one, he breaks through the thicket with tremendous

force" and "men can be tough or courageous just like animals" implying that men are tough and do not easily give in without a fight; this
name is also commonly associated with the proverb "men, like animals, devour each other (or their own kind)" implying that men (such
as the powerful and the influential) can go to gross lengths to destroy,
domineer or oppress of their fellow men [*Ganda*].

Basajjassubi (m) *[bah-sahj-jahs-suh-bih]* "Men are (like) grass"; this
name is commonly associated with the proverbs "men are (like) grass
: they (are used to) tie up themselves" and "men are (like harvested)
grass: one stalk ties up the rest" which is in reference to the hardy grass used for thatching or squeezing out juice from bananas, the name implying that men (such as the powerful and the influential) can
be so unreasonably domineering and oppressive of their fellow men
[*Ganda*].

Basalidde (m) *[bah-saah-lihd-deh]* "They have become disappointed/
regretful/ sorry" [*Ganda*].

Basammula (m) *[bah-sahm-muh-lah]* "They shake off (or reject, or repudiate)"; "they splash (or sprinkle, or scatter)"; this name is commonly associated with the proverb "they (i.e. people) will drive a frog
out of the house (with a stick), but will have no qualms about drinking
the water from the well that the frog dwells in" implying that people
can be so inconsistent and contradictory in their actions [*Ganda*].

Basammulekkere (m) *[bah-sahm-muh-lehk-keh-reh]* "They shake off
(or drive away, or drive out) the large frog"; this name is commonly
associated with the proverb "they (i.e. people) will drive a frog out of
the house (with a stick), but will have no qualms about drinking the
water from the well that the frog dwells in" implying that people can
be so inconsistent and contradictory in their actions [*Ganda*].

Baseka (f) *[bah-seh-kah]* "They (pretentiously) laugh"; this name is
commonly associated with the proverb "they (i.e. people) laugh while
harboring a stinging (caterpillar hair/ or a spicule) hair (in their heart)"
implying that people can smile outwardly but have inner feelings of
malice, or that people often smile outwardly though they are sorrow-
ing inside [*Ganda, Soga*].

Baseke (f/m) *[bah-seh-keh]* "Let them (i.e. the neighbors) laugh/ make
fun": name such as given to a child whose parents imply that they will
continue to ignore the fun made of their condition by neighbors or kin,
since the parents have still managed to survive [The *Ganda, Nyoro,
Soga*] (Beattie 1957: 102).

Basiima (f) *[bah-siih-mah]* "They display gratitude"; this name is commonly associated with the proverb "they display gratitude only while
they are still munching (at your food)" which implies that ingratitude is
commonplace, and that "friends" often desert the one that has become impoverished [*Ganda, Soga*].

Basiimaki (m) *[bah-siih-mah-kih]* "What are they (i.e. people) to be
thankful for?": a name such as given to child born into a family that is

poor, the name implying that those in a situation of poverty are so drained and have little to be thankful for [*Nyoro*] (Beattie 1957: 103).

Basirika (f) *[bah-sih-rih-kah]* "They remain close-mouthed (although they know)" [*Ganda, Soga*].

Batei (f/m) *[bah-tehy]* The name is contracted from *ndakabatei* i.e. "what have I been working for" and is given to one born to a mother whose husband disputingly considers her a good-for-nothing wife whom he has wasted his resources on [*Shona*] (Jackson 1957: 116).

Batindira (f/m) *[bah-tihn-dih-rah]* "They (i.e. people) erect a surrounding framework of trellis protection"; this name is commonly associated with the proverb "they (i.e. people) erect a surrounding framework of trellis protection to just the one (i.e. tree) that has ripened with fruit" which implies that ingratitude is commonplace, that "friends" often desert the one that has become impoverished, and that people tend to not support those they do not hope to profit from [*Ganda*].

Batuuka (f/m) *[bah-tuuh-kah/ baah-tuuh-kah]* "They arrive"; those that arrived; this name is commonly associated with the proverb "upon their arrival, the travelers forget who their travel guides were" which implies that ingratitude is commonplace [*Ganda*].

Batuuse (f/m) *[bah-tuuh-seh]* "Those that have arrived"; this name is commonly associated with the proverb "those that have arrived forget who their travel guides were" which implies that ingratitude is commonplace [*Ganda*, Soga].

Bayita (f) *[bah-yih-tah]* That travel through; that pass by; this name is commonly associated with the proverb "two partners that travel (or pass) together, remind each other" which is synonymous with "two heads are better than one" and contains a message of meriting and fostering a spirit of human cooperation and togetherness; this name is also sometimes associated with the proverb "one that is helpless is like two paupers that walk together" [*Ganda*].

Bazibumbira (m) *[baah-zih-buhm-bih-rah]* "They molded them for"; this name is commonly associated with the proverb "they molded them to crack, but it is (ironically) in the fiery furnace that the pots resiliently survived" and it is usually given to a child born to a parent, most of whose previous offspring died, and whereby there is pessimism (or on the other hand optimism) as to whether this child will survive [The *Ganda*].

Bbwaddene (m) *[bbwahd-deh-neh]* Large dog; this name is commonly associated with a difficult character in the proverb "a big dog is subdued by its owner (or trainer): just as in the situation where sweet potatoes cannot be dug out of the soil with a stick, the hoe which was used to plant them in the first place, will dig them up" implying that it is the one with the expertise or experience in a matter that will best deal with it or solve it [*Ganda*].

Bei (f/m) *[behy]* "Thunder": a name given to a twin, the other named

Mokalikali [*Gombe*] (Daeleman 1977: 190).

Bejjukanya (f) *[behj-juh-kah-ndjh-aah]*/ **Bajjukanya** (f) *[bahj-juh-kah-ndjh-aah]* "They remind each other"; this name is commonly associated with the proverb "two partners that travel (or pass) together, remind each other" which is synonymous with "two heads are better than one" and contains the message of meriting and fostering a spirit of human cooperation and togetherness [*Ganda*].

Bendaki (m) *[behn-dah-kih]* "What is it that they (i.e. the neighbors) want?": the name implies that the neighbors have been so annoying or malicious to the family to which the child so named is born, the bewildered parents wonder what they did wrong or what they can do to please the neighbors [*Nyoro*] (Beattie 1957: 103).

Berabira/ Beerabira (f) *[beh-eh-rah-bih-rah]* "They (i.e. people) forget"; this name is commonly associated with the proverb "upon their arrival, the travelers forget who their travel guides were" which implies that both opportunism and ingratitude are commonplace; this name is also sometimes associated with the proverb "those who close the doors forget that there are still spaces between the door and the wall" implying that there is a tendency for people to dwell on one source of trouble and evil, though they ought to consider the multiple sources [*Ganda*].

Bhekabafowabo (m) *[beh-kah-bah-foh-waah-boh]* "Have respect for your brothers"; "look after your brothers" [*Zulu*] (Koopman 1979: 68).

Bhekani (m) *[uh-beh-kah-nih]* "Look at him": a name such as given to a child suspected by his paternal family of being conceived out of infidelity, to which accusation the child's mother says, "Look at him (i.e. 'the child looks just like my husband')" [The *Zulu*] (Suzman 1994: 263).

Bhekezakhe (m) *[beh-keh-zahk-heh]* "He has regard for his things" [*Zulu*] (Koopman 1979: 160).

Bhekimpilo (m) *[uh-beh-kihm-pih-loh]* "Look after your health": a name such as given to a child whose mother is not properly attentive to her health needs and medical checkup routines, the name exhorting her to take adequate interest in her health status [*Zulu*] (Suzman 1994: 269).

Bhekimthetho (m) *[beh-kihm-sth-eh-th-oh]* "Have regard for the laws" [*Zulu*] (Koopman 1979: 79).

Bhekinkosi (m) *[bheh-kihn-koh-sih]* "He has regard for the Lord" [*Zulu*] (Koopman 1979: 153, 160).

Bhekisisa (m) *[beh-kih-sih-sah]* "Look carefully" [The *Zulu*] (Koopman 1979: 158).

Bhekizitha (m) *[beh-kih-zih-tah]* "He watches out for enemies" [*Zulu*] (Koopman 1979: 160).

Bhekuyise (m) *[beh-kuh-yih-seh]* "He has regard for his father"; "have regard for his father" [*Zulu*] (Koopman 1979: 160).

Bikanga (m) *[bih-kahn-gah]* "They (i.e. things like property or riches)

have refused (i.e. the home)": a name such as given to child born into a family that has degenerated into poverty, the name implying that
the poverty has been a result of losses such as from goats and sheep
dying, crops failing, losing money, and not making profit [The *Nyoro*]
(Beattie 1957: 103).

Bikongoolo (m) *[bih-kohn-goh-oh-loh]* Grimaces; facial expressions of
disgust; this name is commonly associated with the proverb "mocking
(or making facial expressions) does not kill the bull" meaning that
mere words do not frighten the brave or the hardened, and is also
synonymous with "hard words break no bones" and "sticks and stones
may break my bones, but words cannot hurt me" [*Ganda*].

Bikyabyambuzi (m) *[bih-tch-ah-bjaahm-buh-zih]* The neck tendons of
a goat; this name is commonly associated with the proverb "citizens
(or lesser officials) are like the neck tendons of a goat: they do not
refuse to get roped" implying that people may murmur behind the
chief's (or superior official's) back, but they still go on to obey the
superior; this name is also commonly associated with the proverb
"neck tendons of a goat are not grumpy over getting roped" implying
that one can still get hardeningly tolerant of bad conditions and negative criticism (as is compared with the goat which is often roped by
the neck all day, but it heartily grazes) [*Ganda*].

Bileni (f/m) *[bih-leh-nih]* "For the grave": a name such as given to a
child who amongst many in the family cluster group, has been the
first to survive death [*Lugbara*] (Middleton 1961: 35).

Binsangawano (m) *[bihn-sahn-gah-wah-noh]* "They (i.e. the words/
stories/ issues) find me here"; this name is commonly associated with
the proverb "'they (i.e. the words/ stories/ issues) get to me here' is
the talk of the elderly" meaning that the elderly are not so physically
mobile, so they often get information through hearsay other than by
way of personally witnessing the happenings [*Ganda*].

Birabwa (f) *[bih-rah-bwah]* That are noticeable; this name is commonly associated with the proverb "how things are seen is not how they
are evaluated"; this name is also commonly associated with the proverb "what will happen in the future is foreseen by the one who will
live long" [*Ganda*].

Birigenda (m) *[bih-rih-gehn-dah]* "They (i.e. things like property or riches) will (eventually) go": a name such as given to child born into a family that is poor, the name implying that the parents recognize that
wealth is unimportant and may not be a lifetime guarantee to the rich,
and that the rich do not leave with their earthly riches when they pass
away [*Nyoro*] (Beattie 1957: 103).

Biriko (f) *[bih-rih-koh]* "That have a connection with"; this name is
commonly associated with the proverb "accusations for which there is
a witness, cannot be disavowed if the one that has given you away is
of your own household" [*Ganda, Soga*].

Birimumaaso (m) *[bih-rih-muh-maah-soh]* "Things that will happen in the future"; this name is commonly associated with the proverb "what will happen in the future is foreseen by the one who will live long" [*Ganda*].

Bitagase (m) *[bih-tah-gah-seh]* "They would not be of profit": a name such as given to an alarmingly sick child not expected to survive, or to one whose previously born siblings died, or to one born during a time of sorrow whereby the pessimism lingers on [The *Nyoro*] (Beattie 1957: 101).

Bitamazire (m) *[bih-tah-mah-zih-reh]* "They (i.e. the sandals made from banana fiber) have not been adequate": name such as given to an alarmingly sick child not expected to survive, this child compared to the fiber made shoes which are vulnerable to damage and are temporary [*Nyoro*] (Beattie 1957: 101).

Bodo (f/m) *[boh-doh]* Black pot: a name such as given to one of very dark negroid complexion [*Shona*] (Jackson 1957: 120).

Bogere/ Boogere (m) *[boh-oh-geh-reh]* "Let them talk/ gossip"; this name is commonly associated with the proverb "one who says, 'Let them (unyieldingly) talk (about him/ her)' is being told about someone he likes so much" implying that people do not easily accept negative criticism about ones they love or like so much [*Ganda, Soga*].

Bohlale (m) *[boh-lah-leh]* Wisdom [*Sotho*] (Mohome 1972: 178).

Boika (m) *[bohy-kah]* A name given to a parent of twins [*Bolia, Mongo, Ntomba*] (Daeleman 1977: 194).

Boipuso (m) *[bohy-puh-soh]* Independence; freedom [*Sotho*] (Thipa 1986: 288).

Bolo (f/m) *[boh-loh]* "Throw" [*Luo*].

Bonakele (f) *[boh-nah-keh-leh]* "She is visible" [The *Zulu*] (Koopman 1979: 162).

Bongani (m) *[bohn-gaah-nih]* "Be grateful" [The *Zulu*] (Koopman 1979: 158).

Bongani (m) *[uh-bohn-gaah-nih]* "Thanks": a name such as expressing gratitude for the birth of this child [*Zulu*] (Herbert 1995: 6); a name such as given by the named child's grandmother to express that this child was provided by God (since he is borne out of wedlock), or to express gratefulness for her daughter having brought forth the child smoothly; a name such as given by the named child's grandfather to express gratitude for the arrival of yet another boy [*Zulu*] (Suzman 1994: 260).

Bongekile (f) *[bohn-geh-kih-leh]* "She is praiseworthy" [The *Zulu*] (Koopman 1979: 161).

Bongekile (f) *[uh-bohn-geh-kih-leh]* "Thanked": a name such as given by the named child's mother to express gratitude for the arrival of a girl who would help her with household chores [*Zulu*] (Suzman 1994: 260).

Bonginkosi (m) *[bohn-gihn-koh-sih]* "Praise the Lord"; "he is grateful to the Lord"; "he thanks the Lord" [*Zulu*] (Koopman 1979: 160).

Bongomin (m) *[boh-ndgh-oh-mihn]* A name given to one that does not have brothers [*Acholi*] (Nzita 1995: 92).

Borikhoe (m) *[boh-rih-koh-yeh]* Trousers: a name such as given to one whose mother's husband was the first in the family to wear trousers instead of the traditional loin while being wed--this child's mother's name is *Maborikhoe* [*Sotho*] (Ashton 1952: 32).

Boteng (m) *[boh-teh-ndgh]* "There is some": a name such as given to one whose parents had beer to offer a visitor that went to congratulate them following the birth--the other new parents this visitor went to see were not able to offer beer, so their child was named *Haboeo* [*Sotho*] (Ashton 1952: 32).

Budde (m) *[buhd-deh]* Time; weather; occasion; night; this name is sometimes associated with the proverb "the weather conditions as it dawns, are not the same as the conditions of when it gets dark" implying that one should neither be needlessly optimistic nor overly pessimistic because of prevailing conditions; this name is also sometimes associated with the proverb "the weather conditions as it dawns, are not the same as the conditions of when it gets dark: (that is why) the chicken asks its mother what their family and clan totem (or taboo) is" which advises one to inquire about or take care of the important issues as soon as the opportunity, which may never avail itself again, is there--as synonymous with "make hay while the sun shines" [*Ganda*].

Bugagga (f) *[buh-gahg-gah]* Wealthiness; richness; this name is sometimes associated with the proverb "wealth is (like) perspiration: it flows when you are active, and dries up when you rest" [*Ganda*].

Buge (f/m) *[buh-geh]* "Cover it" i.e. the hole [*Luo*].

Bujune (m) *[buh-juh-neh]* "Sorrow": a name such as given to a child born during times of sorrow [*Nyoro*] (Beattie 1957: 100).

Bukaddemagezi (m) *[buh-kahd-deh-mah-geh-zih]* "Old age is wisdom"; this name is commonly associated with the proverb "with old age comes wisdom, but the elderly will not tell you what contributed to their longevity" i.e. because there are contributing factors that are inexplicable, or will not be told--out of shyness or fear of being laughed at [*Ganda*].

Bukalammuli (m) *[buh-kah-lahm-muh-lih]* "It (i.e. tenancy) becomes firmly established by reeds"; this name is commonly associated with the proverb "a new tenant or immigrant cements his welcome by fetching reeds for the landlord" which situation more so applies to the tenant-landlord relationships of the past, and presents the message that it is important to give a new boss or landlord a very good first impression [*Ganda*].

Bukhosi (m) *[buh-koh-siih]* "Chieftaincy" [*Zulu*] (Koopman 1979: 154).

Bukhosibakhe (m) *[buh-koh-sih-bah-keh]* "His chieftaincy" [The *Zulu*] (Koopman 1979: 80).

Bukwetonza/ Bukweetonza (f) *[buh-kweh-eh-tohn-zaah]* That which makes a person irate or grouchy (such as misery or loss); this name is commonly associated with the proverb "misery (or sorrow) makes you irritable" [*Ganda*].

Bukya (f/m) *[buh-tch-aah]* Since; "the day breaks"; this name is commonly associated with the proverb "the weather conditions as it dawns, are not the same as the conditions of when it gets dark" implying that one should neither be needlessly optimistic nor overly pessimistic because of prevailing conditions; this name is also commonly associated with the proverb "the weather conditions as it dawns, are not the same as the conditions of when it gets dark: (that is why) the chicken asks its mother what their family and clan totem (or taboo) is" which advises one to inquire about or take care of the important issues as soon as the opportunity, which may never avail itself again, is there--as synonymous with "make hay while the sun shines" [The *Ganda*].

Bulamutebweweebwa (f) *[buh-lah-muh-teh-bweh-eh-weh-eh-bwaah]* "Life is not given you by yourself"; "it can be hard to take a grip your own life" [*Ganda*].

Buletwenda (m) *[buh-leh-eh-twehn-dah]* "It (i.e. sorrow) is brought forth by the womb": name such as given to an alarmingly sick child not expected to survive [*Nyoro*] (Beattie 1957: 100-101).

Buliggwanga (m) *[buh-lihg-gwahn-gaah]* "Every nation (or ethnic group)"; this name is commonly associated with the proverb "every nation (or ethnic group) has its peculiarities" implying that every social group has its customs, its good and bad qualities, and its problems [*Ganda*].

Bulimarwaki (m) *[buh-lih-mah-rwah-kih]* "What is it that will put an end (i.e. to the sorrow--that seems to be endless)?": name such as given to a child born during a period of misfortune [*Nyoro*] (Beattie 1957: 101).

Bulungi (f) *[buh-luhn-jiih]* Beauty; this name is commonly associated with the proverb "the beauty (of a woman) is not the ticket to a successful marriage" implying that one ought to look beyond the superficial, and instead look at crucial factors such as behavioral characteristics [*Ganda*].

Bulungisiddya (f) *[buh-luhn-jih-sihd-djaah]* "The beauty (of a woman) is not the ticket to a successful marriage": it is implied in this proverbial name that one ought to look beyond the superficial, and instead look at crucial factors such as behavioral characteristics [*Ganda*].

Bulwadda (m) *[buh-lwahd-dah]* Doing for a long time; this name is commonly associated with the proverb "the cumulative effect of walking on a rock for a long time, is a smooth path" which can imply that the lengthy involvement of many can lead to the clearing up of a problem, but it can also result in wearing out of an item [*Ganda*].

Bungukile (f) *[buhn-guh-kih-leh]* (One associated with) being detribalized [*Zulu*] (Koopman 1979: 74).

Buru (m) *[buh-ruuh]* Bull [*Shona*] (Jackson 1957: 120).

Busisiwe (f) *[buh-sih-sih-weh]* "She is blessed"; "the blessed one" [*Zulu*] (Koopman 1979: 162).

Busuma (m) *[buh-suh-mah]* "Corn meal": a name given to one fond of eating corn meal [*Luyia*].

Busungu (f) *[buh-suhn-guuh]* Anger; ire, wrath; this name is sometimes associated with the proverb "anger is (like) a visitor: it comes and goes" [*Ganda*].

Butannaziba (m) *[buh-tahn-nah-zih-bah]* "Before the night"; this name is commonly associated with the proverb "if it is not yet dark (or evening time), do not complain and lose the hope that you will get something to eat" implying that one should not be overly pessimistic because of prevailing conditions [*Ganda*].

Buteraba/ Buteeraba (m) *[buh-teh-eh-rah-bah]* One who little cares about his appearance or mannerisms; sloppiness; this name is commonly associated with the proverb "not checking yourself makes you insult (or blame, or underestimate) one who is superior to you" [The *Ganda*].

Buttibwa (f) *[buht-tih-bwah]* "It (i.e. marriage) is destroyed by"; this name is commonly associated with the proverb "a situation of marriage can only be destroyed by a very crafty person" which situation more so applies to the past when marriages were quite stable [The *Ganda*].

Buttibwamugezi (f) *[buht-tih-bwah-muh-geh-zih]* "It (i.e. marriage) can only be destroyed by a very crafty person"; this name is commonly associated with the proverb "a situation of marriage can only be destroyed by a very crafty person" which situation more so applies to the past when marriages were quite stable [*Ganda*].

Buwambazza (f) *[buh-wahm-bahz-zah]* That which makes a person wander; this name is commonly associated with the proverb "misery (or sorrow) makes one wander" [*Ganda*].

Buyinda (m) *[buh-yihn-dah]* A name given to a rich one [*Luyia*].

Buyisiwanokuthula (f) *[uh-buh-yih-sih-wah-noh-kuh-sth-uh-lah]* "Silence returned": name such as given by the named child's parents to express that since the child was born there have not been any family quarrels [*Zulu*] (Suzman 1994: 261).

Buziba (m) *[buh-zih-bah]* Deep water; open water; "it gets dark"; this name is sometimes associated with the proverb "you do not hang around a hippopotamus in the depth of the waters" implying that it would be highly risky to challenge something big and dangerous in its very own niche (or in conditions it is very familiar with); this name is also sometimes associated with the proverb "the weather conditions as it dawns, are not the same as the conditions of when it gets dark" implying that one should neither be needlessly optimistic nor overly pessimistic because of prevailing conditions; this name is also sometimes associated with the proverb "the weather conditions as it dawns, are not the same as the conditions of when it gets dark: (that is why) the chicken asks its mother what their family and clan totem (or taboo) is" which advises one to inquire about or take care of the important issues as soon as the opportunity, which may never avail itself again, is there--as synonymous with "make hay while the sun shines" [*Ganda*].

Bwangu (f) *[bwahn-guh]* Speed; facility; this name is sometimes associated with the proverb "hastiness in giving makes you give to one that would never hand out anything to you" [*Ganda*].

Bwato/ Bwaato (m) *[bwaah-toh]* Small boats; this name is commonly associated with the proverb "small boats still sink at the very end of the journey when landing" implying that caution other than over-confidence ought to always be exercised since one is still prone to fa-ilure or disaster even after one has seemingly overcome all the diffi-culties and achieved success [*Ganda*].

Bwavu/ Bwaavu (m) *[bwaah-vuh]* Poverty; indigence; this name is sometimes associated with the proverb "poverty is not the same as (or is not as bad as) a debt (or indebtedness)" implying that what belongs to one without a debt is truly his and he can not be charged for being poor, whereas a rich one in debt can face serious charges and even confiscation [*Ganda*].

Bweguyibwa (f) *[bweh-eh-guh-yih-bwah]* That is stooped to or great-ly desired; this name is commonly associated with the saying "marriage is obsequiously stooped to (or desirably honored)" [*Ganda, Soga*].

Bwemage (m) *[bweh-mah-geh]* Without reason (or cause); this name is commonly associated with the saying "to unjustly accuse me (or one), is like accusing the marsh antelope of being in the marsh" whereby the situation of gross false incrimination is compared to acc-using the antelope of being in its very own niche, in which it is only harmlessly grazing, and it is not wrecking havoc on cultivated crops [*Ganda*].

Bweteme (m) *[bweh-teh-meh]* Commitments; pledges; promises; that has cut itself (or oneself); that has cut for itself (or oneself); that has undertaken (to) [*Ganda*].

Bwoga (f/m) *[bwoh-gah]* "Scare me"; "frighten me" [*Luo*].

Byakika (m) *[bjah-tch-ih-kah]* Issues of the clan; this name is comm-only associated with the saying "clan matters are best kept secret" [*Soga*].

Byarufu (m) *[bjah-ruh-fuuh]* "That are of the one that is dead": a name such as given to an alarmingly sick child not expected to survive [*Nyoro*] (Beattie 1957: 102).

Byeitima (m) *[bjehy-tih-mah]* "Those things that involve (or are of) ill will": the parents of a child given this name are heralding the mess-age that the neighbors are so spiteful towards them [*Nyoro*] (Beattie 1957: 104).

Byelamani (f/m) *[bjeh-lah-mah-nih]* "Who to talk to": a name such as given to a newborn whose father died, the mother expressing that as a result she does not have any one to tell and relate her problems to [*Zulu*] (Herbert 1995: 5).

-C-

Caimbasuku (f) *[tch-ah-yihm-bah-suh-kuh]* "The will (or power) of God": this name is commonly associated with the proverb "The will of God is inescapable" and is given to a child some of whose previously born siblings died, or to one born into a family that has recently had deaths [*Ovimbundu*] (Ennis 1945: 3).

Caimile (f) *[tch-ahy-mih-leh]* "It has borne": this name is commonly associated with the expression "It has borne, it falls; a family is born, it perishes" implying that a tree bears fruit and the fruit falls to the ground, and relates to a child who has lost several of her siblings to death [*Ovimbundu*] (Ennis 1945: 6).

Cakuili (f) *[tch-ah-kuh-yih-lih]* "That which you do not know": this name is commonly associated with the proverb "That which you do not know, your own give it to you" implying that even your own family kin can go to extremes to harm you, the name usually given to a child born into a family in which disputes are present [*Ovimbundu*] (Ennis 1945: 5).

Cakusola (f) *[tch-ah-kuh-soh-lah]* "That which you loved": this name is commonly associated with the proverb "That which you loved, you followed the messenger" implying that if the message or action puts you in a selected and more advantageous position *vis-a-vis* that which you love, then you will very willingly accept it--this name is such as given to one whose birth follows the bestowal of an honor on the parents [*Ovimbundu*] (Ennis 1945: 5).

Canjika (f) *[tch-ahn-jih-kah]* "It has become my habit"; "I have become accustomed to it" [*Ovimbundu*] (Ennis 1945: 6).

Capopia (f) *[tch-ah-poh-pjah]* "That which God says": this name is commonly associated with the proverb "That which God says, I do not dispute" and is given to a child some of whose previously born siblings died, or to one born into a family that has recently had deaths [*Ovimbundu*] (Ennis 1945: 3).

Capukulua (f) *[tch-ah-puh-kuh-lwah]* "It is neglected": name such as given to an ill-treated child that is poor and thin [*Ovimbundu*] (Ennis 1945: 6).

Cashephi (f) *[kah-tsh-eh-pih]* "Has she hidden?" [*Zulu*] (Koopman 1979: 162).

Cashile (m) *[tch-ah-tsh-ih-leh]* "Hidden": name such as given to a child who is the product of a "concealed" birth since though when the mother went to hospital she was assured that her time to give birth had not come, when she went back home she produced [The *Zulu*]

(Suzman 1994: 262, 270).

Catava (f) *[tch-ah-tah-vah]* "That which consented": this name is commonly associated with the proverb "That which consented to sleep was protested by pain" whereby sleep is not possible because of the intense pain in the body, implying that often there are cases whereby one has the resources and determination to do something, but an inconveniencing stumbling block persists to not make this possible--perhaps synonymous with the biblical "The spirit is willing, but the body is weak" *[Ovimbundu]* (Ennis 1945: 5).

Cetshwayo (m) *[tch-eht-swaah-yoh]* "The slandered one" *[Zulu]* (Lugg 1968: 13).

Ceyavali (f) *[tch-eh-yah-vah-lih]* "It (i.e. death) has come again": this name is commonly given to a child born after several children in the family or the neighborhood have died, and there is not much optimism about this one surviving *[Ovimbundu]* (Ennis 1945: 7).

Chakide (m) *[tch-ah-kih-deh]* Weasel: name such as given to one with sharpness of sight or expression *[Zulu]* (Koopman 1979: 68, 69).

Chalo (m) *[tch-aah-loh]* Sugar cane patch: one associated with an event (such as a dispute associated with a garden of sugar cane) *[Kaguru]* (Beidelman 1974: 288).

Chando (f/m) *[tch-ahn-doh]* Winter: a name given to one born during winter *[Shona]* (Jackson 1957: 120).

Chauhele (m) *[tch-ah-wuh-heh-leh]* The one with scabies [The *Kaguru*] (Beidelman 1974: 288).

Cheja (f) *[tch-eh-djah]* "We came": a name such as given to one associated with travel, or given to one associated with circumstances that involve being a refugee *[Kaguru]* (Beidelman 1974: 289).

Chemaiyo (f) *[tch-eh-mahy-yoh]* A name given to one born at a time of a beer drinking gathering *[Nandi]* (Hollis 1969: 67).

Chemaket (f/m) *[tch-eh-mah-keht]/* **Chemakut** (f/m) *[tch-eh-mah-kuht]* Examples of animal names given to second born twins, the first born named *Simatua* *[Nandi]* (Hollis 1969: 68).

Chemngeny (f) *[tch-ehm-ndgh-eh-ndjh]* A name given to one born during a time the oxen have just been taken to lick salt rock *[Nandi]* (Hollis 1969: 67).

Chemuike (f) *[tch-eh-muhy-keh]* A name given to one born shortly after a relation is killed *[Nandi]* (Hollis 1969: 67).

Chengeto (f/m) *[tch-ehn-geh-toh]* Holy salvation [The *Shona*] (Jackson 1957: 121).

Chenzira (f) *[tch-en-zih-rah]* "Of the path": a name such as given to a child born close to a road and at a time the mother was on a journey *[Zezuru]* (Marapara 1954: 8).

Chepet (f) *[tch-eh-peht]* A name given to one born in the morning *[Nandi]* (Hollis 1969: 67).

Chepirken (f) *[tch-eh-pihr-kehn]* "One born when the mortars had to be beaten to drown the mothers cries": this likely implies a child of a very painful delivery, or one of a delivery during which the mother's labor pain cries were unusually loud [*Nandi*] (Hollis 1969: 67).

Chepkemboi (f) *[tch-ehp-kehm-bohy]* One born in the evening [The *Nandi*] (Hollis 1969: 67).

Chepkor (f) *[tch-ehp-kohr]* A name given to one born by the roadside [*Nandi*] (Hollis 1969: 67).

Chepruiot (f) *[tch-ehp-ruhy-yoht]* A name given to one born during the night [*Nandi*] (Hollis 1969: 67).

Cheprukut (f) *[tch-ehp-ruh-kuht]* A name given to one born during a period of food scarcity in the land [*Nandi*] (Hollis 1969: 67).

Chepruto (f) *[tch-ehp-ruh-toh]* A name given to one born during a journey [*Nandi*] (Hollis 1969: 67).

Chepsepet (f/m) *[tch-ehp-seh-peht]/* **Cheptiony** (f/m) *[tch-ep-tih-yoh-ndjh]* Examples of animal names given to second born twins, the first born named *Simatua* [*Nandi*] (Hollis 1969: 68).

Chepseta (f/m) *[tch-ehp-seh-tah]* A name given to a child born around the time the father purchased a cow that has a crumpled horn [*Nandi*] (Hollis 1969: 67).

Cheptalil (m) *[tch-ehp-tah-lihl]* God; "God of the Bright Sky"; "that which gleams" [*Nandi*] (Huntingford 1930: 102-103).

Chepunye (m) *[tch-eh-puh-ndjh-eh]* "He who hides his arm": (usually) a post-childhood nickname [*Nandi*] (Hollis 1969: 67).

Chepyator (f) *[tch-ehp-yah-tohr]* A name given to one born very early in the morning i.e. at the time the door is opened [The *Nandi*] (Hollis 1969: 67).

Chezira/ Chezhira (f/m) *[tch-eh-zih-rah]* The one of the path: a name given to one born on the wayside, or born when the parent was on a journey, or born out of wedlock or as a result of infidelity [The *Shona*] (Jackson 1957: 120).

Chibakwa (m) *[tch-ih-bah-kwah]* That is anointed: name such as given to one who is a circumciser, a ritual leader, or some other distinguished person [*Kaguru*] (Beidelman 1974: 288).

Chieng (m) *[tch-yeh-ndgh]* God; creator; the sun; daylight; day [*Luo*] (Huntingford 1930: 102-103).

Chigenda (m) *[tch-ih-gehn-dah]* "Let us go": a name such as given to one who travels frequently (or to one who is originally from elsewhere) [*Kaguru*] (Beidelman 1974: 288).

Chikadiwa (f/m) *[tch-ih-kahn-dih-wah]* "I am just a thing thrown to my husband--he does not love me": a name such as given to one born to a mother who is involved in a dispute with her husband and is far from being in his good books [*Shona*] (Jackson 1957: 116).

Chikira (m) *[tch-ih-kih-rah]* "Deserted": a name such as given to a child born at a time of quarreling and strife between his parents which may have resulted in the mother becoming ostracized/ or to a child born to a mother who characteristically, during the pregnancy, often became angry and refrained from eating [*Pare*] (Omari 1970: 70).

Chilimo (m) *[tch-ih-lih-moh]* A cultivation (or cultivator): a name such as given to one born during the season of cultivating [The *Kaguru*] (Beidelman 1974: 288).

Chilongola (m) *[tch-ih-lohn-goh-lah]* "The first": a name such as given to a first born son/ or to the first boy to be circumcised in the ceremony/ or to the first person to settle in a neighborhood [The *Kaguru*] (Beidelman 1974: 288).

Chimola (m) *[tch-ih-moh-lah]* "The seizer/ breaker of things": a name such as given to one that is strong [*Kaguru*] (Beidelman 1974: 288).

Chinyama (f/m) *[tch-ih-ndjh-ah-mah]* Small piece of meat: name such as given to a child who has lost several of previously born siblings to death and whereby there is pessimism as to whether this one will survive--the name implies that this little child too is just a small piece of meat susceptible to consumption by forces of death, fate, or witchcraft [*Shona*] (Jackson 1957: 118).

Chipiwa (f/m) *[tch-ih-pih-wah]* A gift from God [*Shona*] (Jackson 1957: 121).

Chipo (f) *[tch-ih-poh]* A gift: name such as given to a child born long after the marriage was consummated, so that it was feared that the mother was barren [*Zezuru*] (Marapara 1954: 8).

Chiratidzo (m) *[tch-ih-rah-tihd-zoh]* A sign: a name such as given to a child born into a family with a relatively high number of daughters compared to sons/ or to a child born into a family that does not have any sons [*Zezuru*] (Marapara 1954: 8).

Chirindo (f/m) *[tch-ih-rihn-doh]* A garden or plantation hut that serves as a lookout spot for animals and birds: a name given to one born in a lookout hut [*Shona*] (Jackson 1957: 119).

Chisango (m) *[tch-ih-sahn-goh]* Veld: a name such as given to a child given birth to in the bush [*Zezuru*] (Marapara 1954: 8).

Chitemo (m) *[tch-ih-teh-moh]* Ax: a name such as given to a strong and fierce man [*Kaguru*] (Beidelman 1974: 288).

Chitula (m) *[tch-ih-tuh-lah]* That breaks/ or is broken: a name such as given to one born during times of trouble involving breaking down of social relations [*Kaguru*] (Beidelman 1974: 289).

Chituri (f/m) *[tch-ih-tuh-rih]* Little wooden grain mortar [The *Shona*] (Jackson 1957: 120).

Chiumburu (f/m) *[tch-ih-wuhm-buh-ruh]* A name given to one who is short and pudgy [*Shona*] (Jackson 1957: 120).

Chochorai (f/m) *[tch-tch-oh-rahy]* "Covet our riches--you will see what will happen as a result": a name such as given to one born during a family dispute with neighbors or with kin, this serving as a warning that retaliation, damaged relationships, or evil may accrue if the neighbors or kin do not stop doing the backbiting and coveting that is at the same time giving the family a bad name [The *Shona*] (Jackson 1957: 116).

Chomunorwa (f/m) *[tch-oh-muh-noh-rwah]* "What is all the fighting about?": a name such as given to one born during a puzzling family dispute with kin or neighbors [*Shona*] (Jackson 1957: 116).

Chone (f/m) *[tch-oh-neh]* "Push it"; "move" [*Luo*].

Chune (f/m) *[tch-uuh-neh]* "Force it" [*Luo*].

Chunga (f/m) *[tch-uuh-ndgh-ah]* "Sieve me"; "raise me"; "lift me up" [*Luo*].

Chwangaa (f/m) *[tch-wah-ndgh-aah]* "Annoy me"; "irritate me"; "cross me" [*Luo*].

Ciarunji (f) *[tch-yah-ruhn-jih]* "Of the river": a name given to one born near a river [*Embu*].

Cilehe (f) *[tch-ih-leh-heh]* "Leave it alone": this name is commonly associated with the proverb "Just let it stink, let it be" which is synonymous with "Mind your own business" and implies that you are likely to make the situation worse of a matter that did not concern you in the first place; this name is also commonly associated with the proverb "Let it stink, it is his/ her own" which refers to the custom of keeping a corpse for a long time that leads to non-relatives avoiding the place, though the relatives essentially have to stand it since the corpse is of their own--it implies that one essentially has to come to grips with a repulsive or bad thing as long as it has connection with him or her [*Ovimbundu*] (Ennis 1945: 4).

Cilikonawa (f) *[tch-ih-lih-koh-nah-wah]* "It is in the care of an in-law": this name is associated with the expression "It is in the care of an in-law; it is in the care of a fool" which is metaphorically the lamentation of a disputing woman nursing negative opinion of her husband's family, the name commonly given to such a woman (or a child of such a woman) [*Ovimbundu*] (Ennis 1945: 6).

Cilombo (f) *[tch-ih-lohm-boh]* "Roadside camp": since a roadside camp is a welcome sight for weary travelers, this name implies 'a sight for the sore eye' [*Ovimbundu*] (Ennis 1945: 2).

Cinakavali (f) *[tch-ih-nah-kah-vah-lih]* "Since they do not eat": this name is commonly associated with the proverb "Since they do not eat brambles, they neither cook them nor eat them" implying that one takes on work towards a useful other than a fruitless end [The *Ovimbundu*] (Ennis 1945: 4).

Cinakualile (f) *[tch-ih-nah-kwah-lih-leh]* "That which you did not eat": this name is commonly associated with the proverb "It is not what you did *not* eat that brings on the stomach ache" implying that it is our own actions that lead to sometimes unpleasant consequences, therefore the blame for such should not be assigned to other factors [*Ovimbundu*] (Ennis 1945: 4).

Cinakui (f) *[tch-ih-nah-kuhy]* "That which you do not know": this name is commonly associated with the proverb "That which you do not know, you nevertheless eat" implying that in many situations it is better to quietly (or trustingly) take what you are given (or accept the *status quo*) but which you do not fully understand, otherwise being too inquisitive and critical about it would lead to the worsening of your current situation; the proverb is also advising that if something scarce but desired is presented to you, it is best to take it right away (and perhaps make comments on it later when it is safe in your hands, when you have consumed it, or when you do not need it anymore) [*Ovimbundu*] (Ennis 1945: 4).

Cinakulingi (f) *[tch-ih-nah-kuh-lihn-gih]* "That which you do not do": this name is commonly associated with the proverb "That which you do not do, you do not talk about" implying that people tend to boast about their abilities and achievements other than to speak about their inabilities and failures [*Ovimbundu*] (Ennis 1945: 5).

Cinakupopi (f) *[tch-ih-nah-kuh-poh-pih]* "That which you do not speak about": this name is commonly associated with the proverb "That which you do not talk about, is what you do not do" implying that people tend to boast about their abilities and achievements other than to speak about their inabilities and failures [*Ovimbundu*] (Ennis 1945: 5).

Cinakutela (f) *[tch-ih-nah-kuh-teh-lah]* "That which you are not able to do": this name is commonly associated with the proverb "That which you are not able to do, you do not talk about" implying that people tend to boast about their abilities and achievements other than speak about their inabilities and failures [*Ovimbundu*] (Ennis 1945: 5).

Cinawendela (f) *[tch-ih-nah-wehn-deh-lah]* "That which you went for": this name is commonly associated with the proverb "That which you went for, took away your name" which implies that unlike the home locale where he is known and respected, a worker has to build a reputation there where he finds a job and, he cannot initially depend on favors since he is in the company of strangers--this name appears to relate to a child whose father is a seasonally migrating worker [The *Ovimbundu*] (Ennis 1945: 3).

Cingawove (f) *[tch-ihn-gah-woh-veh]* "That which you do to your own": this name is commonly associated with the proverb "That which you do to your own, you would not do to anybody else" implying that within the tolerance and protection of the family circle, one can dare behave in ways that would otherwise not be tolerated outside the person's family [*Ovimbundu*] (Ennis 1945: 4).

Cingongeva (f) *[tch-ihn-gohn-geh-vah]* "That which causes homesickness": this name is commonly associated with the proverb "That which causes homesickness, throws me into the floods" implying that one who is really homesick will go to tremendous heights to get home [*Ovimbundu*] (Ennis 1945: 4).

Cinofila (f) *[tch-ih-noh-fih-lah]* "That which you die for": this name is commonly associated with the proverb "That which you only die for is what you eat" which is synonymous with "No pain, no gain" and implies that reward comes from sweat and tears, and that laboring for something you really want will not bother you as long as you get to

reap the fruits of your labor (as exemplified by the agonizing and concentrated effort of a hunter for animal meat) [The *Ovimbundu*] (Ennis
1945: 4).

Cinosole (f) *[tch-ih-noh-soh-leh]* "That which you like": this name is
commonly associated with the proverb "That which you like, you do
not eat with a stick" implying that anything that is really desired or
cherished is treated (or ought to be treated) with intimate care and
concern [*Ovimbundu*] (Ennis 1945: 4).

Ciokigi (f) *[tch-yoh-kih-gih]* "Of the eagle": a name given to a proud
one [*Embu*].

Ciokinyua (f) *[tch-yoh-kih-ndjh-wah]* A name given to one who loves
to drink [*Embu*].

Cisanganda (f) *[tch-ih-sah-ndgh-ahn-dah]* "That is left with the fee":
this name is commonly associated with the proverb "The one that is
left with the fee is the doctor" implying that the one who did the work
is the one worthy of getting paid and is synonymous with "No pain, no
gain" and "A man is worthy of his wages" [*Ovimbundu*] (Ennis 1945:
4).

Cisoleukombe (f) *[tch-ih-soh-leh-wuh-kohm-beh]* "That which the
guest wants": this name is commonly associated with the proverb
"That which the guest wants is what is common in the locale he is
visiting, but it does not turn out to be what the host gives" implying
that in going to tremendous lengths to honor a household guest by treating him lavishly, the host disappoints the guest whose likely intention was to have a firsthand experience of and reap from the abundance in the host's country i.e. one's needs and desires are often small and basic, but needlessly extravagant levels are frequently gone
to so as to please and impress the person [*Ovimbundu*] (Ennis 1945:
4).

Cisungwe (f) *[tch-ih-suhn-gweh]* "It is near": this name is commonly
associated with the proverb "Houses are near, but hearts keep to themselves" and is given to a child whose parents are not satisfied with
the attitudes of kin or neighbors towards the family [The *Ovimbundu*]
(Ennis 1945: 3).

Citalala (f) *[tch-ih-tah-lah-lah]* "It is green": this name is commonly
associated with the proverb "Green never gets completely decimated
from the woods, just as the good never gets used up in people" and is
given to a child whose parents are not satisfied with the attitudes of
kin or neighbors towards the family, though they remain optimistic
[*Ovimbundu*] (Ennis 1945: 3).

Citwaal (f/m) *[tch-ih-twaahl]* "The conveyer (of the twins)": name given
to one whose birth precedes that of his or her twin siblings [*Kanyok*]
(Daeleman 1977: 193).

Citwaala (f/m) *[tch-ih-twaah-lah]* "The conveyer (of the twins)": a name
given to one whose birth precedes that of his or her twin siblings [The
Luba] (Daeleman 1977: 193).

Ciyaneke (f) *[tch-ih-yah-neh-keh]* "It will come with the days": this name which implies "Time will tell" is commonly given to a child born after several children in the family or the neighborhood have died, and there is not much optimism that this one will survive [The *Ovimbundu*] (Ennis 1945: 7).

Ciyeva (f) *[tch-ih-yeh-vah]* "You hear it": this name is commonly associated with the proverb "You hear, but you do not do it" implying that often there are issues and resources that we know or hear about which we can advantageously act on, but we just do not i.e. "Performance lags behind knowledge" [*Ovimbundu*] (Ennis 1945: 5).

Coco (f/m) *[tch-oh-tch-oh]* A pet name [*Kongo*] (Ndoma 1977: 97).

Cohila (f) *[tch-oh-hih-lah]* "It is silent": this name is commonly associated with the proverb "It is silence in the young, but in the heart it hurts," which implies that the young are silent over many things that hurt them [*Ovimbundu*] (Ennis 1945: 3).

Cokindaisi (f) *[tch-oh-kihn-dahy-sih]* "That pertaining to railroad tracks": a name such as given to one born close to railroad tracks [The *Ovimbundu*] (Ennis 1945: 7).

Cokoluse (f) *[tch-oh-koh-luh-seh]* "That pertaining to the father's village" [*Ovimbundu*] (Ennis 1945: 7).

Cokombaka (f) *[tch-oh-kohm-bah-kah]* "That pertaining to the coastal town (i.e. *Benguela* in Angola)" [*Ovimbundu*] (Ennis 1945: 7).

Cokoputu (f) *[tch-oh-koh-puh-tuh]* "That pertaining to a foreign land": a name such as given to one born in a foreign locale [*Ovimbundu*] (Ennis 1945: 6).

Cokovenda (f) *[tch-oh-koh-vehn-dah]* "That pertaining to a shop" [*Ovimbundu*] (Ennis 1945: 7).

Cokoviye (f) *[tch-oh-koh-vih-yeh]* "That pertaining to *Viye* (i.e. *Biye* the middle province of Angola)" [*Ovimbundu*] (Ennis 1945: 7).

Cokuvala (f) *[tch-oh-kuh-vah-lah]* "That pertaining to the wife's village" [*Ovimbundu*] (Ennis 1945: 7).

Combo (m) *[tch-ohm-boh]* One of Arabic descent; one associated with the East African coast [*Embu*].

-D-

Dabulamanzi (m) *[dah-buh-lah-maahn-ziih]* "The divider of the waters" [*Zulu*] (Lugg 1968: 13).

Dambudzo (f) *[dahm-buhd-zoh]* Trouble: a name such as given to a child born at a time the parents are in some trouble [The *Zezuru*] (Marapara 1954: 8).

Dande (f/m) *[dahn-deh]* "Its throat" [*Luo*].

Ddiba (m) *[ddih-bah]* Animal skin; animal hide; this name is sometimes associated with the proverb "an animal skin (i.e. one processed to softness) is a result of exertion on the part of the curriers" meaning that hard work is always involved in effecting an outcome that is of good quality or impressive beauty; this name is sometimes associated with the proverb "if you see a dog chasing after one carrying a mat, then surely you will not escape unmolested if it sees you carrying an animal skin" which implies that pertinent lessons and their implications are always directly or indirectly learnt from everyday experiences that advise about risk taking and cautiousness [*Ganda*].

Dedasedlulenathi (m) *[deh-dah-sehd-luh-leh-nah-tih]* "Step aside and let us pass": a name such as given to a child whose mother is a new wife in the polygynous unit, the name content addressed to an older co-wife that was opposed to the marriage [*Zulu*] (Suzman 1994: 269).

Dede (f/m) *[deh-deh]* A pet name [*Kongo*] (Ndoma 1977: 97).

Dede (f/m) *[deh-deh]* Locust; grasshopper; "chase it" [*Luo*].

Delani (m) *[deh-lah-nih]* "Be satisfied" [*Zulu*] (Koopman 1979: 158).

Dembe/ Ddembe (m) *[ddehm-beh]* (At) peace and free from worrying; freedom; opportunity; leisure; quietude; this name is commonly associated with the proverb "those that are at peace are inattentive to potential danger (or do not realize what is coming)" which mirrors the tendency for those that are experienced a lengthy period of peace and prosperity, to drop their guard and not be attentive to the potential threat to their well being that always lurks around; this name is also commonly associated with the proverb "those who are at peace (or are well off) make fun of the one in a state of squalor" [*Ganda*].

Dende (f/m) *[dehn-deh]* "His/ her body" [*Luo*].

Dhabasadha (m) *[tdh-aah-bah-sah-tdh-ah]* What males struggle through; "of the men"; "(troubles/ or sorrows) afflict/ or affect men" [The *Soga*].

Dhabazira (m) *[tdh-aah-bah-zih-rah]* That are attributes, experiences, or strengths of the brave or the heroic [*Soga*].

Dhamufuula (m) *[tdh-aah-muh-fuuh-lah]* "Those that caused one to become"; "those that made one into"; "those that changed one into"; "those that changed one"; "those that altered one"; "those that turned one over"; "those that upset one" [*Soga*].

Dhatemwa (m) *[tdh-aah-teh-mwah]* "They were caused to be cut (or chopped)"; "they were allocated (or allotted, or assessed, or apportioned)" [*Soga*].

Diba (f/m) *[dih-bah]* Dip tank: a name such as given to one born during the time a dip tank was built for the district [*Shona*] (Jackson 1957: 119).

Dibuseng (f) *[dih-buh-seh-ndgh]* "Give them (i.e. the bride price cattle) back": a name such as given to a (usually first) child born to a family involved in disgruntlement such as over the enormity of the bride price put up by the child's mother's family/ or over the child's paternal grandparents' displeasure at the choice of bride or at having been denied adequate involvement in the marriage plans [The *Sotho*] (Mohome 1972: 178).

Didi (f/m) *[dih-dih]* A pet name [*Kongo*] (Ndoma 1977: 98).
Difelile (f) *[dih-feh-lih-leh]* "They (i.e. the bride price cattle) are finished": a name such as given to a (usually first) child born to a family involved in disgruntlement over the enormity of the bride price put up by child's mother's family [*Sotho*] (Mohome 1972: 178).
Digolo (f/m) *[dih-goh-loh]* A name given to a first born [*Luo*].
Dihungwa (f) *[dih-huhn-gwah]* One treated with medicaments for the pregnancy: a name such as given to one whose birth is presumably through the vehicle of magical medicaments [*Kaguru*] (Beidelman 1974: 289).
Dikeledi (f) *[dih-keh-leh-dih]* Tears: name such as given to one whose birth coincides with a period mourning (or with a calamity) [*Sotho*] (Mohome 1972: 175).
Dikeledi (f) *[dih-keh-leh-dih]* Tears: a name such as given to one born at a time a relation dies [*Sotho*] (Thipa 1986: 290).
Dikin (m) *[dih-kihn]* The one that is hilly [*Maasai*].
Dilahlwane (f) *[dih-lah-lwah-neh]* "Forsaken one" [*Sotho*] (Mohome 1972: 177).
Dimakatso (f) *[dih-mah-kaht-soh]* Expressions of wonder: name such as given to one whose birth coincides with happenings that are perplexing [*Sotho*] (Mohome 1972: 175).
Dimba (f/m) *[dihm-bah]* Little blue tit: a name given to one who is physically small [*Shona*] (Jackson 1957: 120).
Dingane (m) *[dihn-gah-neh]* (One associated with) need [The *Zulu*] (Koopman 1979: 73).
Dingase (f) *[dihn-gah-seh]* "Need" [*Zulu*] (Koopman 1979: 156).
Dinuzulu (m) *[dih-nuh-zuh-luh]/ Dinusulu* (m) *[dih-nuh-suh-luh]* "Offend the *Zulus*" [*Zulu*] (Koopman 1979: 75; Lugg 1968: 13).
Dipuo (f) *[dih-puh-woh]* A name given to an older of a set of identical female twins, the younger named *Dipuonyane*; "rumors"; "talks" [The *Sotho*] (Mohome 1972: 179).
Dipuonyane (f) *[dih-puh-woh-ndjh-ah-neh]* Name given to a younger of a set of identical female twins, the older named *Dipuo*; "small rumors"; "small talks" [*Sotho*] (Mohome 1972: 179).
Disebo (f) *[dih-seh-boh]* Acts of gossip [*Sotho*] (Mohome 1972: 177).
Dlabanjani (m) *[dlah-bahn-jaah-nih]* "What kind of people does he overcome?" [*Zulu*] (Koopman 1979: 161).
Dlakunezwe (m) *[dlah-kuh-neh-zweh]* "Food is with the land" [*Zulu*] (Koopman 1979: 160).
Dlezakhe (m) *[dleh-zaah-keh]* "He eats his own things" [The *Zulu*] (Koopman 1979: 160).
Dodo (f/m) *[doh-doh]* A pet name [*Kongo*] (Ndoma 1977: 98).
Dola (f/m) *[doh-lah]* "Bend me" [*Luo*].
Donde (f/m) *[dohn-deh]* "Select it" [*Luo*].
Dongo (f/m) *[dohn-goh]* An evacuated (or abandoned) village: a name

given to one born in a village that was being abandoned or discarded [*Shona*] (Jackson 1957: 120).

Drajoa (f/m) *[drah-joh-wah]* "In the hut of death": name such as given to one born at a time several children in the family cluster group have recently died [*Lugbara*] (Middleton 1961: 35).

Dramadri (f/m) *[drah-mah-tdh-rih]* "For my death": name such as given to a child whose father has been accused of practicing witchcraft and in the process causing deaths [*Lugbara*] (Middleton 1961: 35).

Drateru (f/m) *[drah-teh-eh-ruuh]* "Death wait": a name such as given to a child whose mother is so depressed that she is merely looking forward to dying [*Lugbara*] (Middleton 1961: 36).

Drodroa (f/m) *[droh-droh-wah]* "At the place of leeches": a name such as given to one born to a father who dreamt of drowning in a swamp [*Lugbara*] (Middleton 1961: 35).

Dua (f/m) *[duh-ah]* "River": a name given to a twin, the other named *Ekulu* [*Gombe*] (Daeleman 1977: 190).

Dube (m) *[duuh-beh]* Zebra [*Zulu*] (Hemans 1968: 74; Koopman 1990: 334).

Duduza (f) *[duh-duh-zah]* "Comfort" [*Zulu*] (Koopman 1979: 158).

Duduzile (f) *[duh-duh-zih-leh]* "She has comforted" [*Zulu*] (Koopman 1979: 161).

Dumangeze (m) *[duh-mahn-geh-zeh]* "Be famous through nothing" [*Zulu*] (Koopman 1979: 79).

Dumangi (f) *[duh-mahn-giih]* "Troubles": one that is poor [*Kaguru*] (Beidelman 1974: 289).

Dumazile (f) *[duh-mah-zih-leh]* "She has caused disappointment" [*Zulu*] (Koopman 1979: 161).

Dumisa (m) *[duh-mih-sah]* "That causes it to thunder"; "cause it to thunder" [*Zulu*] (Lugg 1968: 13).

Dumisani (m) *[duh-mih-sah-nih]* "Glorify" [*Zulu*] (Koopman 1979: 158).

Duna (m) *[duh-nah]* Headman: a name such as given to a newborn whose father is pointedly referring to the headman who sold his cows while the father was away and engaged in migratory employment [*Zulu*] (Herbert 1995: 6).

Dzapisi (f/m) *[dzah-pah-sih]* "They (i.e. our houses) are below the surface"; "the houses of down below": a name given to a child born into a family that has lost many of its members to death, the name implying that so many have been buried and make it look like large chunks of households are buried [*Shona*] (Jackson 1957: 118).

Dzimbanheti (f/m) *[dzihm-bahn-heh-tih]* "Thin homes"; "lean houses"; "our home is thin": a name given to a child who has lost several of previously born siblings to death and whereby there is pessimism as to whether this one will survive--the name implies that the population of the household has thinned down as a result of the several deaths [*Shona*] (Jackson 1957: 118).

Dzingesu (f/m) *[dzihn-geh-tsuh]* "You are going to drive us away!": a name given to one born during a family dispute with neighbors, whereby the family tired of the malicious acts or attitude of the neighbors, nurses the prospect of moving away from the locale [*Shona*] (Jackson 1957: 117).

-E-

Egesa (m) *[eh-geh-sah]* A name given to one born during a season of harvesting [*Samia*] (Nzita 1995: 73).

Ejaiya (m) *[eh-jahy-yah]* "Take him to the bush": a name given to an older twin, (the name dramatizing the extent to which twin births are traditionally regarded as ill omens) [*Madi*] (Nzita 1995: 143).

Ejua (m) *[eh-juh-wah]/ Ejurua* (f) *[eh-juh-ruh-wah]* A name given to a twin [*Lugbara*] (Middleton 1961: 35).

Ekabio (f/m) *[eh-kah-bjoh]* "Brown hair": a name such as given to one who at birth has reddish hair [*Lugbara*] (Middleton 1961: 36).

Ekulu (f/m) *[eh-kuh-luuh]* "Bank": a name given to a twin, the other named *Dua* [*Gombe*] (Daeleman 1977: 190).

Ekuva (f) *[eh-kuh-vah]* "The beheading ax of the king" which is, euphemistically, a hoe because the guardian of it is supposed to be a witch [*Ovimbundu*] (Ennis 1945: 7).

Elumbu (f/m) *[eh-luhm-buh]* Mystery: a name such as given to one who is born prematurely and is alarmingly sick [*Ovimbundu*] (Ennis 1945: 7).

Eneku (f/m) *[eh-neh-kuuh]* "You do not see": a name such as given to one whose parents are too short to be noticed in a crowd [*Lugbara*] (Middleton 1961: 35).

Engai (m) *[eh-ndgh-ahy]* God; the rain; the sky [*Maasai*] (Huntingford 1930: 102).

Enyama (f/m) *[eh-ndjh-ah-mah]* Of the hawk: name commonly given to a child who is the product of a pregnancy that involved grievous circumstances, the fetus is believed to have become bewitched when the shadow of the hawk fell upon the mother, and the same shadow may fall upon the child following birth and cause paralysis [The *Ovimbundu*] (Ennis 1945: 2).

Eriaga (f/m) *[eh-rih-yah-gah]* "Caterpillar": name such as given to one whose parents have been so poor that they have had to exclusively eat caterpillars [*Lugbara*] (Middleton 1961: 36).

Eriuwa (m) *[eh-rih-yuh-wah]* God; the sun; the preserver [The *Hanga*] (Huntingford 1930: 102-103).

Esenje (f) *[eh-sehn-jeh]* "Stone": this name is commonly associated with the proverb "A good stone does not see a pounding of maize; a good back does not see a child" which is the lamentation of a childless woman and implies that the way of the world is that desired things often fail to appear even though there exists resources in which they would flourish [*Ovimbundu*] (Ennis 1945: 3).

Eyoru (f/m) *[eh-yoh-ruuh]* "Of witchcraft"; "of 'words'": a name such as given to one whose parents have quarreled with neighbors [*Lugbara*] (Middleton 1961: 36).

-F-

Fakuhlekwa (m) *[fah-kuh-leh-kwah]* "Die, there being laughter" [*Zulu*] (Koopman 1979: 79).

Farirepi (f/m) *[fah-rih-reh-pih]* "We are everywhere unwelcome--where shall we find happiness?": a name given to one born to parents lamenting their not getting along with neighbors or with kin [The *Shona*] (Jackson 1957: 116).

Feku (f/m) *[feh-kuuh]* "Give not": a name such as given to one born to a mother who never gives her husband good or sufficient food [The *Lugbara*] (Middleton 1961: 35).

Felleng (f) *[fehl-leh-ndgh]* "In/ at the wilderness": a name such as given to a child delivered in the wilderness/ or child born at a time the father or a close kin was in the wilderness [*Sotho*] (Mohome 1972: 176).

Fennayatuzza (f) *[fehn-nah-yah-tuhz-zah]* "He/ she brought all of us back" [*Ganda*].

Fikile (f) *[fih-kih-leh]* "She has arrived" [*Zulu*] (Koopman 1979: 161).

Fikile (m) *[fih-kih-leh]* "Arrived" [*Zulu*] (Suzman 1994: 268).

Fisani (m) *[uh-fih-sah-nih]* "What do you wish?" [*Zulu*] (Suzman 1994: 258).

Fuba (m) *[fuh-bah]* "Exert yourself"; "work hard"; "try hard"; "make a great effort [*Ganda, Soga*].

Fudu (m) *[fuh-duuh]* Tortoise [*Zulu*] (Koopman 1979: 69).

Fulathela (m) *[fuh-lah-teh-lah]* "Turn the back" [*Zulu*] (Koopman 1979: 158).

Fulu/ Ffulu (m) *[ffuh-luh]* Very skillful person; one of great expertise; empty or deserted [*Ganda*].

Fumane (f) *[fuh-mah-neh]* "The (right) one that is found": a name that connotes gratitude [*Sotho*] (Mohome 1972: 174).

Fumbe/ Ffumbe (m) *[ffuhm-beh]* The civet cat [*Ganda*].

Funabangi/ Funaabangi (f/m) *[fuh-naah-bahn-jih]* "Get many (such as children, tenants, or subjects)"; this name is commonly associated with the proverb "'get many children (or subjects)' and the noise will increase accordingly" which implies that troubles increase with the numbers of people you get responsibility over; this name is also commonly associated with the proverb "the one who gets many children understands them all"; this name is also commonly associated with the proverb "the one who has the company of many guests would not (or should not) quarrel about a burst of laughter" [*Ganda*].

Gachara (m) *[gah-tch-ah-rah]* Small hand [*Kikuyu*].
Gacheru (m) *[gah-tch-eh-ruh]* Spy [*Kikuyu*].
Gachie (m) *[gah-tch-yeh]* Small river; small pool [*Kikuyu*].
Gaciira (m) *[gah-tch-iih-rah]* One born by the roadside [*Kikuyu*].
Gafabusa (m) *[gah-fah-buh-sah]* "It (i.e. the strength/ sacrifice of the parents) has been spent for nothing": name such as given to an alarmingly sick child not expected to survive, or to one whose previously born siblings died [*Nyoro*] (Beattie 1957: 101).
Gafuma (m) *[gaah-fuh-mah]* Tarnished; having lost color; this name is commonly associated with the proverb "when the teeth become discolored they blame the tobacco; however does the grasshopper (whose teeth are typically discolored) have smoke pipe tobacco?" which mirrors a situation of scapegoating (or placing blame) instead of appropriately taking responsibility for one's actions (such as getting one's teeth discolored because of not cleaning the teeth, blaming the pen for bad handwriting, and blaming wet firewood for not having the food ready) [*Ganda*].
Gakenia (f) *[gah-keh-nyah]* The one who entertains [*Embu*].
Gakii (f) *[gah-kiih]* The one who grinds [*Embu*].
Galuleba/ Galuleeba (m) *[gah-luh-leh-eh-bah]* That (i.e. the water) of the plantain leaf kept in a hole in the ground which may be used as a bath or as a place to keep beer; this name is commonly associated with the proverb "the water of the plantain leafed hole in the ground can only be drunk by a daring person" which images a situation of what would be taking a big risk [*Ganda*].
Galusanja (m) *[gaah-luh-sahn-jah]* (That associated with) dry/ or withered plantain leaves [*Ganda*].
Gambizzi (m) *[gahm-bihz-zih]* Of the pig (or hog) [*Ganda*].
Gamucirai (f/m) *[gah-muh-tch-ih-rahy]* "Receive (i.e. from the Lord)" [*Shona*] (Jackson 1957: 122).
Gamyuka (m) *[gah-mjuuh-kah]* The second in command; the deputy [*Ganda*].
Ganaafa (m) *[gah-naah-fah]* "That (i.e. the bananas) will fail to materialize (into processed juice)"; this name is commonly associated with the proverb "even the bananas that will not eventually materialize into banana-beer, are still catered to, starting with the harvesting of grass to squeeze out their juice for brewing" implying that whatever the circumstances, nothing or no one is to be easily dismissed as being of limited use or hope--the name is usually given to a child born to woman, most of whose previous offspring died, and there being pessimism as to whether this child will survive [*Ganda*].
Gandibukamba (f/m) *[gahn-dih-buh-kahm-bah]* "(My eyes) are heavy with tears" [*Ganda*].
Ganyana (f/m) *[gah-ndjh-ah-nah]* Rich: name such as given to a newborn whose mother is praised for her working hard that has resulted in her wealth [*Zulu*] (Herbert 1995: 5).

Gaongalelwe (m) *[gah-wohn-gah-leh-lweh]* "God would never be sulked against" [*Sotho*] (Moloto 1986: 215).

Gaopotlake (m) *[gah-woh-poht-lah-keh]* "God does not hurry" [*Sotho*] (Moloto 1986: 215).

Gatuimba (m) *[gah-tuh-yihm-bah]* The dull one [*Kikuyu*].

Gatura (m) *[gah-tuh-rah]* A renowned person in the village locale [The *Kikuyu*].

Gawo (f/m) *[gah-woh]* "Stone at" [*Luo*].

Gayita (f) *[gah-yih-tah]* "They (i.e. the teeth) pass by"; this name is commonly associated with the proverb "they (i.e. the teeth) often pass by a saddening event and grin at a good thing" implying that people will still laugh and make jokes during times of disaster or bereavement, though they would not be expected to behave so during such circumstances [*Ganda*].

Gayitakukibi (f) *[gah-yih-tah-kuh-tch-ih-bih]* "They (i.e. the teeth) pass by that which is bad/ unfavorable"; this name is commonly associated with the proverb "they (i.e. the teeth) often pass by a saddening event and grin at a good thing" implying that people will still laugh and make jokes during times of disaster or bereavement, though they would not be expected to behave so during such circumstances [*Ganda*].

Gazini (m) *[gah-zih-nih]* Blood [*Zulu*] (Koopman 1990: 334).

Gbokoru (f/m) *[gboh-koh-ruuh]* "Of the empty place": a name such as given to one whose mother is so poor that she has had to wander around foraging for roots to eat/ or one whose mother has liked to wander away from her husband and into the bush land to look for other men [*Lugbara*] (Middleton 1961: 36).

Gbongo (f/m) *[bohn-goh]* "The big antelope": a name given to a twin, the other named *Mondonga* [*Gombe*] (Daeleman 1977: 190).

Gcinangokubusa (m) *[gah-tch-ih-nahn-goh-kuh-buh-sah]* "End up by reigning" [*Zulu*] (Koopman 1979: 79).

Gcinephi (f) *[gah-tch-ih-neh-pih]* "Where has she finished?" [*Zulu*] (Koopman 1979: 162).

Gebhuza (m) *[geh-buh-zah]* "A warrior who attacks with slashing, thrusting upper cuts like a fighting bull" [*Zulu*] (Lugg 1968: 12).

Ger (m) *[dgehr]* Fierce; "build" [*Luo*].

Gerengbo (f/m) *[geh-reh-ndgh-boh]* "Twin's foot": a name given to the third born child after twin siblings [*Ngbandi*] (Daeleman 1977: 192).

Gero (m) *[dgeh-roh]* Fierceness; building [*Luo*].

Gichuhi (m) *[gih-tch-uh-hih]* Fly whisk [*Kikuyu*].

Giconi (m) *[gih-koh-niih]* Bird [*Embu*].

Gicovi (m) *[gih-koh-vih]* The one who is fond of drinking beer [*Embu*].

Gidelwa (m) *[gih-deh-lwah]* "Be greedy" [*Zulu*] (Koopman 1979: 74).

Gikonyo (m) *[gih-kohn-ndjh-oh]* A big navel [*Kikuyu*].

Gikungi (m) *[gih-kuhn-gih]* The one who gathers [*Embu*].

Githinji (m) *[gih-sth-ihn-jih]* Butchers *[Embu]*.

Gitonga (m) *[gih-tohn-gah]* The wealthy one *[Embu]*.

Gituku (m) *[gih-tuh-kuh]* One notorious for his shady ways; the sly one *[Kikuyu]*.

Godlumthakathi (m) *[gohd-luhm-tah-kah-tih]* "He holds back the wizard"; "hold back the wizard" *[Zulu]* (Koopman 1979: 160).

Gogo (m) *[dgoh-goh]* Log *[Luo]*.

Goli (f) *[goh-lih]* Wealth: a name such as given to one born during a period of abundance/ or to a woman who has a lot of children [The *Kaguru*] (Beidelman 1974: 289).

Golintethe (m) *[goh-lihn-teh-teh]* "Mr. Stork" *[Zulu]* (Koopman 1979: 75).

Goloba/ Golooba (m) *[goh-loh-oh-bah]* The coming to an end (of the day); the setting (of the sun); getting dark *[Ganda]*.

Gologolo/ Ggologolo (m) *[ggoh-loh-goh-loh]* Species of palm tree *[Ganda]*.

Gombararwo (f/m) *[gohm-bah-rwah-rwoh]* "Its (i.e. death's) hole": a name given to a child born into a family that has lost many of its members to death, the name implying that holes are continuously dug for burying the dead *[Shona]* (Jackson 1957: 118).

Gondo (f/m) *[gohn-doh]* Eagle: a name given to one whose head resembles that of an eagle *[Shona]* (Jackson 1957: 120).

Gongobavu/ Ggongobavu (m) *[ggohn-goh-bah-vuh]* That is contorted; that is disfigured; that is crippled *[Ganda]*.

Gonja (m) *[gohn-jah]* Large sweet banana that is either baked or boiled *[Ganda]*.

Gonza (f/m) *[gohn-zah]* Soften; pamper; flatter; make obedient; love; like; wish for *[Ganda]*.

Gonzaabato (f/m) *[gohn-zaah-bah-toh]* "Soften/ or pamper/ or flatter/ or make obedient/ or love/ or like/ or wish for the children (or the young persons)" *[Ganda]*.

Gor (m) *[gohr]* A mythic figure; the name of a great Luo warrior *[Luo]*.

Gotto (m) *[goht-toh]* Crushed; pounded; twisted *[Ganda]*.

Gubadde (f) *[guh-bahd-deh]* "It was"; "it was about to" *[Ganda]*.

Gubagaba (m) *[guh-bah-gah-bah]* "It gives you (all) away"; "it gives you (all) as a present"; "it divides you (all)"; "it distributes/ or apportions you (all)"; "it appoints/ or designates you (all)" *[Ganda]*.

Guda (f/m) *[guh-dah]* "Touch me" *[Luo]*.

Gugu (f) *[guh-guh]* "Treasure" *[Zulu]* (Koopman 1979: 154).

Gugulethu (m) *[guh-guh-leh-tuuh]* "Our treasure" *[Zulu]* (Suzman 1994 : 268; Koopman 1979: 80).

Gulimbula (f) *[guh-lihm-buh-lah]* "It will elude me"; "it will disappear from me"; "I will lack it" *[Ganda]*.

Gumenya (f) *[guh-meh-ndjh-ah]* "It causes to break down"; "it causes to destroy"; "it causes to get fractured"; "it causes to get broken" [The

Ganda].

Gumo (f/m) *[guh-moh]* "Bend" [*Luo*].

Gunadda (m) *[guh-nahd-dah]* "It will come back (or be revivified)"; "more will come" [*Ganda*].

Gungurukwa (f/m) *[guhn-guh-ruh-kwah]* A name given to one who is short and pudgy [*Shona*] (Jackson 1957: 120).

Gunju/ Ggunju (m) *[gguhn-juh]* The name of a species of wild cat; that is cultured (or civilized, or educated, or polished) [*Ganda*].

Gunteese (f) *[guhn-teh-eh-seh]* "It has set me up (or placed me)"; "it has quieted (or calmed) me down" [*Ganda*].

Gutaggwa (m) *[guh-tahg-gwah]* That (i.e. court case) which is not finally settled [*Ganda*].

Gutateganya (m) *[guh-tah-teh-gah-ndjh-ah]* "That (i.e. work) which does not cause to take pains"; this name is commonly associated with the proverb "work which does not involve pain does not result in gain" which is synonymous with "no pain, no gain" [*Ganda*].

Guvamungabo (m) *[guh-vah-muhn-gah-boh]* "Friendship accrues from the shield": this name is commonly associated with the war related proverb in which it is implied that it is common for people who have been fighting together, or arguing with one another, or have been enemies to become comrades when they consequently acknowledge each other's strengths, then compromise and collaborate [*Ganda*].

Guweddeko (m) *[guh-wehd-deh-koh]* "After it (i.e. a tree) has been depleted of"; this name is commonly associated with the proverb "after it (i.e. a tree) has lost all its fruit (or wild figs), the birds shun it)" which images the tendency for people to lose most of the 'friends' upon losing their fortunes [*Ganda*].

Guyidde (m) *[guh-yihd-deh]* "(The beer) has become fermented"; "it has got burnt" [*Ganda*].

Guyiddewa (f) *[guh-yihd-deh-wah]* "In which area is it readily cooked (or fermented, or burned)?" [*Ganda*].

Gwala (m) *[gwah-lah]* Coward [*Zulu*] (Koopman 1990: 334).

Gwayambadde (m) *[gwah-yahm-bahd-deh]* "The body that is clothed/ dressed"; this name is commonly associated with the proverb "a body that is clothed does not go by (or walk) naked" which can imply that one's virtues or vices are apparent regardless of one's outer appearance, or that the appearance and mannerisms of a person speak so much about the person's background, or that not having much (such as the example of a poor person whose only treasures are the clothes on his body), still allows one to fulfill and enjoy much--and therefore one should not unduly worry over being materially poor [*Ganda*].

Gwembeshe (m) *[gwehm-beh-tsh-eh]* "The bow legged one" [*Zulu*] (Lugg 1968: 14).

Gwendisanga (f) *[gwehn-dih-sahn-gah]* "The one that I will come upon/ or meet/ or find" [*Ganda*].

Gwenjira (m) *[gwehn-jih-rah]* "That which I take on (or off, or out, or at, or in)" [*Ganda*].

Gweno (f/m) *[gweh-noh]* Hen; chicken [*Luo*].

Gwerudde (f) *[gweh-eh-ruhd-deh]* "It has made appear (or come out)"; "it has revealed" [*Ganda*].

Gwewajjokulaba (f) *[gweh-wahj-joh-oh-kuh-lah-bah]* "The one you came to see (or greet, or find)" [*Ganda*].

Gweya (f/m) *[gweh-yah]* "Kick me" [*Luo*].

Gwobalira (f) *[gwoh-oh-bah-lih-rah]* "One you take into consideration (or are concerned about, or count in or for)" [*Ganda*].

Gwogabira (f) *[gwoh-oh-gah-bih-rah]* "Whom (or what) you apportion for (or give for)" [*Ganda*].

Gwokebera (f) *[gwoh-oh-keh-beh-rah]* "The one you you examine (or closely inspect)"; "the one you scrutinize/ investigate" [*Ganda*].

Gwokyalya (f) *[gwoh-oh-tch-aah-ljah]* That which you are still feeding on (or consuming); (office) which you are still partaking of [*Ganda*].

Gwoleka (f) *[gwoh-oh-leh-kah]* That which you leave (or abandon); that which you allow/ permit [*Ganda*].

-H-

Haamba (f) *[haahm-baah]* A name given to a parent of twins [*Luba*] (Daeleman 1977: 194).

Haboeo (m) *[hah-boh-eh-yoh]* "There is none": a name such as given to one whose parents did not have beer to offer a visitor that went to congratulate them following the birth--the other new parents this visitor went to see were able to offer beer, so their child was named *Boteng* [*Sotho*] (Ashton 1952: 32).

Hakunavanhu (f/m) *[hah-kuh-nah-vah-nuh]* "There are no people": a name given to a child born into a family that has lost many of its members to death, the name implying that death has alarmingly depopulated the population of the locale [*Shona*] (Jackson 1957: 118).

Hamba (f) *[hahm-bah]* A name given to a parent of twins [*Ntomba*] (Daeleman 1977: 194).

Hambanenkosi (m) *[hahm-bah-nehn-koh-sih]* "He goes with God"; "go with God" [*Zulu*] (Koopman 1979: 161).

Hamundidi (f/m) *[hah-muhn-dih-dih]* "You do not love me": a name given to one born either to a mother lamenting her not being in her husband's good books, or to a parent lamenting over unloving kin or neighbors [*Shona*] (Jackson 1957: 116).

Hamundioni (f/m) *[hah-muhn-dih-yoh-nih]* "You do not notice me"/ "you look past me": a name given to one born either to a mother lamenting her not being in her husband's good books, or to a parent lamenting over despising or unacknowledging kin or neighbors [*Shona*] (Jackson 1957: 116).

Handidzvinzwi (f/m) *[hahn-dihz-vihn-zwih]* "I do not hear what you are saying": a name given to one born either during a family dispute with kin, or during a family dispute with neighbors [*Shona*] (Jackson 1957: 116).

Hapaguti (m) *[hah-pah-guh-tih]* "No satisfaction": name such as given to a child born into a family that has consistently had deaths [*Zezuru*] (Marapara 1954: 8).

Hapazari (f/m) *[hah-pah-zah-rih]* Contraction of *Pasi-hapazari* i.e. "the ground is never filled": a name given to a child born into a family that has lost many of its members to death, the name metaphorically implying that despite the numerous numbers of deaths, the earth indefinitely continues to provide burial ground and never declares that it is too full for more people to die [*Shona*] (Jackson 1957: 118).

Harukundwi (f/m) *[hah-ruh-kuhn-dwih]* "It (i.e. death) is not beaten/ overcome": a name given to a child born into a family that has lost many of its members to death, the name metaphorically implying that death is so draining and taxing and yet it inevitably cannot be stopped [*Shona*] (Jackson 1957: 118).

Harusekwi (f/m) *[hah-ruh-seh-kwih]* "It (i.e. death) is not laughed at": a name given to a child born into a family that has lost many of its members to death, the name metaphorically implying that death is so draining and taxing that there is no place for it to be joked about [*Shona*] (Jackson 1957: 118).

Harushari (f/m) *[hah-ruh-tsh-ah-rih]* "It (i.e. death) does not pick out some": a name given to a child born into a family that has lost many of its members to death, the name metaphorically implying that death is inevitable and indiscriminatingly strikes the rich and poor, sick and healthy, good and bad, and young and old [*Shona*] (Jackson 1957: 118).

Haruzivi (f/m) *[hah-ruh-zih-vih]* "It (i.e. death) does not know (i.e. which house to visit)": name given to a child born into a family that has lost many of its members to death, the name implying that death is inevitable and indiscriminatingly strikes the rich and poor, sick and healthy, good and bad, and young and old [*Shona*] (Jackson 1957: 118).

Hayi (f) *[hah-yih]* "No!" [*Zulu*] (Koopman 1979: 74).

Hlabayidlele (m) *[huh-lah-bah-yihd-leh-leh]* "He slaughters and eats it himself"; "slaughter and then eat it" [*Zulu*] (Koopman 1979: 161).

Hlamusela (m) *[huh-lah-muh-seh-lah]* A name given to a newborn who is the product of a pregnancy alleged by the father to have been caused by another man [*Zulu*] (Herbert 1995: 7).

Hlatshwayo (m) *[huh-lah-tsh-wah-yoh]* "The stabbed one" [The *Zulu*] (Koopman 1990: 336).

Hlawulani (m) *[huh-lah-wuh-lah-nih]* "Make reparations": a name such as given to a child born at a time his maternal family is putting pressure on his father to pay the bride dowry (*lobolo*) that is in arrears [*Zulu*] (Suzman 1994: 262).

Hlelile (m) *[huh-leh-lih-leh]* "Reversed": name such as given to a child born feet first (other than the conventional head first) [*Zulu*] (Suzman 1994: 262).

Hlengiwe (m) *[huh-lehn-gih-weh]* "Rescued": a name such as given to a first child who is the product of a difficult birth that was remedied by a rescuing God [*Zulu*] (Suzman 1994: 263).

Hlomendlini (m) *[hloh-mehn-dlih-nih]* "Arm oneself inside the house" [*Zulu*] (Koopman 1979: 79).

Hluphuyise (m) *[hluh-puh-yih-seh]* "Irritate his father": a name such as given to a child born at a time of discord in the family [The *Zulu*] (Koopman 1979: 68).

Hochi (f/m) *[hoh-tch-ih]* Pig: a name given to one who is short and pudgy, as adapted from the Afrikaans word *otjie* [*Shona*] (Jackson 1957: 120).

Holimali (m) *[hoh-lih-maah-lih]* "He earns money"; "earn money" [*Zulu*] (Koopman 1979: 160).

Hosi (f/m) *[hoh-sih]* Lion: a name given to a twin or triplet, the siblings of the same birth named *Njamba* and/ or *Ngeve* [*Ovimbundu*] (Ennis 1945: 2).

Hosiyinahena (m) *[hoh-sih-yih-nah-heh-nah]* "God is with us": a name such as implying that the parents consider this child a God given reinforcing blessing to the male children they already have [The *Zulu*] (Herbert 1995: 4).

Hulilapi (f) *[huh-lih-lah-pih]* "In which position do I grow?" which expression is metaphorically the lamentation of a woman in a cramped position that would not allow her to express herself, the name commonly given to one who is oppressed and mistreated (or to a child of one who is treated so) [*Ovimbundu*] (Ennis 1945: 6).

Humisa (f/m) *[huh-mih-sah]* "Neglect": disharmony related name such as given by this newborn's mother and expresses her dissatisfaction with the demeanor of her husband whereby he neglects whatever she says [*Zulu*] (Herbert 1995: 6).

Huso (f) *[huh-soh]* "Feigned sadness": this name is commonly associated with the expression "The feigned sadness of a bride," the name usually given to a baby because of fancied resemblance of expression [*Ovimbundu*] (Ennis 1945: 7).

Huwelela (f/m) *[huh-weh-leh-lah]* "Shout!": a disharmony related name such as given by one of this newborn's mother to imply that even when she shouts at her husband, he keeps on doing things the wrong way [*Zulu*] (Herbert 1995: 4).

-I-

Ibanda (m) *[ih-bahn-dah]* That demands debt payments (or reparations); a debt [*Soga*].

Ibvai (f/m) *[ihb-vahy]* "Get away!": a name given to one born either duing a family dispute with kin, or during a family dispute with neighbors [*Shona*] (Jackson 1957: 117).

Idiiro (m) *[ih-diih-roh]* Dining room; dance floor; floor of the assembly; eating place [*Soga*].

Ijara (m) *[ih-jah-rah]* A name given to a child born with more than the normal number of fingers [*Acholi*] (Nzita 1995: 92).

Ikamba (f) *[ih-kahm-bah]* One of (or one associated with) *Akamba* ethnics [*Embu*].

Ikoote (m) *[ih-koh-oh-teh]* Round shouldered; bent; walking with a stoop [*Soga*].

Ilat (m) *[ih-laht]* God; thunder; rain; "God of Thunder"; "God of Rain"; "the Drawer of Water"; "the one that spills the water (thereby causing it to rain" [*Elgeyo, Nandi, Suk*] (Huntingford 1930: 102-103).

Ilumbe (f/m) *[ih-luhm-beh]* "Plantain": a name given to a twin, the other named *Motondo* [*Gombe*] (Daeleman 1977: 190).

Imbayarwo (f/m) *[ihm-bah-yah-rwoh]* "Its (i.e. death's) house": a name given to a child born into a family that has lost many of its members to death, which situation makes it look like death owns and has come to live in the house [*Shona*] (Jackson 1957: 118).

Imbayevu (f/m) *[ihm-bah-yeh-vuh]* The house of clay/ dust/ ashes: a name given to a child born into a family that has lost many of its members to death and whereby there is pessimism as to whether this one will survive, the name metaphorically implying that death has made the household look so delicately built from soft material and that this child will eventually, in inevitability succumb to death [*Shona*] (Jackson 1957: 118).

Imoo (m) *[ih-moh-oh]* Darkness; dusk [*Luo*].

Inababiri (f) *[ih-naah-bah-bih-rih]* "The mother of two/ twins": a name given to a parent of twins [*Hutu, Tutsi, Twa*] (Daeleman 1977: 194).

Inabushuri (f) *[ih-nah-buh-shuh-rih]* "The mother of bull-calves (i.e. triplets)": a name given to a parent of triplets [The *Hutu, Tutsi, Twa*] (Daeleman 1977: 194).

Inakweeji (f) *[ih-nah-kweh-eh-jih]* "The mother of (or the mother) associated with the moon": a name given to a parent of twins (inasmuch as children are traditionally considered to be children of the moon, and the mother as compared to the moon is perceived as carrying prolific seeds in her womb) [*Luba*] (Daeleman 1977: 194).

Inia (f/m) *[ih-nih-yah]* "At night": a name such as given to one whose father went to sleep with his wife at night but refused to help her with work during the day [*Lugbara*] (Middleton 1961: 36).

Intombifuthi (f) *[ihn-tohm-bih-fuh-sth-ih]* "Another girl": a name such as given to a child born into a family with numerically high number of female compared to male children [*Zulu*] (Suzman 1994: 263).

Isae (m) *[ih-saah-yeh]* "The child was born (soon) after a ritual or sacrificial service had been performed for the dracaena tree shrine" [The

Pare] (Omari 1970: 70).

Isansa (m) *[ih-sahn-sah]* A scattering; a spread out; a sprinkling; sowing; strewing; leaf of the wild date palm and used for plaiting (such as baskets and mats) [*Soga*].

Ishemboyo (m) *[ih-tsh-ehm-boh-oh-yoh]* "The father of twins": a name given to a parent of twins [*Hindo*] (Daeleman 1977: 194).

Isoba/ Isooba (m) *[ih-soh-oh-bah]* That walks stealthily or slowly [The *Soga*].

Isoke (m) *[ih-soh-keh]* "Hairy" [*Nyoro*] (Beattie 1957: 99).

Itama (f) *[ih-tah-mah]* Cheek; with prominent cheeks [*Soga*].

Itembe (m) *[ih-tehm-beh]* A species of wild plantain, the seeds from which necklaces are sewn; ease with dealing with; a seizing; a climb; an act/ or performance [*Soga*].

Itima (m) *[ih-tih-mah]* Ill will: the parents of a child given this name are heralding the message that the neighbors are so spiteful towards them [*Nyoro*] (Beattie 1957: 104).

Iyundhu (m) *[ih-yuhn-tdh-uh]/* **Iyunju** (m) *[ih-yuhn-juh]* The cutting down/ or harvesting of plantains [*Soga*].

Izimba (m) *[ih-zihm-bah]* Builder; architect; swelling; of (or associated with) *Buzimba* County [*Soga*].

Izuwa (m) *[ih-zuh-wah]* God; sun; the preserver [*Luyia*] (Huntingford 1930: 102-103).

-J-

Jabu (f) *[jah-buh]* A pet name and abbreviation of *Jabulisiwe*: "she has been made happy" [*Zulu*] (Koopman 1979: 162).

Jabulani (m) *[jah-buh-laah-nih]* "Be happy" [*Zulu*] (Koopman 1979: 158, 164).

Jabulile (m) *[jah-buh-lih-leh]* "Happiness" [*Zulu*] (Suzman 1994: 268); "thanked": name such as given to a child conceived when the mother was relatively advanced in age, the mother thankful to God for this "miracle" [*Zulu*] (Suzman 1994: 269).

Jabulisiwe (f) *[jah-buh-lih-sih-weh]* "She has been made happy" [The *Zulu*] (Koopman 1979: 162).

Jabwiire (m) *[jah-bwiih-reh]* "Go (or go away) at night" [*Soga*].

Jagero (m) *[jah-geh-roh]* "The fierce one" [*Luo*].

Jakinda (m) *[jah-kihn-dah]* "Devoted"; "the diligent one"; "the hardworking one" [*Luo*].

Jakoyo (m) *[jah-koh-yoh]* The cold one; the one of the cold [*Luo*].

Jamba/ Jjamba (m) *[jjahm-bah]* Species of small fish which lives in shallow water [*Ganda*].

Japollo (m) *[jah-pohl-loh]* The one of heaven [*Luo*].

Jasembo (m) *[jah-sehm-boh]* One who helps another walk; one who shepherds [*Luo*].

Jegangeze (m) *[jeh-gahn-zeh-geh]* "He is punished for nothing" [*Zulu*] (Koopman 1979: 161).

Jegereke (f) *[jeh-geh-reh-keh]* One who talks incessantly; what goes on and on [*Ganda*].

Jeke/ Jjeke (m) *[djeh-eh-keh]* In trouble (or difficulty); poverty [*Ganda*].

Jere (f/m) *[jeh-reh]* Jail: a name such as given to one born when the father is in jail [*Shona*] (Jackson 1957: 119).

Jero/ Jeero (m) *[jeh-eh-roh]* Trailing robe; miserable; wretched; in a state of destitution or squalor [*Ganda*].

Jingekwenza (m) *[uh-jihn-geh-kwehn-zah]* "This is the last time!": a name such as given to a child whose father is expressing that he has had enough of his bullying brother [*Zulu*] (Suzman 1994: 267).

Jipiti (m) *[jih-pih-tih]* The name of the son of the first man *Luo* [*Acholi*] (Nzita 1995: 90).

Jjajja (f/m) *[jjahj-jah]* Grandparent; forefather; ancestor; patriarch; matriarch [*Ganda*].

Jjajjawabaana (f/m) *[jjahj-jah-waah-baah-nah]* "Grandparent of (many) children"; "the children's grandparent" [*Ganda*].

Jjengo (m) *[djehn-goh]* Water wave [*Ganda*].

Jomo (m) *[joh-moh]* Those who bring; harbingers; of oil [*Luo*].

Jowi (m) *[joh-wih]* Buffalo [*Luo*].

Jubane (m) *[juh-bah-neh]* "Speed" [*Zulu*] (Koopman 1979: 154).

Jubya/ Jjubya (m) *[jjuh-bjah]* Help; come to the aid of; (the mode of) helping/ or coming to the aid of [*Ganda*].

Juma (m) *[juh-mah]* "Friday": a name given to one born on Friday [The *Luyia*].

Jumba/ Jjumba (m) *[jjuhm-bah]* Zealous; that is diligent or takes great interest in; to become disturbed (or furious, or quarrelsome); large building [*Ganda*].

Junju/ Jjunju (m) *[jjuhn-juh]* Crest/ or crown (on the head of a fowl); the cutting down (or harvesting) of plantains [*Ganda*].

Juru (f/m) *[djuh-ruh]* Brown termite: name such as given to one of light brown complexion [*Shona*] (Jackson 1957: 120).

Jurua (f/m) *[juh-ruh-wah]* "In the place of those that are not of the clan": a name such as given to one born away from one's (i.e. father's) homestead (given that among the *Lugbara* it is traditionally important for the wife to deliver at her husband's homestead) [The *Lugbara*] (Middleton 1961: 35).

Juuko/ Jjuuko (m) *[jjuuh-koh]* That is abrasive (or reverberating) in tone; enragement [*Ganda*].

-K-

Kaara (m) *[kaah-rah]* Small finger [*Kikuyu*].

Kaari (f) *[kaah-rih]* The one who loves to work [*Embu*].

Kaasokampanga (m) *[kaah-soh-kahm-pahn-gah]* The eye of the rooster; this name is commonly associated with the proverb "the sharp/
shrewd eye of the cock: it sees and comprehends through the night"
i.e. the cock dramatizing with crowing, such as recognizes the breaking of the day when nobody else does: the name would therefore imply a very shrewd person [*Ganda*].

Kabaganda (m) *[kah-bah-gahn-dah]* The little one that is of the *Ganda*
ethnics: a name such as given to a child born in *Buganda* territory
[*Nyoro*] (Beattie 1957: 99).

Kabajja (m) *[kah-bahj-jah]* That engages in carpentry work; that chops
(or carves, or cuts) [*Ganda*].

Kabajjo (m) *[kah-bahj-joh]* Chip of wood; a piece of carpentry work
[*Ganda*].

Kabakalinjulira (f) *[kah-bah-kaah-lihn-juh-lih-rah]* "The king will appeal for me (or appeal as my witness)" [*Ganda*].

Kabakalongoosa (f) *[kah-bah-kaah-lohn-goh-oh-sah]* "The king co-
rrects (or causes to improve, or makes better, or makes ready)" [The
Ganda].

Kabakanjagala (f) *[kah-bah-kaahn-jah-gah-lah]* "The king likes (or loves) me" [*Ganda*].

Kabakungu (m) *[kaah-bah-kuhn-guh]* That of (or belonging to) high
ranking chiefs (or officials, or dignitaries) [*Ganda*].

Kabala (m) *[kah-bah-lah]* Fruit; fruitful; spot; stain [*Ganda*].

Kabalangulo (m) *[kah-bah-lahn-guh-loh]* Strop; small whetstone [The
Ganda].

Kabambaala (m) *[kah-bahm-baah-lah]* That interrupts (or interferes);
that injects himself into a conversation; that is mischievous; one that
is unbridled (or reckless, or wild); this name is commonly associated
with the proverb "the mischievous and intrusive one does not allow
the edible locusts to settle down" who in not allowing for the locusts
to be caught images an irascible, impatient, and hasty person [The
Ganda].

Kabambaggulu (m) *[kah-bahm-bahg-guh-luh]* "One who spreads all
over the sky"; this name is commonly associated with the proverb
"one who spreads all over the sky is like one who has thick hairy
growth all over his chest" and the name is typically given to one who
is disputatious, or dominates others by talking loudly and monopolistically [*Ganda*].

Kabanda (m) *[kah-bahn-dah]* One who makes his way through (such
as through a thicket of grass); shed in which bricks are made; moment; space; this name is sometimes associated with the proverb
"one that ably forces his way through a thicket of thorns is also capable of climbing (or jumping through) the thorny hardwooded trees"
which images a fearless person [*Ganda*].

Kabandamajjwa (m) *[kah-bahn-dah-mahj-jwah]* "The one that ably forces his way through a thicket of thorns"; this name is commonly ass-

ociated with the proverb "one that ably forces his way through a thicket of thorns is also capable of climbing (or jumping through) the thorny hardwooded trees" which images a fearless person [*Ganda*].

Kabandu (m) *[kah-bahn-duh]* Very intelligent and daring child [*Ganda*].

Kabanga (m) *[kah-bahn-gah]* Small space; small room; a bit of time; small interval; small opportunity (or chance); the beginning; the establishing; the founding; the constructing [*Ganda*].

Kabangala (m) *[kah-bahn-gah-lah]* (With ears) sticking out; protruding; projecting [*Ganda*].

Kabanvu (m) *[kah-bahn-vuh]* Vat; trough for brewing beer; old wooden trough (or vat) [*Ganda*].

Kabatumaako (f/m) *[kah-baah-tuuh-maah-koh]* "The one who is never to be given orders": a name given to the second child born after twin siblings [*Kongo*] (Daeleman 1977: 192); a name given to the last born of triplets [*Kongo*] (Daeleman 1977: 193).

Kabazaala (m) *[kah-bah-zaah-lah]* "That gave birth to (them)"; that of those who give birth [*Ganda*].

Kabazo (m) *[kah-bah-zoh]* That is used to count (or calculate); that is used to reckon (or consider, or regard) [*Ganda*].

Kabazzi (m) *[kah-bahz-zih]* Small grasshopper with reddish patches on the back and wings; small ax; one who cuts (or chops, or carves); one who makes out of wood, using carpentry tools [*Ganda*].

Kabbula (f/m) *[kahb-buh-lah]* Water lily; one that is scarce [*Ganda*].

Kabeete (m) *[kah-beh-eh-teh]* Viciousness; madness; that has been laid down carelessly [*Ganda*].

Kabege (m) *[kah-beh-geh]* One with folding ears [*Kikuyu*].

Kabejja (f) *[kah-behj-jah]* The name-title of the second wife of the king; favorite wife [*Ganda*].

Kabembula (m) *[kah-behm-buh-lah]* That stretches (or pegs) out (such as a skin to dry) [*Ganda*].

Kabenge (m) *[kah-behn-geh]* Small spell of intense heat [*Ganda*].

Kabengwa (m) *[kah-behn-gwah]* That is heated up [*Ganda*].

Kabi (m) *[kah-bih]* Dangerous; harmful; bad [*Ganda, Soga*].

Kabigi (m) *[kah-bih-jih]* Celebration; merrymaking; rejoicing [*Ganda*].

Kabika (f/m) *[kah-bih-kaah]* "The one that announces/ calls (the twins)": name given to one whose birth precedes that of his or her twin siblings [*Taabwa*] (Daeleman 1977: 193).

Kabindi (m) *[kah-bihn-dih]* Pipe; one that smokes with the use of a pipe [*Ganda*].

Kabinuli (m) *[kah-bih-nuh-lih]* That has been raised/ or raised up; that has been brought up (for consideration); misdirected enthusiasm; infatuation [*Ganda*].

Kabizzi (m) *[kah-bihz-zih]* (Small) pig/ or hog [*Ganda*].

Kabodha/ Kaboodha (m) *[kah-boh-oh-tdh-ah]* That pecks/ henpecks; that picks up (such as termites or edible flying ants); that nags [The

Soga].

Kaboggoza (m) *[kah-bohg-goh-zah]* One who causes them to bark (or to speak harshly); a harsh person [*Ganda*].

Kabogo (m) *[kah-boh-goh]* (Small) buffalo [*Ganda*].

Kabojja (m) *[kah-bohj-jah]* That pecks; that henpecks; that picks up (such as termites or edible flying ants); that nags [*Ganda*].

Kabolu (m) *[kah-boh-luh]* That is dry/ or desiccated/ or overused (such as soil); that is overripe [*Soga*].

Kabongo (m) *[kah-bohm-boh]* Species of fleshy leaved creeping plant that is used to wipe off banana sap [*Ganda*].

Kabonge (m) *[kah-bohn-geh]* Craziness; madness [*Ganda*].

Kabooli (m) *[kah-boh-oh-lih]* That is disowned (or disinherited); that is excommunicated (or ostracized); that is discriminated against (or shown prejudice against) [*Ganda*].

Kaboya (m) *[kah-boh-yah]* The little one that becomes dizzy/ delirious; little one that tosses about restlessly (or becomes disturbed); the little one that becomes troubled; the little one that seethes; (the sick little one) that raves [*Ganda*].

Kabudde (m) *[kaah-buhd-deh]* "Little one of the time (or weather, or occasion)" [*Ganda*].

Kabugo (m) *[kah-buh-goh]* A gift contribution to the family of the deceased; burial shroud; one born during a time of mourning [*Ganda*].

Kabugute (m) *[kah-buh-guh-teh]* Annoyance; hurriedness; harassment [*Ganda*].

Kabula (f/m) *[kah-buh-lah]* A banana species for making beer; slap [*Ganda*].

Kabulattaka (m) *[kah-buh-laht-tah-kah]* "The little one that does not have land property" [*Ganda*].

Kabulindi/ Kaabulindi (m) *[kaah-buh-lihn-dih]* That of (or belonging to) that which is threatening (or unavoidable); that of what they are cautious about (or what is defended against, or what is kept in reserve, or what is awaited) [*Ganda*].

Kabumba (m) *[kah-buhm-bah]* That formed or molded out of clay; potter's clay; molding pots; sculpting; one that molds or sculpts out of clay [*Ganda*].

Kabumbuli (m) *[kah-buhm-buh-lih]* Round and short; rotund (or fat) [*Ganda*].

Kabunga/ Kaabunga (m) *[kaah-buhn-gah]* That rambles or wanders around aimlessly [*Ganda*].

Kabura (f) *[kah-buh-rah]* Of the rains [*Kikuyu*].

Kabuzi (m) *[kah-buh-zih]* (Small) goat; species of plantain [*Ganda*].

Kabwama (m) *[kah-bwaah-mah]* That greets; that welcomes (or receives gladly, or greets enthusiastically); one that crouches down [*Ganda*].

Kabwege (m) *[kah-bweh-geh]* That is huge/ gigantic [*Ganda*].

Kabwijamu (m) *[kah-bwiih-jah-muuh]* "The little one comes right in it (i.e. the misfortune)": a name such as given to a child born during a period of misfortune or bereavement [*Nyoro*] (Beattie 1957: 101).

Kabwimukya (m) *[kah-bwih-muh-tch-aah]* "The little one involved in reviving it (i.e. the sorrow)": a name such as given to a child whose birth reminds the parents of the death of an earlier born child, which death they had began to erase from their minds [The *Nyoro*] (Beattie 1957: 101).

Kabwongera (m) *[kah-bwohn-geh-rah]* "The little one of it (i.e. sorrow) that does increase": name such as given to a child born during a period of misfortune in which children in the family or the neighborhood have recently died, and this one is not expected to survive [*Nyoro*] (Beattie 1957: 101).

Kabyogera (m) *[kah-bjoh-geh-rah]* One who speaks it out [*Soga*].

Kachocho/ Kacocco (m) *[kah-tch-oh-tch-oh]* (Small) teaser or bully; one who pesters [*Ganda*].

Kachuchu/ Kacucu (m) *[kah-tch-uuh-tch-uh]* That loses one's beauty; that loses one's freshness; that fades [*Ganda*].

Kachwamba/ Kacwamba (m) *[kah-tch-wahm-bah]* Escapee; one who flees [*Ganda*].

Kadaali (f/m) *[kah-daah-liih]* The lining of a buttonhole of a long gown *(kkanzu)* worn by males; asparagus fern; the headdress (or tiara) of a bride [*Ganda, Soga*].

Kaddeyo (m) *[kahd-deh-yoh]* "Let it return (or go) there"; "may he/ she go there" [*Ganda*].

Kaddu (m) *[kahd-duh]* Servant; a member of the tiller social class as opposed to the aristocratic cattle keeping class; captive [*Ganda*].

Kaddukibuuka (m) *[kahd-duh-tch-ih-buuh-kah]* Servant of *Kibuuka* the deity associated with war and military affairs [*Ganda*].

Kaddukirizi (m) *[kahd-duh-kih-rih-zih]* That runs to help; that comes to the rescue [*Ganda*].

Kaddulubaale (f) *[kahd-duh-luh-baah-leh]/* **Kaddu-Lubaare** (f) *[kahd-duh-luh-baah-reh]* Name-title of the principal wife of the king; the queen consort; the senior wife of the chief [*Ganda*].

Kaddumukasa (m) *[kahd-duh-muh-kah-sah]* Servant of *Mukasa* the God associated with Lake Victoria [*Ganda*].

Kadduwamala (m) *[kahd-duh-wah-mah-lah]* Servant of *Wamala* a God believed to be helpful in curing; servant of *Wamala* the son of *Musisi* the God associated with earthquakes [*Ganda*].

Kade (m) *[kah-deh]* Small bell [*Ganda*].

Kadihungila (m) *[kah-dih-huhn-gih-lah]* "Surprised": a name such as given to one whose birth, in some aspect, astonished people [*Kaguru*] (Beidelman 1974: 288).

Kafambe (m) *[kah-fahm-beh]* Weakness (usually of the legs); that is caused to be lazy (or idle) [*Soga*].

Kafuluma (m) *[kah-fuh-luh-mah]* That comes out; that goes out [The *Ganda, Soga*].

Kafuma (m) *[kah-fuh-mah]* That tells or recounts (such as a legend, tradition, fable, or tale); that loses color (or becomes tarnished); that fades in memory; that becomes rusty in knowledge and skills; that falls into disrepute [*Ganda*].

Kafumbe (m) *[kah-fuhm-beh]* (One associated with) the civet cat; that is cooked/ boiled [*Ganda*].

Kafumbirwango (f/m) *[kah-fuhm-bih-rwahn-goh]* "The little one that is married to a leopard"; "marrying a leopard" [*Ganda*].

Kafuna (m) *[kah-fuh-nah]* The little one that gets (or obtains, or procures) [*Ganda, Soga*].

Kafunta (m) *[kah-fuhn-tah]* The little one that pounds (or punches, or knocks, or strikes, or beats) [*Ganda, Soga*].

Kafuuma (m) *[kah-fuuh-mah]* Speedy; that goes away at great speed; that is blown away; one whose cooking is delicious [*Ganda*].

Kagaali (m) *[kah-gaah-lih]* Bicycle; a small vehicle; wheelbarrow [The *Ganda, Soga*].

Kagaba (m) *[kah-gah-bah]* That gives away; that gives as a present; that divides (or distributes, or apportions); that appoints (or designates) [*Ganda*].

Kagabane (f) *[kah-gah-bah-neh]* Shared with another; distributed or apportioned; divided up [*Ganda, Soga*].

Kagenzi (f/m) *[kah-gehn-zih]* The departed one; traveler [*Ganda*].

Kagera (f) *[kah-geh-rah]* Apportionment; the name of a river; one that recounts or tells (a story) [*Ganda*].

Kagerekamu (m) *[kah-geh-reh-kah-muh]* One small foot (or toe) [The *Ganda*].

Kagezi (m) *[kah-geh-zih]* That is clever (or wise, or learned) [*Ganda, Soga*].

Kagga (m) *[kahg-gah]* Small river (or stream) [*Ganda*].

Kaggo (m) *[kahg-goh]* One who beats with a small stick (in a children's game involving the use of sticks); a beater; one who with a stick frequently whacks others; name-title of the king's official representative and liaison in relation to the deities and priests, the one who supervised the king's servants in the royal enclosure, who conducted royalty ceremonies, and who in more recent years has been mainly confined to the office of district chief (of *Kyaddondo*) [*Ganda*].

Kaggogo (m) *[kahg-gohg-goh]* One who beats with a small stick (in a children's game involving the use of sticks); a beater; one who with a stick frequently whacks others [*Ganda*].

Kaggwe (m) *[kahg-gweh]* "Let it (or may it) be completed (or ended, or become finished)" [*Ganda*].

Kaggya (f) *[kahj-jah]* Recruit; newcomer [*Ganda*].

Kaggyo (m) *[kahj-joh]* A small fragment of pottery; tile [*Ganda*].

Kagi (m) *[kah-jih]* Small egg [*Ganda*].

Kagiri (m) *[kah-jih-rih]* A species of wild plant [*Ganda*].

Kagodo (m) *[kah-goh-doh]* Thick layer of skin below the hair (of pigs and similar species) [*Ganda*].

Kagogwe (m) *[kah-goh-gweh]* That is caused to stand firm; that is paired/ coupled; that is caused to be afflicted with congenital paralysis (of the spine) [*Ganda*].

Kagole (f/m) *[kah-goh-leh]* A bride that is small in physique; a bride; a (small) bridegroom; mistress of the house; newcomer; recent arrival; newly appointed official; new member; newly ordained priest or minister; the name of a deity [*Ganda, Soga*].

Kagolomolo (m) *[kah-goh-loh-moh-loh]* A narrow neck of the land; an isthmus; canal; narrow channel of water into which boats are launched [*Ganda*].

Kagoma (m) *[kah-goh-mah]* A small drum; a small chiefship; royalty; a small drummer; one who stampedes or rampages around); one who roams the place, moving to and fro [*Ganda, Soga*].

Kagudde (m) *[kah-guhd-deh]* "The little one has fallen"; that has fallen (or occurred, or failed, or occurred, or happened) [*Ganda*].

Kagugube (m) *[kah-guh-guh-beh]* Rejected; refused [*Ganda*].

Kagulu (f/m) *[kah-guh-luh]* (Small) leg [*Ganda, Soga*].

Kagulusi (m) *[kah-guh-luh-sih]* One that causes to gallop (or fly, or frolic) [*Ganda, Soga*].

Kagunda (m) *[kah-guhn-dah]* That throws violently; that stabs; that hurls down; that dashes down [*Ganda*].

Kaguya (m) *[kah-guh-yah]* That beguiles (or dupes); that leads (someone) on [*Ganda, Soga*].

Kahiu (m) *[kah-hjuh]* Knife [*Kikuyu*].

Kaigil (m) *[kahy-gihl]* The one that repeats [*Maasai*].

Kaijabwangu (m) *[kahy-jah-bwahn-guuh]* "It (i.e. the small child) came rapidly": a name such as given to a child whose birth was smooth [*Nyoro*] (Beattie 1957: 99).

Kaijanarwo (m) *[kahy-jah-nah-rwoh]* "It (i.e. the small one) arrived with it (i.e. death)": a name such as given to a child born around the time a close family relative died [*Nyoro*] (Beattie 1957: 102).

Kainanja (m) *[kahy-nahn-jah]* One who is fond of darkness [*Kikuyu*].

Kairugala (m) *[kahy-ruh-gah-lah]* That is (or becomes) black (or darkened); that is with negroid pigmentation [*Soga*].

Kaisokampanga (m) *[kahy-soh-kahm-pahn-gah]* "The eye of the rooster"; this name is commonly associated with the proverb "the sharp/ shrewd eye of the cock: it sees and comprehends through the night" i.e. the cock dramatizing with crowing, such as recognizes the breaking of the day when nobody else does: the name would therefore imply a very shrewd person [*Soga*].

Kajabaga (m) *[kah-jah-bah-gah]* High point of intensity; a climax [The

Ganda].
Kajebede (m) *[kah-jeh-beh-deh]* Soaked; mushy; soggy; lacking consistency (such as in shape) [*Ganda*].
Kajereje (m) *[kah-jeh-reh-jeh]* Small species of bean [*Ganda*].
Kajerenge (m) *[kah-jeh-rehn-geh]* Despised; belittled; derided [*Ganda*].
Kajerero/ Kajeerero (m) *[kah-jeh-eh-reh-roh]* A person that is worthless; nonentity [*Ganda*].
Kaji (m) *[kah-jih]* Small egg [*Ganda*].
Kajimu (m) *[kah-jih-muh]* That is fertile/ fruitful [*Ganda*].
Kajja (f) *[kahj-jah]* "(Here) the little one comes"; newcomer; "the little one arrives"; "it happens" [*Ganda*].
Kajjabuwongwa (m) *[kahj-jah-buh-wohn-gwah]* (Birth) associated with prayer (or dedication, or sacrifice) [*Ganda*].
Kajjabwangu (m) *[kahj-jah-bwahn-guh]* One that comes (or came) fast (or hastily, or prematurely); of a birth that took place quickly; "the little one comes (or came) fast (or hastily, or prematurely)" [*Ganda*].
Kajjakuzimba (m) *[kahj-jah-kuh-zihm-bah]* "The little one came to build (or construct, or edify)" [*Ganda*].
Kajjanenkumbi (m) *[kahj-jah-nehn-kuhm-bih]* "The little one came with (or comes with) a hoe" [*Ganda*].
Kajjankya (m) *[kahj-jahn-tch-aah]* Coming in the morning (or tomorrow); "the little one came (or comes) in the morning" [*Ganda*].
Kajjenke (f) *[kahj-jehn-keh]* Doll; puppet; marionette [*Ganda*].
Kajjula (m) *[kahj-juh-lah]* That dishes up/ or serves (food)/ or uncovers (food); that becomes full (or becomes filled up) [*Ganda*].
Kajoba (m) *[kah-joh-bah]* Messy; soaked [*Ganda*].
Kajogolo (m) *[kah-joh-goh-loh]* Small spear [*Ganda*].
Kajongo (m) *[kah-john-goh]*/ **Kajongolo** (m) *[kah-john-goh-loh]* One that is small, tall, and thin [*Ganda*].
Kajubi (m) *[kah-juh-bih]* That helps (or comes to the aid of) others; that steels oneself; that resolves firmly; that redoubles one's efforts [The *Ganda*].
Kajugo (m) *[kah-juh-goh]* Pen holder; a small bell that is used as an ornament on the neck or on the drums [*Ganda*].
Kajujugwe (m) *[kah-juh-juh-gweh]* That grew up fast; (meat) that is torn off [*Ganda*].
Kajula (m) *[kah-juh-lah]* That wishes for (or yearns for, or desires); that becomes wanting (or misses, or goes without); that becomes deprived (or gets into a state of deprivation); that gets on the point of; that gets on the verge of [*Ganda*].
Kajumba (m) *[kah-juhm-bah]* The name of a royal drum; that is quarrelsome; that becomes vexed (or exasperated, or furious) [*Ganda*].
Kajuna (m) *[kah-juh-nah]* That helps (or assists) [*Ganda*].
Kakadde (m) *[kah-kahd-deh]* One million; that is old [*Ganda*].
Kakaire (m) *[kah-kahy-reh]* One million; that is old [*Soga*].

Kakande (m) *[kah-kahn-deh]* The jungle; (small) deserted stretch of land; (small) wasteland; that was forced (or compelled); that is caused to persist [*Ganda*].

Kakanga (m) *[kah-kahn-gah]* One that scares (or frightens, or startles); one that threatens; that is gripping; that is terrible; that is violent [The *Ganda*].

Kakangula (m) *[kah-kahn-guh-lah]* That raises the voice; that disturbs; that creates an uproar; that raises a price [*Ganda*].

Kakata (m) *[kah-kah-tah]* (Small) head pad; (small) pot pad; (small) ridge of earth dug for planting potatoes [*Ganda*].

Kakazi (f) *[kah-kah-zih]* Small woman; "(it is) a little woman": a preliminary or pet name for one whose parents are lax in going through the naming ceremony (or in giving the child a more descriptive name) [*Ganda, Soga*].

Kakebe (m) *[kah-keh-beh]* (Small) can; (small) tin can; (small) cigarette case; that is trapped; that is circumvented; that is ambushed [*Ganda, Soga*].

Kakeeto (m) *[kah-keh-eh-toh]* The dried hide (or skin) that is sat on [*Ganda*].

Kakembe (m) *[kah-kehm-beh]* That is caused to strut about in a proud and pompous manner [*Ganda*].

Kakenge (m) *[kah-kehn-geh]* That is associated with a throbbing abdominal pain; that is perceived (or noticed, or noted, or suspected) that is suspicious of; that is scented/ smelled [*Ganda*].

Kakete (m) *[kah-keh-teh]* Apron (such as one worn by a carpenter or a cook) [*Ganda*].

Kakinda (m) *[kah-kihn-dah]* A sewing; a stitching [*Ganda*].

Kakindu (m) *[kah-kihn-duh]* Small palm tree [*Ganda*].

Kakireebwe (m) *[kah-kih-reh-eh-bweh]* That of the water lily; that dupes (or becomes limp, or overhangs, or bends) [*Ganda*].

Kakkusa (f/m) *[kahk-kuh-sah]* That satisfies (or satiates) [*Ganda*].

Kakokola (m) *[kah-koh-koh-lah]* Small elbow [*Soga*].

Kakoma (m) *[kah-koh-mah]* That ceases (or stops, or comes to an end); that goes as far as; that reaches; palm pole; the trunk of a wild date palm [*Ganda*].

Kakomo (m) *[kah-koh-moh]* Small bracelet; a small copper wire; the limit; the end [*Ganda, Soga*].

Kakonge (m) *[kah-kohn-geh]* The stump of a tree [*Ganda*].

Kakono (m) *[kah-koh-noh]* A small arm; a small hand; a trunk of an elephant [*Ganda, Soga*].

Kakonya (m) *[kah-koh-ndjh-ah]* That causes to be unable to cook properly; that causes to be stunted in growth (or to not ripen); that causes to be silent in refusal to answer; that causes to remain motionless whilst expected to act (or to sulk) [*Ganda, Soga*].

Kakooto (m) *[kah-koh-oh-toh]* Small edge (such as of a hill or village);

small boundary; small coast; that is bent over; that walks with a stoop [*Ganda*].

Kakooza (m) *[kah-koh-oh-zah]* That tears (or tears off); that causes to suffer greatly; that is of hard times [*Ganda*].

Kakoto (m) *[kah-koh-toh]* Small neck [*Ganda, Soga*].

Kakuku (m) *[kah-kuh-kuh]* A bit of mold [*Ganda, Soga*].

Kakule (m) *[kah-kuh-leh]* (Scornful) burst of laughter [*Ganda*].

Kakulu (f/m) *[kah-kuh-luh]* "Small elder" [*Ganda, Soga*].

Kakulukuku (m) *[kah-kuh-luh-kuh-kuh]* A small and dark termite hill; that rolls in the dirt (or gets soiled, or gets messed up); that tramples (or gets rough on, or crumples) [*Ganda*].

Kakumba (f/m) *[kah-kuhm-bah]* One who marches or struts around; grazing area [*Ganda*].

Kakumirizi (m) *[kah-kuh-mih-rih-zih]* That causes to make a fire; that causes to blow on a fire to keep it going; that works continually at building (a fire); that causes to gather together (or pile together, or heap up) [*Ganda*].

Kakuusa (f/m) *[kah-kuuh-sah]* That is hypocritical; that dupes (or deceives) [*Ganda*].

Kakuya (f) *[kah-kuh-yah]* That makes dirty (or messes up, or crumples) [*Ganda*].

Kakwan-jj (m) *[kah-kwahn-djjh]* Bitter: a nickname such as given to a boy with a habit of biting his brothers [*Kakwa*] (Nzita 1995: 133).

Kakyaama (m) *[kaah-tch-aah-mah]* "The little one that got bent (or twisted)"; this name is commonly associated with the proverb "a little plant that became (or grew) crooked while young, cannot be straightened" implying that it would very difficult during the forthcoming teen and adult stages to undo the harm that was imparted to a child that grew up in an environment devoid of such aspects as proper social training, good education, appreciation, and adequate nutrition [*Ganda*].

Kakyukyu/ Kacuucu (m) *[kah-tch-uuh-tch-uuh]* Grass with sharply stinging and cutting hairy projections; person with such immense power that he is so much feared; "small king" [*Ganda*].

Kalaaki (m) *[kah-laah-tch-ih]* That gasps (or wheezes, or becomes choked up) [*Ganda*].

Kalaba (f/m) *[kah-lah-bah]* That is alert (or perceptive, or awake, or conscious, or alive); that perceives (or sees, or finds, or gets) [*Ganda*].

Kalabalaba (f/m) *[kah-lah-bah-lah-bah]* That is brilliant (or clever); the master (or mistress) of ceremonies; the chairperson; the bodyguard [*Ganda*].

Kalali (m) *[kah-lah-lih]* Loud laughter; a loud laugh; pepper; hot pepper; this name is sometimes associated with the proverb "the one who has the company of many guests would not (or should not) quarrel about a burst of laughter" [*Ganda*].

Kalamazi (f/m) *[kah-lah-mah-zih]* One who makes a pilgrimage (or a journey, or a long trip) [*Ganda*].

Kalambika (f) *[kah-lahm-bih-kah]* That goes (or faces, or proceeds) straight ahead; that stretches out; that lays out straight; that keeps (or holds) straight [*Ganda*].

Kalanda (m) *[kah-lahn-dah]* Small trailing shoot (such as that of the sweet potato); that climbs (or creeps, or spreads); that wanders (or travels) all around; that flourishes [*Ganda*].

Kalangirire (m) *[kah-lahn-gih-rih-reh]* The little one that is prophesied (or announced, or given notice of, or advertised) [*Ganda*].

Kalangirwa (m) *[kah-lahn-gih-rwah]* Deserving (or able) to be given notice of [*Ganda*].

Kalangwa (m) *[kah-lahn-gwah]* The talked about one (or one worth talking about) [*Ganda*].

Kalanzi (m) *[kah-lahn-zih]* Reporter; an announcer; prophet; advertiser [*Ganda*].

Kalasi (m) *[kah-lah-sih]* One who talks loudly and quarrelsomely [The *Ganda*].

Kale (m) *[kah-leh]* Cloud [*Ganda*].

Kaleebu (m) *[kah-leh-eh-buh]* That bends (or overhangs, or droops, or becomes limp, or hangs down, or hangs suspended, or dangles) [The *Ganda*].

Kaleega (m) *[kah-leh-eh-gah]* That tightens (or strains, or draws taut, stretches, or extends, or aims) [*Ganda*].

Kaleet (f/m) *[kaah-leh-eht]* "The conveyer (of the twins)": a name given to one whose birth precedes that of his or her twin siblings [*Kanyok*] (Daeleman 1977: 193).

Kalege (m) *[kah-leh-geh]* One who talks noisily and incessantly [The *Ganda*].

Kalegga (m) *[kah-lehg-gah]* One who loiters (or wanders, or roams) about [*Ganda*].

Kalema (m) *[kah-leh-mah]* The one that is too much for [*Ganda*].

Kalemakansinjo (m) *[kah-leh-mah-kahn-sih-joh]* "The one with the strength of a chisel"; this name is commonly associated with the expression "*Kalema* is (like) a cold chisel--one iron cuts the other" a name-title of the king, originating from the act of King *Kalema* who in 1888 shot dead his brother *Kiweewa* and burnt his corpse [*Ganda*].

Kalemba (m) *[kah-lehm-bah]* One who strolls slowly and leisurely; of the lakes or seas; handkerchief; scarf [*Ganda*].

Kalende (m) *[kah-lehn-deh]* Young mudfish [*Ganda*].

Kalenzi (m) *[kah-lehn-zih]* Small boy; "(it is) a little boy": preliminary or pet name for one whose parents were lax in going through the naming ceremony or giving the child a more descriptive name [*Ganda, Soga*].

Kalevu (m) *[kah-leh-vuh]* (With) a goatee [*Ganda, Soga*].

Kalimba (f/m) *[kah-lihm-bah]* Singer; musician; liar [*Ganda*].

Kalimbwe (m) *[kah-lihm-bweh]* Guano [*Ganda*].

Kalimera (m) *[kah-lih-meh-rah]* "It will sprout (or grow, or become well established)" [*Ganda, Soga*].

Kalimuddungu (m) *[kah-lih-muhd-duhn-guh]* "The little one is in the desert"; "the little one is in the wilderness"; "the little one is in the wasteland"; "it has to do with (or is associated with) *Ddungu*" [The *Ganda*].

Kalinda (f/m) *[kah-lihn-dah]* Waiter; one that looks after the well from which the king's water is drawn [*Ganda*].

Kalindaluzzi (f/m) *[kah-lihn-dah-luhz-zih]* Water well waiter (or keeper); one who looks after the well from which the King's water is drawn [*Ganda*].

Kalindi (m) *[kah-lihn-dih]* A small group (or flock, or band, or crowd, or throng); the ambatch, a light wooded tree that grows in or close to swamps; the grandson of a deceased chief who participated in the ceremonies at the chief's grave [*Ganda*].

Kalingannyana (f) *[kah-lihn-gahn-ndjh-ah-nah]* "the little one is like a calf (in beauty)" [*Ganda*].

Kalinge (m) *[kah-lihn-geh]* That is spied out; that is searched for; that is gone in search of [*Soga*].

Kalinjala (m) *[kah-lihn-jah-lah]* That is experiencing hunger (or famine) [*Ganda*].

Kalinnimula (m) *[kah-lihn-nih-muh-lah]* That drives along (such as a herd or crowd); that pours (or throws) down heavily; that bestows in abundance; that swamps (or overwhelms) [*Ganda*].

Kalinzi (m) *[kah-lihn-zih]* That waits around to exploit an opportunity; a hanger on; an opportunist; that causes to wait (or guard); that waits or guards with (or by means of); that postpones; that defers till later; that is held in reserve [*Ganda*].

Kaliro (m) *[kah-lih-roh]* (Small) fire [*Ganda, Soga*].

Kaliyisa (m) *[kah-lih-yih-sah]* "The little one will cause to go by (or to pass)"; "the little one will overtake"; "the little one will get the better of"; "the little one will prevail over"; "the little one will surpass" [The *Ganda*].

Kalogakalenzi (m) *[kah-loh-gah-kah-lehn-zih]* "That which charms a small boy"; "that which bewitches a small boy" [*Ganda*].

Kalokola (m) *[kah-loh-koh-lah]* One who rescues (or saves, or gives salvation to) [*Ganda, Soga*].

Kalulu (m) *[kah-luh-luh]* Lottery; vote; witty (as the folktale hare) [The *Ganda, Soga*].

Kalumba (m) *[kah-luhm-bah]* Rear seat in a canoe; one that attacks or assaults [*Ganda*].

Kalunda (m) *[kah-luhn-dah]* That herds/ or tends (cattle); that keeps in view; that keeps following (one who does not want to be followed) [*Ganda, Soga*].

Kalungi (f/m) *[kah-luhn-jih]* That is good looking (or good, or beautiful, or handsome, or desirable, or just right) *[Ganda]*.

Kaluusi (f/m) *[kah-luuh-sih]* Female ruminant *[Ganda, Soga]*.

Kalwanire (m) *[kah-lwaah-nih-reh]* That is fought for/ about *[Ganda]*.

Kalwayo (m) *[kah-lwaah-yoh]* Plunder; loot; food taken as an offering to a deity's shrine; clamor; a bad smell; the little one that lingers the-re; the little one that delays; the little one that is late; that is there for a long time; "the little one was there for too long (or was late, or de-layed) there" *[Ganda]*.

Kalwaza/ Kalwaaza (m) *[kahl-waah-zah]* That causes to get sick; that makes ill; that keeps/ houses (a sick person) at *[Ganda, Soga]*.

Kalyango (m) *[kah-ljahn-goh]* (Small) doorway *[Ganda]*.

Kalyankolo (m) *[kah-ljahn-koh-loh]* "That consumes the stumps of ba-nana trees"; "that consumes the epiglottis" *[Ganda]*.

Kalyembula (m) *[kah-ljehm-buh-lah]* That is split in half (or divided do-wn the middle, or divided in half); that eats (or consumes) that which is scarce (or missing) *[Ganda]*.

Kalyemenya (m) *[kah-ljeh-eh-meh-ndjh-ah]* That will humble himself (or apologize, or admit guilt) *[Ganda]*.

Kalyesubula (m) *[kah-ljeh-suh-buh-lah]* (Tree) that will strip itself of bark; that will peel oneself (of the skin); that will flay itself (or oneself) *[Ganda]*.

Kalyomu (m) *[kah-ljoh-oh-muh]* "The little one devours (or eats, or co-nsumes) one"; the little one that is eaten by one *[Ganda]*.

Kalyowa (m) *[kah-ljoh-wah]* One who does a favor (or benefits for); child sent to the king or a distinguished chief to perform services; ob-ligation; favor; benefit *[Ganda]*.

Kamaanya (m) *[kah-maah-ndjh-ah]* Determined (or self willed) person; rogue; rascal *[Ganda]*.

Kamaanyi (m) *[kaah-maah-ndjh-iih]* "The little one of strength"; this na-me is commonly associated with the proverb "that which is strong (or difficult), has to be tackled quickly and courageously" implying that there is always a way to achieve or attack that which may seem to be so difficult, as long as the one pursuing the goal is determined enough--as synonymous with "where there is a will, there is a way" *[Ganda]*.

Kamala (f/m) *[kah-mah-lah]* Finisher; finalizer; completer; that con-sumes (or uses up); that satisfies; that is sufficient for (or adequate for, or enough); that acts to excess; that does to extremes *[Ganda]*.

Kamalabyonna (m) *[kah-mah-lah-bjohn-nah]* "The one who completes (or finishes) all things" i.e. a very powerful person such as a Prime Minister *[Ganda]*.

Kamande (m) *[kah-mahn-deh]* One renowned for dancing *[Embu]*.

Kamanya (m) *[kah-mah-ndjh-ah]* That knows; that knows how to; that learns (or finds out, or learns how to) *[Ganda]*.

Kamanyiro (m) *[kah-mah-ndjh-iih-roh]* That involves getting acquainted (or getting to know each other); that involves getting to know (or to
learn); that involves habituating oneself (or familiarizing oneself with)
[*Ganda*].

Kambaaza/ Kkambaaza (m) *[kkahm-baah-zah]* One who puts on airs;
one who makes himself uncooperative or difficult; who causes to be
arrogant (or cranky); to make sour or bitter [*Ganda*].

Kambagu (m) *[kahm-bah-guh]* That tends to stand up suddenly (or to
start up, or jump up); that tends to arise (or break out suddenly) [The
Ganda].

Kambugu (f/m) *[kah-mbuh-guh]* A species of grass with roots that spread out over a wide area; couch grass [*Ganda*].

Kambundu (f/m) *[kahm-buhn-duh]* A name given to a child believed to
be bewitched since the mother had a flow of blood sometime during
the pregnancy; the child is hence treated with special care that includes ritual performances by the mother which include carrying a rattle and shaking it at the crossroads or when crossing a stream (so as
to contain the spirits) [*Ovimbundu*] (Ennis 1945: 2).

Kamegere (f/m) *[kah-meh-geh-reh]* That is caused to smile; that is caused to have a lively (or attractive, or healthy) appearance; that is thrown (in wrestling); that is defeated; that is overwhelmed [*Ganda*].

Kameke (f) *[kah-meh-keh]* "The blind one": a name such as given to
one with small or squinty eyes [*Ovimbundu*] (Ennis 1945: 6).

Kameketo (m) *[kah-meh-keh-toh]* Aching; crunchy; gnawing; chewing
(something hard); crunching; nibbling [*Ganda*].

Kamenyangabo (m) *[kah-meh-ndjh-ahn-gah-boh]* That destroys the
shield; that shatters the shield; that breaks the shield [*Ganda*].

Kamiapiulu (f) *[kah-mih-yah-pjuh-luh]* "Little cinder": this name is commonly associated with one who is (or feels) so alienated from home
since she is in unfamiliar surroundings (or a name associated with a
child of one in such a situation), or name associated with an oppressed or mistreated woman who does not have many blood relatives
around (that would have remedied her situation), and the name originally (in past times) depicts one who was lost from a caravan [The
Ovimbundu] (Ennis 1945: 6).

Kamogabulungi (m) *[kah-moh-gah-buh-luhn-jih]* That gazes properly
(or well, or nicely, or effectively); that properly displays awareness;
that is nicely lively and hearty; that is properly cognizant [The *Ganda*,
Soga].

Kamohelo (m) *[kah-moh-heh-loh]* Acceptance [*Sotho*] (Mohome 1972:
174).

Kamoze (f/m) *[kah-moh-zeh]* That looks; that displays awareness; to
be lively and hearty [*Soga*].

Kampala (m) *[kahm-pah-lah]* "Of the antelope" one associated with
Kampala the capital city of Uganda, more so when it was a relatively

thriving and more renowned city [*Luyia*].

Kamulegeya (m) *[kah-muh-leh-geh-yah]* That of the weaver bird (or finch); that of hanging loose; that of hanging fingers; that involves a child born with more than the normal number of fingers [*Ganda*].

Kamuswaga (m) *[kaah-muh-swaah-gah]* That harpoons (or spears, or stabs, or pierces) [*Ganda*].

Kamuwanda (f/m) *[kah-muh-wahn-dah]* Of the road: one born while the parent was travelling or while on the way to hospital (to deliver) [*Ganda*].

Kamuwuunyi (m) *[kah-muh-wuuh-ndjh-iih]* That is amazing (or astonishing, or surprising, or stupefying); that makes indistinct sounds; that moans (or groans) [*Ganda*].

Kamuzirizi (f/m) *[kah-muh-zih-rih-zih]* Child with a defective eye [The *Ganda*].

Kamwaka (m) *[kaah-mwaah-kah]* Of the (new) year (or season) [The *Ganda*].

Kamya (f/m) *[kah-mjah]* A name given to one born after twin siblings [*Ganda*].

Kamyoka (m) *[kah-mjoh-kah]* That becomes red (or reddish brown, or tanned); that gets tanned (from the sun); that reddens (with anger); that becomes angry; that becomes discolored (of a bruised part of the body); the second in command; the deputy [*Ganda*].

Kana (f/m) *[kah-nah]* "Without": a name such as given to a child born to father who had not fulfilled the bride dowry payments [*Lugbara*] (Middleton 1961: 35).

Kanaakulya (m) *[kah-naah-kuh-ljah]* That will devour you; "it will eat (or consume) you" [*Ganda*].

Kanaamirira (m) *[kah-naah-mih-rih-rah]* That will swallow using [The *Ganda*].

Kanabbi (m) *[kah-nahb-bih]* A prophet; one that prophesies [*Ganda*].

Kanagwa (m) *[kah-nah-gwah]* "The little one that is thrown away" [The *Nyoro*].

Kanene (f) *[kah-neh-neh]* "That is big": this name is commonly associated with the proverb "It is big--that which is a little thing in the eye" implying that things that appear insignificant or inconsequential to others, can be very significant or hurting on the one directly affected; the proverb also implies that an apparently small or insignificant person or thing can still make a considerable impact [*Ovimbundu*] (Ennis 1945: 5).

Kangavve (m) *[kahn-gahv-veh]* That of the pangolin/ anteater [*Ganda*].

Kangawaza (m) *[kahn-gah-wah-zah]* That causes to become fierce (or violent) [*Ganda*].

Kangongo (f) *[kahn-gohn-goh]* "The one of trouble": a name such as given to one born into a family where there is mourning or sickness [*Ovimbundu*] (Ennis 1945: 7).

Kanindo (m) *[kah-nihn-doh]* "If I sleep" *[Luo]*.

Kanjonjo (f) *[kahn-djohn-djoh]* The humming bird: a name such as given to one who is inquisitive and interfering *[Ovimbundu]* (Ennis 1945: 6).

Kankaka (m) *[kahn-kah-kah]* That is jaundiced; that is intrepid (or bold, or aggressive); that is associated with force (or violence); that speaks violently (or quarrelsomely); that strongly denounces (or criticizes) *[Ganda]*.

Kankoko (f) *[kahn-koh-koh]* (Of or associated with) chickens *[Ganda]*.

Kankoloongo (f/m) *[kaahn-koh-loh-ohn-goh]* The careful one: a name given to the third child born after twin siblings [The *Luwa*] (Daeleman 1977: 192).

Kannalwanga (m) *[kahn-nah-lwahn-gah]* One associated with *Lwanga* the deity whose shrine was on *Bubeke* Island; one that is associated with *Lwanga (Sserwanga) Mukasa* the God associated with Lake Victoria *[Ganda]*.

Kannyamira (m) *[kahn-ndjh-ah-mih-rah]* That becomes overwhelmed with grief (or becomes very sad); the name of a war associated royal fetish *[Ganda]*.

Kannyo (m) *[kahn-ndjh-oh]* (Small) tooth; crisis; climax *[Ganda]*.

Kanoonya (m) *[kah-noh-oh-ndjh-ah]* That looks for (or searches for) *[Ganda]*.

Kansaani (m) *[kahn-saah-nih]* That is fitting (or suitable, or deserves merit) *[Ganda]*.

Kanyango (m) *[kah-ndjh-ahn-goh]* One who loves to touch *[Kikuyu]*.

Kanyeki (m) *[kah-ndjh-eh-kih]* Of the grass *[Kikuyu]*.

Kanyika (m) *[kah-ndjh-ih-kah]* "(Of) the plainland": name such as given to a child conceived or born during the hoeing season in the plainlands *[Pare]* (Omari 1970: 70).

Kapalaga (m) *[kah-pah-lah-gah]* That rushes about excitedly; that is in a very agitated state; that is mischievous; that is unruly; a rascal [The *Ganda*].

Kapasa (m) *[kah-pah-sah]* Small ax *[Soga]*.

Kapere (m) *[kah-peh-reh]* Humorous person; clown; footloose wanderer; the name as equated to 'footloose soldier/ wanderer' or a member of Daniel Mwanga's (the young anticolonialism rebel and king) youthful corps recruited at his court--they would often take the law into their hands and infringe on many traditional mores; military captain--as a nickname for 'Captain,' the name is associated with the British colonial adventurer and fighter Captain (Sir) Frederick Lugard, at that time (late 1800's) in the soon to be British Protectorate territory of *Uganda* *[Ganda, Soga]*.

Kapiinga-Kaba-Mbuuyi (f/m) *[kaah--piih--ndgh-aah-kah-baah-mbuuh-yih]* "The one who reinstates the mother into the normal course of giving birth (that is no longer marked by the sacredness of the birth of twins)": a name given to the fourth child following twin siblings [*Luwa*] (Daeleman 1977: 192).

Kapinga (m) *[kah-pihn-gah]* The top of the hill; one that frustrates; one that is a spoiler [*Ganda*].

Kaptich (m) *[kahp-tih-tch]* One born in kraal country [*Nandi*] (Hollis 1969: 67).

Karani (m) *[kah-raah-nih]* Office person; office clerk [The *Embu*, *Hutu*, *Swahili*, *Tutsi*, *Twa* and several other ethnics of eastern and central Africa].

Karanja (m) *[kah-rahn-jah]* One who is fond of staying outside [The *Kikuyu*].

Kariba (m) *[kah-rih-bah]* The shaker [*Kikuyu*].

Karimi (f) *[kah-rih-mih]* The one who loves to till the land [*Embu*].

Kariuki (m) *[kah-rjuh-kih]* The reincarnated (or reborn) one; a name depicting one named in honor of a child in the family that died [The *Kikuyu*].

Karyoki (m) *[kah-rjoh-kih]* "The one restored to life": a name such as given to one whose preceding siblings died, this child consequently subjected to a ritual to cleanse away death [*Kikuyu*] (Cagnolo 1933: 66).

Kasagala (m) *[kah-sah-gah-lah]* The little one that is loose (or shaky, or slack) [*Ganda*].

Kasaanyi (m) *[kah-saah-ndjh-ih]* A (small) hairy caterpillar; a (small) caterpillar; that is worthy; that qualifies [*Ganda*].

Kasaato (m) *[kah-saah-toh]* That wanders at random (or aimlessly) [*Ganda*].

Kasadha/ Kasaadha (m) *[kah-saah-tdh-ah]* Newly born child; that is small but manly; "(it is) a little (or small) man"; preliminary or pet name for one whose parents were lax in going through the naming ceremony or giving the child a more descriptive name [*Soga*].

Kasagazi (m) *[kah-sah-gah-zih]* Looseness; shakiness; slackness; elephant grass; reed [*Ganda*].

Kasaija (m) *[kah-sahy-jah]* Newly born child; that is small but manly; "(it is) a little (or small) man"; preliminary or pet name for one whose parents were lax in going through the naming ceremony or giving the child a more descriptive name [*Toro*].

Kasajjakaliwano (m) *[kah-sahj-jah-kah-lih-wah-noh]* "The small man is here" [*Ganda*].

Kasaka (m) *[kah-sah-kah]* (Small) thicket; (small) bush; small cooking pot; that forages (for food); a foraging for food; digging up of information [*Ganda*].

Kasala (m) *[kah-sah-lah]* One associated with a person who had so many children [*Luyia*].

Kasalirwe (m) *[kah-sah-lih-rweh]* Decided (or judged) for; that is charged a price; apportioned for [*Ganda*].

Kasamba (m) *[kah-sahm-bah]* Commotion; disturbance; kick; kicker; stomper; (a piece of) floating vegetable matter that forms obstructive masses in a body of water [*Ganda*].

Kasambandege (m) *[kah-sahm-bahn-deh-geh]* Species of twining plant, the large and yellow vetch; "that kicks bell-like ornaments" [The *Ganda*].

Kasana (m) *[kah-sah-nah]* Sunshine [*Ganda, Soga*].

Kasansula (m) *[kah-sahn-suh-lah]* That takes apart (or unravels, or untwists, or unplaits, or uncovers, or reveals) [*Ganda*].

Kasanvu (m) *[kah-sahn-vuh]* Seven thousand; forced labor; small branch; small whip [*Ganda, Soga*].

Kasasa (m) *[kah-sah-sah]* Hardwood tree species on the forest edge; one who scatters (or disperses, or spreads) [*Ganda*].

Kasavu (m) *[kah-sah-vuh]* That is fat [*Ganda, Soga*].

Kasawuli (m) *[kah-sah-wuh-lih]* That is healed (or cured) [*Ganda*].

Kaseka (f) *[kah-seh-kah]* One who laughs; laughter [*Ganda*].

Kasendwa (m) *[kah-sehn-dwah]* That is pushed back (or leveled) [The *Ganda, Soga*].

Kasenene (m) *[kah-seh-eh-neh-neh]* October; small grasshopper [The *Ganda*].

Kasenge (m) *[kah-sehn-geh]* Small room; partition [*Ganda*].

Kasenke (m) *[kah-sehn-keh]* That is associated with (a patch) of grass used for thatching huts and for squeezing out banana juice headed for brewing [*Ganda*].

Kasenyi (f/m) *[kah-seh-ndjh-ih]* Young hen; small swamp; small lowland [*Ganda*].

Kasera (f/m) *[kah-seh-rah]* That of seducing [*Luo*].

Kasinda (f/m) *[kah-sihn-dah]* The (small) earth that blocks the passage behind a burrowing animal: a name given to the first born after twin siblings [*Ovimbundu*] (Ennis 1945: 2).

Katapepo (f) *[kah-tah-peh-poh]* "Go and get water!": this name is commonly associated with the proverb "Go and get water; marriage is about serving!" and the message to the mother of the child named so is that serving is a crucial part of marriage and that she should refrain from participating in discussions involving the child's paternal family [*Ovimbundu*] (Ennis 1945: 3).

Kateke (f) *[kah-teh-keh]* "The days we came": this name is commonly associated with the proverb "The days we came, we ate off dishes; now it comes to eating off wooden bowls" which is synonymous with "We have stayed long and worn out our welcome" and is a message to one who was pleasant to you at first, but is no longer so, following longer acquaintance [*Ovimbundu*] (Ennis 1945: 4-5).

Katum (f/m) *[kah-tuhm]* "That is ordered (or sent, or commissioned)": a name given to the last born of triplets [The *Kanyok*] (Daeleman 1977: 193).

Katuma (f/m) *[kah-tuh-mah]* "That orders (or sends, or commissions)": a name given to the last born of triplets [The *Luba, Luwa*] (Daeleman 1977: 193).

Katumwa/Katumua (f/m) *[kaah-tuuh-mwah/ kaah-tuh-mwaah]/* **Muana -Katumua** (f/m) *[mwaah-nah-kaah-tuuh-mwah]* "The one to whom no orders can be given": a name given to the last born of triplets [*Kongo, Songye*] (Daeleman 1977: 193; Ndoma 1977: 89).

Katumwe (f/m) *[kah-tuh-mweh-eh]* "That has been ordered (or sent, or commissioned)": a name given to the last born of triplets [The *Luba*] (Daeleman 1977: 193).

Katunanzolako (f/m) *[kah-tuh-nahn-zoh-lah-koh]* "The people do not like us" [*Kongo*] (Ndoma 1977: 96).

Katwaal (f/m) *[kah-twaahl]* "The conveyer (of the twins)": name given to one whose birth precedes that of his or her twin siblings [*Kanyok*] (Daeleman 1977: 193).

Katwaala (f/m) *[kah-twaah-lah]* "The conveyer (of the twins)": a name given to one whose birth precedes that of his or her twin siblings [The *Luba*] (Daeleman 1977: 193).

Kavumo (m) *[kah-vuh-moh]* A name given to a child born during the blossoming of a fig tree whose average longevity symbolizes good health and long life [*Pare*] (Omari 1970: 70).

Kaya (f/m) *[kah-yah]* Cousin [*Karamojong*] (Stewart 1993: 64).

Kayieyo (f) *[kahy-yeh-yoh]* The one of the mother [*Maasai*].

Kelesia (f) *[keh-leh-sih-yah]* Church: a name adapted from the European word *ecclesia* and given to one born in a church [*Luyia*].

Kenalemang (m) *[keh-nah-leh-mah-ndgh]* "With whom am I?" [*Sotho*] (Moloto 1986: 215).

Kendo (m) *[kehn-doh]* Stove; cooking place [*Luo*].

Kengera (m) *[kehn-geh-rah]* A name given to a child whose mother's labor pains were uncharacteristically erratic and discontinuous, such that consequently the midwives hardly participated in the eventual delivery [*Pare*] (Omari 1970: 70).

Keya (m) *[keh-yah]* "Strew me"; "scatter me" [*Luo*].

Kganyapa (m) *[kah-gah-ndjh-ah-pah]* Thunderstorm: a name such as given to one whose birth coincides with a period of thunderstorms [*Sotho*] (Mohome 1972: 175).

Kgauhelo (f) *[kah-gahw-heh-loh]* "Mercy!": a name such as given to one born following the death of a preceding sibling [*Sotho*] (Mohome 1972: 174).

Kgosana (m) *[kah-goh-sah-nah]* Small (or minor) chief [The *Sotho*] (Mohome 1972: 179).

Kgosatsana (f) *[kah-goh-saht-sah-nah]* Small (or minor) chieftess [*Sotho*] (Mohome 1972: 179).

Kgotso (m) *[kah-goht-soh]* Peace: name such as given to one born at a time of peace and good social relations amongst kin and (or) neighbors) [*Sotho*] (Mohome 1972: 174).

Khaemba (m) *[kah-yehm-bah]* A name given to one born during a time of millet harvesting [*Luyia*].

Khakhubi (f) *[kah-kuh-bih]* A name given to one born during the season when cowpeas are the main vegetable dish [*Luyia*].

Khamala (f/m) *[kah-mah-lah]* A name given to the second born following his or her twin siblings [*Luyia*] (Wako 1985: 38).

Khamala (f/m) *[kah-mah-lah]* A name given to the second born following the birth of his or her twin siblings, i.e. the one born after *Khisa* [*Luyia*].

Khanda (m) *[kahn-dah]* "The man of brains" [*Zulu*] (Lugg 1968: 13).

Khaukha (f/m) *[kah-wuh-kah]* A name given to a child who is the product of a difficult or unusually long pregnancy [*Luyia*].

Khayongo (m) *[kah-yohn-goh]* A name given to one born in a field overgrowing with *luyongo* weeds [*Luyia*].

Khayelihle (m) *[kah-yeh-lih-leh]* "Nice house" [*Zulu*] (Koopman 1979: 157).

Khehla (m) *[keh-lah]* Old man [*Zulu*] (Koopman 1979: 69).

Khethiwe (f) *[keh-tih-weh]* "She has been chosen"; "the chosen one" [*Zulu*] (Koopman 1979: 162).

Khethokwakhe (m) *[keh-toh-kwaah-keh]* "He chooses his thing" [*Zulu*] (Koopman 1979: 161).

Khisa (f/m) *[tch-ih-sah/ kih-sah]* A name given to one whose birth follows that of his or her twin siblings [*Luyia*].

Khohlwayezakhe (m) *[koh-lwah-yeh-zah-keh]* "Be forgotten by his own things" [*Zulu*] (Koopman 1979: 79).

Khosi (m) *[koh-oh-sih]* Lion: a name given to the older of twin boys, the younger named *Makaanzu* [*Yaka*] (Daeleman 1977: 191); a name given to a triplet [*Yaka*] (Daeleman 1977: 192).

Khulakuhlekwa (m) *[kuh-lah-kuh-leh-kwah]* "He grows up amidst laughter" [*Zulu*] (Koopman 1979: 161).

Khulani (m) *[uh-kuh-lah-nih]* "Grow up": a name such as given by the named child's mother to express to her father and brother that they should act more maturely, now that they have become grandfather and uncle [*Zulu*] (Suzman 1994: 259).

Khuumbu (m) *[kuuhm-buh]* Leopard: a name given to the older of twin boys, the younger named *Nyiimi* [*Yoombe*] (Daeleman 1977: 191).

Khuzwayo (m) *[kuh-zwah-yoh]* The reprimanded one [*Zulu*] (Koopman 1990: 336).

Khwaka (f) *[kwah-kah]* A name given to one born during the weeding season [*Luyia*].

Kiaku (f/m) *[kih-yah-kuuh]* "Yours" [*Kongo*] (Ndoma 1977: 96).

Kibaki (m) *[kih-bah-kih]* Big tobacco leaf [*Kikuyu*].

Kibiika-Mahasa (f/m) *[kiih-biih-kah-maah-hah-sah]* "The one that announces/ calls (the twins)": a name given to one whose birth precedes that of his or her twin siblings [*Luba*] (Daeleman 1977: 193).

Kibika (f/m) *[kiih-bih-kah]* "The one that announces/ calls (the twins)": a name given to one whose birth precedes that of his or her twin siblings [*Saanga*] (Daeleman 1977: 193).

Kibikyo/ Kibiikyo (m) *[tch-ih-biih-tch-oh]* "The bad one that is yours"; this name is commonly associated with the proverbs "that which is bad but is yours is better for you than that which is good but belongs to your neighbor" and "the ugly one (i.e. child) that is yours is of more worth to you than the beautiful one (i.e. child) that is your neighbors" implying that the intrinsic value of something of someone even if seemingly inferior to others, is of great importance (such as the fulfillment of having given birth to a healthy, though unattractive, child) [*Ganda, Soga*].

Kifuba (m) *[tch-ih-fuh-bah]* Chest; strength; breast; bosom; a measure of length (from the center of the chest to the end of the arm; cough or cold in the chest; flu; this name is sometimes associated with the proverb "one who spreads all over the sky is like one who has thick hairy growth all over his chest" and the name is typically given to one who is disputatious, or dominates others by talking loudly and monopolistically [*Ganda, Soga*].

Kigo (m) *[kih-goh]* Fortune teller [*Kikuyu*].

Kija (m) *[kih-jah]* A name given to a child born during a night devoid of moonlight [*Pare*] (Omari 1970: 70).

Kika (f/m) *[tch-ih-kah]* Clan; family; type; kind; deserted kraal; this name is sometimes associated with the proverbs "masters (or elders) are like pillars: once they are removed from the clan, the power of the group crumbles" and "a master (or an elder) is (like) a pillar: once it is removed from the clan, the power of the group crumbles" [The *Ganda*].

Kilak (f) *[kih-lahk]* The name of the daughter of *Jipiti* and mother of *Labongo* who legend has it that he struck his spear into the ground and out came the chiefs of the future *Luo* ethnic groups [The *Acholi*] (Nzita 1995: 90).

Kilonzo (m) *[kih-lohn-zoh]* A name given to a child that makes a lot of noise in the first few nights following his birth [*Pare*] (Omari 1970: 70).

Kilusu (m) *[kih-luh-suh]* The one that exceeds [*Maasai*].

Kiluvia (m) *[kih-luh-vih-yah]* A name given to a child who suffers from alarming bouts of illness and is so close to death in the first few years of his life [*Pare*] (Omari 1970: 70).

Kimaiyo (m) *[kih-mahy-yoh]* A name given to one born at a time of a beer drinking gathering [*Nandi*] (Hollis 1969: 67).

Kimando (m) *[kih-mahn-doh]* Crusher [*Kikuyu*].

Kimanyisho (f) *[kih-mah-ndjh-ih-tsh-oh]* The one that settles [The *Maasai*].

Kimathi (m) *[kih-mah-sth-ih]* One who harvests; one who seeks [The

Kikuyu].

Kimngeny (m) *[kihm-ndgh-eh-ndjh]* A name given to one born during a time the oxen have been taken to lick salt rock [*Nandi*] (Hollis 1969: 67).

Kimuike (m) *[kih-muhy-keh]* A name given to one born shortly after a relation is killed [*Nandi*] (Hollis 1969: 67).

Kingori (m) *[kih-ndgh-oh-rih]* The noisy one [*Kikuyu*].

Kinyanjui (m) *[kih-ndjh-ahn-juhy]* Of the chicken [*Kikuyu*].

Kinyua (m) *[kih-ndjh-wah]* One who drinks [*Embu*].

Kiongi (m) *[kjohn-gih]* One who loves to be breast fed [*Kikuyu*].

Kipet (m) *[kih-peht]* A name given to one born in the morning [*Nandi*] (Hollis 1969: 67).

Kipirken (m) *[kih-pihr-kehn]* "One born when the mortars had to be beaten to drown the mothers cries": this likely implies a child of a very painful delivery, or one of a delivery during which the mother's labor pain cries were unusually loud [*Nandi*] (Hollis 1969: 67).

Kipkarai (f/m) *[kihp-kah-rahy]* A name given to a child born around the time a hornless cow is purchased or looted [*Nandi*] (Hollis 1969: 67).

Kipkatam (m) *[kihp-kah-tahm]* "The left handed one": (usually) a post-childhood nickname [*Nandi*] (Hollis 1969: 67).

Kipkemboi (m) *[kihp-kehm-bohy]* A name given to one born in the evening [*Nandi*] (Hollis 1969: 67).

Kipoiit (m) *[kihp-oh-yiiht]* "The big eared one": (usually) a post-childhood nickname [*Nandi*] (Hollis 1969: 67).

Kipor (m) *[kih-pohr]* A name given to one born by the roadside [*Nandi*] (Hollis 1969: 67).

Kipruiot (m) *[kihp-ruhy-yoht]* Name given to one born during the night [*Nandi*] (Hollis 1969: 67).

Kiprukut (m) *[kihp-ruh-kuht]* A name given to one born during a period there is a food scarcity in the land [*Nandi*] (Hollis 1969: 67).

Kipruto (m) *[kihp-ruh-toh]* A name given to one born during a journey [*Nandi*] (Hollis 1969: 67).

Kipyator (m) *[kihp-yah-tohr]* A name given to one born very early in the morning i.e. at the time the door is opened [*Nandi*] (Hollis 1969: 67).

Kireho (m) *[kih-reh-hoh]* "It is still alive": a name such as given to a child who suffered from an alarming illness, such that the parents were so worried about him surviving [*Pare*] (Omari 1970: 70).

Kiringa (f/m) *[kih-rihn-gah]* "Snake": a name such as given to one whose mother's house was visited by a snake during the pregnancy, or to a child reincarnated more than once [*Embu*].

Kirokimu (m) *[kih-roh-kih-muuh]* "One (more) day/ night": a name such as given to an alarmingly sick child not expected to survive (for even one more night) [*Nyoro*] (Beattie 1957: 101).

Kiseulan (m) *[kih-seh-wuh-lahn]* The one that is fine [*Maasai*].

Kisieku (m) *[kih-sih-yeh-kuuh]* The one that comes fast [*Maasai*].

Kisumo (m) *[kih-suh-moh]* One associated with the Western Kenya and Lake Victoria port-city *Kisumu* [*Luyia*].

Kitaka (m) *[kih-tah-kah]* "Cleanse" i.e. the stomach [*Luo*].

Kitwaala (f/m) *[kih-twaah-lah]* "The conveyer (of the twins)": a name given to one whose birth precedes that of his or her twin siblings [The *Saanga*] (Daeleman 1977: 193).

Kiu (m) *[kih-yuh]* The one that is of a mountain [*Maasai*].

Kola (f/m) *[koh-lah]* The remains from delivery [*Luo*].

Konya (m) *[koh-ndjh-ah]* "Help me" [*Luo*].

Kopito (m) *[koh-pih-toh]* The one of the string [*Maasai*].

Kosale (f) *[koh-sah-leh]* "The one who goes there and back in a day": name such as given to one who is energetic and nimble [*Ovimbundu*] (Ennis 1945: 6).

Kosenge (f) *[koh-sehn-geh]* "The one of the bush": a name such as given to one born in the field or in the woods [The *Ovimbundu*] (Ennis 1945: 7).

Kotsi (m) *[koht-siih]* A danger; an accident: a name such as given to one whose birth coincides with a misfortune in the family [The *Sotho*] (Mohome 1972: 173).

Kperekpere (f/m) *[kpeh-rehk-peh-reh]* "Old sleeping mat": name such as given to one who was given birth to on an old mat since the mother was too poor to afford better conditions [*Lugbara*] (Middleton 1961: 36).

Kudzaishe (f/m) *[kuh-dzah-yih-tsh-eh]* "Praise the Lord" [The *Shona*] (Jackson 1957: 121).

Kufakunesu (m) *[kuh-fah-kuh-neh-suuh]* "Death is with us": a name such as given to a child born to bereaved parents [*Zezuru*] (Marapara 1954: 8).

Kulet (m) *[kuh-leht]* Bladder; (more so in the past,) a container for storing fat [*Maasai*].

Kulya (f/m) *[kuh-ljaah]* Consuming; eating; this name is sometimes associated with the proverb "accumulating wealth does not translate into ceasing to be greedy"; this name is also sometimes associated with the proverb "a mass of people (or a crowd) looks bad when it comes to sharing and eating food, but looks good when it comes to allotting work" meaning that practically in either situation, the food or the work gets finished quickly, and though with the food there will likely be friction over sharing, in the case of the work the synonym "many hands make light work" will likely--human relations hence depend on circumstances that are rarely or never unconditional [*Ganda*].

Kulyennyingi (f) *[kuh-ljehn-ndjh-ihn-jih]* Consuming (or eating) a lot; this name is commonly associated with the proverbs "accumulating wealth does not translate into ceasing to be greedy," "eating a lot (of meat) does not translate into ceasing to desire" and "eating a lot does not translate into getting fat: otherwise the hen which eats all day would be as big as the cow" [*Ganda*].

Kumba (m) *[kuhm-bah]* Elbow [*Luo*].

Kumbelembe (f) *[kuhm-beh-lehm-beh]* "You are not well kept": name such as given to an ill-treated child that is poor and thin [*Ovimbundu*] (Ennis 1945: 6).

Kumbirai (f/m) *[kuhm-bih-rahy]* "Ask (i.e. the Lord)" [*Shona*] (Jackson 1957: 122).

Kundisai (f/m) *[kuhn-dih-sahy]* "Make me a victor" [*Shona*] (Jackson 1957: 121).

Kundu (m) *[kuhn-duuh]* A name given to one born after several of his preceding siblings died while infants [*Luyia*].

Kunene (m) *[kuh-neh-neh]* The right hand side [*Zulu*] (Koopman 1990: 336).

Kuruhira (m) *[kuh-ruh-hih-rah]* "Giving to it (i.e. death) a valuable present": the name implies that to bear a child is to give a present to the phenomenon of death, the name usually given to an alarmingly sick child not expected to survive [*Nyoro*] (Beattie 1957: 102).

Kusahila (m) *[kuh-sah-hih-lah]* "Finishing up food": one born during a famine [*Kaguru*] (Beidelman 1974: 288).

Kuseni (m) *[kuh-seh-nih]* "In the morning" [The *Zulu*] (Koopman 1979, 155).

Kutsirai (f/m) *[kuht-sih-rahy]* "Join together in insulting me (or inflicting evil upon me)": a name given to one born either during a dispute with backbiting and insulting kin or neighbors, or with kin or neighbors suspected of conspiring against the family [*Shona*] (Jackson 1957: 117).

Kutukhulu (m) *[kuh-tuh-kuh-luh]* A name given to one born after all of his preceding siblings died [*Luyia*].

Kutukutu (m) *[kuh-tuh-kuh-tuh]* A name given to a child of large body size [*Luyia*].

Kwahle (m) *[kwah-leh]* Lizard [*Zulu*] (Herbert 1995: 5).

Kwanya (m) *[kwah-ndjh-ah]* "Pick me up" [*Luo*].

Kwazikwakhe (m) *[kwah-zih-kwah-keh]* "(Of) his knowledge" [*Zulu*] (Koopman 1979: 157).

Kwenzakwabo (m) *[kwehn-zah-kwaah-boh]* "(Of) their doing" [*Zulu*] (Koopman 1979: 157).

Kwoba (m) *[kwoh-bah]* A name given to one born during a mushroom season [*Luyia*].

Kyalo (m) *[tch-aah-loh]* Village; large estate; the countryside; this name is sometimes associated with the proverb "the village of an elderly person is called 'too much' (or 'abundance')" implying that whether it comes to eating food, working, walking, and so forth, he always says 'it is too much for me!'; this name is also sometimes associated with the proverb "two masters (or elders) of the same village, that are jealous of each other, will not guarantee peace in the village" [The *Ganda*].

Labongo (m) *[lah-boh-ndgh-oh]* The name of the son of *Jipiti* and grandson of *Luo*---legend has it that Labongo struck his spear into the ground and out came the chiefs of the future *Luo* ethnic groups [The *Acholi*] (Nzita 1995: 90).

Ladur (f) *[lah-durh]* Name given to a child whose mother experienced difficult and painful birth labor pains that involved administration of herbs and divination; consequently, the child's umbilical cord became buried under a rubbish heap [*Acholi*] (Nzita 1995: 92).

Ladwong (f) *[lah-dwoh-ndgh]* A name given to a child whose mother experienced difficult and painful birth labor pains that involved administration of herbs and divination; consequently, the child's umbilical cord became buried under an *odwong* tree [The *Acholi*] (Nzita 1995: 92).

Langalibalele (m) *[lahn-gah-lih-bah-leh-leh]* "The sun is hot" [The *Zulu*] (Koopman 1979: 78).

Langalihle (m) *[lahn-gah-lih-leh]* "Christmas day": name such as given to a child born on Christmas [*Zulu*] (Suzman 1994: 270).

Langelile (m) *[lahn-geh-lih-leh]* "Nice day" [*Zulu*] (Koopman 1979: 80).

Langeni (m) *[lahn-geh-nih]* Sun [*Zulu*] (Koopman 1990: 334).

Layat (f) *[lah-yaht]* A name given to one whose mother experienced difficult and painful birth labor pains that involved administration of herbs [*Acholi*] (Nzita 1995: 91).

Lazalina (m) *[lah-zah-lih-nah]* "It came and rained" [*Zulu*] (Koopman 1979: 161).

Lebetsa (m) *[leh-beh-tsah]* "The one who strikes": an initiation name [*Sotho*] (Mohome 1972: 184).

Ledama (m) *[leh-dah-mah]* The one that is born during the day [The *Maasai*].

Leeto (m) *[leh-eh-toh]* Journey: a name such as given to a child born to a parent (or close kin) on a journey [*Sotho*] (Mohome 1972: 176).

Leeya (m) *[leh-eh-yah]* Being lazy (or idle); to loaf; civilian; ordinary [*Soga*].

Lefu (m) *[leh-fuuh]* Death: a name such as given to one whose birth coincides with a period of death/ or with deaths in the family [*Sotho*] (Mohome 1972: 175).

Lefufa (m) *[leh-fuh-fah]* Jealousy: name such as given to a child born at a time of social discord within the family or with neighbors [*Sotho*] (Mohome 1972: 177).

Lefuma (m) *[leh-fuh-mah]* Poverty: name such as given to a child born during times of poverty [*Sotho*] (Mohome 1972: 177).

Lehana (m) *[leh-hah-nah]* "The one who refuses": an initiation name [*Sotho*] (Mohome 1972: 184).

Lehlwa (m) *[leh-lwah]* Snow: a name such as given to one born during snow conditions [*Sotho*] (Thipa 1986: 289).

Lekgotla (m) *[lehk-goht-lah]* Court of law: a name such as given to a child born during a time of social discord within the family or with neighbors [*Sotho*] (Mohome 1972: 177).

Lekonko (m) *[leh-kohn-koh]* The one of the grandmother [*Maasai*].

Lelengues (m) *[leh-lehn-gwehs]* The one of the animal; the great one [*Maasai*].

Lema (f/m) *[leh-mah]* "Loves me": a name such as given to one whose father loves his wife [*Lugbara*] (Middleton 1961: 36); a ritual related name traditionally conferred on a child following its initiation [*Kongo*] (Ndoma 1977: 90).

Lembe (f) *[lehm-beh]* A ritual related name traditionally conferred upon the child following its initiation [*Kongo*] (Ndoma 1977: 90).

Lenepa (m) *[leh-neh-pah]* "The one who hits on the target": an initiation name [*Sotho*] (Mohome 1972: 184).

Lenkai (m) *[lehn-kahy]* The one that is of God [*Maasai*].

Lenzile (f) *[lehn-zih-leh]* "It has acted" [*Zulu*] (Koopman 1979: 162).

Lepapa (m) *[leh-pah-pah]* The one of the father [*Maasai*].

Leperes (m) *[leh-peh-rehs]* The one with (or the one associated with) the species of grass *ilperes* [*Maasai*].

Lerato (f) *[leh-rah-toh]* Love: a name such as given to one born at a time of peace and good social relations amongst kin and/ or neighbors [*Sotho*] (Mohome 1972: 174).

Lerato (f/m) *[uh-leh-rah-toh]* "Love" [*Sotho*] (Suzman 1994: 263, 270).

Lerole (m) *[leh-roh-leh]* "Great Drought" [*Sotho*] (Thipa 1986: 288).

Lerole (m) *[leh-roh-leh]* Wind; dust: a name given to one born during dusty, windy, or drought conditions [*Sotho*] (Thipa 1986: 289).

Lesarge (m) *[leh-sahr-geh]* The bloody [*Maasai*].

Leteipa (m) *[leh-tehy-pah]* A name given to one born in the evening [*Maasai*].

Letlama (m) *[leht-lah-mah]* "The one who unites (or binds)": an initiation name [*Sotho*] (Mohome 1972: 184).

Letsatsi (m) *[leh-tsah-tsih]* Sun: a name such as given to one born during a period of intense sunshine conditions [The *Sotho*] (Thipa 1986: 289).

Limbere (m) *[lihm-beh-reh]* God; "the friendly one" [*Luyia*] (Huntingford 1930: 103).

Linda (m) *[lihn-dah]* "Wait" [*Zulu*] (Koopman 1979: 158, 164).

Lindi (m) *[lihn-dih]* The ambatch tree; an opportunist; hanger on; one who waits around to exploit any opportunity; that is waited for; that causes to wait for [*Ganda*].

Lindiwe (f) *[lihn-dih-weh]* "She has been awaited"; "the awaited one" [*Zulu*] (Koopman 1979: 162).

Lindiwe (m) *[lihn-dih-weh]* "Waited": a name such as implying that the parent has so much desired this birth of one of male gender--can imply a first born boy among several older female siblings [The *Zulu*] (Herbert 1995: 4); "awaited": a name such as implying that though some of this newborn's siblings died, the parents wait patiently with the hope that this and the subsequent children will survive and grow to healthy maturity [*Zulu*] (Suzman 1994: 263).

Liuva (m) *[lih-yuh-vah]* God; sun; the preserver [*Luyia*] (Huntingford 1930: 102-103).

Livanga (f) *[lih-vahn-gah]* "Be the first": this name is commonly associated with the proverb "Be the first to think, do not be the first to eat" implying that In many situations it is best to be skeptical, and to reflect on the situation other than quickly involve yourself in it or jump to a favoring conclusion--this is synonymous with "Look before you leap" and "Slow but sure wins the race"; this name is also commonly associated with the proverb "Be the first to eat, do not be the first to think" which somewhat contradicts the above and implies that if something scarce but desired is presented to you, it is best to take it right away, otherwise someone else will take it or you will lose the appetite for it--you then can later perhaps reflect and make comments on it when it is safe in your hands, when you have consumed it, or when you do not need it anymore (which can be applied to delicious food and to enjoying what you can out of life) [*Ovimbundu*] (Ennis 1945: 4).

Lolobo (m) *[loh-loh-boh]* "Of the soil": a name given to a child whose previously born siblings died--the named child's umbilical cord and placenta are traditionally both buried in the house under a cooking pot previously used for keeping water, and this is so as to keep them out of reach of wizards and other ill wishers that would use them to downgrade the health of the child and the fertility of the mother [*Iteso, Langi*] (Nzita 1995: 132).

Longoli (m) *[loh-ndgh-oh-lih]* Of the ox with the black hide [The *Jie/ Karamojong*] (Gulliver 1952: 74).

Lopero (f/m) *[loh-peh-roh]* A name given to one that is born at night [*Karamojong*] (Nzita 1995: 119).

Lore (m) *[loh-reh]* "Lock it"; "close it" [*Luo*].

Lubabu (m) *[luh-bah-buh]* Something terrible (or awesome); that which produces a burning sensation [*Ganda*].

Lubabule (m) *[luh-bah-buh-leh]* That is done quickly; that is singed (or scorched) [*Soga*].

Lubadde (f/m) *[luh-bahd-deh]* "It was about to happen (to him)"; "it was going to happen"; "it nearly happened"; "it has been" [*Ganda*].

Lubaga (m) *[luh-bah-gah]* A fastening that is loose; the laying out of the first stages of; the drafting of a bill; a temporary action [*Ganda*].

Lubalaza (m) *[luh-bah-lah-zah]* Porch; verandah [*Ganda, Soga*].

Lubambula (m) *[luh-bahm-buh-lah]* That stretches out/ or pegs out (such as an animal skin to dry); that pulls up (such as a nail); that unpegs; that tears off; that takes the skin off [*Ganda*].

Lubandi (m) *[luh-bahn-dih]* Master; person in authority; that belongs to others; that causes to turn off; that causes to cut across; that causes to make one's way through (such as a thicket of grass) [The *Ganda*, *Soga*].

Lubanga (m) *[luh-bahn-gah]* The constructor; the establisher; founder; seat of a paddler in a canoe [*Ganda*].

Lubanja (m) *[luh-bahn-jah]* That demands debt payments [*Ganda*].

Lubeerenga (m) *[luh-beh-eh-rehn-gah]* "Always help (or assist) it/ him"; "let it always be (like that)" [*Ganda*].

Lubega (m) *[luh-beh-gah]* A carving; a serving or helping of food; the back; of a portion; to spy; to detect [*Ganda*].

Lubembe (m) *[luh-behm-beh]* Crust (on burnt food); burnt portion adhering to the pan; (formation of) a crust or scab; a coagulation; a swarming; an abundance [*Ganda*].

Lubende (m) *[luh-behn-deh]* That is frightened (or afraid); that fears (or honors, or respects) [*Ganda*].

Lubimbi (f) *[luh-bihm-bih]* A day's cultivation; this name is sometimes associated with the proverb "if many congratulate you for your work, then your day's cultivation is at it's end (or it has reached a very commendable level)" [*Ganda*].

Lubinga (m) *[luh-bihn-gah]* One who drives (or chases) away [*Ganda*].

Lubira (m) *[luh-bih-rah]* That is warmed up; (food) that is warmed over [*Ganda*].

Lubogo (m) *[luh-boh-goh]* Buffalo [*Ganda*, *Soga*].

Lubojje (m) *[luh-bohj-jeh]* That is (or was) pecked; that is (or was) henpecked; that is (or was) nagged [*Ganda*].

Lubondo (f) *[luh-bohn-doh]* A ritual related name traditionally conferred upon the child following its initiation [*Kongo*] (Ndoma 1977: 90).

Lubongebonge (m) *[luh-bohn-geh-bohn-geh]* A borderline case of craziness (or madness); that tends to whirl (or spin) around.

Luboobi (m) *[luh-boh-oh-bih]* That has been subjected to a long period of cooking; that is thoroughly cooked; a species of millipede; that of one whose taboo is drinking and using rainwater i.e. one (*Muboobi*) of the Rainwater clan (*Ababoobi*) [*Ganda*].

Lubowa (m) *[luh-boh-wah]* Security held for the payment of a debt [*Ganda*].

Luboyera (m) *[luh-boh-yeh-rah]* A pest; nuisance; or hanger on; one that encircles (or engulfs, or surrounds) [*Ganda*].

Lubuga (f) *[luh-buh-gah]* The name-title of the queen sister; the queen-dowager [*Ganda*].

Lubuga (f/m) *[luh-buh-gah]* Co-heir of an important person [*Ganda*].

Lubulwa (m) *[luh-buh-lwah]* Being without (a necessity); absent or difficult to find [*Ganda*].

Lubumba (m) *[luh-buhm-bah]* Liver; the molder; the Creator [*Ganda*].

Lubungo (f) *[luh-buhn-goh]* A species of tough but pliable wood: a name such as given to one who is flexible in some ways, yet is resilient and is therefore considered the ideal female [The *Kaguru*]

(Beidelman 1974: 288).

Lubuulwa (m) *[luh-buuh-lwah]* Danger (or trouble) [*Ganda*].

Lubuzi (m) *[luh-buh-zih]* Goat [*Ganda*].

Lubwama (m) *[luh-bwah-mah]* That greets; that welcomes (or receives gladly, or greets enthusiastically); one that crouches down [*Ganda*].

Ludidi (m) *[luh-dih-dih]* Porridge mash [*Zulu*] (Koopman 1990: 336).

Lufu (m) *[luh-fuuh]* Fog; mist [*Soga*].

Lufuka (m) *[luh-fuh-kah]* That spills (or pours) [*Soga*].

Lufula (m) *[luh-fuh-lah]* Slaughterhouse [*Ganda, Soga*].

Lufwalula (m) *[luh-fwah-luh-lah]* A name given to a first born boy [The *Luyia*].

Lugaba (m) *[luh-gah-bah]* The giver; God; that gives away (or gives as a present, or divides, or distributes, or apportions, or designates) [The *Ganda*].

Lugaje (m) *[luh-gah-jeh]* That is caused to be dark brown or reddish in color; that is caused to be languid (or inert, or lazy) [*Ganda*].

Lugalama (m) *[luh-gah-lah-mah]* Looking up; raising the head; inclined on one side [*Ganda*].

Lugalambi (m) *[luh-gah-lahm-bih]* One who is indifferent (or negligent, or takes matters lightly) [*Ganda*].

Lugano (m) *[luh-gah-noh]* "Much": a name such as given to one whose birth, in some way, astonished people [*Kaguru*] (Beidelman 1974: 288).

Lugasa (m) *[luh-gah-sah]* Useful; profitable [*Ganda, Soga*].

Lugaya (m) *[luh-gah-yah]* Scorning; despising; having contempt for [*Ganda, Soga*].

Lugayaavu (m) *[luh-gah-yaah-vuh]* Laziness; idleness; that is lazy (or idle) [*Ganda, Soga*].

Lugayizi (m) *[luh-gah-yih-zih]* That is scornful (or contemptuous); that involves scorn (or contempt) [*Ganda, Soga*].

Lugemankofu (m) *[luh-geh-mahn-koh-fuh]* That which wards off (or catches) guinea fowls [*Soga*].

Lugemwa (m) *[luh-geh-mwah]* Immunization; inoculation; forestalling; averting; warding off (such as a disease, bad weather, or a calamity) [*Ganda*].

Lugendo (m) *[luh-gehn-doh]* "Journey": a name such as given to one born during times of a lot of traveling/ or one whose parents at the time of his birth were refugees fleeing trouble [*Kaguru*] (Beidelman 1974: 289).

Lugeye (m) *[luh-geh-yeh]* The colobus monkey; that is talked about behind one's back [*Ganda*].

Lugobe (m) *[luh-goh-beh]* That is driven away (or dismissed, or chased, or defeated, or steered, or sought) [*Ganda, Soga*].

Lugogo (m) *[luh-goh-goh]* Fresh plantain fiber [*Ganda*].

Lugogoma (m) *[luh-goh-goh-mah]* Huge; very long [*Ganda*].

Lugoloobi (m) *[luh-goh-loh-oh-bih]* The coming to an end (of the day); the setting (of the sun); getting dark; that makes (the day) come to an end; that makes (the sun) set; that makes it get dark [*Ganda*].

Lugonda (m) *[luh-gohn-dah]* Being docile and obedient; yielding; that is pliable; able to be softened [*Ganda, Soga*].

Lugonja (m) *[luh-gohn-jah]* A species of large and sweet tasting banana that is baked or boiled [*Ganda*].

Lugono (m) *[luh-goh-noh]* Sound sleep [*Ganda*].

Lugonvu (m) *[luh-gohn-vuh]* That is soft (or tender, or docile, or obedient, or pliable, or polite, or weak, or easy, or simple) [The *Ganda, Soga*].

Lugoomye (f/m) *[luh-goh-oh-mjeh]* "It has become crooked (or bent, or warped, or wrecked, or bent down)" [*Ganda, Soga*].

Lugoonya (m) *[luh-goh-oh-ndjh-ah]* Crocodile [*Ganda*].

Lugoye (f) *[luh-goh-yeh]* A cloth; a fabric; material; a garment; hunting net [*Ganda*].

Lugudde (m) *[luh-guhd-deh]* "It has fallen (or happened, or occurred, or failed)" [*Ganda*].

Lugugule (f/m) *[luh-guh-guh-leh]* A rumbling (or thundering) that makes a thumping sound [*Ganda*].

Lugulu (f/m) *[luh-guh-luh]* (With a peculiarity of) a long leg [*Soga*].

Lugulukira (m) *[luh-guh-luh-kih-rah]* One who is top-heavy; that is lopsided; that leans to one side [*Ganda, Soga*].

Luguma (m) *[luh-guh-mah]* That is firm (or solid); that is faithful; that is brave (or courageous); that is daring; that has the nerve (or boldness) to [*Ganda, Soga*].

Lugumba (m) *[luh-guhm-bah]* A long bone; a gathering in a group; a congregation [*Ganda*].

Lugumya (m) *[luh-guh-mjaah]* That gives reassurance to; that makes firm (or encourages, or heartens, or cheers on) [*Ganda*].

Lugunju (m) *[luh-guhn-juh]* Species of wild cat; that is cultured (or civilized, or educated, or polished) [*Ganda*].

Luguza (m) *[luh-guh-zah]* That causes to buy; that buys with; that buys using [*Ganda*].

Lugwa (m) *[luh-gwah]* That falls (or happens, or occurs); that fails; a rope [*Ganda, Soga*].

Lugwanye (m) *[luh-gwaah-ndjh-eh]* "It is (or has been) appropriately suitable (or fitting for)" [*Ganda*].

Lugyaayo (m) *[luh-jaah-yoh]* "That fits there"; "that is appropriately suitable there"; "that is fitting there"; "that corresponds there" [*Ganda, Soga*].

Lujaganya (m) *[luh-jah-gah-ndjh-ah]* That rejoices; that is exultant (or happy, or jubilant) [*Ganda*].

Lujumba (m) *[luh-juhm-bah]* That becomes vexed (or exasperated, or furious); that quarrels [*Ganda*].

Luka (m) *[luh-kah]* Small net for trapping wild fowls; weave; plait [The *Ganda*].

Lukaaga (m) *[luh-kaah-gah]* Six hundred [*Ganda*].

Lukaayi (m) *[luh-kaah-yih]* Piece of gourd used as scoop; bitterness; protestation; disputation; that is (or causes to be) bitter (or sour, or unpleasant to the taste); that is (or causes to be) enraged (or quarrel-some; a situation that has become (or is caused to become) serious (or bad) [*Ganda*].

Lukaddiye (m) *[luh-kahd-dih-yeh]* That has become old (or aged); that has become worn out [*Ganda*].

Lukajaju (m) *[luh-kah-jah-juh]* Shriveled up person [*Ganda*].

Lukakamwa (m) *[luh-kah-kah-mwaah]* Endowed with meekness [The *Ganda*].

Lukalu (m) *[luh-kah-luh]* Dry land; land; continent [*Ganda, Soga*].

Lukambagire (m) *[luh-kahm-bah-gih-reh]* That which is caused to be sour (or acrid, or bitter); that is caused to be arrogant (or conceited) [*Ganda*].

Lukanga (m) *[luh-kahn-gah]* That frightens (or shocks, or startles, or threatens); that is gripping (or terrible, or violent); a punishment; a ch-astisement; a disciplinary action; correction; that involves dealing ha-rshly with; of the basket woven from grass [*Ganda*].

Lukau (m) *[luh-kahw]* A ritual related name traditionally conferred up-on the child following its initiation [*Kongo*] (Ndoma 1977: 90).

Lukazilubi (f) *[luh-kah-zih-luh-bih]*/ ***Lukazirubi*** (f) *[luh-kah-zih-ruh-bih]* "The woman who is bad (or evil, or dangerous, or ugly, or in bad shape)" [*Ganda*].

Lukeberwa (m) *[luh-keh-beh-rwah]* One that is so good looking that he deserves to be looked at over and over again with awe; a very hand-some king [*Ganda*].

Lukenge (m) *[luh-kehn-geh]* Swelling of the feet [*Ganda*].

Lukenku (m) *[luh-kehn-kuh]* Excessively sweet beer; beer made using very little sorghum; dense growth [*Ganda*].

Luketa (m) *[luh-keh-tah]* A cut off; that is cut down [*Ganda*].

Lukhozi (m) *[luh-koh-zih]* Black eagle [*Zulu*] (Koopman 1990: 336).

Lukhulwini (m) *[luhk-huh-lwih-nih]* "One in a thousand" [The *Zulu*] (Koopman 1979: 71).

Lukindu (m) *[luh-kihn-duh]* Wild date palm; sewn or stitched [*Ganda*].

Lukiza (m) *[luh-kih-zah]* That causes to surpass (or exceed, or be more than, or be superior to); that excels (or surpasses) in; pubic hair [*Ganda*].

Lukoda (f/m) *[luh-koh-dah]* Left handedness [*Soga*].

Lukoko (m) *[luh-koh-koh]* Chicken; hen; that involves getting out of hand (or being impossible to handle); that involves intractableness (or incorrigibility) [*Ganda*].

Lukolongo (m) *[luh-koh-lohn-goh]* Long line; that is long [*Ganda*].

Lukoma (m) *[luh-koh-mah]* A palm tree; palm tree pole; a coming to an end (or a cessation, or a going as far as, or a reaching) [*Ganda*].

Lukomwa (m) *[luh-koh-mwah]* "It is caused come to an end"; "it can be made to cease"; "it is enabled to stop"; "the end"; a cessation; a reaching out/ or going as far as [*Ganda*].

Lukomya (m) *[luh-koh-mjaah]* That causes to end (or to cease, or to stop) [*Ganda*].

Lukondo (m) *[luh-kohn-doh]* A name given to a very light complexioned one [*Luyia*].

Lukonge (m) *[luh-kohn-geh]* Stump of a tree; an obstacle; stumbling block [*Ganda*].

Lukoni (m) *[luh-koh-nih]* Pipestem euphorbia tree [*Ganda*].

Lukooba (m) *[luh-koh-oh-bah]* A species of tree with white flowering; a large spear [*Ganda*].

Lukoombo (f/m) *[luh-koh-ohm-boh]* "The cleaning" i.e. the 'the one who cleans the womb': a name given to the second child born after twin siblings [*Kongo*] (Daeleman 1977: 192); "causing to be concave": name given to the last born of quadruplets [*Kongo*] (Daeleman 1977: 193).

Lukooto (m) *[luh-koh-oh-toh]* Boundary; coast; the edge (such as of a hill or a village) [*Ganda*].

Lukooya (m) *[luh-koh-oh-yah]* That causes to become tired (or fatigued); that causes to become weary; that causes to get fed up [The *Ganda*, *Soga*].

Lukooyi (m) *[luh-koh-oh-yih]* That causes to become tired (or fatigued); that causes to become weary; that causes to get fed up; women's cloth wear about three or four yards [*Ganda*, *Soga*].

Lukowe (f) *[luh-koh-weh]* Eyelash [*Ganda*].

Lukubaga (m) *[luh-kuh-bah-gah]* That which consoles (or sympathizes with, or comforts); consolation; sympathizing with; comforting [The *Ganda*].

Lukubiro (f) *[luh-kuh-bih-roh]* A beating; where beating (or striking, or knocking) is done [*Ganda*].

Lukukirizi (m) *[luh-kuh-kih-rih-zih]* That causes to hide/ conceal (such as an object) [*Ganda*].

Lukukumula (m) *[luh-kuh-muh-lah]* That creates an abundance; that assembles a collection [*Ganda*, *Soga*].

Lukungo (m) *[luh-kuhn-goh]* An assembling; a collecting; a bringing together; a roundup (such as of suspects); a raid [*Ganda*].

Lukusa (m) *[luh-kuh-sah]* Permission; permit [*Ganda*, *Soga*].

Lukuube (m) *[luh-kuuh-beh]* Poor and wretched person [*Ganda*].

Lukuuta (m) *[luh-kuuh-tah]* That rubs (or smears, or scrubs) [*Ganda*].

Lukuyege (m) *[luh-kuh-yeh-geh]* The worker termite; that is associated with worker termites [*Ganda*].

Lukwago (m) *[luh-kwaah-goh]* Scratching; clawing [*Ganda*].

Lukwaju (m) *[luh-kwah-juh]* That is strong willed (or aggressive, or daring) [*Ganda*].

Lukwakula (m) *[luh-kwaah-kuh-lah]* That seizes (or grasps, or snatches away, or takes away) [*Ganda*].

Lukwangu (m) *[luh-kwahn-guh]* Stone [*Ganda*].

Lukwanzi (f/m) *[luh-kwahn-zih]* Necklace; string of beads [*Ganda*].

Lukyamuzi (m) *[luh-tch-aah-muh-zih]* A species of barkcloth tree [The *Ganda*].

Lulama (m) *[luh-lah-mah]* That involves being in good health/ or surviving (or living) after an illness; that involves flourishing; that involves turning out well (such as of an object which is being constructed) [*Ganda, Soga*].

Lulangwa (m) *[luh-lahn-gwah]* That is talked about; that is worth talking about; that is announced (or advertised, or prophesied, or given notice of) [*Ganda*].

Luleeba (f) *[luh-leh-eh-bah]* Plantain leaf placed in a hole in the ground which may be used as a bath or as a place to store beer; this name is sometimes associated with the proverb "the water of the plantain leafed hole in the ground can only be drunk by a daring person" which images a situation of what would be taking a big risk [The *Ganda*].

Luliika (m) *[luh-liih-kah]* That is edible [*Ganda, Soga*].

Luluga (m) *[luh-luh-gah]* Walking cane; cane used to administer a beating; a species of creeping plant [*Ganda*].

Lulume (m) *[luh-luh-meh]* Reincarnated; touched; bitten [The *Ganda, Soga*].

Lulunda (m) *[luh-luhn-dah]* Herding/ tending (cattle); keeping in view; stalking [*Ganda, Soga*].

Lulyolyo (f/m) *[luh-ljoh-ljoh]* A denouncement; an accusation (in secret); family; race; genealogy [*Ganda*].

Lumaama (m) *[luh-maah-mah]* Weedy plant whose flowers are dried and powdered to make snuff [*Ganda*].

Lumala (m) *[luh-mah-lah]* A finisher; a finalizer; a completer; that consumes (or uses up); that satisfies; that is sufficient for (or adequate for, or enough); that acts to excess; that does to extremes [*Ganda, Soga*].

Lumansi (m) *[luh-mahn-sih]* That scatters (or sprinkles, or pours); a scattering (or sprinkling, or pouring); that acts in a vain and ostentatious manner; that puts on airs [*Ganda*].

Lumanyika (m) *[luh-mah-ndjh-ih-kah]* Famous; well known; (able to become) known (or recognized) [*Ganda*].

Lumasa (m) *[luh-mah-sah]* That shines (or glitters, or sparkles) [The *Ganda*].

Lumberwente (m) *[luhm-beh-rwehn-teh]* "Scourge of the cows" [The *Ganda*].

Lumbuye (m) *[luhm-buh-yeh]* That is short and is the object of contempt [*Ganda*].

Lume (m) *[luh-meh]* Mist; dew [*Ganda*].

Lumfuankenda (f/m) *[luhm-fuh-wahn-kehn-dah]* "Have mercy on me!" : name such as given to one whose mother took a relatively long time to achieve this pregnancy [*Kongo*] (Ndoma 1977: 90).

Lumfuuwa (m) *[luhm-fuuh-waah]* "It blows me away" [*Ganda*].

Lumiramwenge (m) *[luh-mih-rah-mwehn-geh]* Alcoholic; alcohol swallower (or consumer) [*Ganda*].

Lumunye (m) *[luh-muh-ndjh-eh]* (That with a peculiarity of) the pupil of the eye; (one that) stares (others) square in the eye; the yellow billed African kite, a species of hawk; a species of reddish orange flowered plant with carrot like roots that are white [*Ganda*].

Lumweno (m) *[luh-mweh-eh-noh]* Smile [*Ganda*].

Lundi (m) *[luhn-dih]* At another time; sometimes [*Soga*].

Lungephi (m) *[uh-luhn-geh-pih]* "Where was she good?": a name such as given by the named child's mother to express that her mother-in-law pretends to be nice to some people, but is nasty to her [The *Zulu*] (Suzman 1994: 259).

Lungisana (m) *[uh-luhn-gih-sah-nah]* "We get along": a name such as given by the named child's paternal grandmother to express to her daughter-in-law (*makoti*) that though she did not approve of her before, since the *makoti* bore a son, the relationship has improved [*Zulu*] (Suzman 1994: 259).

Lungu (m) *[uh-luhn-guuh]* Joint of finger [*Zulu*] (Koopman 1990: 336).

Lunguse/ Lunguuse (f) *[luhn-guuh-seh]* (A body part) that has become bruised and swollen [*Ganda*].

Lunia (f/m) *[luh-nih-yah]* "At the killing": a name such as given to one whose mother is alleged to be a sorceress and in the process caused the death of a woman [*Lugbara*] (Middleton 1961: 36).

Lunja (m) *[luhn-jah]* That has been moved aside (or has veered, or has swerved, or has deviated) [*Ganda*].

Lunjaabwa (m) *[luhn-jaah-bwah]* That is diluted (or watered down); that has been caused to lose meaning [*Ganda*].

Lunkuse (f) *[luhn-kuh-seh]* Impoverished [*Ganda*].

Lunnamunnyu (m) *[luhn-nah-muhn-ndjh-uh]* A species of large plantain [*Ganda*].

Lunnyo (m) *[luhn-ndjh-oh]* Long tooth; drying rack (such as for coffee or cotton); stretcher; bier; a stretch of barren soil [*Ganda*].

Lunyago (m) *[luh-ndjh-ah-goh]* Shaft of a spear [*Ganda*].

Lusaaka (m) *[luh-saah-kah]* The beating (of barkcloth in the first stage of its processing); the mallet used in the beating (of barkcloth in the first stage of its processing) [*Ganda*].

Lusajjalubi (m) *[luh-sahj-jah-luh-bih]*/ *Lusajjarubi* (m) *[luh-sahj-jah-ruh -bih]* A man who is bad (or evil, or dangerous, or ugly, or in bad shape) [*Ganda*].

Lusambya (m) *[luh-sahm-bjah]* A species of yellow flowered hardwood tree [*Ganda*].

Lusati (f/m) *[luh-sah-tih]* "Stalk of maize": a name given to a child born after the father died [*Ovimbundu*] (Ennis 1945: 2).

Lusekera (m) *[luh-seh-keh-rah]* That laughs at; that smiles at [*Ganda*].

Lusembo (m) *[luh-sehm-boh]* The last; the final; that is at the end; that supports (or backs up, or recommends, or is in favor of) [*Ganda*].

Lushaba (m) *[luh-tsh-ah-bah]* Ferocious temper; fidgety person [*Zulu*] (Koopman 1990: 336).

Lusiba (m) *[luh-sih-bah]* That ties (or imprisons, or binds, or fastens, or locks, or preserves, or reserves, or packs up, or bolts, or bars) [The *Ganda*].

Lusinga (m) *[luh-sihn-gah]* That excels (surpasses, or exceeds); excellence; a pledge (or bet, or vow); that of the *Basinga* clan [*Ganda*].

Lusiola (m) *[luh-sjoh-lah]* A name given to one born under the tree species *lusiola* also known as the *Nandi* flame [*Luyia*].

Lusoboya (m) *[luh-soh-boh-yah]* That moves slowly (or carefully) [The *Ganda*].

Lusoke (m) *[luh-soh-keh]* That is filled in with (or inserted in with) [The *Ganda*].

Lusolo (m) *[luh-soh-loh]* Body rash; animal (in a piteous or emaciated state) [*Ganda*].

Lusuku (f/m) *[luh-suh-kuh]* Plantain/ banana garden (or plantation); this name is sometimes associated with the proverb "the beautiful (or the good) are like fresh banana leaves: new ones always sprout out and never cease to exist in the banana plantation" implying that there will always be beautiful people, and that however ugly or bad the circumstances get, there are elements of beauty and good that always emerge [*Ganda*].

Lusula (m) *[luh-suh-lah]* That spends the night; that sleeps; that stays; that dwells [*Ganda*].

Lusundo (m) *[luh-suhn-doh]* An agitation; a churn up; a shaking; a worry; a pump up; a toss about; a ramble about [*Ganda*].

Luswa (m) *[luh-swaah]* Termite hill; the termite; the white ant; like a termite i.e. naked; authentic; pure; genuine [*Ganda*].

Luswabi (m) *[luh-swaah-bih]* That makes scarce (or insufficient) [The *Ganda*].

Luswata (m) *[luh-swaah-tah]* Burning; hurting; itching [*Ganda*].

Lutabi (m) *[luh-tah-bih]* Unity; mixture; joining together [*Ganda*].

Lutakoma (m) *[luh-tah-koh-mah]* That is endless (or infinite, or ceaseless) [*Ganda*].

Lutakome/ Lutaakome (m) *[luh-taah-koh-meh]* That will go on endlessly (or infinitely, or without stopping, or ceaselessly, or all the time) [*Ganda*].

Lutalo (m) *[luh-tah-loh]* Battle; war; that involves ranging or lining one-self up for battle; that involves steadying oneself for combat (or for a dangerous venture); that involves charging (or attacking) [*Ganda*].

Lutaya/ Lutaaya (m) *[luh-taah-yah]* That travels (or roams) around without restricting himself; that is preoccupied; that circumcises; that urges; that prevails on; that pesters [*Ganda*].

Lutazigwa (m) *[luh-tah-zih-gwah]* That is not easily tracked down (or hunted down, or scouted out, or spied on) [*Ganda*].

Luteete (m) *[luh-teh-eh-teh]* A net trap made of grass [*Ganda*].

Lutembe (f/m) *[luh-tehm-beh]* A necklace made from the seeds of a wild banana plant [*Ganda, Soga*].

Lutemye (m) *[luh-teh-mjeh]* That has cut (or chopped) [*Ganda, Soga*].

Lutereke (f) *[luh-teh-reh-keh]* Package; parcel; that is put aside (or reserved, or stored) [*Ganda, Soga*].

Luthuli (m) *[luh-sth-uh-lih]* Dust [*Zulu*] (Koopman 1990: 334, 336).

Lutiba (m) *[luh-tih-bah]* A wooden bowl; a round and flat papyrus basket; mold (for bricks) [*Ganda*].

Lutonnya (m) *[luh-tohn-ndjh-ah]* That involves raining (or coming do-wn, or dripping, or leaking) [*Ganda*].

Luttamaguzi (m) *[luht-tah-mah-guh-zih]* "It kills (or destroys) trading"; "it kills (or destroys) merchandise" [*Ganda*].

Lutuulu (m) *[luh-tuuh-luh]* That is associated with madness (or fero-city, or sullenness, or stubbornness); that is associated with middle age [*Ganda*].

Lutwama (m) *[luh-twaah-mah]* That greets (us); that welcomes (us)/ or receives (us) gladly/ or greets (us) enthusiastically [*Ganda*].

Luutu (m) *[luuh-tuh]* Large amount; large mass; that pursues vigorous-ly; that beats a drum; that becomes greedy [*Ganda*].

Luvamubaima (f) *[luh-vah-muh-bah-yih-maah]* That comes from am-ongst (or is associated with) the *Hima* people [*Ganda*].

Luvannyuma (f) *[luh-vahn-ndjh-uh-mah]* Afterwards; later; after [The *Ganda*].

Luvule (m) *[luh-vuh-leh]* Iroko, a species of timber tree, the wood of which highly resists termite attack and is often employed as a sub-stitute for teak [*Ganda*].

Luvuuma (m) *[luh-vuuh-mah]* That makes a rumbling sound; that hiss-es/ or whizzes; immature (plantain) [*Ganda*].

Luwaca (m) *[luh-wah-tch-ah]* That is pleasingly spread out [The *Zulu*] (Koopman 1990: 336).

Luwaga (m) *[luh-wah-gah]* A name-title of the king; one who supports (or backs up, or encourages); staunch supporter; prop post [*Ganda*].

Luwalana (m) *[luh-wah-lah-nah]* That feuds or dislikes with hostility [*Ganda*].

Luwalira (m) *[luh-wah-lih-rah]* That moves reluctantly (or hangs back, or drags one's feet, or resists, or refuses) [*Ganda*].

Luwandagga (m) *[luh-wahn-dahg-gah]* Wanderer; drizzle of rain [The *Ganda*].

Luwangiza (m) *[luh-wahn-gih-zah]* That fits in/ or sets upright (such as construction poles) [*Ganda*].

Luwangula (m) *[luh-wahn-guh-lah]* The conqueror; that defeats (or conquers, or becomes victorious over, or wins over); that overcomes difficulties; name-title of a king; name-title designation of a great chief; designation of a major calamity such as a famine or epidemic [*Ganda*].

Luwawu (m) *[luh-wah-wuh]* Rough leaf of a tree species that is used as sandpaper: a name commonly given to a tough person [*Ganda*].

Luwayo (m) *[luh-wah-yoh]* A conversation; a chat; a talk [The *Ganda*, *Soga*].

Luwedde (f/m) *[luh-wehd-deh]* "It is over"; completed; complete; that is finished; that is exhausted/ or worn out [*Ganda*].

Luweero (m) *[luh-weh-eh-roh]* A truce; a cessation of hostilities; a piece of mind; a relaxation; a calming down [*Ganda*].

Luweekula (m) *[luh-weh-eh-kuh-lah]* The taking from off the back (of children being carried on there); an unloading; a depriving of [The *Ganda*].

Luwemba (m) *[luh-wehm-bah]* Red cloth; a spread; that covers up (or over) [*Ganda*].

Luwemberedde (m) *[luh-wehm-beh-rehd-deh]* That is covering (it or them) up/ or over [*Ganda*].

Luwemberera (m) *[luh-wehm-beh-reh-rah]* That covers up (or over) [*Ganda*].

Luwenda (m) *[luh-wehn-dah]* Path; border strip between two pieces of land; way; means; method; plan; opportunity; that involves flattering (or inciting); stern (or the rear end) of a ship or boat [*Ganda*].

Luwerekera (m) *[luh-weh-reh-keh-rah]* That accompanies (or escorts, or sees off); that goes along with as a companion or an associate; that accompanies part of the way [*Ganda*, *Soga*].

Luwero (m) *[luh-weh-roh]* Top board of a canoe.

Luwondera (m) *[luh-wohn-deh-rah]* A pursuit; following after; following; that pursues (or follows, or follows after) [*Ganda*].

Luwooma (f/m) *[luh-woh-oh-mah]* "It is pleasant (or nice, or attractive)" [*Ganda*, *Soga*].

Luwugge (m) *[luh-wuhg-geh]* Sawdust; a thin and dusty substance; ashy substance that forms on young plantain leaves [*Ganda*].

Luwuliza (m) *[luh-wuh-lih-zah]* That causes to hear (or make listen); that causes to feel (or sense, or perceive); that makes obey; that hears news of [*Ganda*, *Soga*].

Luwungwe (m) *[luh-wuhn-gweh]* A hurriedness; a briefness [*Ganda*].

Luwuukya (m) *[luh-wuuh-tch-ah]* That chokes with rage; that swells; that eats compulsively; that eats all the time [*Ganda*].

Luwuuzambugo (m) *[luh-wuuh-zahm-buh-goh]* The beating (or the beater) in the processing of barkcloth/ or barkcloth clothing [*Ganda*].

Luwuzambugo (m) *[luh-wuh-zahm-buh-goh]* That causes to have an aversion to barkcloth (or barkcloth clothing) [*Ganda*].

Luyana (f) *[luh-yah-nah]* A cry; a cry of mourning; calf; heifer [The *Ganda*].

Luyege (m) *[luh-yeh-geh]* That is held up (or propped, or supported) [*Ganda*].

Luyenje (m) *[luh-yehn-jeh]* The cockroach; that moves about aimlessly (or roams around, or floats about, or totters); that is weak (or exhausted, or tired) [*Ganda*].

Luyiga/ Luiga (f) *[luh-yih-gah]* A learner; neophyte; the mode of learning [*Ganda*].

Luyiika (m) *[luh-yiih-kah]* That involves pouring out (or being poured out, or spilling, or overflowing, or falling down, or collapsing); that involves the pouring out in a group (of people); that involves the failing (or the coming to naught) of a plan [*Ganda*].

Luyima (m) *[luh-yih-maah]* Of the aristocratic cattle keeping people, the *Hima*; that stands up; that is situated [*Ganda*].

Luyimbazi/ Luyimbaazi (m) *[luh-yihm-baah-zih]* That causes (the eyes) to grow dim with age; that causes to be blinded; that combines (or ties together, or joins together); that does in addition to; singer [*Ganda*].

Luyinda (m) *[luh-yihn-dah]* (The weather) that is menacing or threatening [*Ganda*].

Luyogera (m) *[luh-yoh-geh-rah]* That speaks (or talks, or says) [The *Ganda*, *Soga*].

Luyombo (m) *[luh-yohm-boh]* A grouping of indiscriminately gathered up items; quarrel; strife; contention [*Ganda*, *Soga*].

Luyombya (m) *[luh-yohm-bjaah]* One who (or that which) incites people into quarreling (or into losing their tempers) [*Ganda*].

Luyonga (m) *[luh-yohn-gah]* Burnt out remains of food; sparks from a fire [*Ganda*].

Luyuzambugo (m) *[luh-yuh-zahm-buh-goh]* "The one who (or that which) tears up barkcloth" [*Ganda*, *Soga*].

Luzige (m) *[luh-zih-geh]* Locust; that is applied cosmetics to; that is darkened; that is tracked down (or hunted down, or scouted out, or spied on) [*Ganda*].

Luzinda (m) *[luh-zihn-dah]* That raids (or invades, or attacks); that involves raiding (or attacking, or invading); species of tall forest tree [*Ganda*].

Luzinga (m) *[luh-zihn-gah]* That folds, wraps up, or surrounds [*Ganda*, *Soga*].

Luzingo (m) *[luh-zihn-goh]* A roll; a scroll; a volume (of a book); a wrapping up; that is folded up; that is coiled; that is surrounded around [*Ganda, Soga*].

Luzira (m) *[luh-zih-rah]* Unit of measurement of approximately one meter that is used by herdsmen; that involves heroism (or bravery); that involves taboo (or abhorrence, or scorning) [*Ganda*].

Luzuyo (f/m) *[luh-zuh-yoh]* "No telling": a name such as given to one whose mother was visited by her parents whose intent to come she had not been told, and on their arrival she was not present to welcome them and to cook and serve them food (which is a serious breach of kinship etiquette) [*Lugbara*] (Middleton 1961: 36).

Luzze (m) *[luhz-zeh]* A return; a resurgence; "it has come back (or gone back, or returned)" [*Ganda*].

Luzzi (m) *[luhz-zih]* Water well; river; large stream [*Ganda*].

Lwabidongo (m) *[lwah-bih-dohn-goh]* "Because of (or by reason of, or on account of) guitars (or banjos/ or stringed instruments)" [*Ganda*].

Lwabiriza (m) *[lwah-bih-rih-zah]* That of which causes to weep (or mourn); that of what is caused to play around; that of what is caused to walk at a fast pace; that of which is caused to roll over and over (on the ground); that of which is hurled [*Ganda, Soga*].

Lwabulanga (m) *[lwah-buh-lahn-gah]* That of the upright (or the vertically placed); that of (or because of) the mouth organ/ the harmonica; that of (or because) of the small insects found on corn cobs; that used to disappear (or become lost, or go astray, or become lacking, or become missing) [*Ganda*].

Lwabutatendwa (f) *[lwah-buh-tah-tehn-dwah]* On account of (or because of) not being praised; a need for praise; a time of not praising [*Ganda*].

Lwaga (m) *[lwah-gah]* One who fits in/ installs/ loads (such as bullets in a gun) [*Ganda*].

Lwajuuka (f) *[lwah-juuh-kah]* One who booms (or gets enraged, or gets harsh in tone); that involves enragement; a time of enragement [*Ganda*].

Lwakabeete (m) *[lwah-kah-beh-eh-teh]* That of viciousness; that of what has been laid down carelessly [*Ganda*].

Lwakanya (m) *[lwah-kah-ndjh-ah]* That of an abundance (or an increase); that of amassment [*Ganda*].

Lwakirenzi (m) *[lwah-tch-ih-rehn-zih]* That of boyishness (or boys) [*Ganda, Soga*].

Lwakkalaaza (m) *[lwahk-kah-laah-zah]* That of anger (or irritation, or irascibility) [*Ganda*].

-M-

Maadhi (m) *[maah-dhih]* Water [*Soga*].

Maalo (m) *[maah-loh]* Smearings; smearings on; plasterings on; that of villages (or large estates, or the rural countryside) [*Ganda*].

Maanyi (m) *[maah-ndjh-iih]* Strength; power; energy; this name is sometimes associated with the proverb "men are (like) wild animals: when you pursuingly follow into the bush after one, he breaks through the thicket with tremendous force"; this name is also sometimes associated with the proverb "those that block (or close off) the path must be very powerful, just as are those that open up the path" which refers to pioneers, revolutionaries, stubborn persons, and decisive persons [*Ganda*].

Maato (m) *[maah-toh]* Boats; canoes; steamers; ships; brewing vats [*Ganda*].

Mabale (m) *[mah-bah-leh]* That are few; that are easily counted [The *Soga*].

Mabanga (f/m) *[mah-bahn-gah]* (Empty) spaces; blanks [The *Ganda, Soga*].

Mabele (m) *[mah-beh-leh]* A name given to one born during a period of cattle milk abundance [*Luyia*].

Mabikke (m) *[mah-bihk-keh]* That are covered up (or closed, or covered) [*Ganda*].

Mabinda (f) *[mah-bihn-dah]* A ritual related name traditionally conferred upon the child following its initiation [*Kongo*] (Ndoma 1977: 90).

Mabingo (m) *[mah-bihn-goh]* The acts involving chasing (or driving away) [*Ganda, Soga*].

Mabira (m) *[mah-bih-rah]* Forested [*Ganda, Soga*].

Mabiriizi (m) *[mah-bih-riih-zih]* (With a peculiarity of) the ribs; the sides of the body [*Ganda*].

Mabizi (m) *[mah-bih-zih]* That cause (food) to be warmed over; that cause to be warmed up [*Ganda*].

Mabodla (m) *[mah-bohd-lah]* The one (supposedly) able to divide the sea with a rod [*Zulu*] (Lugg 1968: 13).

Maborikhoe (f) *[mah-boh-rih-koh-yeh]* The mother associated with trousers: a name such as given to one who got wedded to a man who was the first in the family to wear trousers instead of the traditional loin while being wed [*Sotho*] (Ashton 1952: 32).

Mabumba (m) *[mah-buhm-bah]* The process of molding (clay) [The *Ganda*].

Mabunduggu (m) *[mah-buhn-duhg-guh]* Emptyings out; pourings out (or down) in large quantities; spillings [*Ganda*].

Mabuqwini (m) *[mah-buh-kwih-nih]* "In loose soil" [*Zulu*] (Koopman 1979: 71).

Mabuzi (m) *[mah-buh-zih]* The acts of a goat [*Ganda*].

Mabwa (m) *[mah-bwah]* Wounds; the acts of a dog [*Gisu, Soga*].

Mabwazara (f/m) *[mah-bwah-zah-rah]* "The caves are all full": a name given to a child born into a family that has so lost many of its members to death, which situation makes it look like the caves where they are buried are full [*Shona*] (Jackson 1957: 118).

Mabwibwi (f/m) *[mah-bwih-bwih]* A name given to one born early in the morning [*Luyia*].

Machaka (m) *[mah-tch-ah-kah]* A name given to one born in a bushy area [*Luyia*].

Macharia (m) *[mah-tch-ah-rih-yah]* Those who seek [*Embu*].

Machingura (f/m) *[mah-tch-ihn-guh-rah]* To look for a wife: a name such as given to one born during a time the father was out looking for an additional woman to marry [*Shona*] (Jackson 1067: 119).

Madongo (m) *[mah-dohn-goh]* That involves stringed instruments (or guitars, or banjos, or harps, or harp players, or musicians) [*Ganda*].

Madungu (m) *[mah-duhn-guuh]* Deserts; wastelands; wilderness areas; ulcer of the outer ear [*Ganda*].

Maduudu (m) *[mah-duuh-duh]* The datura plant [*Ganda*].

Maende (f/m) *[mah-yehn-deh]* A name given to one afflicted by jiggers during childhood [*Luyia*].

Mafumiro (m) *[mah-fuh-mih-roh]* That involve the telling/ or recounting of (such as legends, traditions, fables, or tales); that involve fading (or the losing of color, or becoming tarnished); that involve fading (of memories)/ or becoming rusty (in knowledge or skills); that involve falling into disrepute [*Ganda*].

Mafutabirye (m) *[mah-fuh-taah-bih-rjeh]* Ointment; grease; oil [The *Ganda*].

Magaga (m) *[mah-gah-gah]* One who feeds another [*Luo*].

Magak (f/m) *[mah-gah-tk]* Zebra [*Luo*].

Magala (m) *[mah-gah-lah]* To shout; become bewildered; get into a frenzy; revolt; to become listless or inattentive [*Ganda*].

Magambe (m) *[mah-gahm-beh]* That has been told (or reported, or said) [*Ganda*].

Maganda (m) *[mah-gahn-dah]* Peculiarities of the *Ganda* ethnics [The *Ganda*].

Maganga (m) *[mah-gaahn-gah]* Processes in treating a sickness [The *Ganda*].

Maganyi (m) *[mah-gah-ndjh-ih]* Authorization; permission [*Ganda*].

Magatto (m) *[mah-gaht-toh]* An adding; a joining; a combining; a uniting; a unifying; a putting together; shoes; boots; sandals [*Ganda*].

Magaya (f/m) *[mah-gah-yah]* Difficulties/ or endurances: a name such as given to one who has experienced several misfortunes/ or one whose birth involved discomforting labor/ or one born to an ill mother [*Kaguru*] (Beidelman 1974: 288, 289).

Magaya (m) *[mah-gah-yah]* That involve scorning (or despising, or having contempt for) [*Ganda*].

Magembe (m) *[mah-gehm-beh]* Lies; that is associated with traps for large animals [*Ganda*].

Magemeso (m) *[mah-geh-meh-soh]* That enable to catch; that cause to be immunized (or inoculated); that cause to forestall (or avert, or ward off) [*Soga*].

Magera (m) *[mah-geh-rah]* A mashed food combination of beans (or bean soup, or bean sauce); that are precise (or measured, or definite); recounted (stories, proverbs, or parables) [*Soga*].

Magero (m) *[mah-geh-roh]* Miracles; wonders; marvels: a name commonly given to one born with visible teeth in the mouth, with more or fewer fingers than normal, or some other atypical feature/ or to a first born of a woman of a relatively advanced age [*Ganda*].

Magero (m) *[mah-geh-roh]* One who builds [*Luo*].

Mageza (m) *[mah-geh-zah]* Trials and tribulations; tryings [*Ganda*].

Magezi (m) *[mah-geh-ziih]* Braininess; wisdom; knowledge; judiciousness; this name is sometimes associated with the proverb "with old age comes wisdom, but the elderly will not tell you what contributed to their longevity" i.e. because there are contributing factors that are inexplicable, or will not be told (such as out of shyness or fear of being laughed at) [*Ganda*].

Magimbi (m) *[mah-jihm-bih]* Sharp and hairy projection on elephant grass (or on sugar cane foliage, or on a caterpillar) [*Ganda, Soga*].

Magino (m) *[mah-gih-noh]* Pampering; the giving of excessive freedom to; spoiling [*Ganda, Soga*].

Magoba (m) *[mah-goh-bah]* Profits; interest; arrivals; landings; reachings ashore; drivings away; dismissals; chasings; victories; seekings; this name is sometimes associated with the proverb "small boats still sink at the very end of the journey when landing" implying that caution other than overconfidence ought to always be exercised since one is still prone to failure or disaster even after one has seemingly overcome all the difficulties and achieved success [*Ganda*].

Magogo (m) *[mah-goh-goh]* Vomiting; retch.

Magu/ Mmagu (m) *[mmah-guh]* Craziness; devilishness (such as that of children); with a distracted look; with a tendency towards distraction; restlessness; that looks around suddenly [*Ganda*].

Magulunnyondo (m) *[mah-guh-luhn-ndjh-ohn-doh]* Hammer-like legs: a name such as given to a person with muscular/ or powerful/ or large legs; a name-title of the king [*Ganda*].

Magunda (m) *[mah-guhn-dah]* Stabbings; throwings down that involve violence; hurlings down; dashings down [*Ganda*].

Magwanya/ Magwaanya (m) *[mah-gwaah-ndjh-ah]* That are suitable (or fitting) [*Ganda*].

Magwenzi (f/m) *[mah-gwehn-zih]* Small bushes: a name such as given to one conceived in a bush, or born out of wedlock or as a result of infidelity [*Shona*] (Jackson 1957: 120).

Mahlomola (m) *[mah-loh-moh-lah]* Grief: a name such as given to one whose birth coincides with a period of mourning/ or coincides with a calamity [*Sotho*] (Mohome 1972: 175).

Mahungo (m) *[mah-huhn-goh]* "Therapies": a name such as given to one whose birth is presumably through the vehicle of magical medicaments that the mother in the attempt to conceive, was treated with [*Kaguru*] (Beidelman 1974: 289).

Maido (m) *[mahy-doh]* Groundnuts; peanuts [*Soga*].

Mainga (f/m) *[mah-yihn-gah]* A name given to one born to a mother who often grumbled and argued during the pregnancy [*Luyia*].

Maingano (m) *[mah-yihn-gah-noh]* A name given to a very argumentative boy [*Luyia*].

Maitha (f) *[mahy-sth-ah]* The one of the enemy [*Embu*].

Majala (m) *[mah-jah-lah]* Magnificence; showiness; making a display [*Ganda*].

Majanja (m) *[mah-jahn-jah]* Insolence; effrontery; aggressiveness; nosiness [*Ganda*].

Majecha (f) *[mah-jeh-tch-ah]* Sands: a name such as given to a child born into a family that is victim to high infant mortality, given that dead infants are traditionally buried in the sand near a river [*Zezuru*] (Marapara 1954: 8).

Majolo (m) *[mah-joh-loh]* Bee eater [*Ganda*].

Majuma (f) *[mah-juh-mah]* A name given to one born on Friday [*Luyia*].

Majuru (m) *[mah-juh-ruh]* White ants: a name such as given to one born into a family in which the children often die young i.e. they "are soon eaten by white ants" [*Zezuru*] (Marapara 1954: 7).

Majuta (m) *[mah-juh-tah]* "Disappointments": a name such as given to one born during times of trouble [*Kaguru*] (Beidelman 1974: 288).

Majwajwa (m) *[mah-jwah-jwah]* Clown; joker; jester [*Ganda*].

Majwala (m) *[mah-jwah-lah]* That involve being adorned; that involve being well dressed [*Ganda*].

Majwenge (m) *[mah-jwehn-geh]* Fringes; manes; long hair [*Ganda*].

Maka (m) *[mah-kah]* Home; household; house [*Ganda*].

Makaanzu (m) *[mah-kaahn-zuh]* "(The one who holds the lion [i.e. *nkosi*] by his) feet": a name given to the younger of twin boys, the older named *Nkosi* [*Kongo*] (Daeleman 1977: 191); "(the one who holds the lion [i.e. *khosi*] by his) feet": a name given to the younger of twin boys, the older named *Khosi* [*Yaka*] (Daeleman 1977: 191); a name given to a triplet [*Yaka*] (Daeleman 1977: 192).

Makaatu (m) *[mah-kaah-tuh]* Gone sour [*Ganda*].

Makaayi (m) *[mah-kaah-yih]* That is associated with pieces of gourds used as scoops; bitterness; protestation; disputation; that is (or causes to be) bitter (or sour, or unpleasant to the taste); that is (or causes to be) enraged (or quarrelsome); a situation that has become (or is caused to become) serious/ or bad [*Ganda*].

Makala (m) *[mah-kah-lah]* Charcoal; that involve becoming dry (or drying up, or withering, or wasting away, or stiffening, or growing rigid); that involve becoming well established (or becoming firm, or becoming resolute, or standing up for oneself) [*Ganda*].

Makalo (m) *[mah-kah-loh]* Wondering: a name such as given to one whose birth coincides with happenings that are perplexing [*Sotho*] (Mohome 1972: 175).

Makanaga (m) *[mah-kah-nah-gah]* That are associated with a hardwood species of thorny tree; that are associated with a tree species whose wood is frequently converted into mallets, pestles, and poles [*Ganda*].

Makanga (m) *[mah-kahn-gah]* That frighten (or startle, or threaten); that are gripping (or terrible, or violent); punishments; chastisements; disciplinary actions; corrections; dealings of harshness with [*Ganda*].

Makanhu (m) *[mah-kah-nuh]* A name given to one born during the sesame planting season [*Luyia*].

Makayagga (m) *[mah-kah-yahg-gah]* Acts of devouring; instances that are overwhelming [*Ganda*].

Makayu (m) *[mah-kah-yuh]* Ill temper; bad disposition; sourness.

Makechemu (m) *[mah-keh-tch-eh-muh]* Manacles: a name such as given to a child likely born soon after the arrest of his father on some charge and who was then tied up to prevent him from escaping [The *Zezuru*] (Marapara 1954: 8).

Makerere (f) *[mah-keh-eh-reh-reh]* Lateness; the first things done in the morning (after having gone to bed with the intention of doing them) [*Ganda*].

Makesa (f) *[mah-keh-sah]* Harvesting; cutting down for harvest [The *Ganda, Soga*].

Makgokolotso (f) *[mah-kah-goh-koh-loht-soh]* "Collected/ gathered things": a name such as given to a child born out of wedlock/ or one born of an infidel mother (or wife) [*Sotho*] (Mohome 1972: 177).

Makhese (m) *[mah-keh-eh-seh]* A name given to one born in a sheep pen; a name given to a boy who loves herding sheep [*Luyia*].

Makhokolotsa (f) *[mah-koh-koh-loh-tsah]* Rubbish: an unpleasant name given to one whose previous born sibling was stillborn or died before weaning, this attributed to sorcery--this name is a means to safeguard the named "by making a show of neglecting it in the hope of lulling the sorcerer's vigilance" [*Sotho*] (Ashton 1952: 33).

Makhosazana (f) *[mah-koh-sah-zah-nah]* "Young ladies" [The *Zulu*] (Koopman 1979: 154).

Makhosonke (m) *[mah-koh-sohn-keh]* "All chiefs"; "chiefs: all of them" [*Zulu*] (Koopman 1979: 157).

Makiino (m) *[mah-chee-noh]* Sarcasm; sneers; tauntings [The *Ganda, Soga*].

Makindu (m) *[mah-kihn-doo]* Stitches [*Ganda*].

Makoe (m) *[mah-koh-yeh]* A name given to one whose mother has a fondness for *makoe* vegetables; a name given to one born in a field with *makoe* plants [*Luyia*].

Makokha (f/m) *[mah-koh-kah]* A name given to one born in a locale in which several children have died at infancy [*Luyia*].

Makona (m) *[mah-koh-nah]* A name given to a lazy one who sleeps so excessively that he is said to be able to eat while sleeping [*Luyia*].

Makonzi (m) *[mah-kohn-zih]* Physical stuntedness; that involve being unprogressive; emaciation [*Ganda*].

Makooba (m) *[mah-koh-oh-bah]* Ending; coming in last [*Ganda*].

Makoosi (m) *[mah-koh-oh-sih]* Courses of study (as adapted from the European word "courses") [*Ganda*].

Makozi (m) *[mah-koh-zih]* Industriousness; involving hard work [The *Ganda*].

Makubuya (m) *[mah-kuh-buh-yah]* Acts of silliness (or stupidity) [The *Ganda*].

Makula (m) *[mah-kuh-lah]* Food presented to the king; something magnificent or wondrous; a gorgeous looking man; "(good) growth" [The *Ganda*].

Makumba (m) *[mah-kuhm-bah]* Marches; struttings around; swaggerings [*Ganda*].

Makumbi (m) *[mah-kuuhm-bih]* One that likes to show off; one that marches or struts about; elephant snout fishes [*Ganda*].

Makya (m) *[mah-tch-aah]* Early morning; dawning (of day); letting up (of rain); ending (of famine) [*Ganda*].

Male (m) *[mah-leh]* Clouds; that sings well or is associated with (*malenge* which are) small wind instruments (or reed pipes) of bamboo [*Ganda*].

Malefu (f) *[maah-leh-fuh]* "The mother associated with death": a name given to one born at a time a relation dies [*Sotho*] (Thipa 1986: 290).

Malege (m) *[mah-leh-geh]* Tested; tried [*Ganda*].

Malehlwa (f) *[maah-leh-lwah]* "The mother associated with snow": a name given to one born during snow conditions [*Sotho*] (Thipa 1986: 289).

Malembe (m) *[mah-lehm-beh]* That involve strolls (or leisurely walks); that involve peace (or periods of peace, or times of safety); that are associated with the era (or period) [*Ganda*].

Malembo (m) *[mah-lehm-boh]* Strolls; leisurely walks [*Ganda*].

Malenge (m) *[mah-lehn-geh]* Measured; apportioned; well cut; small wind instruments (or reed pipes) of bamboo [*Ganda*].

Malerole (f) *[maah-leh-roh-leh]* "The mother associated with a big drought" [*Sotho*] (Thipa 1986: 288).

Malevu (m) *[mah-leh-vuh]* One with an abundance of beards [*Ganda, Soga*].

Malinzi (m) *[mah-lihn-zih]* That involves causing to wait (or to guard); that involves guarding with (or by means of); that involves opportunists (or hangers on) [*Ganda, Soga*].

Maliwa (m) *[mah-lih-wah]* Payments for damages; reparations; compensations [*Ganda, Soga*].

Maloine (m) *[mah-lohy-neh]* "I cannot go there"; "I will not go there" [*Maasai*].

Maluge (m) *[mah-luh-geh]* The crown of the head (having hair while the rest of the head is shaven) [*Ganda*].

Malumba (m) *[mah-luhm-bah]* Attacks; verbal assaults; routings [The *Ganda*].

Malunda (m) *[mah-luhn-dah]* Herding; tending; followings around [The *Ganda*].

Malungu (m) *[mah-luhn-guh]* Wildernesses; wastelands; deserts; that are associated with *Ddungu* the God linked to hunters and animals [*Ganda*].

Malyakungabo (m) *[mah-ljah-kuuhn-gah-boh]* "The profits that accrue from the shield"; "the gains from fighting/ or raiding" [*Ganda*].

Malyante (f) *[mah-ljaahn-teh]* That involve eating (or consuming cattle) [*Ganda*].

Mamaropene (f) *[mah-mah-roh-peh-neh]* A name given to one who becomes betrothed when many in her in-law family are no longer alive [*Tlokwa-Sotho*] (Kruger 1937: 107).

Mamello (f/m) *[mah-mehl-loh]* Perseverance: a name such as given to a child born during times of hardship/ or name given to a first-born whose father struggled hard to win over the love of the mother [The *Sotho*] (Mohome 1972: 176).

Mamisha (m) *[mah-mih-tsh-ah]* A collection of villages [The *Zulu*] (Koopman 1979: 69).

Mamoribula (f) *[mah-moh-rih-buh-lah]* "The one who came to uncover (the home of her older sister): a name given to one who gets married where her older sister who died was married [*Tlokwa-Sotho*] (Kruger 1937: 107).

Manata (f/m) *[mah-naah-tah/ mah-naah-taah]* "The carrier (of the twins)": a name given to one whose birth precedes that of his or her twin siblings [*Yaka*] (Daeleman 1977: 193).

Mandazi (m) *[mahn-daah-zih]* A snack mixture of wheat flour, baking soda, and sugar that is fried in small portions [*Ganda*].

Mandisa (m) *[mahn-dih-sah]* "Increase" [*Zulu*] (Suzman 1994: 268).

Mandla (m) *[mahn-dlah]* "(He has) strength"; the name can also be an abbreviation of *Mandlenkosi*: "Strength of the Lord" [*Zulu*] (Koopman 1979: 154, 163).

Mandlakapheli (m) *[mahn-dlah-kah-peh-lih]* "Strength never finishes" [*Zulu*] (Koopman 1979: 78).

Mandlakhe (m) *[uh-mahn-dlah-keh]* "His power": name such as given to a child whose father is proud of his power to have a son [The *Zulu*] (Suzman 1994: 258).

Mandlenkosi (m) *[mahnd-lehn-koh-sih]* "Strength of the Lord" [*Zulu*]

(Koopman 1979: 156, 163).

Mangaala (m) *[maahn-gaah-lah]* In open spaces (or openings, or open areas, or emptiness) [*Ganda*].

Mangosuthu (m) *[mahn-goh-suh-tuh]* "Lies of the *Suthu* faction"; "he stands through the *Suthu* faction" [*Zulu*] (Koopman 1979: 157, 161).

Mankankanana (m) *[mahn-kahn-kah-nah-nah]* "One who speaks through his nose" [*Zulu*] (Lugg 1968: 14).

Mankenda (f/m) *[mahn-kehn-dah]* Sadness [*Kongo*] (Ndoma 1977: 96).

Mankumba (m) *[mahn-kuhm-bah]* Infertility/ or barrenness (of the soil) [*Ganda*].

Mannyangalya (m) *[mahn-ndjh-ahn-gah-ljah]* "I take on (or acquire) names"; "I take on (or acquire) a reputation" [*Ganda*].

Mannyowennu (m) *[mahn-ndjh-oh-weh-nuh]* (That with) strong jaws [*Ganda*].

Manqoba (m) *[mahn-kwoh-bah]* "Overcome": a name such as given to signify that this named child's father was badly injured, but he subsequently recovered and all his enemies died [*Zulu*] (Suzman 1994: 269).

Mantombi (f) *[mahn-tohm-bih]* "Girl" [*Zulu*] (Koopman 1979: 155).

Mantotole (f) *[mahn-toh-toh-leh]* One whose parents in law are not involved in her marriage arrangement (as would be the traditional method) so that her marriage is regarded as insecure and vulnerable [*Tlokwa-Sotho*] (Kruger 1937: 107).

Mantwa (m) *[mahn-twah]* War [*Sotho*] (Thipa 1986: 288).

Manyiginya (m) *[mah-ndjh-ih-gih-ndjh-ah]* Phantoms: a name such as given to a child that is ugly or deformed [*Zezuru*] (Marapara 1954: 8).

Manywanto (m) *[mah-ndjh-wahn-toh]* The teats; nipple of a bottle; pacifier [*Ganda*].

Manzekhofi (m) *[mahn-zeh-koh-fee]* "The (hot) water for the coffee" [*Zulu*] (Lugg 1968: 14).

Mapaseka (f) *[mah-pah-seh-kah]* "The mother associated with Passover/ Easter": a name given to one born during Passover or Easter [*Sotho*] (Thipa 1986: 289).

Mapera/ Mapeera (m) *[mah-peh-eh-rah]* Guavas [*Ganda*].

Mapesa (m) *[mah-peh-sah]* "Moneys": a name given to one with a fondness for money [*Luyia*].

Mapfumo (m) *[mahp-fuh-moh]* Spears: name such as given to a child born shortly after his parents were involved in an assault [*Zezuru*] (Marapara 1954: 8).

Mapuseletso (f) *[maah-puh-seh-leh-tsoh]* The mother associated with reward (or compensation): a name given to one who has lost two or more preceding siblings to death, the name implying that this child serves as welcome restitution, by the action of God or the ancestors, for the deceased [*Sotho*] (Thipa 1986: 290).

Mara (f) *[mah-rah]* One who has experienced rough times i.e. "the one the Almighty has dealt bitterly with" [*Ovimbundu*] (Ennis 1945: 5).

Marambu (f/m) *[mah-rahm-buh]* Bones: a name such as given to a newborn whose skinny features are compared to those of a skeleton [*Zulu*] (Herbert 1995: 5).

Maranga (m) *[mah-rah-ndgh-ah]* "The one who stares (or looks) at me" [*Luo*].

Marango (m) *[mah-rahn-goh]* A name given to one whose parent (or some family associate) has characteristically large thighs [*Luyia*].

Marapara (m) *[mah-rah-pah-rah]* Sable antelope: name such as given to a child born to a father who is a renowned hunter of wild beasts [*Zezuru*] (Marapara 1954: 8).

Mareba (m) *[mah-reh-bah]* A name given to one who is very inquisitive [*Luyia*].

Marendepese (f) *[maah-rehn-deh-peh-seh]* "The mother associated with rinderpest": name adapted from the European word "rinderpest" [*Sotho*] (Thipa 1986: 288).

Mariuki (m) *[mah-rjuh-kih]* The reincarnated one; the one reborn [The *Embu*].

Marufu (f/m) *[mah-ruh-fuh]* Deaths: a name given to a child born into a family that has lost many of its members to death [*Shona*] (Jackson 1957: 118).

Marufudza (f/m) *[mah-ruh-fuh-dzah]* "You have been herding death": a name such as given to a child born into a family that has lost many of its members to death, as compared to one herding cattle in large numbers [*Shona*] (Jackson 1957: 118).

Masaamba (m) *[mah-saahm-bah]* "That one who clears the path (through the high grass) (for the twins)": a name given to one whose birth precedes that of his twin siblings [The *Kongo*] (Daeleman 1977: 193).

Masafu (m) *[mah-sah-fuh]* A name given to one born in the bush and whereby leaves were used to cover him; a name given to one who was abandoned in the bush [*Luyia*].

Masagazi (m) *[mah-sah-gah-zih]* Looseness; shakiness; slackness; elephant grass; reeds [*Ganda*].

Masajjage (m) *[mah-sahj-jah-geh]* "His manly ways"; manliness; strength; bravery [*Ganda*, *Soga*].

Masaka (m) *[mah-sah-kah]* Sorghum; moving around to obtain food for purchase or in exchange for services; foraging for food; digging up (or ferreting) information [*Ganda*].

Masanafu (m) *[mah-sah-nah-fuuh]* (That associated with) the species of reddish brown soldier ants that bite fiercely [*Ganda*].

Masanda (m) *[mah-sahn-dah]* Rubber or sap in its natural state [The *Ganda*, *Soga*].

Masanja (m) *[mah-sahn-djah]* A name given to one born in a banana plantation [*Luyia*].

Masanso (m) *[mah-sahn-soh]* Sowings; scatterings; spreadings [The *Ganda*].

Masawi (m) *[mah-saah-wih]* Grass/ or tares: a name such as given to a child not expected to live long i.e. similar to grass or tares will soon wither away and die [*Zezuru*] (Marapara 1954: 8).

Masawuli (m) *[mah-sah-wuh-lih]* Healing; curing [*Ganda*].

Masegi (m) *[mah-seh-jih]* That involve bald patches running back from both sides of the forehead [*Ganda*].

Masemani (f/m) *[mah-tseh-mah-nih]* "You despised me": a name depicting regret that is intended to remind a kin or neighbor that the scorn in the past directed to this child's parent (who may now be in an enviable position) is still remembered and felt [The *Shona*] (Jackson 1957: 117).

Masembe (m) *[mah-sehm-beh]* That are last; supporting; backings up; recommendations; favoring [*Ganda*].

Masengere (m) *[mah-sehn-geh-reh]* A court; a tribunal; the waste from smelting; reddish brown rock found in barren areas; appealing; (well) laid out; (put) in order; aligned [*Ganda*].

Masenseke (m) *[mah-sehn-seh-keh]* That are exhausted (or fatigued, or broken down); torn to pieces [*Ganda*].

Masepa (f) *[mah-seh-pah]* Human excrement: an unpleasant name given to one whose previous born sibling was stillborn or died before weaning, this attributed to sorcery--this name is a means to safeguard the named "by making a show of neglecting it in the hope of lulling the sorcerer's vigilance" [*Sotho*] (Ashton 1952: 33).

Maseruka (m) *[mah-seh-ruh-kah]* Imperceptible movements forward; pushings forward, bit by bit [*Ganda*].

Mashayemhlana (m) *[mah-tsh-ah-yehm-lah-nah]* "Mr. Back Lasher": this started out as a nickname for a magistrate prone to impose lashes [*Zulu*] (Lugg 1968: 14).

Masi (m) *[mah-sih]* The one of the hair [*Maasai*].

Masiembe (m) *[mah-tsih-yehm-beh]* A name given to one who loves to eat the fatty mutton of sheep tails [*Luyia*].

Masiga (m) *[mah-sih-gah]* Planting season; stones, bricks, or balls of clay arranged for a wood fireplace for cooking; the cooking area of a stove or oven; the largest subdivisions of clans [*Samia, Soga*].

Masika (m) *[mah-tsih-kah]* A name given to one born during a funeral [*Luyia*].

Masikat (f/m) *[mah-tsih-kaht]* Midday: name such as given to one born during the middle of the day [*Shona*] (Jackson 1957: 120).

Masiki (m) *[mah-sih-kih]* That involve logs (or stumps); that involve the party held for the groom or the bride on the night before the wedding [*Ganda, Soga*].

Masilo (m) *[mah-sih-loh]* The older of a set of identical male twins, the younger named *Masilonyane* [*Sotho*] (Mohome 1972: 179).

Masilonyane (m) *[mah-sih-loh-ndjh-ah-neh]* The younger of a set of identical male twins, the older named *Masilo* [The *Sotho*] (Mohome
1972:179).

Masimong (f) *[mah-sih-moh-ndgh]* An older of a set of identical female twins, the younger named *Masingwaneng*; "at the fields" [*Sotho*]
(Mohome 1972: 179).

Masindano (m) *[mah-sihn-dah-noh]* A name given to one born during
mashindano sports competitions [*Luyia*].

Masinde (m) *[mah-sihn-deh]* A name given to one born during the circumcision season [*Luyia*].

Masingisa (m) *[mah-sihn-gih-sah]* "The one who shakes things": name
such as given to one who is fierce (or powerful) [*Kaguru*] (Beidelman
1974: 288).

Masingo (f/m) *[mah-sihn-goh]* A name given to one born in a cattle
kraal [*Luyia*].

Masingwaneng (f) *[mah-sih-ndgh-wah-neh-ndgh]* The younger of a
set of identical female twins, the older named *Masimong*; "at the small fields" [*Sotho*] (Mohome 1972: 179).

Masiwa (f) *[mah-sih-wah]* "The fatherless one": a name given to one
born after her father died [*Shona*].

Masoma (m) *[mah-soh-mah]* That involve reading/ or studying/ or
practicing (religion)/ or attending church [*Ganda, Soga*].

Masonga (m) *[mah-sohn-gah]* Proddings; piercings; pokings; pointings
out; sharp pains; causes; reasons; matters; affairs [*Ganda, Soga*].

Masoto/ Masooto (m) *[mah-soh-oh-toh]* Muddy; mud [*Ganda*].

Masulubu (m) *[mah-suh-luh-buh]* (With a prominent) mustache [The
Ganda, Soga].

Maswa (m) *[mah-swaah]* Authenticity; genuineness; purity [*Ganda*].

Maswabi (m) *[mah-swah-bih]* Sadness/ grief: name given to one born
at a time a relation dies [*Sotho*] (Thipa 1986: 290).

Maswanku (m) *[mah-swahn-kuuh]* Eating (or chewing) noisily; smack-
ing one's lips in satisfaction or anticipation; snatching [*Ganda*].

Mata (m) *[mah-tah]* A ritual related name traditionally conferred upon
the child following its initiation [*Kongo*] (Ndoma 1977: 90).

Matabi (m) *[mah-tah-bih]* Branches; boughs; branches (of an association) [*Ganda*].

Matala (m) *[mah-tah-lah]* A name given to one born in a cattle kraal
[*Luyia*].

Mateega (m) *[mah-teh-eh-gah]* Lying in wait; in a position to ambush;
being on the lookout for; bewitching [*Ganda*].

Mateete (m) *[mah-teh-eh-teh]* A type of fine grass placed on the floors
of houses [*Ganda*].

Matega (f) *[mah-teh-gah]* The setting of a trap; trapping; strain; a foul
of tripping (in soccer) [*Ganda, Soga*].

Matembe (m) *[mah-tehm-beh]* The fruits of the wild plantain; putting on an act; performing; seizing; climbing up [*Ganda*].

Matete (m) *[mah-teh-teh]* A name given to one born during the season of grasshoppers [*Luyia*].

Matete (m) *[mah-teh-teh]* "All this" [*Luo*].

Matete (m) *[mah-teh-teh]* "Finished"; "completed": name such as given to one who gives funeral orations, or to one who skillfully officiates at ceremonies during which affairs are settled [The *Kaguru*] (Beidelman 1974: 289).

Mathunzini (m) *[mah-tuhn-zih-nih]* "Among shadows" [*Zulu*] (Koopman 1979: 71).

Matimba (m) *[mah-tihm-bah]* "Strength": a name such as implying that the birth of this child of male gender depended on the assisting strength of God [*Zulu*] (Herbert 1995: 4).

Mativengerei (f/m) *[mah-tih-vehn-geh-rehy]* "Why have you been hating us?": a name given to one born during a family dispute with kin or neighbors, whereby the family is so perplexed at the malicious acts or attitude of kin or neighbors [*Shona*] (Jackson 1957: 117).

Matlakala (f) *[maht-lah-kah-lah]* Garbage; litter: name such as given to a child born out of wedlock/ or one born of an infidel mother (or wife) [*Sotho*] (Mohome 1972: 177).

Matovu (m) *[mah-toh-vuh]* Thistle [*Ganda*].

Matshediso (f) *[maht-tsh-eh-dih-soh]* "(Expressions of) consolation": a name such as given to one born following the death of a preceding sibling [*Sotho*] (Mohome 1972: 174).

Matshediso (f) *[mah-tsh-eh-dih-soh]* "The mother who has consoled us"/ "the mother who has made us cross (over)": name such as given to one who has lost two or more preceding siblings to death, the name implying that this child serves as welcome solace, by the action of God or the ancestors, for the family of the deceased [*Sotho*] (Thipa 1986: 290).

Matshwele (m) *[uh-mah-tsh-weh-leh]* "Chicks": a name such as implying that this child is born into a family of many children [The *Zulu*] (Suzman 1994: 263).

Matte (m) *[maht-teh]* Rude (or stern, or grouchy) in behavior [*Ganda*].

Matulumi (m) *[mah-tuh-luh-mih]* "Decorations": name such as given to one who decorates (or makes things attractive) [*Kaguru*] (Beidelman 1974: 288).

Matumbwe (m) *[mah-tuhm-bweh]* (One with a peculiarity of large) loins (or calves of the legs) [*Ganda*].

Matumpaggwa (m) *[mah-tuhm-pahg-gwah]* a bullheaded, obstinate person; person with large and protruding ears [*Ganda*].

Maturu (f/m) *[mah-tuh-ruh]* A name given to one who loves to suckle and is weaned late [*Luyia*].

Matusongua (f/m) *[mah-tuh-sohn-gwah]* "What we have been shown":

a name such as given to one whose mother took a relatively long time to achieve this pregnancy [*Kongo*] (Ndoma 1977: 90).

Matutu (m) *[mah-tuh-tuh]* Prominence; fame; the sharp tips of a species of grass (used for thatching and squeezing out banana juice for
brewing) [*Ganda*].

Matwaala (m) *[mah-twaah-lah]* "That convey (the twins)": name given
to one whose birth precedes that of his or her twin siblings [The *Yaka*]
(Daeleman 1977: 193).

Matwale (m) *[mah-twaah-leh]* Taken charge of; captured; a colony; do-
mains [*Ganda*].

Matwenge (m) *[mah-twehn-geh]* Laughter [*Ganda*].

Mavakala (m) *[mah-vah-kah-lah]* A ritual related name traditionally conferred upon the child following its initiation [*Kongo*] (Ndoma 1977:
90).

Maviiri (m) *[mah-viih-rih]* (One with) disheveled (or unshaven, or prominent) hair on the head [*Ganda*].

Mavu (f/m) *[mah-vuh]* Lumps of soil: a name such as given to a child
born into a family that has lost many of its members to death and
whereby there is pessimism as to whether this one will survive, the
name metaphorically implying that the child is so fragile looking and
vulnerable just like lumps of soil [*Shona*] (Jackson 1957: 118).

Mavu (f) *[mah-vuuh]* Soil: a name such as given to a child not expected to live long and who will therefore soon be buried i.e. in the
soil [*Zezuru*] (Marapara 1954: 8).

Mavugo (m) *[mah-vuh-goh]* (The one who is loudly) talkative in mannerism [*Ganda*].

Mavumengwana (m) *[mah-vuh-meh-ndgh-wah-nah]* The one who sub-
mits to the orders of the leopard (or the commander) [*Zulu*] (Lugg
1968: 13).

Mavuuma (m) *[mah-vuuh-mah]* Rumbling (or wheezing) noises [The
Ganda].

Mawa (m) *[mah-wah]* "Beer": a name such as given to a child born at a
time there was a beer party at the family home/ or to a child whose
mother (frequently) drank beer during the pregnancy [*Pare*] (Omari
1970: 70).

Mawa (m) *[mah-waah]* Thorns; spikes; spines; a very strong beer that
is fermented in a calabash inside the house [*Ganda, Soga*].

Mawaayira (m) *[mah-waah-yih-rah]* That involve slandering (or accusing falsely); that involves adding (or adding to, or supplementing)
[*Ganda*].

Mawagi (m) *[mah-wah-jih]* That are firm (or well supported); encou-
ragement; supporters [*Ganda*].

Mawale (m) *[mah-wah-leh]* That is stubborn (or intractable, or rebellious); trousers [*Ganda*].

Mawalo (f) *[mah-wah-loh]* Turns; shifts [*Ganda, Soga*].

Mawanda (m) *[mah-wahn-dah]* One that causes it to rain (or to pour down); spiting out; blurting out; ejecting; throwing out [*Ganda, Soga*].

Mawanga (m) *[mah-wahn-gah]* Countries; nations; tribes; ethnic groups [*Ganda*].

Mawangwe (m) *[mah-wahn-gweh]* That is made naturally (or properly) [*Ganda*].

Mawano (m) *[mah-wah-noh]* Astonishing; marvelous; unheard of [The *Ganda, Soga*].

Mawawa (m) *[mah-wah-wah]* Gadflies; wings; edible mushroom [The *Ganda, Soga*].

Maweerere (m) *[mah-weh-eh-reh-reh]* That is supportingly given; that is bestowed with luck/ or fortune [*Ganda, Soga*].

Mawejje (m) *[mah-wehj-jeh]* Calm; cool-headed; well behaved [The *Ganda*].

Mawemuko (f/m) *[mah-weh-muh-koh]* That involves shame (or disgrace) [*Ganda*].

Mawerere (m) *[mah-weh-reh-reh]* That involves placing (of a child into the care of one other than the parents, to be brought up) [The *Ganda, Soga*].

Maweta (m) *[mah-weh-tah]* (Finger) rings; bends; turns [*Ganda, Soga*].

Mawogola (m) *[mah-woh-goh-lah]* That are broken off (or snapped off) [*Ganda*].

Mawu (m) *[mah-wuuh]* Animal skins; carpets made of animal skins [*Soga*].

Mawuba (m) *[mah-wuh-bah]* Overlooking; slippings out of unintended acts; failings; misses [*Ganda*].

Mawuwani (f/m) *[mah-wuh-wah-nih]* July: name such as given to one born during a cold day that is compared to the cold seasonal conditions of July [*Zulu*] (Herbert 1995: 5).

Maxangu (f/m) *[mah-ksahn-guh]* Problems: a name such as given to a newborn who is a product of a problematic pregnancy during which its mother was often sick, or a name given to one born around the time the parents had to move away from their locale because of war [*Zulu*] (Herbert 1995: 5).

Maya (f) *[maah-yah]* Ostrich [*Ganda*].

Mayala (m) *[mah-yah-lah]* Reaching abundance; multiplying; spreading (or laying) out [*Ganda, Soga*].

Mayambala (m) *[mah-yahm-bah-lah]* (Modes of) dressing [*Ganda*].

Mayega (m) *[mah-yeh-gah]* (The instance/ or process of) feeling unwell [*Ganda*].

Mayemba (m) *[mah-yehm-bah]* Noisy and fool mannered talk; ranting; witchcraft substances [*Ganda*].

Mayembe (m) *[mah-yehm-beh]* Horns of animals; spirits associated with fetishes; hexes; spells [*Ganda*].

Mayengo (m) *[mah-yehn-goh]* Lake or ocean waves; mix of water waves of lakes (or oceans); that is stirred and dissolved; that is diluted [*Ganda*].

Mayenje (m) *[mah-yeh-ehn-jeh]* Moving about aimlessly; tottering; reeling; roaming around; floating about; (the acts of) cockroaches [The *Ganda*].

Mayimbo (m) *[mah-yihm-boh]* Singing; joining (or combining) with [*Ganda*].

Mayinja (m) *[mah-yihn-jah]* Rocks; stones; phonograph records [The *Ganda*].

Mayirwa (m) *[mah-yih-rwah]* That involve making rippling noises/ or gurglings of water/ or rumblings (such as of waterfalls or the sea); that involve snorting (or snoring, or wheezings, or purring) [*Ganda*].

Mayite (m) *[mah-yih-teh]* That are called (or called to, or named); that are described as; that are invited [*Ganda*].

Mayito (m) *[mah-yih-toh]* Calling upon; passing (by or through) [The *Ganda*].

Mayobyo (m) *[mah-yoh-bjoh]* Species of edible green plants which have white flowering [*Soga*].

Mayoga (m) *[mah-yoh-gah]* Congratulations; all the way; that are associated with the rock rabbit (or the hyrax, or the cony) [*Ganda*].

Mayu (f/m) *[mah-yuh]* A name given to a child who has a prefers fresh as opposed to sour (fermented) milk [*Luyia*].

Mayugi (m) *[mah-yuh-jih]* Hunting bells [*Ganda*].

Mayumba (m) *[mah-yuhm-bah]* Houses; homes [*Ganda*].

Mayungwe (m) *[mah-yuuhn-gweh]* That are joined (or connected) together; (bones) set [*Ganda*].

Mazibuko (m) *[mah-zih-buh-koh]* Fjords [*Zulu*] (Koopman 1990: 334).

Mazime (m) *[mah-zih-meh]* Annihilated; extinguished; having lost luster [*Ganda*].

Mazinga (m) *[mah-zihn-gah]* (Acts of) surrounding (or encircling, or wrapping, or folding, or coiling) [*Ganda*].

Mazzi (f/m) *[mahz-zih]* Water; this name is sometimes associated with the proverb "they (i.e. people) will drive a frog out of the house (with a stick), but will have no qualms about drinking the water from the well that the frog dwells in" implying that people can be so inconsistent and contradictory in their actions [*Ganda*].

Mbabaali (m) *[mbah-baah-lih]* Rushings about; acting hastily and rashly; that is all in a dither; that become uncontrollable (or unruly) [The *Ganda*].

Mbabazane (m) *[mbah-bah-zah-neh]* "Mr. Stinging Nettle": this started out as a nickname for a magistrate who meted out punishment in a quiet and gentle manner, but whose sentences always had a sting in their tails [*Zulu*] (Lugg 1968: 14).

Mbafaakoki (f) *[mbah-faah-koh-oh-tch-iih]* "What concern/ or interest do I have for them/ or for (all of) you?"; "what do I care about them/

or (all of) you?"; "why should I pay them/ or (all of) you any attention?" [*Ganda*].

Mbaga (m) *[mbah-gah]* Wedding; feast; banquet [*Ganda*].

Mbago (m) *[mbah-goh]* Hoe [*Soga*].

Mbagu (m) *[mbah-guh]* That is tough (or aggressive, or indomitable, or hard boiled); starting up/ or jumping up (suddenly) [*Ganda*].

Mbagumidde (f) *[mbah-guh-mihd-deh]* "I remain boldly courageous in confronting them"; "I remain faithfully tolerant of them"; "I remain firm in waiting for them" [*Ganda*].

Mbajja (m) *[mbahj-jah]* Mode of carpentry activity; "I engage in carpentry activity"; one who walks fast; one who walks clumsily [*Ganda*].

Mbakebuse (f) *[mbah-keh-buh-seh]* "I looked back over my shoulder at them/ or you" [*Ganda*].

Mbalabyebungi (f) *[mbah-lah-bjeh-buhn-jih]* "I have viewed them as having abundance"; "I see them as having numerical strength"; "I recognize your having a lot" [*Ganda*].

Mbalangu (m) *[mbah-lahn-guh]* One who speaks (or strikes) forcibly; intrepid (or bold, or brusque) person [*Ganda*].

Mbaleka (f) *[mbah-leh-kah]* "I leave (or abandon) them"; "I permit (or allow) them"; "I leave/ or abandon you (all)"; "I permit/ or allow you (all)" [*Ganda, Soga*].

Mbalinda (f) *[mbah-lihn-dah]* "I wait for them/ or for (all) of you"; "I await them/ or await (all) of you" [*Ganda, Soga*].

Mbalire (m) *[mbah-lih-reh]* Counted; numbered; that is rare (or scarce); that is well considered [*Ganda*].

Mbalule (m) *[mbah-luh-leh]* Beer processing bananas not yet ripe [The *Soga*].

Mbalyowere (f) *[mbah-ljoh-weh-reh]* One they do a favor to (or a benefit for); "I would perform an obligation on their behalf" [*Ganda*].

Mbambeni (m) *[mbahm-beh-nih]* "Hold him" [*Zulu*] (Koopman 1979: 164).

Mbangeni (m) *[mbah-ndgh-eh-nih]* "Quarrel over him" [The *Zulu*] (Koopman 1979: 159).

Mbani/ Mbaani (m) *[mbaah-nih]* "Who am I (to do it)?"; "who would I be (to do it)?"; "what would my capacity be (to do it)?" [*Ganda, Soga*].

Mbanja (m) *[mbahn-jah]* "I demand payment of a debt" [*Ganda*].

Mbanzira (m) *[mbahn-zih-rah]* "I would be rejecting (or scorning, or refusing)" [*Ganda*].

Mbare (m) *[mbah-reh]* Squirrel [*Embu*].

Mbarikoi (m) *[mbah-rih-kohy]* The brown complexioned one [*Maasai*].

Mbatidde (f) *[mbah-tihd-deh]* "I am frightened of them"; "I am afraid of you"; one who is fearful [*Ganda*].

Mbatudde (f) *[mbah-tuhd-deh]* "I sit around waiting for them/ or (all of) you" [*Ganda*].

Mbatunuulire (f) *[mbah-tuh-nuuh-lih-reh]* "Let me look at them/ or (all of) you"; "that I may look at them"; one that looks intently [*Ganda*].

Mbawadde (f) *[mbah-wahd-deh]* "I have given them/ or (all of) you"; one who is giving [*Ganda*].

Mbawonye (f) *[mbah-woh-ndjh-eh]* "I have successfully got rid of them/ or (all of) you"; "I have escaped them/ or (all of) you" [*Ganda*].

Mbaziira (m) *[mbah-ziih-rah]* "I block (or impede) their progress"; "I reject (or scorn, or forbid) them" [*Ganda*].

Mbazzi (m) *[mbahz-zih]* Ax; this name is sometimes associated with the proverb "they demand a butchering ax for it (i.e. the cow), while it continues to munch on the grass (in the field)" which exemplifies a situation in which one in danger does not heed a warning [*Ganda*].

Mbeegeyedde (f) *[mbeh-eh-geh-yehd-deh]* "I have talked about them behind their backs"; "I have slandered them" [*Ganda*].

Mbeekeka/ Mbekeka (f) *[mbeh-eh-keh-kah]* "I (as a young child) can be carried on the back" [*Ganda, Soga*].

Mbeeraba (f) *[mbeh-eh-rah-bah]* "I compare them to myself"; "I see them in my shoes"; "I reflect myself on them" [*Ganda*].

Mbeewoze (f) *[mbeh-eh-woh-zeh]* "I have borrowed (money) or got credit from them/ or you" [*Ganda*].

Mberege (m) *[mbeh-reh-geh]* Small, reddish colored pig; a name commonly given to a very intelligent and daring child [*Ganda*].

Mberenge (m) *[mbeh-reh-ehn-geh]* Corn nuts (or popcorn); a name commonly given to a very intelligent and daring child [*Ganda*].

Mbhekeni (m) *[mbeh-keh-nih]* "Look after him" [*Zulu*] (Koopman 1979: 159).

Mbigidde (m) *[mbih-gihd-deh]* "I have overburdened (or overloaded) myself"; "I have filled to the brim" [*Ganda*].

Mbiikire (m) *[mbiih-kih-reh]* (Eggs) laid out for (or on behalf of); under the protection or influence of Roman Catholic nuns [*Ganda*].

Mbikimye (f) *[mbih-tch-ih-mjeh]* "I have fetched them (i.e. the things)" [*Ganda*].

Mbilime (f) *[mbih-lih-meh]* "Runner": a name such as given to one whose parents had to run to a native doctor to obtain magical therapy to assist in conceiving or giving birth to her [The *Kaguru*] (Beidelman 1974: 289).

Mbira (m) *[mbih-rah]* Forests; bead; "I become warmed up" [*Ganda, Soga*].

Mbiridde (f) *[mbih-rihd-deh]* "I have eaten (or consumed) them (i.e. the things)" [*Ganda*].

Mbirinze (f) *[mbih-rihn-zeh]* "I am waiting for them"; "I wait for them" [*Ganda*].

Mbizi (m) *[mbih-zih]* Of the water; to drop in water [*Ganda*].

Mbizzi (m) *[mbihz-zih]* Pig; hogs; this name is commonly associated with the proverb "people are like (the teeth of) wild hogs: their teeth have a laughing appearance on the outside, but inwardly the wild hogs are killers" implying that people can smile outwardly but have inner feelings of malice [*Ganda*].

Mbobimbo (m) *[mboh-bihm-boh]* That are foamed up; overflowed; pampered; babied [*Ganda*].

Mbogga (f/m) *[mbohg-gah]* That takes on an attractive appearance and whose skin is as fair and healthy as that of a baby [*Ganda*].

Mbogo (m) *[mboh-goh]* Buffalo [*Embu*].

Mbogo (m) *[mboh-goh]* Buffalo; name commonly given to a first born boy [*Ganda*].

Mboneko (m) *[mboh-neh-koh]* Appearance [*Ganda*].

Mbongeleni (m) *[mboh-ndgh-eh-leh-nih]* "Be grateful on his behalf"; "be grateful for him" [*Zulu*] (Koopman 1979: 159).

Mbookolo (f/m) *[mboh-oh-oh-koh-oh-loh]* Name given to either a twin or a triplet [*Ntomba*] (Daeleman 1977: 192).

Mboolanyi (m) *[mboh-oh-lah-ndjh-ih]* That involves expelling (such as from a clan); that involves disinheriting (or excommunicating, or disowning, or ostracizing); that involves discriminating (or showing prejudice against) [*Ganda*].

Mbooy (f/m) *[mboh-ohy]* A name given to an older twin [The *Bushong*] (Daeleman 1977: 190).

Mbowa/ Mboowa (m) *[mboh-oh-wah]* Of noble birth; free born; of the upper class [*Ganda*].

Mbowanye (f/m) *[mboh-wah-ndjh-eh]* A confiscation/ or appropriation/ or seizure (mostly as security surety for payment of a debt); "I have held as security for payment of a debt" [*Ganda*].

Mboyo (f/m) *[mboh-yoh]* Name given to an older twin [*Hindo, Mongo, Ntomba*] (Daeleman 1977: 190); a name denoting the reincarnation of a maleficent spirit, and which name is given to both twin sisters [*Topoke*] (Daeleman 1977: 190); a name given to a triplet [*Ntomba*] (Daeleman 1977: 192).

Mbucu (f/m) *[mbuh-tch-uh]* A name given to one whose birth follows that of his or her twin siblings [*Tetela*] (Daeleman 1977: 191); a name given to a triplet [*Tetela*] (Daeleman 1977: 192).

Mbugayamunyoro (m) *[mbuh-gah-yah-muh-ndjh-oh-roh]* "The council (or court of law) of the *Nyoro* ethnic"; "the enclosure of a *Nyoro* chief"; "the cattle fountain that belongs to a *Nyoro* ethnic" [*Ganda*].

Mbuku (m) *[mbuh-kuh]* Hare [*Embu*].

Mbundu (f) *[mbuhn-duuh]* "Mist": this name is commonly associated with the proverb "The mist of the coast is the rain of the upland" which can be equated to "one man's meat is another man's poison," implying people vary in their ways and desires including customs; the name is also commonly associated with the proverb "I am an old person of the mountain: I greet the mist of the morning" which implies that one has to be in very close association with another so as to adequately get acquainted with this person [*Ovimbundu*] (Ennis 1945:

3).

Mbutela (f/m) *[mbuh-teh-lah]* A name given to the youngest of quad-
ruplets/ or to a child whose birth follows that of twin siblings [*Tetela*]
(Daeleman 1977: 192).

Mbuuyi (f/m) *[mbuuh-yiih]* A name given to an older twin [*Luba, Luwa*]
(Daeleman 1977: 190).

Mbuy (f/m) *[mbuhy]* A name given to an older twin [The *Kanyok*]
(Daeleman 1977: 190).

Mbuyu (f/m) *[mbuh-yuh]* A name given to an older twin [The *Luba*]
(Daeleman 1977: 190).

Mchithwa (m) *[muh-tch-ih-sth-wah]* The discarded one/ the one thrown
away: a name such as given to a child born at a time of discord in the
family [*Zulu*] (Koopman 1979: 155).

Mdogo (m) *[muh-doh-goh]* "The small one": a name given to a child of
small body size [*Luyia*].

Mduduzi (m) *[muh-duh-duh-zih]* "The comforter" [The *Zulu*] (Koopman
1979: 164).

Mduduzibhekisa (m) *[uhm-duh-duh-zih-beh-kih-sah]* "Comforter looks
after things": a name such as given by the named child's parents to
express that the child is considered one that will look after things
carefully, and see to it that they are proper [The *Zulu*] (Suzman 1994:
261).

Mdumazi (m) *[muh-duh-mah-zih]* "The one that disappoints" [The *Zulu*]
(Koopman 1979: 155).

Mechi (f/m) *[meh-tch-ih]* "Water": a name given to one born at the well
[*Luyia*].

Meeli (m) *[meh-eh-lih]* The one that is not smeared [*Maasai*].

Mehlabuka (m) *[meh-lah-buh-kah]*/ **Mehlayabuka** (m) *[meh-lah-yah-
buh-kah]* "The eyes are watching" [*Zulu*] (Koopman 1979: 159).

Mehlo (m) *[meh-hloh]* "(He has) striking eyes" [*Zulu*] (Koopman 1979:
71).

Mehlokazulu (m) *[meh-loh-kah-zuh-luh]* "The eyes of the *Zulu* ethnics"; "the *Zulu* watchdog" [*Zulu*] (Lugg 1968: 13).

Meleji (m) *[meh-leh-jih]* The one that cannot be cheated [*Maasai*].

Melelek (m) *[meh-leh-lehk]* The one that is not easy to deal with [The
Maasai].

Meliyo (f) *[meh-lih-yoh]* The one that is not lonely [*Maasai*].

Memruti (m) *[mehm-ruh-tih]* The one that cannot be bypassed [The
Maasai].

Memuzi (m) *[meh-muh-zih]* A child whose birth is a surprise, not expected [*Maasai*].

Mengi (f/m) *[mehn-gih]* "Many": a name such as given to one born following the mother having frequently miscarried [*Kaguru*] (Beidelman
1974: 289).

Menya (m) *[meh-ndjh-ah]* "Allow to light" [*Luo*].

Merumo (m) *[meh-ruh-moh]* The one that is not visible *[Maasai]*.

Meshuki (m) *[meh-tsh-uh-kih]* One that cannot be ventured *[Maasai]*.

Mesi (f) *[meh-sih]* A name given to the older of a set of identical female twins, the younger named *Mesinyane*; fumes of smoke *[Sotho]* (Mohome 1972: 179).

Mesinyane (f) *[meh-sih-ndjh-ah-neh]* A name given to the younger of a set of identical female twins, the older named *Mesi*; small fumes of smoke *[Sotho]* (Mohome 1972: 179).

Metho (f/m) *[meh-sth-oh]* Drinking *[Luo]*.

Mfanawafuthi (m) *[mfah-nah-wah-fuh-tih]* "Another boy"; "a boy again" *[Zulu]* (Koopman 1979: 157).

Mfaniseni (m) *[uhm-fah-nih-seh-nih]* "Who did he look like?": a name such as given by the named child's mother who responds, to her mother-in-law's allegations that this child is borne out of infidelity, by asking "If my child does not look like my husband, then who does the child look like?" *[Zulu]* (Suzman 1994: 259).

Mfanomhlophe (m) *[mfah-nohm-loh-peh]* "A pale complexioned boy" *[Zulu]* (Koopman 1979: 157).

Mfanufikile (m) *[mfah-nuh-fih-kih-leh]* "A boy has arrived" [The *Zulu*] (Koopman 1979: 159, 166).

Mfulathelwa (m) *[mfuh-lah-teh-lwah]* "The shunned one" [The *Zulu*] (Koopman 1979: 155).

Mfumo (m) *[uhm-fuh-moh]* "Leader": a name such as implying that this boy born is regarded as a leader who is grounds for building on, as well as for the continuity of, the family name--can imply a first born boy in the family *[Zulu]* (Herbert 1995: 3).

Mfumu-Katumwa (f/m) *[mfuuh-muuh-kaah-tuuh-mwah]* "The chief that is ordered/ sent/ commissioned": a name given to the last born of triplets *[Kongo]* (Daeleman 1977: 193).

Mgcineni (m) *[muhg-tch-ih-neh-nih]* "Take care of him" [The *Zulu*] (Koopman 1979: 79).

Mghanga (m) *[muhg-hahn-gah]* "(Traditional) medicine-man": a name such as given to a child whose mother was administered herbs by a traditional doctor to enable her to conceive *[Pare]* (Omari 1970: 70).

Mhashu (f/m) *[mah-tsh-uuh]* Locusts: a name given to one born during a locust invasion period *[Shona]* (Jackson 1957: 119).

Mhlakuvana (m) *[mlah-kuh-vah-nah]* "The little castor oil plant that frequently pops off": a name such as given to one likened to the castor seeds when discharged from the pod upon ripening *[Zulu]* (Lugg 1968: 12).

Mhute (f/m) *[muh-teh]* Mist: a name given to a child born into a family that has lost many of its members to death and whereby there is pessimism as to whether this one will survive, the name metaphorically implying that the child is so fragile looking and vulnerable to disappearing just like mist *[Shona]* (Jackson 1957: 118).

Micere (f) *[mih-tch-eh-reh]* A name given to one who loves to travel

[*Embu*].

Midlayi (m) *[mihd-lah-yih]* Killer [*Zulu*] (Herbert 1995: 5).

Midolu (m) *[mih-doh-luuh]* "One that you cannot see coming" [*Maasai*].

Miguda (f/m) *[mih-guh-dah]* "Touch me" [*Luo*].

Migui (m) *[mih-guhy]* Arrows [*Embu*].

Mikka (m) *[mihk-kah]* Blowing (from the mouth); wind instrument tunes; this name is commonly associated with the proverb "the horn blowers blow their instruments in harmony" which urges the spirit of community and cooperation as exemplified by horn blowers who are of different background and character, yet they work together to produce a fine tune [*Ganda*].

Mirimo/ Mirimu (m) "Work"; "tasks"; "employment"; "business"; this name is sometimes associated with the proverb "a mass of people (or a crowd) looks bad when it comes to sharing and eating food, but looks good when it comes to allotting work" meaning that practically in either situation, the food or the work gets finished quickly, and though with the food there will likely be friction over sharing, in the case of the work the synonym "many hands make light work" will likely apply--human relations hence depend on circumstances that are rarely or never unconditional [*Ganda*].

Misha (m) *[miih-tsh-ah]* Village [*Zulu*] (Koopman 1979: 69).

Mivule (m) *[mih-vuh-leh]* The iroko timber trees whose wood is very resistant to termite attack and is used as a substitute for teak; this name is sometimes associated with the proverb "men are like iroko timber trees: they shed (or lose) their leaves, but they do regrow their thick foliage" implying that people experience both good and bad days and times; this name is also sometimes associated with the proverb "men are like iroko timber trees: they shatter but they also make firm" implying that men can be remarkably good and of great use, but on the other hand they can be so malicious and damaging [*Ganda*].

Mkede (f/m) *[mkeh-deh]* "Quarrel": a name such as given to a child conceived or born at a time of contention between the parents [*Pare*] (Omari 1970: 70).

Mkenya (m) *[muh-keh-ndjh-ah]* "One of Kenyan nationality": one associated with the nation Kenya, as adapted from the word *Mukenya* used in Uganda and standing for "Kenyan" [*Luyia*].

Mkhethwa (m) *[mkeh-twah]* "Chosen one" [The *Zulu*] (Koopman 1979: 155).

Mkholiseni (m) *[mkoh-lih-seh-nih]* "Deceive him" [The *Zulu*] (Koopman 1979: 159).

Mkhombiseni (m) *[mkohm-bih-seh-nih]* "Show him the way" [*Zulu*] (Koopman 1979: 79).

Mlaho (m) *[mlah-hoh]* "Case": a name such as given to a child born at a time there was a court case in the family/ or to a child born to parents that were involved in court cases during the pregnancy [*Pare*] (Omari 1970: 70).

Mlaleni (f) *[mlah-leh-nih]* "Place her" [*Zulu*] (Koopman 1979: 159).

Mlamuli (m) *[mlah-muh-lih]* The mediator [*Zulu*] (Koopman 1979: 73).

Mlavwasi (m) *[mlah-vwah-sih]* A name given to a child whose birth involved problems/ or to a child who became alarmingly sick that there was little hope he would survive [*Pare*] (Omari 1970: 70).

Mlomokawudli (m) *[mloh-moh-kah-wuhd-lih]* "The mouth does not eat" [*Zulu*] (Koopman 1979: 159).

Mlonyeni (m) *[mloh-ndjh-eh-nih]* "In the mouth" [The *Zulu*] (Koopman 1979: 155).

Mlungisi (m) *[uhm-luhn-gih-sih]* "Set things right": name such as given to a child born to parents whose family relationship has markedly improved from the deteriorated state it was in [*Zulu*] (Suzman 1994: 267).

Mlungunengweyini (m) *[mluhn-guh-nehn-gweh-yih-nih]* "What has the white man been offended by?" [*Zulu*] (Koopman 1979: 159).

Mmadikeledi (f) *[mmah-dih-keh-leh-dih]* "The mother of *Dikeledi*"; "the mother that is of tears"; "the one of tears": a name such as given to one whose birth coincides with a period of mourning/ or coincides with a calamity [*Sotho*] (Mohome 1972: 175).

Mmafelleng (f) *[mmah-fehl-leh-ndgh]* "The mother of *Felleng*"; "the mother in (or at) the wilderness"; "the one in/ at the wilderness": a name such as given to a child delivered in the wilderness/ or to a child born at a time the father or a close kin was in the wilderness [*Sotho*] (Mohome 1972: 176).

Mmakganyapa (f) *[mmah-kah-gah-ndjh-ah-pah]* Mother of *Kganyapa*; "the mother that is of a thunderstorm"; "the one of a thunderstorm": a name such as given to one whose birth coincides with a period of thunderstorms [*Sotho*] (Mohome 1972: 175).

Mmaleeto (f) *[mmah-leh-eh-toh]* "The mother of *Leeto*"; "the mother that is of a journey"; "the one of a journey": a name such as given to a child born to a mother or to a father (or close kin) on a journey [The *Sotho*] (Mohome 1972: 176).

Mmalefu (f) *[mmah-leh-fuuh]* "The mother of *Lefu*"; "the mother that is of death"; "the one of death": a name such as given to one whose birth coincides with a period of death/ or deaths in the family [*Sotho*] (Mohome 1972: 175).

Mmamamello (f) *[mmah-mah-mehl-loh]* "The mother of *Mamello*"; "the mother that is of perseverance"; "the one of perseverance": a name such as given to a child born during times of hardship/ or to a first-born whose father struggled hard to win over the love of the mother [*Sotho*] (Mohome 1972: 176).

Mmamookgo (f) *[mmah-moh-ohk-goh]* "The mother of *Mookgo*"; "the mother that is the tear"; "the one of the eye tear": a name such as given to one whose birth coincides with a period of mourning/ or with a calamity [*Sotho*] (Mohome 1972: 175).

Mmantsho (f) *[mmahn-tsh-oh]* "The mother that is black"; "the one that is black" [*Sotho*] (Mohome 1972: 183).

Mmantwa (f) *[mahn-twah]* "The mother that is of the war"; "the one of the war" [*Sotho*] (Mohome 1972: 183).

Mmaphehello (f) *[mmah-peh-ehl-loh]* "The mother of *Phehello*"; "the mother that is of persistence"; "the one of persistence": name such as given to a child born during times of hardship/ or to a first-born whose father struggled hard to win over the love of the mother [The *Sotho*] (Mohome 1972: 176).

Mmapule (f) *[mmah-puh-leh]* "The mother of *Pule*"; "the mother that is (born) in rain"; "the one that is (born) in rain": a name such as given to one born on a rainy day [*Sotho*] (Mohome 1972: 182, 183).

Mmasefako (f) *[mmah-seh-fah-koh]* "The mother of *Sefako*"; "the mother that is of hail"; "the one of hail": a name such as given to one whose birth coincides with a period of hailstorm activity [The *Sotho*] (Mohome 1972: 175).

Mmasehloho (f) *[mmah-seh-loh-hoh]* "The mother of *Sehloho*"; "the mother that is of disaster"; "the one of disaster": name such as given to one whose birth coincides with a period of calamity [The *Sotho*] (Mohome 1972: 175).

Mmaserame (f) *[mmah-seh-rah-meh]* "The mother of *Serame*"; "the mother that is of the cold" "the one of the cold": a name such as given to one whose birth coincides with a weather period of coldness [*Sotho*] (Mohome 1972: 175).

Mmatatello (f) *[mmah-tah-tehl-loh]* "The mother of *Tatello*"; "the mother that is of persistence"; "the one of insistence": a name such as given to a child born during times of hardship/ or to a first-born whose father struggled hard to win over the love of the mother [The *Sotho*] (Mohome 1972: 176).

Mmathalala (f) *[mmah-sth-ah-lah-lah]* "The mother associated with the Great Fever" [*Sotho*] (Thipa 1986: 288).

Mmathota (f) *[mmah-toh-tah]* "The mother of *Thota*"; "the mother that is of the plain"/ "the one of the plain": a name such as given to a child delivered in plain countryside/ or one born when the father or a close kin was in the plain [*Sotho*] (Mohome 1972: 176).

Mmatiisetso (f) *[mmah-tiih-seht-soh]* "The mother of *Tiisetso*"; "the mother that is of endurance"/ "the one of endurance": name such as given to a child born during times of hardship/ or to a first-born whose father struggled hard to win over the love of the mother [The *Sotho*] (Mohome 1972, 176).

Mmatladi (f) *[mmah-tlah-dih]* "The mother of *Tladi*"; "the mother that is of lightning"/ "the one of lightning": a name such as given to one whose birth coincides with a period of lightning [The *Sotho*] (Mohome 1972: 175).

Mmatselane (f) *[mmah-tseh-lah-neh]* "The mother of *Tselane*"; "the mother that is of the small road"/ "the one of the small road": a name such as given to a child delivered along a road [The *Sotho*] (Mohome

1972, 176).

Mmatseleng (f) *[mmah-tseh-leh-ndgh]* "The mother of *Tseleng*"; "the mother on (or at) the road"; "the one on/ at the road": a name such as given to a child delivered along a road [*Sotho*] (Mohome 1972: 176).

Mmatshepiso (f) *[mmah-tsh-eh-pih-soh]* "The mother of *Tshepiso*"; "the mother that is of promise"; "the one of promise" [The *Sotho*] (Mohome 1972: 181).

Mmatsie (f) *[mmah-tsih-yeh]* "The mother of *Tsie*"; "the mother that is of the locust"/ "the one of the locust": a name such as given to one whose birth coincides with a locust invasion [*Sotho*] (Mohome 1972: 175).

Mmatshepo (f) *[mmah-tsh-eh-poh]* "The mother of *Tshepo*"; "the mother that is of hope"; "the mother that is of trust."; "the one of hope"; "the one of trust" [*Sotho*] (Mohome 1972: 181).

Mmatumelo (f) *[mmah-tuh-meh-loh]* "The mother of *Tumelo*"; "the mother that is of belief"; "the one of belief": a name such as given to a child born during times of hardship during which there is still hope for a situation of success and normalcy/ or to a first-born whose father struggled hard to win over the love of the mother [The *Sotho*] (Mohome 1972: 176).

Mntwana (f) *[muhn-twah-nah]* "Child" [*Zulu*] (Koopman 1979: 154).

Mobanda (f/m) *[moh-baahn-dah]* "The short dry season": name given to a twin, the other named *Yanga* [*Gombe*] (Daeleman 1977: 190).

Modiehi (f) *[moh-dih-yeh-hih]* Delayer; the delayed one: a name such as given to a child who is the product of an unduly long pregnancy period with the birthdate long overdue [*Sotho*] (Mohome 1972: 177).

Modise (m) *[moh-dih-seh]* "The herdsman": (though the source gives this name a scanty glance, given that girls are in part traditionally associated with acquisition of cattle for the family by way of dowry, which acquired cattle would metaphorically place a male sibling into the position of a herdsman, the source seems to imply that this name is appropriately given to) the first born male among a disproportionately large number of preceding female siblings/ or a child born into a family with a disproportionately high ratio of female to male children [*Sotho*] (Mohome 1972: 179-180).

Mogore (f) *[moh-goh-reh]* "The one that is bought": a name such as given to one whose preceding siblings died, this child consequently subjected to a ritual to cleanse away death [*Kikuyu*] (Cagnolo 1933: 66).

Mohanuwa (f) *[moh-hah-nuh-wah]*/ **Mohanwe** (m) *[moh-hah-nweh]* "The disclaimed one": a name such as given to a child born out of wedlock/ or one born of an infidel mother (or wife) [*Sotho*] (Mohome 1972: 177).

Mohlalefi (m) *[moh-lah-leh-fih]* "Wise one" [*Sotho*] (Mohome 1972: 178).

Mohloki (m) *[moh-loh-kih]* "One who needs" [*Sotho*] (Mohome 1972:

177).

Mohlouwa (m) *[moh-loh-wuh-wah]* "The hated one": a name such as given to a child born during a time of social discord within the family or with neighbors *[Sotho]* (Mohome 1972: 177).

Mohome (m) *[moh-hoh-meh]* Hoe; plow *[Sotho]* (Mohome 1972: 179).

Moiketsi (m) *[mohy-keht-sih]* "The one who lets himself down": name such as given to a (usually first) child born to a family involved in disgruntlement such as over the enormity of the bride price put up by the child's mother's family/ or over the child's paternal grandparents' displeasure at the choice of bride or at having been denied adequate involvement in the marriage plans *[Sotho]* (Mohome 1972: 178).

Moitheri (f) *[mohy-sth-eh-rih]* "The one who planned his own marriage": a name such as given to a (usually first) child born to a family involved in disgruntlement over the child's paternal grandparents' having been denied adequate involvement in the marriage plans [The *Sotho*] (Mohome 1972: 178).

Mojalefa (m) *[moh-jah-leh-fah]* "The inheritor": name such as given to the eldest son; a name such as given to the first born male among a disproportionately large number of preceding female siblings *[Sotho]* (Mohome 1972: 179-180).

Mokalikali (f/m) *[moh-kah-lih-kah-lih]* "Lightning": a name given to a twin, the other named *Bei* [*Gombe*] (Daeleman 1977: 190).

Mokoto (f/m) *[moh-koh-toh]* "A thing of naught": a derogatory name given to one who has lost two or more preceding siblings to death, the name (paradoxically) intended to devalue and hence serve as protection for this child through dissuading the forces of evil and death from taking such a "useless" child away *[Sotho]* (Thipa 1986: 290).

Mokxadi (f) *[mohk-sah-dih]* One who has an older sister [The *Tlokwa-Sotho*] (Kruger 1937: 107).

Mola (f/m) *[moh-lah]* "Crawl on me" [*Luo*].

Molefi (m) *[moh-leh-fih]* A name given to the older of a set of identical male twins, the younger named *Molefinyane*; the payer [The *Sotho*] (Mohome 1972: 179).

Molefinyane (m) *[moh-leh-fih-ndjh-ah-neh]* Name given to the younger of a set of identical male twins, the older named *Molefi*; small payer [*Sotho*] (Mohome 1972: 179).

Molelekeng (f) *[moh-leh-leh-keh-ndgh]* "Expel her (i.e. the bride)!": a name such as given to a (usually first) child born to a family involved in disgruntlement such as over the enormity of the bride price put up by the child's mother's family/ or disgruntlement over the child's paternal grandparents' displeasure at the choice of bride or at having been denied adequate involvement in the marriage plans [The *Sotho*] (Mohome 1972: 178).

Monase (f) *[moh-nah-seh]* "Jealousy" [*Zulu*] (Koopman 1979: 156).

Mondonga (f/m) *[mohn-dohn-gah]* "The small antelope": name given to a twin, the other named *Gbongo* [*Gombe*] (Daeleman 1977: 190).

Monono (f) *[moh-noh-noh]* Prosperity [*Sotho*] (Mohome 1972: 174).

Monyatsi (m) *[moh-ndjh-aht-sih]* "One who despises": a name such as given to a child born during a time of social discord within the family or with neighbors [*Sotho*] (Mohome 1972: 177).

Mookgo (f) *[moh-ohk-goh]* Eye tear: a name such as given to one whose birth coincides with a period of mourning/ or with a calamity [*Sotho*] (Mohome 1972: 175).

Mopeleko (f) *[moh-peh-leh-koh]* "Save me": this name is associated with the expression "Save me! I do not have any relatives to save me" which is metaphorically the cry of an oppressed or mistreated woman who does not have many blood relatives around (or cry of a child of one in such a situation), or of a child who is an orphan, or of a slave (in past times) who does not see any alternative refuge to her present situation, or of a slave (in past times) who is being sold or being made a hostage [*Ovimbundu*] (Ennis 1945: 6).

Mopotlaki (m) *[moh-poht-lah-kih]* "The one who hurries": a name such as given to a child who is the product of a premature birth [*Sotho*] (Mohome 1972: 177).

Moreithi (m) *[moh-rehy-sth-ih]*/ ***Mureithi*** (m) *[muh-rehy-sth-ih]* Shepherd; herdsman [*Kikuyu*] (Cagnolo 1933: 226-227; Stewart 1993: 94).

Moremi (m) *[moh-reh-mih]* A cultivator; an agriculturist [The *Kikuyu*] (Cagnolo 1933: 227).

Moromodi (m) *[moh-roh-moh-dih]* A name given to the older of a set of twins, one of which is a girl named *Moromotsane* [*Sotho*] (Mohome 1972: 179).

Moromotsane (f) *[moh-roh-moht-sah-neh]* A name given to the younger of a set of twins, one of which is a boy named *Moromodi* [*Sotho*] (Mohome 1972: 179).

Moselantja (f) *[moh-seh-lahnt-jah]* Dog's tail: this derogatory/ non-human name given to a child whose preceding sibling or siblings died, there being pessimism as to whether this one will survive, is however intended to effectuate the opposite of its literal meaning [*Sotho*] (Mohome 1972: 176).

Moselantja (f) *[moh-seh-lahnt-jah]* Dog's tail: derogatory name given to one who has lost two or more preceding siblings to death, the name (paradoxically) intended to devalue and hence serve as protection for this child through dissuading the forces of evil and death from taking such a "useless" child away [*Sotho*] (Thipa 1986: 290).

Moselantja (f) *[moh-seh-lahnt-jah]* Dog's tail: an unpleasant name given to one whose previous born sibling was stillborn or died before weaning, this attributed to sorcery--the name is a means to safeguard this child "by making a show of neglecting it in the hope of lulling the sorcerer's vigilance" [*Sotho*] (Ashton 1952: 33).

Mosele (f) *[moh-seh-leh]* Tail: this derogatory/ non-human name given to a child whose preceding sibling or siblings died, there being pessimism as to whether this one will survive, is however intended to effectuate the opposite of its literal meaning [*Sotho*] (Mohome 1972: 176, 179).

Mosemodi (f) *[moh-seh-moh-dih]* A name given to the older of a set of identical female twins, the younger named *Mosemotsane* [*Sotho*] (Mohome 1972: 179).

Mosemotsane (f) *[moh-seh-moht-sah-neh]* A name given to the younger of a set of identical female twins, the older named *Mosemodi* [*Sotho*] (Mohome 1972: 179).

Mosiuwa (m) *[moh-sih-yuh-wah]* The forsaken one; the one left behind; a name such as given to the younger of a set of twins, one of which is a girl named *Ntshiuwa* [*Sotho*] (Mohome 1972: 175).

Mosuoe (m) *[moh-suh-woh-yeh]* The circumciser/ the one in charge of conducting a circumcision ceremony, and in charge of the boys' initiation lodge (*mophato*): a name such as given to one born soon following the conducting of the first ever initiation ceremony in the family home [*Sotho*] (Ashton 1952: 32, 318).

Mosuwe (m) *[moh-suh-weh]*/ **Mosuwetsane** (f) *[moh-suh-weht-sah-neh]* The teacher [*Sotho*] (Mohome 1972: 179).

Motondo (f/m) *[moh-tohn-doh]* "Banana": a name given to a twin, the other named *Ilumbe* [*Gombe*] (Daeleman 1977: 190).

Motsamai (m) *[moht-sah-mahy]* The traveler; walker; the one who travels: name such as given to a child born to a mother traveling/ or one born at a time the father or a close kin was traveling [The *Sotho*] (Mohome 1972: 171, 176).

Motseki (m) *[moht-seh-kih]* "The one who disputes": a name such as given to a child born during a time of social discord within the family or with neighbors [*Sotho*] (Mohome 1972: 177).

Motshewa (f) *[moht-sheh-wah]* "The ridiculed one" [*Sotho*] (Mohome 1972: 177).

Moturi (m) *[moh-tuh-rih]* The blacksmith [*Kikuyu*] (Cagnolo 1933: 228).

Mozambi (m) *[moh-zahm-bih]* God [*Kakwa, Lugbara*].

Mpabaisi (m) *[mpah-bahy-sih]* "I give to killers": the parent of a child given this name is heralding the message that by bringing forth a child, the parent has presented an opportunity for malicious and antagonistic neighbors to inflict their toll on a helpless being [The *Nyoro*] (Beattie 1957: 104).

Mpagi (m) *[mpah-jih]* Pillar; post; pole; this name is commonly associated with the proverbs "masters (or elders) are like pillars: once they are removed from the clan, the power of the group crumbles" and "a master (or an elder) is (like) a pillar: once it is removed from the clan, the power of the group crumbles" [*Ganda*].

Mpande (m) *[mpahn-deh]* "The root (of future kings)" [The *Zulu*] (Lugg 1968: 13).

Mphathi (m) *[mpah-sth-ih]* Guardian; the manager; controller [*Zulu*] (Koopman 1979: 155).

Mpho (f) *[mpoh]* "Gift"; name given to the older of a set of twins, one of which is a boy named *Neo* [*Sotho*] (Mohome 1972: 179).

Mpia (f/m) *[mpih-yah]* Name given to a twin or to a triplet [*Ntomba*] (Daeleman 1977: 192).

Mpiiga (m) *[mpiih-gah]* Envy; jealousy; this name is sometimes associated with the proverb "two masters (or elders) of the same village, that are jealous of each other, will not guarantee peace in the village" [*Ganda*].

Mpisi (m) *[mpih-sih]* Hyena; hyena; this name is commonly associated with the proverb "people are like (the teeth of) hyenas: their teeth have a laughing appearance on the outside, but inwardly the hyenas are killers" implying that people can smile outwardly but have inner feelings of malice [*Ganda*].

Mpiyenzani (m) *[mpih-yehn-zah-nih]* "What is the army doing?" [*Zulu*] (Koopman 1979: 159).

Mpiyonke (m) *[mpih-yohn-keh]* "Whole army" [*Zulu*] (Koopman 1979: 157).

Mputela (f/m) *[mpuh-teh-lah]* A name given to one whose birth follows that of his or her twin siblings [*Ntomba*] (Daeleman 1977: 191); a name given to a triplet [*Ntomba*] (Daeleman 1977: 192).

Mputu (f/m) *[mpuuh-tuh/ mpuh-tuuh]* Name given to one whose birth follows that of his or her twin siblings [*Bolia, Luba, Luwa, Ntomba*] (Daeleman 1977: 191); a name given to a triplet [*Ntomba*] (Daeleman 1977: 192).

Mputu-Abaangi (f/m) *[mpuuh-tuh-ah-baahn-gih]* A name given to one whose birth follows that of his or her twin siblings [*Luwa*] (Daeleman 1977: 191).

Mputunkanga (f/m) *[mpuh-tuuhn-kahn-gah]* Name given to one whose birth follows that of his or her twin siblings [*Bolia*] (Daeleman 1977: 191); a name given to a triplet [*Ntomba*] (Daeleman 1977: 192).

Mpuuta-Miloongo (f/m) *[mpuuh-taah-mih-loh-ohn-goh]* "Pacemaker of the rows": name given to one whose birth precedes that of his or her twin siblings [*Luwa*] (Daeleman 1977: 193).

Mramba (m) *[mrahm-bah]* A name given to a child conceived or born during the season of harvesting and processing thread from the baobab trees [*Pare*] (Omari 1970: 71).

Msawenkosi (m) *[msah-wehn-koh-sih]* "Mercy of the Lord" [The *Zulu*] (Koopman 1979: 164).

Mshadweni (m) *[muh-tsh-ah-dweh-nih]* "At the wedding" [The *Zulu*] (Koopman 1979: 155).

Mshitu (m) *[muh-tsh-ih-tuuh]* A name given to a child born during the season of boys' initiation ceremonies [*Pare*] (Omari 1970: 71).

Mshoniseni (m) *[mtsh-oh-nih-seh-nih]* "Make him disappear" [*Zulu*] (Koopman 1979: 159).

Mthandeni (m) *[muh-tahn-deh-nih]* "Love him" [*Zulu*] (Koopman 1979: 159).

Mthethuthini (m) *[mteh-tuh-tih-nih]* "What does the law say?" [*Zulu*] (Koopman 1979: 159).

Mthwalose (f) *[muh-twah-loh-seh]* "Burden" [*Zulu*] (Koopman 1979: 156).

Mthwazi (m) *[mtwah-zih]* "Mr. Monkey Rope": this started out as a nickname for a tall and thin man [*Zulu*] (Lugg 1968: 14).

Mubukusu (f/m) *[muh-buh-kuh-suh]* One associated with the *Luyia* group known as the *Bakusu* [*Luyia*].

Muchadzingesu (f/m) *[muh-tch-ahn-dzihn-geh-tsuh]* "You are going to drive us away!": name given to one born during a family dispute with kin or neighbors, whereby the family tired of the malicious acts or attitude of the kin or neighbors, nurses the prospect of moving away from the locale or severely limiting contact with kin [*Shona*] (Jackson 1957: 117).

Muchangi (m) *[muh-tch-ahn-gih]* One who moves about; one who travels frequently [*Embu*].

Muchato (f) *[muh-tch-ah-toh]* Marriage: a name such as given to a child born on a wedding anniversary [*Zezuru*] (Marapara 1954: 8).

Muchemi (f/m) *[muh-tch-eh-mih]* Crybaby [The *Shona*] (Jackson 1957: 120).

Muchemi (m) *[muh-tch-eh-mih]* The careful one; one who treads softly [*Kikuyu*].

Mucheso (m) *[muh-tch-eh-soh]* "Playing game": name given to a child who likes to toy about in games [*Luyia*].

Muchinji (m) *[muh-tch-ihn-jih]* Butcher; fool [*Kikuyu*].

Muchoki (m) *[muh-tch-oh-kih]* The reincarnated (or reborn) one; one named in honor of a child in the family that died [*Kikuyu*].

Mucina (m) *[muh-tch-ih-nah]* The one who sets fires [*Embu*].

Mudyiwa (f/m) *[muh-djih-wah]* "The one eaten up (i.e. by witches)": a name given to a child born into a family that has lost many of its members to death and whereby there is pessimism as to whether this one will survive, the name metaphorically implying that the child will soon, upon death, be at the mercy of sorcerers [The *Shona*] (Jackson 1957: 118).

Mufupi (m) *[muh-fuh-pih]* "The short one": a name given to a child of short height [*Luyia*].

Mugagga (m) *[muh-gahg-gah]* The wealthy one; this name is commonly associated with the proverb "it is the one who is wealthy that is liked (or loved)" which images the tendency for those who are materially well endowed to be better regarded than those who have little [*Ganda*].

Mugandanswa (f/m) *[muh-gahn-dahn-swah]* "A *Ganda* ethnic is (like) edible flying ants"; this name is commonly associated with the proverb "a *Muganda* is (like) edible flying ants: the ants cover their backs with fragile wings, whilst their stomachs hang out bare)" implying that the *Ganda* ethnics (or people in general/ or relations) harbor a false sense of protection, or that they superficially look harmless and kind with the soft wing covering though inwardly they are coarse and stingy; this name is commonly associated with the proverb "the *Ganda* ethnic is (like) edible flying ants: they throw their shields onto their backs" which is a humorous statement that the *Ganda*, in carrying a shield on his back (which was more commonplace with men in the past), has the appearance of the edible flying ants with their wings folded [*Ganda*].

Mugeni (f/m) *[muh-geh-niih]* "Stranger": a name such as given to one born in a strange country or a place of strangers, possibly during the parents' attempt to flee difficulties [*Kaguru*] (Beidelman 1974: 289).

Mugenyi (m) *[muh-geh-ndjh-ih]* Guest; stranger; visitor; this name is sometimes associated with the proverb "the visitor that was invited arrives with ease and spontaneity, approaching noisily and uninhibited"; this name is also sometimes associated with the proverb "anger is (like) a visitor: it comes and goes"; this name is also sometimes associated with the proverb "a visitor puts you in debt" meaning that with the arrival of a visitor, one often goes to borrow from a neighbor so as to be able to give the visitor a proper treat [*Ganda*].

Mugezi (m) *[muh-geh-zih]* Smart/ or clever person; a wise person; that is learned; this name is sometimes associated with the proverb "even the very intelligent one can fail, for even the ears cannot sense smell"; this name is also sometimes associated with the proverb "a situation of marriage can only be destroyed by a very crafty person" which situation more so applies to the past when marriages were very stable [*Ganda*].

Mugo (m) *[muh-goh]* Fortune teller; medicine man [*Embu, Kikuyu*].

Mugoli (m) *[muh-goh-lih]* "Rich one": name such as given to one born during a period of abundance [*Kaguru*] (Beidelman 1974: 288).

Muguwa (m) *[muh-guh-wah]* Rope; tug-of-war event; to steal a goat (with the assistance of a rope); this name is sometimes associated with the proverb "citizens (or lesser officials) are like the neck tendons of a goat: they do not refuse to get roped" implying that people may murmur behind the chief's (or superior official's) back, but they still go on to obey the superior; this name is also sometimes associated with the proverb "neck tendons of a goat are not grumpy over getting roped" implying that one can still get hardeningly tolerant of bad conditions and negative criticism (as is compared with the goat which is often roped by the neck all day, but it heartily grazes) [The *Ganda*].

Muhanda-Ngabo (m) *[muh-haahn-dahn-gah-boh]* The one that lards shields [*Hutu, Tutsi, Twa*].

Muhashyi (m) *[muh-haah-shjih]* The one pursuing money (through forcible fining); "the one after money": this begun as a nickname for the police commissioner, an *administrateur* in the European colonial

territoire in Central Africa--he was responsible for security and he beat, jailed, and fined locals [*Hutu, Tutsi, Twa*].

Muhaya (m) *[muh-hah-yah]* One of (or one associated with) the *Haya*
ethnics [*Hutu, Tutsi, Twa*].

Muhindila (m) *[muh-hihn-dih-lah]* "The one that closes": name such as
given to one who in the group is the last to be circumcised [*Kaguru*]
(Beidelman 1974: 288).

Muhle (f/m) *[muuh-leh]* "He is handsome"; "she is beautiful" [The *Zulu*]
(Koopman 1979: 74, 163).

Muhongo (f/m) *[muh-hohn-goh]* A name given to a child who is the
product of an unusual pregnancy (during which the mother who is th-
en to wear a cap with strings of beads that fall down over her face,
consulted a herbalist for treatment) [*Ovimbundu*] (Ennis 1945: 2).

Muindi (m) *[muh-yihn-dih]* Albino [*Embu*].

Muita (m) *[mwiih-tah]* One who kills; a ruthless one [*Kikuyu*].

Mujere (f/m) *[muh-jeh-reh]* Of the jail: name such as given to one born
when the father is in jail [*Shona*] (Jackson 1957: 119).

Mukadde (f/m) *[muh-kahd-deh]* Elder; parent; old person; that is old;
elder of the church; minister; this name is sometimes associated with
the proverb "'they (i.e. the words/ stories/ issues) get to me here' is
the talk of the elderly" meaning that the elderly are not so physically
mobile, so they often get information through hearsay other than by
way of personally witnessing the happenings; this name is also sometimes associated with the proverb "the village of an elderly person is
called 'too much' (or 'abundance')" implying that whether it comes to
eating food, working, walking, and so forth, he always says 'it is too
much for me!' [*Ganda*].

Mukami (f) *[muh-kah-mih]* The one who milks; "the milker": a name
such as given to one who loves to milk cows [*Embu, Kikuyu*].

Mukanga (f/m) *[muuh-kaahn-gah]* A name given to one whose birth
follows that of his or her twin siblings [*Tetela*] (Daeleman 1977: 191).

Mukejuwa (f) *[muh-keh-eh-juh-wah]* "The spouse of the sun"/ "the
one of the sun": name such as given to one that is beautiful [*Kaguru*]
(Beidelman 1974: 288).

Mukewa (m) *[muh-keh-wah]* A name given to one born in a *mukewa*
plain [*Luyia*].

Mukhebi (m) *[muh-keh-bih]* Circumciser; one associated with a circumciser [*Luyia*].

Mukhuyu (f/m) *[muh-kuh-yuh]* A name given to one born under a fig
tree [*Luyia*].

Mukhwana (f/m) *[muh-kwaah-nah]* A name given to the first born of
twins [*Gisu, Luyia*] (Wako 1985: 38).

Mukiwa (m) *[muh-kih-wah]* "The one that is poor": name such as given
to one born during times of famine [*Kaguru*] (Beidelman 1974: 289).

Mukoko (f/m) *[muh-koh-koh]* "With a hand": a name such as given to a child born while holding his or her head with the hand [The *Kongo*] (Ndoma 1977: 89).

Mukora (m) *[muh-koh-rah]* The deviant one [*Kikuyu*].

Mukulumpagi (m) *[muh-kuh-luhm-pah-jih]* "An elder (or a leader) is a pillar"; this name is commonly associated with the proverb "a master (or an elder) is (like) a pillar: once it is removed from the clan, the power of the group crumbles" [*Ganda*].

Mukundi (m) *[muh-kuhn-dih]* The one who drinks [*Embu*].

Mukungi (m) *[muh-kuhn-gih]* One that is keen; one who treads softly [*Kikuyu*].

Mukuria (m) *[muh-kuh-rjah]* One who walks fast [*Kikuyu*].

Mukwalufu (m) *[muh-kwah-lah-fuuh]* A name given to one who washes excessively, i.e. takes a bath more than twice a day [*Luyia*].

Mulaa (f/m) *[muh-laah]* "Touch me" [*Luo*].

Mulaha (m) *[muh-lah-hah]* A name given to one born under a tree of the species *kumulaa* [*Luyia*].

Mulemwa (m) *[muh-leh-mwah]* "The rejected one": a name such as given to one whose circumstances of birth are disputed [The *Kaguru*] (Beidelman 1974: 289).

Mulenju (m) *[muh-lehn-juh]* This manifestation of a supernatural said to have come from the neighboring *Bunyoro* territory and said to have fallen on the *Alur* ethnics and placed them in trances, is also the nickname of the British colonialist adventurer and warrior Samuel Baker [*Alur*] (Southall 1951: 187).

Muliro (m) *[muh-lih-roh]* A fire; this name is commonly associated with the proverb "blood or kinship relations are (like) fire: although the fire dwells in the house, it hates the house and sometimes burns it down" [*Ganda*].

Mulongo (f/m) *[muh-lohn-goh]* Name given to the second born of twins [*Gisu, Luyia*] (Wako 1985: 38).

Mulongo (f/m) *[muuh-lohn-goh]* A name given to the second born following the birth of his or her twin siblings, i.e. the one born after *Khisa* [*Luyia*].

Mulongwa (m) *[muh-lohn-gwah]* "The one that is talked about": name such as given to one whose birth is the subject of a lot of talk [The *Kaguru*] (Beidelman 1974: 289).

Mumamisha (m) *[muh-mah-mih-tsh-ah]* "In a collection of villages" [*Zulu*] (Koopman 1979: 69).

Mumbi (f) *[muhm-bih]* Creator; the name of the mother of the *Kikuyu* people [*Kikuyu*].

Mumma (m) *[muhm-mah]* Oath [*Luo*].

Mundeyi (m) *[muhn-deh-yih]* "One who makes turns": a name given to one whose growth is not smooth, and instead lingers at times, so he turns out to be stunted [*Shona*] (Jackson 1957: 120).

Munene (m) *[muh-neh-neh]* One who leads; one with leadership qualities; leader [*Embu, Kikuyu*].

Munghunga (m) *[muhn-guhn-gah]* Circumciser: a name such as given to one who is clever and skilled [*Kaguru*] (Beidelman 1974: 288).

Mungu (f) *[muhn-guh]* Ghost: this name is commonly associated with the expression "The lory of a ghost: speak to the lory so that the lory may explain" whereby traditionally the lory is the one that brings the message of the ghost of one from a distance away who has died, the name commonly given to one born at a time the family receives bad tidings [*Ovimbundu*] (Ennis 1945: 7).

Munialo (m) *[muhn-yah-loh]* A name given to a baby of small body size [*Luyia*].

Muniokano (m) *[muhn-yoh-oh-kaah-noh]* A struggle (such as with a task); a troubling of oneself; that involves taking trouble [*Soga*].

Muntongathenjwa (m) *[muhn-toh-ndgh-ah-tehn-jwah]* The person who cannot be trusted [*Zulu*] (Koopman 1979: 157).

Muntukafi (m) *[uh-muhn-tuh-kah-fih]* "One does not die (i.e. despite the circumstances)": a name such as given by the named child's mother who, in response to her parents' disgruntlement over her bearing this child out of wedlock, became depressed and slept in bed and did not eat for a long period of time--nevertheless she did not die despite the psychological pressure [*Zulu*] (Suzman 1994: 261).

Muntukazibona (m) *[muhn-tuh-kah-zih-boh-nah]* "A person does not see himself" [*Zulu*] (Koopman 1979: 159).

Muntuwasembo (m) *[muhn-tuh-wah-sehm-boh]* Person from *Mboland* [*Zulu*] (Koopman 1979: 157).

Muntuyedwa (m) *[muhn-tuh-yeh-dwah]* "The only person"; "a lone person" [*Zulu*] (Koopman 1979: 157).

Munyi (m) *[muh-ndjh-iih]* Rhino [*Embu*].

Munyika (m) *[muh-ndjh-ih-kah]* "The one of the bush": a name such as given to a hunter [*Kaguru*] (Beidelman 1974: 288).

Muponisi (m) *[muh-poh-nih-sih]* Savior: a name such as implying that the birth of this child registered relief to the mother who was sick and overburdened during the pregnancy [*Zulu*] (Herbert 1995: 4).

Murangi (f) *[muh-rahn-gih]* Bamboo; an overseer [*Embu*].

Murango (m) *[muh-rahn-goh]* Door [*Embu*].

Murathi (m) *[muh-rah-sth-ih]* Fortune teller; medicine man [*Embu*].

Muriitui (m) *[muh-riih-tuhy]* One who looks after livestock; shepherd [*Embu, Kikuyu*].

Murimi (m) *[muh-rih-mih]* One who loves to till (or dig) the land; farmer; one who tills the land [*Embu, Kikuyu*].

Muriuki (m) *[muh-rjuh-kih]* The reincarnated (or reborn) one; one named in honor of a child in the family that died [*Embu, Kikuyu*].

Murugi (f) *[muh-ruh-gih]* The one who loves to cook [*Embu, Kikuyu*].

Musa (m) *[muh-sah]* Mercy; kindness [The *Zulu*] (Koopman 1979: 154, 155).

Muse (m) *[muh-seh]* "Elder": pet name adapted from the Swahili name
-title *Mzee* [*Luyia*].

Musha (m) *[muh-tsh-ah]* Village [*Zulu*] (Koopman 1979: 69).

Musiwanda (m) *[muh-sih-wahn-dah]* "Last born (son)" [The *Kaguru*]
(Beidelman 1974: 288).

Musiyiwa (f/m) *[muh-sih-yih-wah]* "The one left behind": name such as
given to a child born after the father died, or to a child born to a mother who dies soon after the delivery [*Shona*] (Jackson 1957: 118).

Musongwe (m) *[muh-sohn-gweh]* "Fearless one" [*Kaguru*] (Beidelman
1974: 288).

Musore (m) *[muh-soh-reh]* One who squeezes his way through [*Luo*].

Musulwa (m) *[muh-suh-lwah]* The unwanted one: name such as given
to one whose parenthood is disputed/ or one born during troubling
times [*Kaguru*] (Beidelman 1974: 289).

Musumba (m) *[muh-suhm-bah]* Bachelor [*Luo*].

Musumi (m) *[muh-suh-mih]* "The one who fetches food": a name such
as given to one who is a good provider [*Kaguru*] (Beidelman 1974:
288).

Musungu (f/m) *[muh-suhn-guh]* "White person"/ "European": a name
such as given to a very light complexioned child [*Luyia*].

Muswaamba (f/m) *[muuh-swaahm-bah]* A name given to one whose
birth follows that of his or her twin siblings [*Luba, Luwa*] (Daeleman
1977: 191).

Mutegi (m) *[muh-teh-gih]* The competent fisherman [*Embu*].

Mutekhele (f/m) *[muh-teh-keh-leh]* A name given to a child that is
sickly [*Luyia*].

Muthama (m) *[muh-sth-ah-mah]* Wanderer [*Kikuyu*].

Muthanje (f) *[muh-sth-ahn-jeh]* "Reed": a name such as given to one
born near reeds [*Embu*].

Muthee (m) *[muh-sth-eh-eh]* The elderly one; elder [*Embu*].

Muthinji (m) *[muh-sth-ihn-jih]* Butcher [*Embu*].

Muthiora (m) *[muh-sth-yoh-rah]* The cunning one [*Kikuyu*].

Muthoni (f) *[muh-sth-oh-nih]* "In-law"/ "mother-in-law": one named in
respect of the father's in-law i.e. the named child's maternal grandmother [*Embu, Kikuyu*].

Mutitu (f) *[muh-tih-tuuh]* Forest [*Embu*].

Mutoka (m) *[muh-toh-kah]* "Motor car": the name is adapted from the
European words, and is given to one born during (or to one associated with) the period motor vehicles were introduced or first seen
in the locale [*Luyia*].

Mutoro (m) *[muh-toh-roh]* A name given to one born soon after a ritual
ceremony [*Luyia*].

Mutswangiwa (m) *[muht-swahn-gih-wah]* "Looked for": a name such
as given to a child born to a mother that took medicaments to make
her fertile [*Zezuru*] (Marapara 1954: 8).

Mutua (f/m) *[muh-tuh-wah]* A name given to a last born [*Luyia*].

Mutugi (m) *[muh-tuh-gih]* Overseer; one who cares for [*Embu*].

Mutuinji (m) *[muh-tuh-yihn-jih]* Butcher; fool [*Kikuyu*].

Mutuiri (m) *[muh-tuhy-rih]* The one who feeds livestock [*Embu*].

Muturi (m) *[muh-tuh-rih]* Blacksmith [*Embu, Kikuyu*].

Muugi (m) *[muuh-gih]* The intelligent one [*Kikuyu*].

Muzikawukho (m) *[muh-zih-kah-wuh-koh]* "There is no family/ home" [*Zulu*] (Koopman 1979: 160).

Mvuria (m) *[mvuh-rih-yah]* Rhino [*Embu*].

Mwaluko (m) *[mwah-luh-koh]* Name given to one whose wounds from getting circumcised took a relatively long time to heal [The *Kaguru*] (Beidelman 1974: 288).

Mwambu (m) *[mwahm-buh]* The name of the first man (as synonymous with the biblical Adam) [*Luyia*].

Mwanda (f/m) *[mwahn-dah]* Gazelle [*Luo*].

Mwangala (m) *[mwahn-gah-lah]* A name given to one born after all of his preceding siblings died [*Luyia*].

Mwaniki (m) *[mwah-nih-kih]* One who spreads bee hives; a bee keeper [*Embu, Kikuyu*].

Mwanjuka (m) *[mwaah-ndjh-uh-kah]* That of a newcomer; of the newcomers [*Kikuyu*].

Mwari (m) *[mwah-rih]* Teacher [*Embu*].

Mwennyango (f) *[mwehn-ndjh-ahn-goh]* Species of coarse grass, the nettle; this name is commonly associated with the proverb "people with sound minds and healthy bodies still get stung by the nettle while they see it" implying that people will still run into the trouble they have clearly envisioned; this name is also commonly associated with the proverb "the *Ganda* ethnics are (like) the stinging nettle: they get stung on it while seeing it with their open eyes" implying that the *Ganda* (or people in general) will ridiculously carry out acts that they fully know are detrimental to themselves such as befriending bad elements and being hospitable to thieves [*Ganda*].

Mwingwa (m) *[mwihn-gwah]* "The one chased away": a name such as given to one whose parenthood is disputed by some [The *Kaguru*] (Beidelman 1974: 288).

Mwongia (f) *[mwohn-gih-yah]* The one who soothes [*Embu*].

Mzikawupheli (m) *[muh-zih-kah-wuh-peh-lih]* "The family does not end" [*Zulu*] (Koopman 1979: 159).

Mzilikazi (m) *[muh-zih-lih-kaah-zih]* "The great abstainer": one possibly born during a period of want [*Zulu*] (Lugg 1968: 13).

Mziwakithi (m) *[muh-zih-wah-kih-tih]* "Homestead of our place" [*Zulu*] (Koopman 1979: 157).

Mziwandile (m) *[muh-zih-wahn-dih-leh]* "Family has increased" [*Zulu*] (Koopman 1979: 159, 166).

Mziwenhlanhla (m) *[muh-zih-weh-nlah-nlah]* "House of fortune/ luck"

[*Zulu*] (Koopman 1979: 156).
Mzungezi (m) *[muh-zuhn-geh-zih]* The one that surrounds; the one that causes to surround [*Zulu*] (Koopman 1979: 155).

-N-

Naababinge (f) *[nnaah-bah-bihn-geh]* "(The spouse of/ or one ass-ociated with/ or one prominent among) those that are chased (or driven away)" [*Ganda*].

Naabalende (f) *[nnaah-bah-lehn-deh]* "(The spouse of/ or one ass-ociated with/ or one prominent among) those that stroll (or go slowly, or are lazy)"; "(the spouse of/ or one affiliated with/ or one prominent amongst) those associated with mudfish" [*Ganda*].

Naabi (f) *[nnaah-bih]* That involves washing oneself (or cleaning up); that involves getting money the easy way [*Ganda*].

Naaliisanga (f) *[nnaah-liih-saahn-gah]* "I will always feed (them)"; "I will always enable (them) to eat"; "I will always cater to (their) nut-ritional needs" [*Ganda*].

Naanyu (f) *[naah-ndjh-uh]* The one that waits [*Maasai*].

Naasisho (m) *[naah-tsih-tsh-oh]* The one that works [*Maasai*].

Naata (m) *[naah-tah]* The one who has [*Maasai*].

Naava (f) *[nnaah-vah]* Daughter of a princess and a commoner [The Ganda].

Naayita (f) *[nnaah-yih-tah]* "I will pass (or move) around"; "I will call (or invite, or name, or describe as)" [*Ganda*].

Nabaagadde (f) *[nnah-baah-gahd-deh]* Name-title of the official fem-ale guardian of the Goddess and fetish *Nantaba* [*Ganda*].

Nabaaliyo (f) *[nnah-baah-lih-yoh]* "They were there" [*Ganda*].

Nababaazi (f) *[nnah-bah-baah-zih]* Surgeons; those that operate on (a patient); those that skin (or flay); those that butcher (an animal); those that cut up (or dismember) [*Ganda*].

Nababazzi (f) *[nnah-bah-bahz-zih]* Carpenters; those that engage in carpentry work; those that make (out of wood using carpentry tools); those that carve (or chop, or cut) [*Ganda*].

Nababi (f) *[nnah-bah-bih]* The bad ones [*Ganda*].

Nababibnge (f) *[nnah-bah-bihn-geh]* "They are chased away (or pur-sued)" [*Ganda*].

Nabadda (f) *[nnah-bahd-dah]* "Those that resurge (or recover, or co-me back)" [*Ganda*].

Nabagasere (f) *[nnah-bah-gah-seh-reh]* "Let them boil it up" [*Ganda*].

Nabagereka (f) *[nnah-bah-geh-reh-kah]* The wife of the king; ones that assess the value of (or apportions) [*Ganda*].

Nabageya (f) *[nnah-bah-geh-yah]* "They make slanderous state-ments" [*Ganda*, *Soga*].

Nabaggala (f) *[nnah-bahg-gah-lah]* Those who close the entrances;

those that shut (or enclose, or bring to an end, or discontinue) [The *Ganda*].

Nabaggya (f) *[nah-bahj-jah]* Ones who uproot or pick crops (and take them away) [*Ganda*].

Nabaka/ Naabaka (f/m) *[nnaah-bah-kah]* "The one that is extremely beautiful"; grasp; catch; lay hold on [*Ganda*].

Nabakeni (f) *[nah-bah-keh-nih]* "Of visitors": a name such as given to one born when there is a presence of visitors [*Luyia*].

Nabakka (f/m) *[nnah-bahk-kah]* "The one that is extremely beautiful"; "those that descend (or sink)" [*Ganda*].

Nabakooza (f) *[nnah-bah-koh-oh-zah]* That tear (or tear off); that cause to suffer greatly; that are of hard times [*Ganda*].

Nabakyala (f) *[nnah-bah-tch-aah-lah]* Queen; senior wife [*Ganda*].

Nabala (m) *[nnah-bah-lah]* "I produced/ bore (such as fruit, or rice, or other food crops)" [*Ganda, Soga*].

Nabaleera (f) *[nnah-bah-leh-eh-rah]* Those that have embroidered designs on the front a long dress type [*Ganda*].

Nabali (m) *[nnah-bah-lih]* (One associated with) gluttons/ eaters [The *Ganda*].

Nabaloga (f) *[nnah-bah-loh-gaah]* "Those that heal (others)"; "those that bewitch (or charm, or put spells on)" [*Ganda, Soga*].

Nabalongo (f) *[nnah-bah-lohn-goh]* Mother of more than one set of twins; wife [*Ganda*].

Nabaluga (f) *[nnah-bah-luh-gah]* Those that administer beatings with canes; those that use walking sticks [*Ganda*].

Nabambonge (f) *[nnah-baahm-bohn-geh]* "Those that are crazy"; "those that whirl around" [*Ganda*].

Nabana (f) *[nnah-bah-nah]* Daughter of a princess and a commoner [*Ganda*].

Nabanaku (f) *[nnah-bah-nah-kuh]* Those who are distraught (or in misery, or in poverty) [*Ganda*].

Nabanakulya/ Nnabanakulya (f) *[nnah-bah-naah-kuh-ljah]* "They will devour you" [*Ganda*].

Nabangala (f) *[nah-bahn-gah-lah]* A name given to one born after all of his preceding siblings died [*Luyia*].

Nabangi (m) *[nah-bahn-gih]* A name given to one whose birth follows that of his twin siblings [*Luyia*].

Nabanjala (f) *[nnah-bahn-jah-lah]* "Those of famine (or hunger)"; ones born during hunger (or famine, or a dry season); "they spread out to dry" [*Ganda*].

Nabankema (f) *[nnah-bahn-keh-mah]* "They tempt me"; "they put me to test" [*Ganda*].

Nabankuuma/ Nnabankuuma (f) *[nnah-bahn-kuuh-mah]* "They watch over/ or guard/ or protect me" [*Ganda*].

Nabasa (f) *[nnah-bah-sah]* Omnipotent [*Ganda*].

Nabasaaku/ Nnabasaaku (f) *[nnah-bah-saah-kuh]* Those that beat severely (or unmercifully); those that attack; those who beat (tree bark into barkcloth in the first processing stage)" *[Ganda]*.

Nabasaasanya (f) *[nnah-bah-saah-saah-ndjh-aah]* Distributors; "they spread it"; "they cause to scatter (or disperse)" *[Ganda]*.

Nabasaku/ Nnabasaku (f) *[nnah-bah-sah-kuh]* Those that beat severely (or unmercifully); those that attack; those that forage (for food); those that travel a distance to obtain food either by paying in money (or in exchange for services); those that dig up information *[Ganda]*.

Nabasenya (f) *[nnah-bah-seh-ndjh-ah]* "Those that are picky and brush over (such as food) with a display of reluctance"; "those that brush/ clean (such as teeth)" *[Ganda]*.

Nabasinga (m) *[nnah-bah-sihn-gah]* "Those who bet (or pledge, or vow)"; "those that are excellent"; "those that surpass"; of the *Basinga* clan members *[Ganda]*.

Nabasoba (f) *[nnah-bah-soh-bah]* "Those who go wrong (or are wrong)"; "those who are over and above"; "those who become pregnant before marriage"; "those who lose shape" *[Ganda]*.

Nabatanzi (f) *[nnah-bah-tahn-zih]* "(Of) those who fine" *[Ganda]*.

Nabategere (f) *[nnah-bah-teh-geh-reh]* Those that they have arranged for (or prepared for, or made ready for) *[Ganda]*.

Nabatte (m) *[nnah-baht-teh]* "Let them (or may they) kill (or murder, or destroy, or ruin, or abolish, or annul)"; of those that are killed [The Ganda].

Nabattu (f) *[nnah-baht-tuh]* Small packages; small packets *[Ganda]*.

Nabawanire (f) *[nnah-bah-wah-nih-reh]* That are held up (or supported, or propped up, or sustained); (assisting hunters) that are divided one's spoil with [Ganda, Soga].

Nabayaza/ Nnabayaza (f) *[nnah-bah-yah-zah]* That make abundant (or cause to spread, or cause to multiply, or cause to increase); those that search (such as a house or a person); those that search for *[Ganda]*.

Nabayengo (f) *[nnah-bah-yehn-goh]* Those that are associated with water waves *[Ganda]*.

Nabayiga (f) *[nnah-bah-yih-gah]* Learners *[Ganda]*.

Nabazika (f) *[nnah-bah-zih-kah]* Run wild/ or overgrown (with weeds or excess vegetation) *[Ganda]*.

Nabaziwa (f) *[nnah-bah-zih-zah]* "They give them" *[Ganda]*.

Nabazze (f) *[nnah-bahz-zeh]* "They have returned (or come back)"; "they have gone back" *[Ganda]*.

Nabbaale (f) *[nnahb-baah-leh]* A deity; the heavens; the sky *[Ganda]*.

Nabbamba/ Nnabbamba (m) *[nnahb-bahm-bah]* That is vast (or extensive); that stretches out; the name of a deity *[Ganda]*.

Nabbanda (f) *[nnahb-bahn-dah]* Hollow stemmed perennial mountain bamboo [*Ganda*].

Nabbanja/ Nnabbanja (f) *[nnahb-bahn-jah]* Debt; the demand for payment of a debt [*Ganda*].

Nabbengo/ Nnabbengo (f) *[nnahb-behn-goh]* Large millstone; large grindstone; large scale for weighing sacks (or bags) of produce such as of sugar and coffee berries [*Ganda*].

Nabbona (f) *[nnahb-boh-nah]* Collar (or band) of metal or wood; insulator for telegraph wires; the sports discuss [*Ganda*].

Nabboola (f) *[nnahb-boh-oh-lah]* An expulsion (from a clan); a disowning; a disinheriting; an excommunication; an ostracizing; a discrimination; a showing of prejudice against [*Ganda*].

Nabbosa (f) *[nnahb-boh-sah]* Perfect looking; perfectly beautiful [The *Ganda*].

Nabbubi/ Nnabbubi (f) *[nnahb-buh-bih]* The spider [*Ganda*].

Nabbumba (f) *[nnahb-buhm-bah]* Clay; potter's clay [*Ganda*].

Nabbuto (f) *[nnahb-buh-toh]* (With) a large belly [*Ganda*].

Nabeefunye (f/m) *[nnah-beh-eh-fuh-ndjh-eh]* The name of a species of small caterpillar; "they are folded up (or wrinkled, or crumpled)"; "they have folded themselves up" [*Ganda*].

Nabembe/ Nnabembe (f) *[nnah-behm-beh]* Crust (on burnt food); burnt portion adhering to the pan; (formation of) a crust or scab; a coagulation; a swarming; an abundance [*Ganda*].

Nabembezi/ Nnabembezi (f/m) *[nnah-behm-beh-zih]* That is handled with care (or treated with consideration) [*Ganda*].

Nabembezo (m) *[nnah-behm-beh-zoh]* Handled with care; treated with consideration [*Ganda*].

Nabibia (m) *[nah-bih-bih-yah]* A name given to one born at a blacksmith's home [*Luyia*].

Nabibooge (f) *[nnah-bih-boh-oh-geh]* A species of edible plants resembling spinach but having smaller leaves [*Ganda*].

Nabibbubu (f) *[nnah-bih-buhb-buh]* Species of tall grasses that have prickly spicules [*Ganda*].

Nabiddo (f) *[nnah-bihd-doh]* Grasses; tufts; weeds [*Ganda*].

Nabifuufu (f) *[nnah-bih-fuuh-fuh]* One who moves quickly; one who moves ceaselessly; (like) dust [*Ganda*].

Nabifwo (f) *[nah-bih-fwoh]* A name given to one born outside the house in the bush [*Luyia*].

Nabigavu (f) *[nnah-bih-gah-vuh]* That are shut (or closed) [*Ganda*].

Nabigotto (f) *[nnah-bih-goht-toh]* That are mashed up (or crushed, or pounded) [*Ganda*].

Nabijugo (f) *[nnah-bih-juh-goh]* The bell ringers; pen holders [The *Ganda*].

Nabikaajumbe (f) *[nnah-bih-kaah-juhm-beh]* Old straws spread on the floor of a house; hut thatching straws [*Ganda*].

Nabikamba (m) *[nnah-bih-kahm-bah]* Urine [*Ganda*].

Nabikande (f) *[nnah-bih-kahn-deh]* Deserted stretches of land; waste-lands; name-title of the royal chief midwife [*Ganda*].

Nabikofu (f) *[nnah-bih-koh-fuh]* (Like/ or of) guinea fowls [*Ganda*, *Soga*].

Nabikolo (f) *[nnah-bih-koh-loh]* Roots; tree bases [*Ganda*].

Nabikoni (f) *[nnah-bih-koh-nih]* The pipe stem euphorbia trees from which are obtained sticky sap said to be useful in healing warts [The *Ganda*].

Nabikono (f) *[nnah-bih-koh-noh]* Arms of the lake (or sea); estuaries; bays; with a peculiarity of the arms [*Ganda*].

Nabiku (f) *[nnah-bih-kuh]* Bed bugs; large pieces of dead wood; old pieces of firewood.

Nabikuku (f) *[nnah-bih-kuh-kuh]* A skin disease characterized by a rash and excessive itching [*Ganda*].

Nabikukuzi (f) *[nnah-bih-kuh-kuh-zih]* That cause to become moldy; that cause to mildew [*Ganda*].

Nabikyalo (f) *[nnah-bih-tch-aah-loh]* (That associated with) the vill-age/ or the rural countryside/ or the large estate; visits [*Ganda*].

Nabilai (m) *[nah-bih-lahy]* A name given to a handsome child [*Luyia*].

Nabinene (f) *[nnah-bih-neh-neh]* "Large ones"; "big ones" [*Ganda*].

Nabinyale (f) *[nnah-bih-ndjh-ah-leh]* Sootiness; soot; lint; small part-icles of dust that float in the air [*Ganda*].

Nabinyansi (f) *[nnah-bih-ndjh-ahn-sih]* That are in the manner of the native (or the indigenous, or the local, or the national, or the citizen) [*Ganda*].

Nabira/ Nnabira (f) *[nnah-bih-rah]* That becomes warmed up; (food) that becomes warmed over [*Ganda*].

Nabirimu (f) *[nnah-bih-rih-muh]* Those which contain; those which make sense; those that have value [*Ganda*].

Nabiriyo/ Nnabiriyo (m) *[nnah-bih-rih-yoh]* "That are there" [*Ganda*].

Nabirongo (f) *[nnah-bih-rohn-goh]* That are associated with twins [*Ganda*].

Nabiruka (f) *[nnah-bih-ruh-kah]* That slip away (or glide away, or fly away, or disappear); that are associated with a parish (or a sub-district); small nets for capturing (such as guinea fowls); weavings; plaitings [*Ganda*].

Nabirumbi (f) *[nnah-bih-ruhm-bih]* Young sugar canes; young eleph-ant grasses [*Ganda*].

Nabirya (f) *[nnah-bih-rjah]* "I ate (or consumed) them"; "they eat (or consume)" [*Ganda*].

Nabirye (f) *[nnah-bih-rjeh/ naah-bih-rjeh]* Mother of twins [The *Ganda*, *Soga*].

Nabiryo (f) *[nnah-bih-rjoh]* The pumpkin vines; the gourd vines; that is associated with profitable ventures; that is of or associated with the family (or the race, or the genealogy, or the lineage, or the pedigree)

[*Ganda, Soga*].

Nabisaalu (f) *[nnah-bih-saah-luh]* Rush marsh grasses; patches of rushes; marshes; the lacustrine pratincol birds [*Ganda*].

Nabisaaniiko/ Nnabisaaniiko (f) *[nnah-bih-saah-niih-koh]* The planet Jupiter; liter; trash [*Ganda*].

Nabisaanyi (f) *[nnah-bih-saah-ndjh-ih]* The hairy caterpillars; the caterpillars [*Ganda*].

Nabisenke (f) *[nnah-bih-seh-ehn-keh]* Having a film covering over the eyes; afflictions on the pupil and the iris [*Ganda*].

Nabisere (f) *[nnah-bih-seh-reh]* (Liquids) boiling; that are watery (or diluted, or soggy); that have diminished (or declined, or exhausted, or weakened, or become limp); that are bewitched [*Ganda*].

Nabisiga (f) *[nnah-bih-sih-gah]* That are associated with sowing (or the planting season); that are associated with the stones, bricks, or balls of clay arranged for a wood containing fireplace for cooking; that are associated with the cooking area of a stove or oven; that involve staying by the hearth; wakeful sittings up for a long time; that are associated with the largest subdivisions of clans [*Ganda*].

Nabisubi (f) *[nnah-bih-suh-bih]* Grass [*Ganda*].

Nabisunsa (f) *[nnah-bih-suhn-sah]* Leaves of the pumpkin (or vine gourd) that are eaten as relish [*Ganda*].

Nabiswa (m) *[nah-bih-swah]* "Of ant hills" a name such as given to one born in an environment of ant hill abundance [*Luyia*].

Nabiswazzi/ Nnabiswazzi (f) *[nnah-bih-swahz-zih]* That are tasteless; that are of poor quality [*Ganda*].

Nabitaba (f) *[nnah-bih-tah-bah]* Puddles; temporary convergences of water; stagnant waters following a rainfall [*Ganda*].

Nabitaka (f) *[nnah-bih-tah-kah]* Earth; that are brown; that are earth colored [*Ganda*].

Nabitakuli (f) *[nnah-bih-tah-kuh-lih]* Busybodies; those who though busy, do not accomplish much; restlessness; that are scratched [The *Ganda*].

Nabitali (f) *[nnah-bih-tah-lih]* That are not (what they purport to be); that are without; that are not to be [*Ganda*].

Nabitalo (f) *[nnah-bih-tah-loh]* Associated with wonders (or miracles): a name commonly given to one who is the first born to a woman of a relatively advanced age, or one born with visible teeth in the mouth, or born with more fingers than normal, or one born with some other atypical body feature [*Ganda*].

Nabiteete (f) *[nnah-bih-teh-eh-teh]* Fine grass carpeting on the floors of houses [*Ganda*].

Nabitengero (f) *[nnah-bih-tehn-geh-roh]* That involve nervousness (or frightfulness, or trepidation) [*Ganda*].

Nabitimpa (m) *[nnah-bih-tihm-pah]* Beatings; whippings; thrashings [*Ganda*].

Nabitoogo (f) *[nnah-bih-toh-oh-goh]* Stalks of papyrus [The *Ganda, Soga*].

Nabitosi (f) *[nnah-bih-toh-sih]* Wet clay; alluvium [*Ganda, Soga*].

Nabitula (f) *[nnah-bih-tuh-lah]* (Associated with) a species of delicious fruits that have sepals that cause a choking sensation when being removed [*Ganda*].

Nabitungo (f) *[nnah-bih-tuhn-goh]* Sewings; threading on a string; attachments [*Ganda*].

Nabitunzi (f) *[nnah-bih-tuhn-zih]* That cause or enable to sell (or to make bargains); the means by which to sell (or to bargain); selling; the means by which to sew (or to thread); that causes to sew [The *Ganda*].

Nabitwere (f) *[nnah-bih-tweh-reh]* Beer during the fermentation process [*Ganda*].

Nabiwande (f) *[nnah-bih-wahn-deh]* That are spit out; that are hurled out forcibly [*Ganda*].

Nabiweeke (f) *[nnah-bih-weh-eh-keh]* That are carried on the back; that are lifted and thrown (such as in wrestling or in some other struggle) [*Ganda*].

Nabiweke (f) *[nnah-bih-weh-keh]* Grains; seeds; pills [*Ganda*].

Nabiwemba (f) *[nnah-bih-wehm-bah]* Coverings up; spreadings out; swarmings all over [*Ganda*].

Nabiwoko (f) *[nnah-bih-woh-koh]* A species of evergreen shrubs, the leaves of which are highly poisonous [*Ganda*].

Nabiyiki (f) *[nnah-bih-yih-kih]* A species of creeping plant whose seeds are used in a game (*mweso*) [*Ganda*].

Nabiyonga (f) *[nnah-bih-yohn-gah]* Sparks from a grass fire; pieces of burnt paper flying in the air [*Ganda*].

Nabona (m) *[nnah-boh-nah]* That experiences trouble [*Soga*].

Nabowa (f) *[nnah-boh-wah]* The convolvulus, a species of climbing plant [*Ganda*].

Nabubi/ Nnabubi (f/m) *[nnah-buh-bih]* That are of evil (or wickedness); that are of badness (or inferiority, or ugliness) [*Ganda*].

Nabudobona (f) *[nnah-buh-doh-boh-nah]* A going to waste; a mess up; a bungle; a talking of nonsense [*Ganda*].

Nabuggala (f) *[nnah-buhg-gah-lah]* That close off (the entrance or the exit); the closer [*Ganda*].

Nabuggamu (f) *[nnah-buhg-gah-muh]* Sheltering from (the sun or the rain) [*Ganda*].

Nabugo (f) *[nnah-buh-goh]* Small leopards; small enclosures; small kraals; small fences enclosing cattle; small brinks (or rims, or edges) [*Ganda, Soga*].

Nabugulu (m) *[nnah-buh-guh-luh]* (With the peculiarity) of small legs [*Ganda, Soga*].

Nabuguzi (f) *[nnah-buh-guh-zih]* That involves commercialism; merchant; buying; trade; commercial dealing [*Ganda*].

Nabugwaamu (f/m) *[nnah-buh-gwaah-muh]* Intruders; interloper; "I fell right into it"; "I fell upon it"; "I fell right into the occurrence"; "they fall into/ or upon it" [*Ganda*].

Nabukalu (f) *[nnah-buh-kah-luh]* That are dry (or stiff, or hard); aridness of the ground; distinctness or clarity of voices [*Ganda*].

Nabukeera (f) *[nnah-buh-keh-eh-rah]* That get up early; "I went for it (or them) early"; "I started on it (or them) early" [*Ganda*].

Nabukenya (f) *[nah-buh-keh-ndjh-ah]/* ***Nabukekenyi*** (f) *[nnah-buh-keh-keh-ndjh-ih]* One who with violence, hurls to the ground (such as during wrestling); one who acts reluctantly or ungraciously; killings [*Ganda*].

Nabukome (f) *[nnah-buh-koh-meh]* Cloudy weather; cloudy day [The *Ganda*].

Nabukomeko (f) *[nnah-buh-koh-meh-koh]* That are touched; that are come up to; that are rebuked; that cannot be controlled; that are insubordinate; "that is where they stop"; "stop at those"; those which are arranged (or put in compact form, or stacked) [*Ganda*].

Nabukuuku (f) *[nnah-buh-kuuh-kuh]* Scraps of firewood; one that carries out without hesitation; one who acts in a straightforward (or forceful) manner [*Ganda*].

Nabukwanzi (f) *[nnah-buh-kwahn-zih]* Strings of beads; necklaces; small beads generally made of plant seeds [*Ganda*].

Nabukya (f) *[nnah-buh-tch-ah]* "It dawns"; "(the rain) lets up"; "(the famine) ends" [*Ganda*].

Nabukyu (f) *[nnah-buh-tch-uh]* Dregs in beer [*Ganda*].

Nabula (f) *[nnah-buh-lah]* One that goes astray (or disappears, or becomes missing, or is lacking); one that is lost to; "I went astray"; "I disappeared"; "I became missing"; "I became lacking"; "I became lost" [*Ganda*].

Nabulagala (f/m) *[nnah-buh-lah-gah-lah]* Leaves; foliage; medicines; drugs; chemicals [*Ganda*].

Nabulega (f) *[nnah-buh-leh-gah]* To taste or try; overdue pregnancy [*Ganda*].

Nabulekwe (f) *[nnah-buh-leh-kweh]* Forcefulness; wholeheartedness; relentless determination [*Ganda*].

Nabulime (f) *[nnah-buh-lih-meh]* That are cultivated (or farmed, or dug); a cultivation [*Ganda*].

Nabulo/ Nnabulo (f) *[nnah-buh-loh]* Millet [*Ganda*].

Nabulwana (f) *[nnah-buh-lwah-nah]* "The small ones fight (or struggle, or make war)" [*Ganda*].

Nabulya (f) *[nnah-buh-ljah]* "I ate (or consumed)"; "I took up high office" [*Ganda*].

Nabuna/ Nnabuna (f) *[nnah-buh-nah]* That spreads (or spreads over, or reaches all over); (food) that is enough to go around; that gets ones share; that gets enough; that participates; "I went (or reached all over, or spread over)" [*Ganda*].

Nabunga/ Nabbunga (f/m) *[nnahb-buhn-gah]* One who rambles (or wanders around) aimlessly [*Ganda*].

Nabunje (f) *[nnah-buhn-jeh]* The seeds of a fruit resembling a large dark olive, and which seeds are used as spinning tops [*Ganda*].

Nabunnya (f) *[nnah-buhn-ndjh-aah]* Small holes; small gutters; decoys [*Ganda*].

Nabusoga/ Nnabusoga (f) *[nnah-buh-soh-gah]* One of (or one associated with) *Soga* ethnics, or the *Busoga* territory [*Ganda, Soga*].

Nabuswala (m) *[nnah-buh-swah-lah]* Those that become disgraced; those that are put to shame; those that become ashamed [The *Ganda, Soga*].

Nabuta (f) *[nnah-buh-tah]* That stagger around aimlessly; that are at loss; that are in a state of confusion; that are at the end of their wits [*Ganda*].

Nabuto (f) *[nnah-buh-toh]* "Young ones"; "mother of young ones" [*Ganda*].

Nabutono (f) *[nnah-buh-toh-noh]* Slim or small girl [*Ganda, Soga*].

Nabutunzi (f) *[nnah-buh-tuhn-zih]* Tailoring; merchandising; trading; selling [*Ganda*].

Nabututu (f) *[nah-buh-tuh-tuh]* A name given to one whose weight, as a baby, is below normal [*Luyia*].

Nabuuma (f) *[nnah-buuh-mah]* One associated with money; one associated with small machines (or tools, or instruments, or devices) [*Ganda*].

Nabuuso (f/m) *[nnah-buuh-soh]* (With a peculiarity of) small eyes [The *Ganda*].

Nabuwembo (f) *[nnah-buh-wehm-boh]* Spread around; a spread out; a cover up [*Ganda*].

Nabuwufu (f) *[nnah-buh-wuh-fuh]* One who tracks (or traces, or gives direction); pawprints; footprints; tracks [*Ganda*].

Nabuwule (f) *[nnah-buh-wuh-leh]* One who has experienced temporary aversions to (such as to certain foods) [*Ganda*].

Nabuyira (f) *[nnah-buh-yih-rah]* Rippling noises; gurglings (of water); rumblings/ roars (such as of waterfalls or big fires); snortings; snorings; wheezings; purrings [*Ganda*].

Nabwaga (f/m) *[nnah-bwah-gah]* "They melt" [*Ganda*].

Nabwami (f) *[nnah-bwaah-mih]* Honored (or powerful) woman; power; authority; high position [*Ganda*].

Nabwana/ Nabwaana (f/m) *[nnah-bwaah-nah]* (Parent of/ or owner of) children that are small in physique [*Ganda*].

Nabwanda (m) *[nnah-bwahn-dah]* (That is associated with) a species of weed which spreads rapidly and is difficult to eliminate; (that is associated with) small pieces of charcoal (or coal) [*Ganda, Soga*].

Nabwato/ Nabwaato/ Nnabwato (f) *[nnah-bwaah-toh]* Small boats; small canoes; small ships; small steamers; small brewing vats [The *Ganda*].

Nabwavu/ Nnabwaavu (f) *[nnah-bwaah-vuh]* Poverty; indigence [The *Ganda*].

Nabweggamu/ Nnabweggamu (f) *[nnah-bwehg-gah-muh]* Sheltering from (the sun or the rain) [*Ganda*].

Nabweteme (f) *[nnah-bweh-teh-meh]* Commitments; pledges; promises; that has cut itself (or oneself); that has cut for itself (or oneself); that has undertaken (to) [*Ganda*].

Nabwile (f) *[nah-bwih-leh]* "The one of the night": a name such as given to one born in the depth of night [*Luyia*].

Nabwire (f) *[nah-bwih-reh]* "The one of the night": a name such as given to one born in the night [*Samia*] (Nzita 1995: 73).

Nabwiso/ Nabwiiso (f/m) *[nnah-bwiih-soh]* (With a peculiarity of) small eyes [*Soga*].

Nabwoba (f) *[nah-bwoh-bah]* A name given to one born during a season of mushroom abundance [*Luyia*].

Nabyalo (f) *[nnah-bjaah-loh]* Villages; large estates; rural areas; countryside areas [*Ganda*].

Nabyoloolo (f) *[nnah-bjoh-loh-oh-lah]* The helping/ or giving assistance to (such as a poor person or one in difficulty) [*Ganda*].

Nabyonga (f) *[nnah-bjohn-gah]* A species of large and venomous caterpillars that are hairy [*Ganda*].

Nabyuma (f) *[nnah-bjuuh-mah]* Irons; metals; machinery; machines; tools; devices [*Ganda*].

Nacheke/ Naceke (m) *[nnah-tch-eh-keh]* That is of an ongoing (or continuing) rainfall; that makes a rattling (or creaking, or chugging) sound; that rings (such as a bell) [*Ganda*].

Nachwa/ Nacwa (f) *[nnah-tch-wah]* One who flees or escapes; the sound of cutting or rustling movements [*Ganda*].

Nadogo/ Naddogo (f) *[nnahd-doh-goh]* Sorcerer; healer; witchcraft; magic; magician; object or combination of objects used to produce magic effects [*Ganda*].

Nadosoito (m) *[nah-doh-tsohy-toh]* The one with red stones [*Maasai*].

Naduli (m) *[nnah-duh-lih]* Indian hemp seed [*Ganda*].

Nadupoi (f) *[nah-duh-pohy]* The one that is redeemed [*Maasai*].

Naeku (f) *[nah-yeh-kuh]* The one that comes very early [*Maasai*].

Nafula (f) *[nah-fuh-lah]* A name given to one born during a rainy season [*Luyia*].

Nafuna (f) *[nah-fuh-nah]* A name given to one who is of a breech birth i.e. one born feet first (as opposed to the conventional head first); a name given to one who is born soon following the death of a child in the home [*Luyia*].

Nagabandule (f) *[nnah-gah-bahn-duh-leh]* That was broken open (or snapped open, or opened forcefully) [*Ganda*].

Naganga (f) *[nnah-gaahn-gah]* One who treats a sickness; herbalist [*Ganda, Soga*].

Nagawa (f) *[nnah-gah-wah]* Associated with the patas monkey.

Nagawonye/ Nnagawonye (m) *[nnah-gah-woh-ndjh-eh]* That has been cured (or healed, or has escaped it, or got saved from it, or escaped from it, or got rid of it); "I have been cured (or healed) from it"; "I escaped it"; "I got saved from it"; "I escaped from It" [*Ganda*].

Nagawonyi/ Nnagawonyi (m) *[nnah-gah-woh-ndjh-ih]* That has been cured (or healed, or has escaped it, or got saved from it, or escaped from it, or got rid of it) [*Ganda*].

Nagaya (f/m) *[nnah-gah-yah]* "I harbored contempt (for)/ or scorned" [*Ganda*].

Nagayi/ Naggayi (f) *[nnahg-gah-yih]* Scorn; contempt; sloth; idleness; boredom [*Ganda*].

Nagenda (m) *[nnah-gehn-dah]* One who went forth [*Ganda*].

Nageza (f/m) *[nnah-geh-zah]* "I tried (or tested, or put to test)"; "I took as an example (or compared, or took into account)" [*Ganda, Soga*].

Nagezza (f/m) *[nnah-gehz-zah]* "I caused to become fat (or obese)"; "I caused to increase (or to become greater)" [*Ganda*].

Naggenda/ Nnaggenda (m) *[nnahg-gehn-dah]* One that goes (or goes away) [*Ganda*].

Naggendo (f) *[nnahg-gehn-doh]* Long voyage; long trip [*Ganda*].

Naggombwa (m) *[nnahg-gohm-bwah]* A plaiting of reeds; that is tied crosswise; that is intertwined; that is entangled; that is complicated; that is desired [*Ganda*].

Naggugu (f) *[nnahg-guh-guh]* A species of water grass; a large load/ or burden [*Ganda*].

Naggulu (f) *[nnahg-guh-luh]* Heaven; the sky; lightning [*Ganda*].

Naggulumbya (m) *[nnahg-guh-luhm-bjah]* That shakes (or causes to shake); that tosses about (or causes to toss about); that rumbles (or causes to rumble); that rattles (or causes to rattle); that creates an uproar; that bothers; that causes to be agitated [*Ganda*].

Nagujja/ Nnagujja (f) *[nnah-guhj-jah]* "It comes"; "it arrives"; "it happens" [*Ganda*].

Nagula/ Nnagula (f) *[nnah-guh-lah]* That buys (or purchases) [The Ganda].

Nagutta/ Nnagutta (f/m) *[nnah-guht-tah]* "(Amongst those) I will perform rituals of blood-brotherhood with, (some will conspire against me through causing others to harm me)" [*Ganda*].

Nagwala (f) *[nnah-gwah-lah]* "It becomes abundant (or increases, or multiplies, or spreads)" [*Ganda*].

Nagwovuma (f) *[nnah-gwoh-oh-vuh-mah]* The one you insult (or revile, or slander); "the one you are abusive towards" [*Ganda*].

Nagyawa (f) *[nnah-jaah-waah]* "Where shall I fit (in)/ or be fitting?";

"where shall I be suitable (or appropriate)?"; "what shall I be con-gruent with?" [*Ganda*].

Nainguran (m) *[nah-yihn-guh-rahn]* The one that plays [*Maasai*].

Naini (f) *[nahy-nih]* The one that waits [*Maasai*].

Naipanoi (f) *[nahy-pah-nohy]* The one that is easy to send [*Maasai*].

Nairuko (f) *[nahy-ruh-koh]* The one that responds [*Maasai*].

Nairuma (f) *[nnahy-ruh-mah]* That bites (or pinches); that hurts (or is in pain, or is aching); one who charges with a fault [*Soga*].

Naisae (f) *[nah-yih-saah-yeh]* "The child was born (soon) after a ritual or sacrificial service had been performed for the dracaena tree sh-rine" [*Pare*] (Omari 1970: 70).

Naisarusaru (f) *[nahy-tsah-ruh-sah-ruh]* The one that comes very fast [*Maasai*].

Naiscae (f) *[nahy-tsk-ah-yeh]* The one whose body is soft (or tender) [*Maasai*].

Naisha (f) *[nahy-tsh-ah]* A name given to a child whose mother's la-bor pains were uncharacteristically erratic and discontinuous, so con-sequently the midwives did not participate that much in the eventual delivery [*Pare*] (Omari 1970: 70).

Naishorua (f) *[nahy-tsh-oh-ruh-wah]* The one that has been given [*Maasai*].

Naisula (f) *[nahy-tsuh-lah]* The one that has excelled [*Maasai*].

Naitareu (f) *[nahy-tah-rehw]* The one who escorts [*Maasai*].

Najeke/ Najjeke (f) *[nnahj-jeh-keh]* In trouble or difficulty; poverty [*Ganda*].

Najemba/ Najjemba (f) *[nnahj-jehm-bah]* Witchcraft substance; that talks in a noisy and foolish manner; that talks nonsense; that rants [*Ganda*].

Najembe/ Najjembe (f) *[nahj-jehm-beh]* Large horn (of an animal); fetish; spirit associated with a fetish; spell; hex [*Ganda*].

Najengo/ Najjengo (m) *[nnahj-jehn-goh]* Water wave [*Ganda*].

Najja (f/m) *[nnahj-jah]* "I came (at a bad time)": a name commonly given to a child born following the father's death [*Ganda*].

Najjakulya (m) *[nnahj-jah-kuh-ljah]* "I came to eat (or acquire, or usurp power)" [*Ganda*].

Najjalwambi (f/m) *[nnahj-jah-lwah-mbih]* "I came at a bad time": a na-me commonly given to a child born following the father's death [The *Ganda*].

Najjamalenge (f/m) *[nnahj-jah-mah-lehn-geh]/ Najjanannenge* (f/m) *[nnahj-jah-nahn-nehn-geh]/ Najjannenge* (f/m) *[nnahj-jahn-nehn-geh]* "I came with feet first": a name commonly given to a child born feet first (as opposed to the conventional head first) from the womb [The *Ganda*].

Najjambuubu (f/m) *[nnahj-jahm-buuh-buh]* "My birth was associated with indigestion (or stomach rumbling)" [*Ganda*].

Najjinda (f) *[nahj-jihn-dah]* Menacing/ threatening (weather) [*Ganda*].

Najjoba (f) *[nnahj-joh-bah]* Tuft of hair on a shaven head; the crest of a bird (especially the crested crane) [*Ganda*].

Najjoge (f) *[nnahj-joh-geh]* A species of tall forest tree [*Ganda*].

Najuuka/ Najjuuka (f) *[nnahj-juuh-kah]* One who talks in an abrasive, abusive or reverberating in tone; one who becomes enraged [*Ganda*].

Najuuko/ Najjuuko (f) *[nnahj-juuh-koh]* Abrasive or reverberating in tone; enragement [*Ganda*].

Najuuma/ Najjuuma (f) *[nnahj-juuh-mah]* That becomes furious (or angry); that goes wild; that is rebellious [*Ganda*].

Najuumwa/ Najjuumwa (f/m) *[nnahj-juuh-mwah]* That is caused to become furious (or angry); that is caused to go wild; that is caused to be rebellious [*Ganda*].

Nakaake (f) *[nnah-kaah-keh]* "Let it burn (or blaze, or light up, or shine)"; "let flare up in anger"; "let it be burned up"; "let suffer from immense hunger (or thirst)" [*Ganda*].

Nakaana (m) *[nnah-kaah-nah]* Small child; baby [*Ganda, Soga*].

Nakaasa (f) *[nnah-kaah-sah]* A fiercely biting species of black soldier ant [*Ganda*].

Nakaayi (f) *[nnah-kaah-yih]* (Small) dried plantain fiber; bitterness; or sourness [*Ganda*].

Nakabaale (f/m) *[nnah-kah-baah-leh]* Small deity; small stone [*Soga*].

Nakabalira (f/m) *[nnah-kah-bah-lih-rah]* Species of medium sized tree [*Ganda*].

Nakambagiza (f/m) *[nnah-kah-bahm-bah-gih-zah]* One who interrupts (or interferes); one who injects himself/ herself into a conversation [*Ganda*].

Nakabanda/ Nnakabanda (f) *[nnah-kah-bahn-dah]* A species of sweet potato; one who makes his way through (such as through a thicket of grass); climber; shed in which bricks are made; moment; space [*Ganda*].

Nakabango (f) *[nnah-kah-bahn-goh]* The shaft of a small spear; small spear; piece [*Ganda, Soga*].

Nakabazzi (f) *[nnah-kah-bahz-zih]* (Small) grasshopper with reddish patches on the back and wings [*Ganda*].

Nakabba (f) *[nnah-kahb-bah]* The lining of a long dress *(kkanzu)* worn by males [*Ganda*].

Nakaberenge (f) *[nnah-kah-beh-reh-ehn-geh]* Very intelligent and daring child; corn nuts or popcorn [*Ganda*].

Nakabiri (f) *[nnah-kah-bih-rih]* One of small body weight [The *Ganda, Soga*].

Nakabiti (f) *[nnah-kah-bih-tih]* A string of beads [*Ganda*].

Nakabo (f) *[nnah-kah-boh]* Small bug [*Ganda*].

Nakabogo (f) *[nnah-kah-boh-goh]* Small buffalo [*Ganda*].

Nakabonge (f) *[nnah-kah-bohn-geh]* Craziness; madness [*Ganda*].

Nakabugo/ Nnakabugo (f) *[nnah-kah-buh-goh]* The red tailed monkey; gift contribution to the family of the deceased; burial shroud [The *Ganda*].

Nakabungo (f) *[nnah-kah-buhn-goh]* Fruit of the rubber vine [*Ganda*].

Nakabuye (f) *[nnah-kah-buh-yeh]* That is caused to be naive; that is abducted (by the spirit) [*Ganda*].

Nakachwa/ Nakacwa (f) *[nnah-kah-tch-wah]* One who flees or escapes; the sound of cutting or rustling movements; one associated with the reign of the King Chwa [*Ganda*].

Nakaddu (f/m) *[nnah-kahd-duh]* Servant; member of the cultivator social class as opposed to the aristocratic cattle keeping class; captive [*Ganda*].

Nakafenke (f) *[nah-kah-fehn-keh]* One that eats up (or gobbles up, or stuffs oneself with) [*Ganda*].

Nakafu (f) *[nnah-kah-fuh]* A small and niggardly portion (or helping) of food [*Ganda*].

Nakafumbe (f) *[nnah-kah-fuhm-beh]* (One associated with) the civet cat [*Ganda*].

Nakagembe (f) *[nnah-kah-gehm-beh]* Trap for large animals [*Ganda*].

Nakagga (f) *[nnah-kahg-gah]* Small river (or stream) [*Ganda*].

Nakaggala (m) *[nnah-kahg-gah-lah]* The little one that closes (the entrance); the little one that shuts (or encloses, or brings to an end, or discontinues) [*Ganda*].

Nakaggwe (f) *[nnah-kahg-gweh]* "Let it be finished"; "may it be completed"; "may it be ended" [*Ganda*].

Nakagiri (f) *[nnah-kah-gih-rih]* A species of wild plant [*Ganda*].

Nakagulire (f) *[nnah-kah-guh-lih-reh]* One that was bought (or purchased) for [*Ganda*].

Nakajubi (f) *[nnah-kah-juh-bih]* That helps (or comes to the aid of) others [*Ganda*].

Nakajugo (f) *[nnah-kah-juh-goh]* The bell ringer; pen holder; small bell used as an ornament on the neck or on drums [*Ganda*].

Nakakaawa (f) *[nnah-kah-kaah-wah]* A small one that is bitter (or sour, or unpleasant to the taste); a small one that becomes quarrelsome (or enraged); a small situation that becomes serious (or bad) [*Ganda*].

Nakakakkulu (m) *[nnah-kah-kahk-kuh-luh]* (The small one) that walks very fast (or is in a great hurry); (the small one) that leads (someone) away in a hurry [*Ganda*].

Nakakande (f) *[nnah-kah-kahn-deh]* The jungle; (small) deserted stretch of land; (small) wasteland; that was forced (or compelled); that is caused to persist [*Ganda*].

Nakakanga (f) *[nnah-kah-kahn-gah]* One that scares (or frightens, or startles); one that threatens; that is gripping; that is terrible; that is violent [*Ganda*].

Nakake/ Nnakake (f/m) *[nnah-kah-keh]* That was forced (or compelled) [*Ganda*].

Nakakenyi (f) *[nnah-kah-keh-ndjh-ih]* That causes to violently hurl to the ground (such as during wrestling); that causes to act reluctantly (or ungraciously); that causes to kill [*Ganda*].

Nakakinzi (f) *[nnah-kah-kihn-zih]* A small sewing in many places; a small bit of sewing done quickly; a small embroidering [*Ganda*].

Nakakoole (f) *[nnah-kah-koh-oh-leh]* That has been uprooted; that has been weeded out [*Ganda*].

Nakakungu (f) *[nnah-kah-kuhn-guh]* The little one that is a high ranking official (or a dignitary); the little one that is rich [*Ganda*].

Nakakweya (f) *[nnah-kah-kweh-yah]* One who drags the feet; one who drags along the ground [*Ganda*].

Nakalago (f/m) *[nnah-kah-lah-goh]* (One with the peculiarity) of a small neck (or small throat) [*Ganda*].

Nakalagwe (f) *[nnah-kah-lah-gweh]* One associated with the people of *Karagwe* [*Ganda*].

Nakalangirire (f) *[nnah-kah-lahn-gih-rih-reh]* That is proclaimed (or announced, or given public notice of, or advertised) [*Ganda, Soga*].

Nakalanzi (f) *[nnah-kah-lahn-zih]* Reporter; announcer; prophet; advertiser [*Ganda*].

Nakalawa (f) *[nnah-kah-lah-wah]* The beat (or sound) of drums; the sounding of an alarm [*Ganda*].

Nakalemba (f) *[nnah-kah-lehm-bah]* One who strolls slowly and leisurely; of the lakes or seas; handkerchief; scarf [*Ganda*].

Nakalembe (f) *[nnah-kah-lehm-beh]* A respite; a little bit of peace; that walks slowly (or leisurely); that approaches carefully (or slowly); that deals carefully with [*Ganda*].

Nakalembi (f) *[nnah-kah-lehm-bih]* That causes to stroll slowly and leisurely [*Ganda*].

Nakaliika (f/m) *[nah-kah-liih-kah]* That is edible (or fit for consumption); that exacts payment from; that demands fulfillment of a commitment by; that puts pressure on [*Ganda*].

Nakaliisa (f) *[nnah-kah-liih-sah]* Lark; pipit; yellow wagtail [*Ganda*].

Nakalo (f) *[nnah-kah-loh]* Finger millet [*Ganda*].

Nakalyana/ Nnakalyana (f) *[nnah-kah-ljah-nah]* One that is insolent; childishness [*Ganda*].

Nakalyowa (f) *[nnah-kah-ljoh-wah]* One who does a favor for; one who benefits for; one associated with a child sent to the king or a distinguished chief to perform services; obligation; favor; benefit [The *Ganda*].

Nakamanya/ Nakamaanya (f) *[nnah-kah-maah-ndjh-ah]* Determined, self willed person; rogue; rascal [*Ganda*].

Nakamanyisa (f) *[nnah-kah-mah-ndjh-ih-sah]* That causes to know; that informs [*Ganda*].

Nakamatte (f) *[nnah-kah-maht-teh]* One that is rude, grouchy, or stern in behavior [*Ganda*].

Nakame (f) *[nnah-kah-meh]* That has been milked [*Ganda*].

Nakamo (f) *[nnah-kah-moh]* One that is highly skilled (or very proficient); an expert [*Ganda*].

Nakamu (f) *[nnah-kah-muh]* One (little thing) [*Ganda*].

Nakampi (f) *[nnah-kahm-pih]* Short person [*Ganda*]

Nakamwa (f) *[nnah-kah-mwah]* Mouth [*Ganda*].

Nakamyuka (f) *[nnah-kah-mjuh-kah]* That becomes red (or reddish brown, or tanned); that gets tanned (from the sun); that reddens (with anger); that becomes angry; that becomes discolored (of a bruised part of the body); the second in command; the deputy [*Ganda*].

Nakanaku (f) *[nnah-kah-nah-kuh]* One who is distraught (or in misery, or in poverty) [*Ganda*].

Nakandi (f) *[nnah-kahn-dih]* The name of a species of yam [*Ganda*].

Nakanga (f/m) *[nnah-kahn-gah]* "I scared (or frightened, or startled)"; "I threatened"; that is gripping; that is terrible; that is violent [*Ganda*].

Nakango/ Nnakango (f) *[nnah-kahn-goh]* (Small) frame of a door (or window) [*Ganda*].

Nakangu/ Nnakangu (f) *[nnah-kahn-guh]* A name given to one born with visible teeth in the mouth; that is fast [*Ganda*].

Nakangubi (f) *[nnah-kahn-guh-bih]* One that is of darkness (or hardships, or pressures, or difficulties, or uncertainties) [*Ganda*].

Nakanninga (f) *[nnah-kahn-nihn-gah]* (With a small) nail [*Ganda*].

Nakanwagi (f) *[nnah-kahn-waah-jih]* "The little one that is supported (or backed up, or encouraged, or inserted firmly, or propped up)" [*Ganda*].

Nakanyaakaali/ Nakanyakaali (m) *[nnah-kah-ndjh-aah-kaah-lih]* "An abundance (or increase) that there was" [*Ganda*].

Nakanyale (m) *[nnah-kah-ndjh-ah-leh]* Lint; soot; small particles of dust that float in the air [*Ganda*].

Nakanyiga (f) *[nnah-kah-ndjh-ih-gah]* That oppresses (or squeezes, or presses); that dresses a wound [*Ganda*].

Nakanyigo (m) *[nnah-kah-ndjh-ih-goh]* Narrow pass; tight situation [*Ganda*].

Nakanyike (f) *[nnah-kah-ndjh-ih-keh]* That is sad (or sorrowful); sadness; sorrow [*Ganda*].

Nakanyolo (f) *[nnah-kah-ndjh-oh-loh]* A small drumstick; door handle [*Ganda*].

Nakanyoro (f) *[nnah-kah-ndjh-oh-roh]* The little one of (or associated with) the *Nyoro* ethnics [*Ganda*].

Nakanywa/ Nnakanywa (f) *[nnah-kah-ndjh-wah]* Small tendon [The *Ganda*].

Nakasaala (f) *[nnah-kah-saah-lah]* That leads (or goes first); that makes a hissing noise (or sizzling noise, or clangs, or hums); that engages in (Islamic) prayer [*Ganda*].

Nakasaawula (m) *[nnah-kah-saah-wuh-lah]* That beats (or thrashes, or slashes down) [*Ganda*].

Nakasala (f) *[nnah-kah-sah-lah]* That cuts (or cuts up, or slaughters, or divides, or apportions, or allots, or abbreviates, or crosses, or decides) [*Ganda*].

Nakasalirwe (f) *[nnah-kah-sah-lih-rweh]* Decided or judged for; charged a price; apportioned for [*Ganda*].

Nakasenge/ Nnakasenge (f) *[nnah-kah-sehn-geh]* Small room; partition.

Nakase (f) *[nnah-kah-seh]* An infinitely large number; one hundred million [*Ganda, Soga*].

Nakasese (f) *[nnah-kah-seh-seh]* Red tailed finch [*Ganda*].

Nakasi (f) *[nnah-kah-sih]* Small country (or land) [*Ganda*].

Nakasiga (f) *[nnah-kah-sih-gah]* One who sows or plants seeds in; of the planting season [*Ganda*].

Nakasinde (f) *[nnah-kah-sihn-deh]* That runs very fast; the sound of footsteps, thumping, or of tramping of the feet; the noise from gun fire and explosives detonation; (small) expedition [*Ganda*].

Nakasiyo/ Nnakasiyo (f) *[nnah-kah-sih-yoh]* An ingredient that seasons (or flavors); an ingredient added to (food or drink to flavor it such as salt to meat or sorghum to beer); millet mashed into beer [*Ganda*].

Nakasolo (f) *[nnah-kah-soh-loh]* Small mammal; a stepladder used in the construction of a house or in the picking of cotton [*Ganda, Soga*].

Nakasolya (f) *[nnah-kah-soh-ljah]* The roof of house; (one associated with) a head of a clan [*Ganda, Soga*].

Nakasonge/ Nnakasonge (f) *[nnah-kah-sohn-geh]* That is prodded (or poked, or pierced, or pointed out) [*Ganda*].

Nakaswa (f/m) *[nnah-kah-swah]* Real; genuine; authentic; pure; indigenous [*Ganda*].

Nakataba (f) *[nnah-kah-tah-bah]* A small puddle; a small pool; a small pond; one who unites (or joins together); a sewing (or stitching together); a joining together [*Ganda*].

Nakatana (m) *[nnah-kah-tah-nah]* An inadvertent source of an accident; that causes to be infected (or to fester, or to grow septic) [The *Ganda*].

Nakatandagira/ Nakatandaggira (f/m) *[nnah-kah-tahn-dahg-gih-rah]* A throw down; a hurl down; laying low [*Ganda*].

Nakatanza (f/m) *[nnah-kah-tahn-zah]* That fines a person; that imposes a fine on; that fines for [*Ganda*].

Nakate/ Nnakate (f) *[nnah-kah-teh]* Small cow [*Ganda*].

Nakatema (f/m) *[nnah-kah-teh-mah]* The one that cuts (or chops) into pieces" [*Ganda*].

Nakatemwa (f) *[nnah-kah-teh-mwah]* That can be cut (or chopped) into pieces; a small allocation (or allotment of money, or assessment, or apportionment) [*Ganda*].

Nakatereka (f) *[nnah-kah-teh-reh-kah]* That puts away (or puts aside, or or lays up, or stores, or deposits money, or reserves) [*Ganda*].

Nakati (f) *[nnah-kah-tih]* Small tree; small stick [*Ganda*].

Nakato (f) *[nnah-kah-toh]* A name given to the second born of female twins [*Ganda*].

Nakato (f/m) *[nnah-kah-toh]* One with (or one associated with) a young one (or small) one [*Ganda*].

Nakatudde (f) *[nnah-kah-tuhd-deh]* That is seated; that is residing (or dwelling) [*Ganda*].

Nakatumba (f) *[nnah-kah-tuhm-bah]* The month of March; bundle (of cloth); porter's load; burden [*Ganda*].

Nakatuza (f) *[nnah-kah-tuh-zah]* That makes sharp [*Ganda*].

Nakavubu (f) *[nnah-kah-vuh-buh]* Small hippopotamus [*Ganda*].

Nakavuma (f) *[nnah-kah-vuh-mah]* Profits; booty [*Ganda*].

Nakawa (f) *[nnah-kah-wah]* "I gave it"; "I gave to it" [*Ganda*].

Nakawanguzi (f) *[nnah-kah-wahn-guh-zih]* Winner; victor; conqueror [*Ganda*].

Nakawere (f) *[nnah-kah-weh-reh]* Type of plantain given woman who has very recently given birth to a child; mother of recently born infant [*Ganda, Soga*].

Nakawesa/ Nakaweesa (f) *[nnah-kah-weh-eh-sah]/* **Nakawesi/ Nakaweesi** (f) *[nnah-kah-weh-eh-sih]* Blacksmith; iron smith [*Ganda*].

Nakawombe (f) *[nnah-kah-wohm-beh]* That is humble (or meek, or docile) [*Ganda*].

Nakawooya (f) *[nnah-kah-woh-oh-yah]* That appeases (or calms down, or pacifies, or speaks softly to) [*Ganda*].

Nakawooza (f) *[nnah-kah-woh-oh-zah]* Tax collector; that taxes; that levies (taxes, customs duty, tariffs, dues) [*Ganda*].

Nakawoza (f) *[nnah-kah-woh-zah]* One who pleads her case (in court); that causes to cool down; that causes to calm down; that causes to lose interest [*Ganda*].

Nakawuba (f) *[nnah-kah-wuh-bah]* That overlooks (or misses); that (unintentionally) slips by; that loses color; that changes beyond recognition [*Ganda*].

Nakawuka (f) *[nnah-kah-wuh-kah]* Small insect; bug; germ; microbe [*Ganda*].

Nakawunda (f) *[nnah-kah-wuhn-dah]* That decorates; that adorns; that embellishes [*Ganda*].

Nakawunde (f) *[nnah-kah-wuhn-deh]* Decorated; adorned; embellished [*Ganda*].

Nakawundo (f) *[nnah-kah-wuhn-doh]* Small bat [*Ganda*].

Nakawunga/ Nnakawunga (f) *[nnah-kah-wuhn-gah]* That nets/ catches (flying insects such as lake flies with a net); commeal; flour meal [*Ganda*].

Nakawungu (f) *[nnah-kah-wuhn-guh]* Young eagle [*Ganda*].

Nakaye (f) *[nnah-kah-yeh]* "Let it become weary (or tired, or exhausted)" [*Ganda*].

Nakayemba (f) *[nnah-kah-yehm-bah]* That talks in a noisy and foolish manner; that talks nonsense; that rants [*Ganda*].

Nakayenga (f) *[nnah-kah-yehn-gah]* That twists about; that is slow in doing something; that is stirred and dissolved (or diluted, or mixed) [*Ganda*].

Nakayijja (f) *[nnah-kah-yihj-jah]* Small stone anvil [*Ganda*].

Nakayiki (f) *[nnah-kah-yih-tch-ih]* Creeping plant, the seeds of which are used in playing a numbers game [*Ganda*].

Nakayima (f) *[nnah-kah-yih-mah]* One of (or one associated with) the *Hima* people; a beautiful girl of small physique who has a slender nose said to resemble that of the cattle associated *Hima* people [The *Ganda, Soga*].

Nakayita (f) *[nnah-kah-yih-tah]* One who passes (or moves) around; one who calls (or invites, or names, or describes as) [*Ganda*].

Nakayiwa (f) *[nnah-kah-yih-wah]* That spills (or pours out, or pours away, or flows out); that develops a rash [*Ganda*].

Nakayiza (f) *[nnah-kah-yih-zah]* One involved in teaching or learning; that causes to learn [*Ganda*].

Nakayombya (f) *[nnah-kah-yohm-bjah]* That makes lose one's temper; that quarrels with; that causes to quarrel [*Ganda*].

Nakayonga/ Nnakayonga (m) *[nnah-kah-yohn-gah]* Ash; a species of fern; loin cloth; warrior; black; black-like; very dark [*Ganda*].

Nakayonge/ Nnakayonge (m) *[nnah-kah-yohn-geh]* That is caused to be ashen (or black, or very dark) [*Ganda*].

Nakaza/ Nnakaza (f) *[nnah-kah-zah]* To cause to dry; to make firm; to make certain of (or to confirm, or to affirm); to know well; to pronounce well; to name (or to nickname, or to dub); "I caused to dry"; "I made firm"; "I affirmed"; "I learnt well"; "I pronounced well" [*Ganda*].

Nakazaana (f/m) *[nnah-kah-zaah-nah]* That is in servitude [*Ganda*].

Nakazadde (f) *[nnah-kah-zahd-deh]* (Small) parent; honored mother; mother of many children; mother of important person [*Ganda*].

Nakazibwe (f) *[nnah-kah-zih-bweh]* Descendant of (or one associated with) the *Bazibwe* people [*Ganda*].

Nakazimba (f) *[nnah-kah-zihm-bah]* That becomes furious (or angry); that swells up; constructor; builder; architect; that builds (or constructs); that edifies [*Ganda*].

Nakazinga (f) *[nnah-kah-zihn-gah]* Island [*Ganda*].

Nakedi (f/m) *[nah-keh-dih]* A name given to an only child (in the house) [*Tlokwa-Sotho*] (Kruger 1937: 107).

Nakedi (m) *[nah-keh-dih]* Skunk: this derogatory/ non-human name given to a child whose preceding sibling or siblings died, there being pessimism as to whether this one will survive, is however intended to effectuate the opposite of its literal meaning [*Sotho*] (Mohome 1972: 176).

Nakerebwe (f) *[nnah-keh-reh-bweh]* The squirrel [*Ganda*].

Nakhanu (f) *[nah-kah-nuh]* A name given to one born during the sesame planting season [*Luyia*].

Nakhumicha (f) *[nah-kuh-mih-tch-ah]* A name given to one born during the planting season [*Luyia*].

Nakhungu (f) *[nah-kuhn-guh]* A name given to one born during an invasion by army worms [*Luyia*].

Nakibaala (f) *[nnah-tch-ih-baah-lah]* A hill of *(mbaala)* termites [The *Ganda*].

Nakibalo (f) *[nnah-tch-ih-bah-loh]* A calculation; a counting; that is reckoned (or taken into consideration, or regarded) [*Ganda*].

Nakibe (f) *[nnah-tch-ih-beh]* The jackal [*Ganda*].

Nakibengo (f) *[nnah-tch-ih-behn-goh]* Sharpened; filled to the brim; lower millstone; large grindstone; a scale for weighing sacks (or bags) of produce such as of sugar and coffee berries [*Ganda*].

Nakibenje (f) *[nnah-tch-ih-behn-jeh]* Accident; misfortune [*Ganda*].

Nakiberu (f) *[nnah-tch-ih-beh-ruh]* That topples (or overturns, or exposes oneself, or is lifted and dropped, or is overturned) [*Ganda*].

Nakibinga/ Nnakibinga (m) *[nnah-tch-ih-bihn-gah]* One that chases (or drives) away [*Ganda*].

Nakibinge/ Nnakibinge (f/m) *[nnah-tch-ih-bihn-geh]* One that is chased or driven away [*Ganda*].

Nakibirango (f) *[nnah-tch-ih-bih-rahn-goh]* Species of plant; species of large snake [*Ganda*].

Nakibombo (f) *[nnah-tch-ih-bohm-boh]* One who (in shame or humiliation) takes off or runs away [*Ganda*].

Nakibondwe (f) *[nnah-tch-ih-bohn-dweh]* One that is docile (or quiet, or peaceful, or bashful, or glum).

Nakiboneka (f) *[nnah-tch-ih-boh-neh-kah]* One born during the appearance of a new moon; appearance; that is noticeable; that is visible [*Ganda*].

Nakibongo (f) *[nnah-tch-ih-bohn-goh]* Chipped off; knocked off; notched; (hair) partially cut; a piece cut or broken off [*Ganda*].

Nakibowa (f) *[nnah-tch-ih-boh-wah]* Security held for the payment; that is confiscated (or appropriated) [*Ganda*].

Nakiboya (f) *[nnah-tch-ih-boh-yah]* That becomes dizzy (or delirious); that raves; that tosses about restlessly; that becomes disturbed (or troubled); that seethes (or gets in turmoil) [*Ganda*].

Nakibungo (f) *[nnah-tch-ih-buhn-goh]* (Cattle) dung hill [*Ganda*].

Nakibuule (f) *[nnah-tch-ih-buuh-leh]* A banana that is cooked; that is thrashed (or beaten, or beaten hard, or thrown to the ground); (cattle) that is raided; that is associated with bachelorhood (or losing one's wife through separation or desertion); that is associated with a poor boy (or a poor kid) [*Ganda, Soga*].

Nakibwa (f) *[nnah-tch-ih-bwah]* Sore; open wound [*Ganda*].

Nakidde (f) *[nnah-tch-ihd-deh]* "Let it come back (or reappear)"; cloudy weather; overcast weather [*Ganda*].

Nakiddu (f) *[nnah-tch-ihd-duh]* Servitude; captivity [*Ganda*].

Nakide (f) *[nnah-tch-ih-deh]* The bell [*Ganda*].

Nakifamba (f) *[nnah-tch-ih-fahm-bah]* Having weakness (in the legs) [*Ganda*].

Nakigala (f) *[nnah-tch-ih-gah-lah]* The stock (or butt) of a gun [The *Ganda*].

Nakigalala (f) *[nnah-tch-ih-gah-lah-lah]* A house with a partition [The *Ganda*].

Nakiganda (f) *[nnah-tch-ih-gahn-dah]* Large heap or bundle; relating to the customs, mannerisms, fashion or style of the *Ganda* ethnics [*Ganda*].

Nakiggala (f) *[nnah-tch-ihg-gah-lah]* Deaf person; one that closes [*Ganda*].

Nakiggwe (f) *[nnah-tch-ihg-gweh]* "Let it come to an end (or get completed or finished)" [*Ganda*].

Nakigo (f) *[nnah-tch-ih-goh]* A fenced enclosure; fort; yard; stockade; a parish [*Ganda*].

Nakigoye (m) *[nnah-tch-ih-goh-yeh]* Cloth [*Ganda*].

Nakigozi (f) *[nnah-tch-ih-goh-zih]* Cloth used to cover an infant; barkcloth employed to carry an infant on the back [*Ganda*].

Nakigudde (f) *[nnah-tch-ih-guhd-deh]* That has fallen; that has happened (or occurred); that has failed (such as in an examination) [The *Ganda*].

Nakiguli (f) *[nnah-tch-ih-guh-lih]* A large cage; an animal cage [The *Ganda*].

Nakiisi (f) *[nnah-tch-iih-sih]* "Each"; "every" [*Ganda*].

Nakiiso (m) *[nnah-tch-iih-soh]* (With a peculiarity of) the eye [*Ganda*].

Nakija (f) *[nah-kih-jah]* A name given to a child born during a night devoid of moonlight [*Pare*] (Omari 1970: 70).

Nakijjo (f) *[nnah-kihj-joh]* A marvel; a prodigy; a strange thing; a sensation [*Ganda*].

Nakijoba (f) *[nnah-tch-ih-joh-bah]* One who creates confusion (or commotion); one who arranges for a great feast or banquet; one who gets soaked; one who gets messy such as with mud or liquids; the crest of the crested crane bird; the tuft of hair on a shaven head [The *Ganda*].

Nakikofu (f/m) *[nnah-tch-ih-koh-fuh]* With characteristics (or the color) of the guinea fowl [*Ganda, Soga*].

Nakiku (f) *[nnah-tch-ih-kuh]* Old piece of firewood; big piece of dead wood; bed bug [*Ganda*].

Nakikulwe (f) *[nnah-tch-ih-kuh-lweh]* To be outstanding; expert; renowned; notorious; tadpole [*Ganda*].

Nakilwadde (f) *[nnah-tch-ih-lwahd-deh]* That is sick (or ill); a sickness (or illness) [*Ganda*].

Nakilyowa (f) *[nnah-tch-ih-ljoh-wah]*/ **Nakiryowa** (f) *[nah-tch-ih-rjoh-wah]* One who does a favor for; one who benefits for; one associated with a child sent to the king or a distinguished chief to perform services; obligation; favor; benefit [*Ganda*].

Nakima/ Nnakima (f) *[nnah-tch-ih-mah]* "I fetched (or went to get, or went for)"; "that fetches (or goes to get, or goes for)" [*Ganda*].

Nakimaka/ Nnakimaka (f) *[nnah-tch-ih-mah-kah]* That tends to stare hard (or fixedly) [*Ganda*].

Nakimbugwe (f) *[nnah-tch-ihm-buh-gweh]* One associated with the keeper of the king's umbilical cord; one associated with a chief [The *Ganda*].

Nakimera (f) *[nnah-tch-ih-meh-rah]* That sprouts; that grows; that becomes well established (in a position); a gift to (or from) God; name-title of one of the king's principal wives, one traditionally provided by the Edible Grasshopper (*Nseenene*) Clan [*Ganda*].

Nakio (f) *[nah-kih-yoh]* A name given to a child born during the night [*Pare*] (Omari 1970: 71).

Nakivona (f) *[nah-kih-voh-nah]* A name given to a child who "had a hard time in her early life" [The *Pare*] (Omari 1970: 71).

Nalamae (f) *[nah-lah-mah-yeh]* The one that people are a part of [The *Maasai*].

Nalangu (f) *[nah-lahn-guh]* The one that crosses [*Maasai*].

Nalepo (m) *[nah-leh-poh]* The one that is yielding [*Maasai*].

Naliaka (f) *[nah-lih-yah-kah]* A name given to one born during a weeding season [*Luyia*].

Nalotuesha (f) *[nah-loh-tweh-tsh-ah]* The one that comes (or is born) when it is raining [*Maasai*].

Nam (f/m) *[nahm]* Lake; ocean [*Luo*].

Namaemba (f) *[nah-mah-yehm-bah]* A name given to one born during a time of millet harvesting [*Luyia*].

Namalwa (f) *[nah-mah-lwah]* "Of beer": a name given to one born at a time of a beer drinking festival [*Luyia*].

Namarimba (m) *[nah-mah-rihm-bah]* A name given to one whose hearing and talking abilities are impaired [*Luyia*].

Namarome (f) *[nah-mah-roh-meh]* A name given to one born during the clearing of virgin land [*Luyia*].

Namasaka (m) *[nah-mah-tsah-kah]* One associated with a plant species *saka* made into vegetables that taste bitter, so the name is commonly given to a child who is very short tempered; a name given to one whose parents are fond of eating *saka* vegetables [*Luyia*].

Namatirai (f/m) *[nah-mah-tih-rahy]* "Cleave to the Lord" [The *Shona*]

(Jackson 1957: 121).

Nambakha (f/m) *[nahm-bah-kah]* A name given to a very social and talkative person [*Luyia*].

Nambande (f) *[nahm-bahn-deh]* A name given to one born during the harvesting of *chimbande* nuts [*Luyia*].

Namelok (m) *[nah-meh-lohk]* The sweet one [*Maasai*].

Namerae (f) *[nah-meh-rah-yeh]* The one that is born at a time folk are drinking beer (or getting drunk) [*Maasai*].

Namghanga (f) *[nahm-gahn-gah]* (One associated with the) tradition-al medicine-man: a name such as given to a child whose mother was administered herbs by a traditional doctor to enable her to conceive [*Pare*] (Omari 1970: 70).

Namramba (f) *[nah-muh-rahm-bah]* Name given to a child conceived or born during the season of harvesting and processing of thread fr-om the baobab trees [*Pare*] (Omari 1970: 71).

Namshitu (f) *[nahm-tsh-ih-tuh]* A name given to a child born during the season of boys' initiation ceremonies [*Pare*] (Omari 1970: 71).

Namulekhwa (f) *[nah-muh-leh-kwah]* "The one left (or abandoned)": a name given to one whose mother dies soon after giving birth to her, or to one whose parent (or parents) died when she was very young [*Luyia*].

Namunane (m) *[nah-muh-nah-neh]* A name given to one born during a rainy season [*Luyia*].

Namuno (m) *[nah-muh-noh]* A name given to one whose teeth are ch-aracteristically large [*Luyia*].

Namunyak (f) *[nah-muh-ndjh-ahk]* The blessed one [*Maasai*].

Namunyele (f) *[nah-muh-ndjh-eh-leh]* Name given to one whose birth follows that of her twin siblings [*Luyia*].

Namutie (f) *[nah-muh-tjeh]* The one that has come late [*Maasai*].

Namvua (f) *[nahm-vuh-wah]* A name given to a child born during the rainy season [*Pare*] (Omari 1970: 71).

Namvumo (f) *[nahm-vuh-moh]* Name given to a child born during the blossoming of a fig tree whose average longevity symbolizes good health and long life [*Pare*] (Omari 1970: 70).

Namwaka (f) *[nah-mwaah-kah]* A name given to a child born of an unduly long pregnancy period [*Pare*] (Omari 1970: 71).

Namwenye (m) *[nah-mweh-ndjh-eh]* "Himself": name such as given to a child born without the assistance of midwives i.e. one who came by himself [*Pare*] (Omari 1970: 71).

Nanana (f) *[nah-nah-nah]* The one whose body is soft (or tender) [The *Maasai*].

Nandi (f) *[uh-nahn-dih]* "Nice" [*Zulu*] (Suzman 1994: 254).

Nanditi (f) *[nahn-dih-tih]* A name given to a child of small body size [*Luyia*].

Nangari (m) *[nah-ndgh-ah-rih]* The one that is thrown to the ground

[*Maasai*].

Nangekhe (f) *[nah-ndgh-eh-keh]* A name given to one whose weight, as a baby, is below normal; name given to a child of small body size [*Luyia*].

Nange (m) *[nah-ndgh-eh]* A name given to a stingy person [*Luyia*].

Nangendo (m) *[nah-ndgh-ehn-doh]* "Of journeys": name given to one born at a time the mother is visiting; one associated with a habitual visitor [*Luyia*].

Nangila (f) *[nah-ndgh-ih-lah]* "Of a road/ path": a name given to one born at a time the mother was on a journey; name given to one born on a wayside [*Luyia*].

Nangol (m) *[nah-ndgh-ohl]* The strong one [*Maasai*].

Nang'oni (f) *[nah-ndgh-oh-nih]* A name given to one who is lazy and slow at work [*Luyia*].

Nangosole (f) *[nah-ndgh-oh-soh-leh]* "The cloth you like": this name is commonly associated with the proverb "The cloth you like is not the one that appears" implying that many things that are rare, unattainable, far away, or are out of our reach tend to be excessively prized, this synonymous with "Forbidden fruit is sweetest" and "Absence makes the heart grow fonder" [*Ovimbundu*] (Ennis 1945: 5).

Nangulu (m) *[nah-ndgh-uh-luh]* An appellation given to one born in the *Chingulu* hills [*Luyia*].

Nangwe (f) *[nah-ndgh-weh]* A name given to one born after several of her preceding siblings died [*Luyia*].

Nanjala (f) *[nah-ndjh-ah-lah]* "Of hunger": a name given to one born during a period of famine [*Luyia*].

Nanjamba (f) *[nah-ndjh-ahm-bah]* "The mother of twins" [*Ovimbundu*] (Ennis 1945: 2).

Nanjaya (f) *[nah-ndjh-ah-yah]* A name given to one who is characteristically cheerful, and is liked by everybody [*Luyia*].

Nanjekho (f) *[nah-ndjh-eh-koh]* "Of laughter": a name such as given to one who often laughs happily [*Luyia*].

Nankondo (f) *[nahn-kohn-doh]* A name given to a child conceived or born during a time of war [*Pare*] (Omari 1970: 71).

Nankulo (f) *[nahn-kuh-loh]* "Herbs": a name such as given to a child conceived following her mother taking herbs to enhance the process, and which child was administered herbs to enable it to survive [*Pare*] (Omari 1970: 71).

Nanyama (f) *[nah-ndjh-ah-mah]* "Of meat": a name such as given to one born at a time there is plenty of meat to eat [*Luyia*].

Nanyika (f) *[nahn-ndjh-ih-kah]* "(Of) the plainland": a name such as given to a child conceived or born during the hoeing season in the plainlands [*Pare*] (Omari 1970: 70).

Nanyikal (f) *[nah-ndjh-ih-kahl]* The one that there is closeness to [The *Maasai*].

Nanyiku (m) *[nah-ndjh-ih-kuh]* The one that comes closer [*Maasai*].

Nanzighe (f) *[nahn-zih-geh]* "Locusts": name such as given to a child conceived or born during a period of invasion by locusts [The *Pare*] (Omari 1970: 71).

Nanzovu (f) *[nahn-zoh-vuh]* "The big one": a name such as given to a big size newborn [*Pare*] (Omari 1970: 71).

Napono (f) *[nah-poh-noh]* The one that adds [*Maasai*].

Naramat (f) *[nah-rah-maht]* The one that caves [*Maasai*].

Nasaka (f) *[nah-tsah-kah]* A name given to one born during a season when there is an abundance of the species *saka* eaten as vegetables; a name given to one whose parents are fond of eating *saka* vegetables [*Luyia*].

Nasaye (m) *[nah-sah-yeh]* God; "one to whom prayer is made" [*Luyia*] (Huntingford 1930: 103).

Nasenan (f) *[nah-seh-nahn]* The one that is fine [*Maasai*].

Nashipae (f) *[nah-tsh-ih-pah-yeh]*/ **Nashipai** (f) *[nah-tsh-ih-pahy]* The one that people rejoice over [*Maasai*].

Nasiebanda (f/m) *[nah-tsjeh-bahn-dah]* A name given to a child who is the product of an unusually long pregnancy period [*Luyia*].

Nasieku (f) *[nah-tsyeh-kuh]* The one that hurries up [*Maasai*].

Nasike (f) *[nah-sih-keh]* A name given to one born during a locust invasion (or season) [*Luyia*].

Nasimbikiti (f/m) *[nah-sihm-bih-kih-tih]* A name given to a child of very short, dwarfish, height [*Luyia*].

Nasimiyu (f) *[nah-sih-mih-yuh]* A name given to one born during a dry season [*Luyia*].

Nasipwoni (f) *[nah-sih-pwoh-nih]*/ **Nasipwondi** (f) *[nah-sih-pwohn-dih]* A name given to one born in a sweet potato plantation [*Luyia*].

Naswa (f) *[nah-swah]* A name given to one born during a season when there is an abundance of edible white ants [*Luyia*].

Nataana (f) *[nah-taah-nah]* The one that is near [*Maasai*].

Natembeya (m) *[nah-tehm-beh-yah]* Of traveling: name such as given to one whose mother likes traveling around [*Luyia*].

Navuri (f) *[nah-vuh-rih]* A name given to a child conceived or born during a short season of rain [*Pare*] (Omari 1970: 71).

Navwasi (f) *[nahv-wah-sih]* A name given to a child whose birth involved problems/ or to a child who became alarmingly sick that there was little hope she would survive [*Pare*] (Omari 1970: 70).

Nayaemkop (m) *[nah-yah-yehm-kohp]* The proud one; the one that takes up more land [*Maasai*].

Nayioloang (f) *[nah-yih-yoh-loh-wah-ndgh]* One who knows home; one who recognizes and upholds the importance of home [*Maasai*].

Ndabaisendlini (m) *[uhn-dah-bahy-sehn-dlih-nih]* "This is the last time!": a name such as given to a child born into a polygamous unit where there is marked tension between the co-wives [*Zulu*] (Suzman

1994: 267).

Ndabakayise (m) *[ndah-bah-kah-yih-seh]* "His father's affair" [*Zulu*] (Koopman 1979: 80).

Ndabazakhe (m) *[ndah-bah-zaah-keh]* "(Of) his affairs" [The *Zulu*] (Koopman 1979: 157).

Ndakabatei (f/m) *[ndah-kah-bah-tehy]* "What have I been working for?": a name given to one born to a mother whose husband disputatiously considers her a good-for-nothing wife on whom he has wasted his resources [*Shona*] (Jackson 1957: 116).

Ndakadashe (f/m) *[ndah-kah-dah-tsh-eh]* "I have loved the Lord" [The *Shona*] (Jackson 1957: 121).

Ndalo (f/m) *[ndah-loh]* Form [*Luo*].

Ndanatsiwa (f/m) *[ndah-nah-tsih-wah]* "I have been cleansed" [*Shona*] (Jackson 1957: 121).

Ndasiala (f) *[ndah-sih-yah-lah]* "I am left (with)": this name is associated with the expression "I am left with you and it does not comfort the weeping" which is metaphorically the lamentation of an oppressed or mistreated woman who does not have many blood relatives around (or of a child of one in such a situation), or of a child who is an orphan, or of a slave (in past times) who does not see any alternative refuge to her present situation [*Ovimbundu*] (Ennis 1945: 6).

Ndasvika (f/m) *[ndah-svih-kah]* "I have arrived at the goal" [*Shona*] (Jackson 1957: 121).

Ndawayikho (m) *[ndah-wah-yih-koh]* "There is no space" [The *Zulu*] (Koopman 1979: 160).

Ndawokayise (m) *[ndaah-woh-kah-yih-seh]* "His father's place" [*Zulu*] (Koopman 1979: 157).

Ndazabantu (m) *[ndah-zah-bahn-tuh]* "People's affairs" [The *Zulu*] (Koopman 1979: 156).

Ndege (f/m) *[ndeh-geh]* Airplane [*Luo*].

Ndegwa (m) *[ndeh-gwah]* Bull [*Embu, Kikuyu*].

Ndekenya (f/m) *[ndeh-eh-keh-eh-ndjh-ah]* A name given to the third child born after twin siblings [*Luwa*] (Daeleman 1977: 192).

Ndere (m) *[ndeh-reh]* The one that is brownish in complexion [*Maasai*].

Nderi (m) *[ndeh-rih]* Eagle; vulture [*Embu*].

Nderitu (m) *[ndeh-rih-tuh]* The heavy one [*Kikuyu*].

Ndiane (m) *[ndjah-neh]* "I have eaten with them": name such as given to one who has moved to dwell in a settlement to which he does not properly belong [*Kaguru*] (Beidelman 1974: 288).

Ndinatsei (f/m) *[ndih-nah-tsehy]* "Cleanse me" [*Shona*] (Jackson 1957: 121).

Ndisukeleni (f/m) *[ndih-suh-keh-leh-nih]* "Leave me": a disharmony related name such as given by this newborn's grandmother to imply that her daughter-in-law (i.e. the newborn's mother) who is a problem to her ought to leave her alone [*Zulu*] (Herbert 1995: 4, 6).

Ndlazi (m) *[ndlah-zih]* Mousebird [*Zulu*] (Koopman 1990: 336).

Ndlebende (m) *[ndleh-behn-deh]* "Mr. Long Ears" *[Zulu]* (Lugg 1968: 14).

Ndlela (m) *[ndleh-lah]* Way; path *[Zulu]* (Koopman 1990: 336).

Ndlovu (m) *[ndloh-vuh]* Elephant *[Zulu]* (Koopman 1990: 336).

Ndo (m) *[ndoh]* "Of a thumping blow" *[Zulu]* (Koopman 1979: 163).

Nduduzo (m) *[uhn-duh-duh-zoh]* Comforter [The *Zulu]* (Suzman 1994: 268, 269).

Ndumiseni (m) *[uhn-duh-mih-seh-nih]* "Progress": name such as given (to a first born) by the named child's mother to express that her husband came from a proper and commendable household from which he was the first to go to school and become a teacher *[Zulu]* (Suzman 1994: 261).

Nduva (f) *[nduh-vah]* The lory parrot: this name is commonly associated with the expression "The lory of a ghost: speak to the lory so that the lory may explain" whereby traditionally the lory is the one that brings the message of the ghost of one from a distance away who has died, the name commonly given to one born at a time the family receives bad tidings *[Ovimbundu]* (Ennis 1945: 7).

Ndwiga (m) *[ndt-wih-gah]* Giraffe *[Embu]*.

Ndyanabo (m) *[ndjah-naah-boh]* "I eat (together) with them": the name is usually given to a child whose parents imply that though they are aware of the hatred of neighbors and kin towards them, the parents carry on and strive to maintain social solidarity with the antagonists *[Nyankore, Nyoro]* (Beattie 1957: 104).

Nekesa (f) *[neh-keh-sah]* A name given to one born during a period of harvesting *[Luyia, Samia]*.

Nekoye (f) *[neh-koh-yeh]* An honorific name given to a beautiful girl *[Luyia]*.

Nelongo (f) *[neh-lohn-goh]* "The mother of triplets" [The *Ovimbundu]* (Ennis 1945: 2).

Nelugendo (f) *[neh-luh-gehn-doh]* "Traveler": a name such as given to one born when her mother was on a journey *[Kaguru]* (Beidelman 1974: 288).

Nene (f/m) *[neh-neh]* A pet name *[Kongo]* (Ndoma 1977: 98).

Nenko (f) *[nehn-koh]* A name given to a child associated with a period in which there were lots of monkeys in the area [The *Pare]* (Omari 1970: 71).

Neo (m) *[neh-woh]* A present; a name given to the younger of a set of twins, one of which is a girl (named *Mpho*) *[Sotho]* (Mohome 1972: 179).

Neshika (f) *[neh-tsh-ih-kah]* A name given to a child born during a long rainy season *[Pare]* (Omari 1970: 71).

Ngabo (m) *[ngah-boh]* Shields; shield; this name is sometimes associated with the proverb "the *Ganda* ethnics are (like) edible flying ants: they throw their shields onto their backs" which is a humorous statement that the *Ganda*, in carrying shields on their backs (which was more commonplace with men in the past), have the appearance of the edible flying ants with their wings folded [*Ganda*].

Ngagumuntu (m) *[uhn-gah-guh-muhn-tuh]* "As large as a man": name such as given to a child of large size [*Zulu*] (Suzman 1994: 254).

Ngai (m) *[ndgh-ahy]* God; the rain; the sky [*Maasai*] (Huntingford 1930: 102).

Ng'ang'a (m) *[ndgh-ah-ndgh-ah]* The tough one [*Kikuyu*].

Ngangehlathi (m) *[ndgh-ahn-geh-lah-tih]* "As big as a forest" [*Zulu*] (Koopman 1979: 155).

Ngari (m) *[ndgah-rih]* Tiger [*Embu*].

Ngatia (m) *[ndgah-tjah]* Of the animal [*Kikuyu*].

Ngbo (f/m) *[ndgh-boh]* Snake: a name given to a twin [The *Ngbandi*] (Daeleman 1977: 190).

Ngendalelie (f) *[ngehn-dah-leh-lih-yeh]* "Whom shall I go with?": this name is commonly associated with the expression "Whom shall I go with? I shall not go with them" which is metaphorically the lament-ation of an oppressed or mistreated woman who does not have many blood relatives around (or of a child of one in such a situation), or of a child who is an orphan, or of a slave (in past times) who does not see any alternative refuge to her present situation [The *Ovimbundu*] (Ennis 1945: 6).

Ngeso (m) *[ndgeh-soh]* Saturday [*Luo*].

Ngeve (f) *[ndgeh-veh]* Hippopotamus [*Ovimbundu*] (Ennis 1945: 2).

Ngeve (f/m) *[ndgeh-veh]* Hippopotamus: a name given to a twin or trip-let, the siblings of the same birth named *Hosi* and/ or *Njamba* [The *Ovimbundu*] (Ennis 1945: 2).

Nghaminyigwe (m) *[ndgh-ah-mih-ndjh-ih-gweh]* "The one that is not known": a stranger [*Kaguru*] (Beidelman 1974: 288).

Nghenakwe (m) *[ndgh-eh-nah-kweh]* "The one who perceives on his own": a name such as given to one distinguished for his independ-ence [*Kaguru*] (Beidelman 1974: 288).

Ngila (f) *[ndgih-lah]* Pathway; road: a name such as given to one born whereby there is doubting suspicion as to whether the mother's hus-band is the father [*Luyia*].

Ngima (f) *[ndgih-mah]* Monkey [*Embu*].

Ngisila (f/m) *[ndgh-ih-sih-lah]* "The one that comes for/ after": a name given to the second child born after twin siblings [*Kongo*] (Daeleman 1977: 192); a name given to a last born of triplets [*Kongo*] (Daeleman 1977: 193).

Ngobese (m) *[uhn-goh-beh-seh]* Bogwood [The *Zulu*] (Koopman 1990: 336).

Ngole (f/m) *[ndgh-oh-leh]* A name given to the third child born after tw-in siblings [*Hindo*] (Daeleman 1977: 192).

Ngolela (f/m) *[ndgh-oh-oh-leh-eh-laah]* The straightening of something crooked: a name given to the second child born after twin siblings [*Luwa*] (Daeleman 1977: 192).

Ngongo (f) *[ngohn-goh]* Trouble: a name such as given to one born into a family where there is mourning or sickness [*Ovimbundu*] (Ennis 1945: 7).

Ngonidzashe (f/m) *[uhn-goh-nih-dzah-tsh-eh]* "The grace of the Lord" [*Shona*] (Jackson 1957: 121).

Ngoroi (m) *[ndgoh-rohy]* The name of a monkey species [*Embu*].

Ngula (f) *[ndguh-lah]* "The color": this name is commonly associated with the expression "The color of morning," the name usually given to one born very early in the morning--at cockcrow [*Ovimbundu*] (Ennis 1945: 7).

Ngwadi (f) *[ndgh-wah-dih]* A letter [*Shona*] (Jackson 1957: 122).

Ngwako (m) *[ndgh-wah-koh]/* **Ngwakwana** (f) *[ndgh-wah-kwah-nah]* A name given to one whose previously born sibling died [*Tlokwa-Sotho*] (Kruger 1937: 107).

Ngwane (m) *[ndgh-wah-neh]* Cuttlefish [*Zulu*] (Koopman 1990: 336).

Ngweela (f) *[ndgh-weh-eh-lah]* A name given to the fourth child born after twin siblings [*Hindo*] (Daeleman 1977: 192).

Ngwenya (m) *[ndgh-weh-ndjh-ah]* Crocodile [*Zulu*] (Hemans 1968: 74; Koopman 1990: 336).

Ngwono (m) *[ndgh-woh-noh]* Mercy [*Luo*].

Nhamagwa (m) *[nah-mah-gwah]* "The one who suffers" [The *Kaguru*] (Beidelman 1974: 288).

Nhlamulo (f/m) *[unh-lahm-loh]* "Answer": a name such as implying that the parent considers the birth of this child a prayer answer from the assisting Lord [*Zulu*] (Herbert 1995: 4).

Nhlanhla (m) *[uhn-lah-nh-lah]* "Lucky": name such as given to a child whose mother is considered lucky since she nearly died while giving birth to him [*Zulu*] (Suzman 1994: 262).

Nhlanhla (m) *[nlah-nlah]* Luck; good luck [*Zulu*] (Koopman 1979: 154, 156).

Nhloko (m) *[uhn-loh-koh-oh]* "Headgear": a name such as given to a child whose mother's way of dressing is considered sloppy or un-appealing, the name exhorting her to dress properly [*Zulu*] (Suzman 1994: 269).

Nhomagwa (m) *[noh-mah-gwah]* "The one that is hurt/ sick": a name such as given to one who is sickly during his childhood [The *Kaguru*] (Beidelman 1974: 288).

Nikisai (f/m) *[nih-kih-sahy]* "Spread out in the open": a name such as given to one born during a family dispute with kin or neighbors, whereby the child's parent expresses dismay at the kin's or neighbors' consistent backbiting and spreading rumors about the child's parent that would even progress to the level of enticing the forces of witchcraft to encroach upon and malice the parent [*Shona*] (Jackson 1957: 117).

Njabulomzwandile (m) *[ndjah-buh-lohm-zwahn-dih-leh]* "Happiness at the enlarged family": a name such as given by the parents of the named to express gratitude for a good and large family (upon the birth of this fifth child) that translates to more brains and other resources [*Zulu*] (Suzman 1994: 261).

Njagi (m) *[ndjah-gih]* Zebra [*Embu*].

Njakupiti (f) *[ndjah-kuh-pih-tih]* "A path that you do not pass through": this name is commonly associated with the proverb "A path you do not pass through, you do not close it (but you just merely look at it)" implying that it is not logical for you to prevent others from following a path simply because you yourself do not adopt it; this name is also commonly associated with the proverb "A path you do not pass through, you do not clear it of stumps" implying that it is not logical for you to waste time clearing a path that you do not intend to walk in [*Ovimbundu*] (Ennis 1945: 4).

Njamba (f/m) *[ndjh-ahm-bah]* Elephant: name given to a twin or triplet, the siblings of the same birth named *Hosi* and/ or *Ngeve* [The *Ovimbundu*] (Ennis 1945: 2).

Njau (m) *[ndjh-ahw]* Calf [*Embu*].

Njengabantu (m) *[njehn-gah-bahn-tuuh]* "Just like people" [The *Zulu*] (Koopman 1979: 71).

Njengoyise (m) *[njehn-goh-yih-seh]* "Just like his father" [The *Zulu*] (Koopman 1979: 155).

Njeri (f) *[ndjeh-rih]* One who loves to move about; one who loves to visit; visitor [*Embu, Kikuyu*].

Njeru (f/m) *[ndjeh-ruh]* Locusts: a name given to one born during a locust invasion period [*Shona*] (Jackson 1957: 119).

Njeru (m) *[ndjeh-ruuh]* Hyena [*Embu*].

Njiru (m) *[ndjih-ruh]* Rhino; black [*Embu*].

Njobe (m) *[njoh-beh]* The marsh antelope; this name is sometimes associated with the saying "to unjustly accuse me (or one), is like accusing the marsh antelope of being in the marsh" whereby the situation of gross false incrimination is compared to accusing the antelope of being in its very own niche, in which it is only harmlessly grazing, and not wrecking havoc on cultivated crops [*Ganda*].

Njodzi (m) *[njoh-dzih]* Disaster: a name such as given to a child born to a mother who "experienced great troubles during her confinement" --'confinement' likely refers to the period of a few days following giving birth during which a new mother is traditionally required by many African societies to stay indoors [*Zezuru*] (Marapara 1954: 8).

Njogu (m) *[ndjoh-guh]* Elephant [*Embu, Kikuyu*].

Njoka (f/m) *[ndjoh-kah]* "Snake": a name given to one whose mother's house was visited by a snake during the pregnancy, or to a child reincarnated more than once [*Embu*].

Njoki (f) *[ndjoh-kih]* The one reborn; "the one who returns"; "the reincarnated one" [*Embu, Kikuyu*].

Njuka (m) *[ndjuh-kah]* Newcomer [*Kikuyu*].

Njukura (m) *[ndjuh-kuh-rah]* A name given to one born during a period when there is an abundance of food [*Luyia*].

Njunju (f) *[ndjh-uhn-juh]* The name of a species of large mushroom: a name such as given to a deliberate and rather languid person [The *Ovimbundu*] (Ennis 1945: 6).

Njura (f) *[ndjuh-rah]* The one who swings [*Embu*].

Nkamoheleng (f) *[nkaah-moh-heh-leh-ndgh]* "(You all) accept/ welcome me!" [*Sotho*] (Mohome 1972: 174).

Nkamunu (f) *[ndkah-muh-nuh]* The tiny one [*Maasai*].

Nkandangulu (m) *[nkahn-dahn-guh-luh]* The pig's hide [The *Kongo*] (Ndoma 1977: 96).

Nkaniyakhe (m) *[nkah-nih-yaah-keh]* "(Of) his obstinacy" [The *Zulu*] (Koopman 1979: 157).

Nkfutela (f) *[nkfuh-teh-lah]* A name given to the second child born after twin siblings [*Hindo*] (Daeleman 1977: 192).

Nkfutu (f/m) *[nkfuh-tuuh]* A name given to one whose birth follows that of his or her twin siblings [*Hindo*] (Daeleman 1977: 191).

Nkini (f) *[nkih-nih]* The small one [*Maasai*].

Nkiponyi (m) *[nkih-poh-ndjh-ih]* The one that is not pushed [*Maasai*].

Nkisikatumwe (f/m) *[nkih-sih-kaah-tuuh-mweh]* "That has been sent/ ordered/ commissioned": name given to the last born of triplets [The *Saanga*] (Daeleman 1977: 193).

Nkomo (m) *[nkoh-moh]* Cattle; beast; head of cattle [*Zulu*] (Hemans 1968: 74; Koopman 1990: 336).

Nkomokazikho (m) *[nkoh-moh-kah-zih-koh]* "The cattle are not here": a name such as given to a child born during a drought [The *Zulu*] (Koopman 1979: 68).

Nkoomba (f/m) *[nkoh-ohm-bah]* "I clean (the womb of the ritual anomaly of the twins-birth)": name given to one whose birth follows that of his or her twin siblings [*Luba, Saanga*] (Daeleman 1977: 191).

Nkosenye (m) *[nkoh-seh-ndjh-eh]* "Another chief" [*Zulu*] (Koopman 1979: 157).

Nkosi (m) *[nkoh-sih]* Chief [*Zulu*] (Koopman 1990: 336).

Nkosi (m) *[nkoh-oh-sih]* Lion: a name given to an older twin, the younger named *Makaanzu* [*Kongo*] (Daeleman 1977: 191).

Nkosikayikhonzi (m) *[nkoh-sih-kah-yih-kohn-zih]* "The chief is not respectful"; "the Lord/ chief does not respect" [*Zulu*] (Koopman 1979: 159).

Nkosinathi (m) *[nkoh-sih-nah-tih]* "The Lord is with us" [The *Zulu*] (Koopman 1979: 160).

Nkosingiphile (m) *[nkoh-sihn-gih-pih-leh]* "The Lord has given me" [*Zulu*] (Koopman 1979: 166).

Nkosiyapha (m) *[nkoh-sih-yaah-pah]* "The Lord gives" [The *Zulu*] (Koopman 1979: 159, 164).

Nkotoi (m) *[nkoh-tohy]* The one of the way [*Maasai*].

Nkuku (f/m) *[nkuh-kuh]* Hen; chicken [*Zulu*] (Herbert 1995: 5).

Nkukuu (m) *[nkuh-kuuh]* The one of the wild animal [*Maasai*].

Nkululekosebenzani (m) *[uhn-kuh-luh-leh-koh-seh-behn-zah-nih]* "Be free but continue working": a name such as given by the named child's parents to express that they consider that upon the birth of the previous (third born) child, they felt they had fulfilled their social obligation of starting a family but, they were committed to continuing to work hard for the good of their children [*Zulu*] (Suzman 1994: 261).

Nkunzebomvu (m) *[nkuhn-zeh-bohm-vuh]* "Red bull" [*Zulu*] (Koopman 1979: 157, 164).

Nkurufi (m) *[nkuh-ruh-fih]* A name given to a child born during a cock crow in the early morning [*Pare*] (Omari 1970: 71).

Nlaandu/ Nlandu (f/m) *[nlaahn-duh]* "The next one"/ "the one who follows the footsteps (of the twins)"/ "the one that follows": a name given to one whose birth follows that of his or her twin siblings [The *Kongo*] (Daeleman 1977: 191; Ndoma 1977: 89).

Nnume (m) *[nnuh-meh]* Male animal; bull; this name is sometimes associated with the proverb "mocking (or making facial expressions) does not kill the bull" meaning that mere words do not frighten the brave or the hardened, and is also synonymous with "hard words break no bones" and "sticks and stones may break my bones, but words cannot hurt me" [*Ganda*].

Nobantu (f) *[noh-bahn-tuh]* "People" [*Zulu*] (Koopman 1979: 155).

Nobathonyile (f) *[noh-bah-toh-ndjh-ih-leh]* "Miss. Enchantment" [The *Zulu*] (Lugg 1968: 14).

Nodoli (f) *[noh-doh-lih]* "Dolly": a name such as given to a beautiful child, the name adapted from the European word [The *Zulu*] (Suzman 1994: 269).

Nokuthula (f) *[noh-kuh-tuh-lah]* Quietude; peace [*Zulu*] (Koopman 1979: 155).

Nolwandle (f) *[noh-lwahn-dleh]* Sea; ocean [*Zulu*] (Koopman 1979: 155).

Nomali (m) *[noh-mah-lih]* The one that is wealthy [*Maasai*].

Nomasonto (f) *[noh-mah-sohn-toh]* "Born on Sunday" [The *Zulu*] (Suzman 1994: 270).

Nomathemba (f) *[noh-mah-tehm-bah]* "Hope" [*Zulu*] (Koopman 1979: 155).

Nomhle (f) *[nohm-leh]* "Beauty" [*Zulu*] (Suzman 1994: 268, 269).

Nomusa (f) *[noh-muh-sah]* Kindness [*Zulu*] (Suzman 1994: 268, 269).

Nomusa (f) *[noh-muh-sah]* Mercy; kindness [*Zulu*] (Koopman 1979: 155-156).

Nomvula (f) *[nohm-vuh-lah]* "In the rain" [*Zulu*] (Suzman 1994: 268).

Nomvula (f) *[noh-mvuh-lah]* "Rain" [*Zulu*] (Koopman 1979: 155).

Nondwayiza (m) *[nohn-dwah-yih-zah]* "The crane": a name such as given to one who is long legged and walks in a stately manner that is likened to a crane [*Zulu*] (Lugg 1968: 14).

Nonhlanhla (f) *[noh-nlah-nlah]* "(Good) luck" [*Zulu*] (Koopman 1979: 154).

Nonhlanhla (f) *[noh-nlah-nlah]* "Lucky" [*Zulu*] (Suzman 1994: 268).

Noolarami (f) *[noh-oh-lah-rah-mih]* The one with many domestic animal herds [*Maasai*].

Noolarin (f) *[noh-oh-lah-rihn]* The one of rain [*Maasai*].

Noonkishu (f) *[noh-ohn-kih-tsh-uh]* The one that has cows [*Maasai*].

Nozinyathi (f) *[noh-zih-ndjh-ah-tih]* "Miss. Buffalo": a name such as given to one who is somewhat rotund or plump and is likened to a young buffalo cow [*Zulu*] (Lugg 1968: 12, 13).

Nseemo (f/m) *[nseh-eh-moh]* "Lightning": a name given to a twin, the other named *Nzasi* [*Yaka*] (Daeleman 1977: 190).

Nsekanabo (m) *[nseh-kah-nah-boh]/* **Nshekanabo** (m) *[ntsh-eh-kah-nah-boh]* "I laugh alongside (or with) them": a name given to a child whose parents imply that, though the antagonists may not think so, the parents are aware of the hostility of neighbors or kin towards them [*Kiga, Nyankore, Nyoro*] (Beattie 1957: 104).

Nsengo (f/m) *[nsehn-goh]* Hoe: a "non-human" and usually temporary name given to a newborn [*Kongo*] (Ndoma 1977: 89).

Nsiimba (f/m) *[nsiihm-bah]* Wild cat: a name given to an older twin, the younger named *Nzuzi* [*Kongo*] (Daeleman 1977: 191); a name given to a first-born of triplets [*Kongo*] (Daeleman 1977: 193).

Nsiko (m) *[nsih-koh]* Bush; jungle; uncultivated land; this name is sometimes associated with the proverb "men are (like) wild animals: when you pursuingly follow into the bush after one, he breaks through the thicket with tremendous force" implying that men are tough and do not easily give in without a fight [*Ganda*].

Nsimba (f/m) *[nsiihm-bah]* "The one that holds": a name given to an older twin, the younger named *Nzuzi* [*Kongo*] (Ndoma 1977: 89).

Nsongi (f/m) *[nsohn-gih]* A name given to one whose birth precedes that of his or her twin siblings [*Ntomba, Bolia*] (Daeleman 1977: 193).

Nsonzi (m) *[nsohn-zih]* Small mudfish that resembles an eel; this name is sometimes associated with the proverb "the involvement of many people results in a killing catch of the tiny mudfishes" which is synonymous with "many hands make light work" [*Ganda*].

Nsumba (m) *[nsuhm-bah]* Moth: a name such as given to a newborn whose father considers the friendly man he works with as like a moth to him [*Zulu*] (Herbert 1995: 5).

Nsumbu (m) *[nsuhm-buuh]* A ritual related name traditionally conferred upon the child following its initiation [*Kongo*] (Ndoma 1977: 90).

Nsunda (f/m) *[nsuuhn-dah]* "The one that sinks": name such as given to a child that is born legs first (as opposed to the conventional head first) from the womb [*Kongo*] (Ndoma 1977: 89).

Ntai (m) *[ntahy]* A name given to the older of a set of identical male twins, the younger named *Ntainyane* [*Sotho*] (Mohome 1972: 179).

Ntainyane (m) [*ntah-yih-ndjh-ah-neh*] A name given to the younger of a set of identical male twins, the older named *Ntai* [*Sotho*] (Mohome 1972: 179).

Ntarumanye (m) [*ntah-ruh-mah-ndjh-eh*] "I do not comprehend it (i.e. death)": the name implies that the parents are so bewildered and ignorant as to why the phenomenon of death took away a family member so young, and is given to a child whose earlier born sibling passed away [*Nyoro*] (Beattie 1957: 102).

Nthabiseng (f) [*ntah-bih-seh-ndgh*] "Make me happy!"; a name given to the younger of a set of twins, one of which is a boy (named *Thabiso*) [*Sotho*] (Mohome 1972: 179).

Nthofeela (m) [*ntoh-feh-eh-lah*] "(Simply) just a thing": this derogatory/ non-human name given to a child whose preceding sibling or siblings died, there being pessimism as to whether this one will survive, is however intended to effectuate the opposite of its literal meaning [*Sotho*] (Mohome 1972: 176).

Nthuseng (f) [*ntuh-seh-ndgh*] "(You all) help me!" [*Sotho*] (Mohome 1972: 174).

Nti (f/m) [*ntih*] Tree: a "non-human" and usually temporary name given to a newborn [*Kongo*] (Ndoma 1977: 89).

Ntja (f) [*int-jah*] Dog: an unpleasant name given to one whose previous born sibling was stillborn or died before weaning, this attributed to sorcery--the name is a means to safeguard this child "by making a show of neglecting it in the hope of lulling the sorcerer's vigilance" [*Sotho*] (Ashton 1952: 33).

Ntja (m) [*int-jah*] Dog: a derogatory name given to one who has lost two or more preceding siblings to death, the name (paradoxically) intended to devalue and hence serve as protection for this child through dissuading the forces of evil and death from taking such a "useless" child away [*Sotho*] (Thipa 1986: 290).

Ntjantja (f) [*ntjahn-tjah*] "Doggy dog": this derogatory/ non-human name given to a child whose preceding sibling or siblings died, there being pessimism as to whether this one will survive, is however intended to effectuate the opposite of its literal meaning [*Sotho*] (Mohome 1972: 176).

Ntokozo (m) [*uhn-toh-koh-zoh*] "Joy": a name such as given by the named child's mother to signify that she is happy and thankful to God that she has bore this boy that was so much longed for, given that the numbers of the family's female children are very high compared to those of the male ones [*Zulu*] (Suzman 1994: 268).

Ntombazana (f) [*ntohm-bah-zah-nah*] "Small girl" [*Zulu*] (Koopman 1979: 154).

Ntombebomvu (f) [*ntohm-beh-bohm-vuh*] "Red complexioned girl" [*Zulu*] (Koopman 1979: 157, 164).

Ntombenhle (f) [*ntohm-beh-nleh*] "Pretty girl" [*Zulu*] (Koopman 1979:

157).

Ntombenkulu (f) *[ntohm-behn-kuh-luh]* "Big girl" [*Zulu*] (Koopman 1979: 157).

Ntombi (f) *[ntohm-bih]* "Girl" [*Zulu*] (Koopman 1979: 154).

Ntombifikile (f) *[ntohm-bih-fih-kih-leh]* "A girl has arrived" [The *Zulu*] (Koopman 1979: 160, 164).

Ntombifile (f) *[ntohm-bih-fih-leh]* "A girl has died" [*Zulu*] (Koopman 1979: 160).

Ntombikanina (f) *[ntohm-bih-kah-nih-nah]* "Girl of her mother"; "(her) mother's girl" [*Zulu*] (Koopman 1979: 157).

Ntombikayise (f) *[ntohm-bih-kah-yih-seh]* "Girl of her father"; "(her) father's girl" [*Zulu*] (Koopman 1979: 157, 164).

Ntombise (f) *[ntohm-bih-seh]* "Girl" [*Zulu*] (Koopman 1979: 156).

Ntombiyesichaka (f) *[uhn-tohm-bih-yeh-sih-tch-ah-kah]* Destitute girl : a name such as given to one born when the mother was destitute [*Zulu*] (Suzman 1994: 269).

Ntombizabantu (f) *[ntohm-bih-zah-bahn-tuh]* "Girls of the people" [*Zulu*] (Koopman 1979: 157).

Ntombizibuyile (f) *[ntohm-bih-zih-buh-yih-leh]* "The girls have come back" [*Zulu*] (Koopman 1979: 160).

Ntombizodwa (f) *[ntohm-bih-zoh-dwah]* "Only girls" [*Zulu*] (Koopman 1979: 158, 162).

Ntombizonke (f) *[ntohm-bih-zohn-keh]* "All girls" [*Zulu*] (Koopman 1979: 162).

Ntshediseng (f) *[ntsh-eh-dih-seh-ndgh]* "Console me!" [The *Sotho*] (Mohome 1972: 174).

Ntshiuwa (f) *[ntsh-ih-yuh-wah]* The forsaken one; the one left behind; a name given to the older of a set of twins, one of which is a boy (named *Mosiuwa*) [*Sotho*] (Mohome 1972: 175, 179).

Ntswaki (f) *[nt-swah-kih]* "The mixer": (though the source gives this name a scanty glance, given that an ideally desired African family situation is for there to be an equitable mix in number of male relative to female children, the source seems to imply that this name is appropriately given to) the first born female among a disproportionately large number of preceding male siblings/ or a child born in a family with a disproportionately high ratio of male to female children [*Sotho*] (Mohome 1972: 179-180).

Ntungunono (m) *[ntuhn-guh-noh-noh]* "Mr. Secretary Bird": this started out as a nickname for a tall and thin man that strides like a bird [*Zulu*] (Lugg 1968: 14).

Numanawa (f) *[nuh-mah-nah-wah]* "I shall send an in-law": this name is commonly associated with the expression "Whom shall I send? I shall send an in-law since I do have a relative" which is metaphorically the lamentation of an oppressed or mistreated woman who does not have many blood relatives around (or a child of one in such a situation) [*Ovimbundu*] (Ennis 1945: 6).

Numelie (f) *[nuh-meh-lih-yeh]* "Whom shall I send?": this name is commonly associated with the expression "Whom shall I send? I shall send an in-law since I do have a relative" which is metaphorically the lamentation of an oppressed or mistreated woman who does not have many blood relatives around (or a child of one in such a situation) [*Ovimbundu*] (Ennis 1945: 6).

Nvubu (m) *[nvuh-buh]* Hippopotamus; this name is sometimes associated with the proverb "you do not hang around a hippopotamus in the depth of the waters" implying that it would be highly risky to challenge something big and dangerous in its very own niche (or in conditions it is very familiar with) [*Ganda*].

N'wangilazi (m) *[uhn-wahn-gih-lah-zih]* Glass [*Zulu*] (Herbert 1995: 5).

Nyabilo (f/m) *[ndjh-ah-bih-loh]* That of charms; that of taste [*Luo*].

Nyabola (f/m) *[ndjh-ah-boh-lah]* One who throws away [*Luo*].

Nyaduwo (f/m) *[ndjh-ah-duh-woh]* One who disorganizes (or disturbs) [*Luo*].

Nyadwe (f) *[ndjh-ah-dweh]* Of the moon [*Luo*].

Nyadwe (f) *[ndjh-ah-dweh]* "The moon's daughter": one who is very beautiful, and also the nickname of the wife of the British colonialist adventurer and warrior Samuel Baker [*Acholi*] (Southall 1951: 187).

Nyadwi (f) *[ndjh-ah-dwih]* "The moon's daughter": one who is very beautiful, and also the nickname of the wife of the British colonialist adventurer and warrior Samuel Baker [*Alur*, as adapted from the *Acholi* name *Nyadwe*] (Southall 1951: 187).

Nyaga (m) *[ndjh-ah-gah]* Ostrich [*Embu*].

Nyagutuii (f) *[ndjh-ah-guh-tuh-yiih]* One who loves to walk [*Kikuyu*].

Nyakallo (f/m) *[ndjh-ah-kahl-loh]* Merriment [*otho*] (Mohome 1972: 174).

Nyakech (f/m) *[ndjh-ah-ketch]* The harsh one; the sour one [*Luo*].

Nyakota (f/m) *[ndjh-ah-koh-tah]* One who rolls up tobacco [*Luo*].

Nyakwaka (f/m) *[ndjh-ah-kwah-kah]* One who embraces [*Luo*].

Nyalwal (f/m) *[ndjh-ah-lwahl]* "The one of the red soil" [*Luo*].

Nyamayedenga (m) *[ndjh-ah-mah-yeh-dehn-gah]* Flesh of the heavens: a name given to a child who is not expected to live long i.e. "his body will soon be the flesh of the Heavens" [*Zezuru*] (Marapara 1954: 7).

Nyamiti (f) *[ndjh-ah-mih-tih]* "Medicine": a name such as given to one whose birth is presumably through the vehicle of magical therapy [*Kaguru*] (Beidelman 1974: 288).

Nyamu (m) *[ndjh-ah-muh]* Animal [*Kikuyu*].

Nyandene (f/m) *[ndjh-ahn-deh-neh]* One that is associated with the locale *Ndene* [*Luo*].

Nyangomboyo (f) *[ndjh-ah-ndgh-oh-ohm-boh-oh-yoh]* "The mother of twins": a name given to a parent of twins [*Hindo*] (Daeleman 1977: 194).

Nyaradzaomunashe (f/m) *[ndjh-ah-rah-dzoh-muh-nah-sheh]* "Comfort in the Lord" [*Shona*] (Jackson 1957: 121).

Nyasaye (m) *[ndjh-ah-sah-yeh]* God; "one that is worshipped" [*Luo*] (Huntingford 1930: 103).

Nyasene (f/m) *[ndjh-ah-seh-neh]* Of hate: one who hates [*Luo*].

Nyashadzashe (f/m) *[ndjh-ah-tsh-ah-dzah-tsh-eh]* "The grace of the Lord" [*Shona*] (Jackson 1957: 122).

Nyawawa (f/m) *[ndjh-ah-wah-wah]* Evil spirits: name given to one born at a time the spirits of a twin birth are being chased away [*Luo*].

Nyawira (f) *[ndjh-ah-wih-rah]* One who loves to work [*Embu, Kikuyu*].

Nyawose (m) *[ndjh-ah-woh-seh]* "Foot" [*Zulu*] (Koopman 1979: 156).

Nyelani (f/m) *[ndjh-eh-lah-nih]* "Emit stool onto me": a disharmony related name such as given by one of this newborn's grandparents to imply that the daughter-in-law (i.e. the newborn's mother) is so disrespectful and is not be expected to change her ways [*Zulu*] (Herbert 1995: 4, 6).

Nyendwoha (m) *[ndjh-ehn-dwoh-hah]* "By whom am I loved?": the parent of a child given this name is heralding the message that no one seems to like him/ her [*Nyoro*] (Beattie 1957: 104).

Nyengeterai (f/m) *[ndjh-ehn-geh-teh-rahy]* "Cleanse me" [The *Shona*] (Jackson 1957: 121).

Nyenjura (m) *[ndjh-ehn-juh-rah]* "Of the rain": a name such as given to a child born during a period of rainfall [*Nyoro*] (Beattie 1957: 99).

Nyiimi (m) *[ndjh-iih-mih]* "The worm subsisting on human (or animal) flesh": a name given to the younger of twin boys, the older named *Khuumbu* [*Yoombe*] (Daeleman 1977: 191).

Nyokabi (f) *[ndjh-oh-kah-bih]* One from amongst the *Maasai* ethnics [*Kikuyu*].

Nyokana (m) *[uh-ndjh-oh-kah-nah]* "Little snake": name such as given to one born around the time a small snake is seen or killed [*Zulu*] (Suzman 1994: 254).

Nyongo (f/m) *[ndjh-ohn-goh]* Direction; course [*Luo*].

Nyooko (m) *[ndjh-oh-oh-koh]* Gall: a name such as given to one born during a period of drought [*Sotho*] (Ashton 1952: 32).

Nyuot (m) *[ndjh-uh-woht]* Heavy rainstorm: name such as given to one born during a heavy rainstorm [*Nuer*] (Evans-Pritchard 1948: 167).

Nyuto (f/m) *[ndjh-uh-toh]* One associated with the locale *Nyuto* [*Luo*].

Nzara (f/m) *[ndzah-rah]* Famine/ hunger: a name given to one born during a period of food shortages [*Shona*].

Nzasi (f/m) *[ndzh-zaah-sih]* "Thunder": name given to a twin, the other named *Nseemo* [*Yaka*] (Daeleman 1977: 190).

Nzinga (f/m) *[ndzh-iihn-gah]* "The one that rolls up": a name such as given to a child born with the umbilical cord rolled up around its body [*Kongo*] (Ndoma 1977: 89).

Nzita (m) *[nzih-tah]* "I kill"; "I would kill"; "I am killing" [*Ganda*].

Nzota (f) *[ndzh-oh-tah]* A name given to a child conceived or born during a period of large-scale famine [*Pare*] (Omari 1970: 71).

Nzovu (m) *[ndzh-oh-vuh]* "The big one": a name such as given to a big size newborn [*Pare*] (Omari 1970: 71).

Nzusi (f) *[ndzh-uh-sih]* The serval (cat): a name given to the younger of twin girls, the older named *Tsiimba* [*Yaka*] (Daeleman 1977: 191); a name given to a triplet [*Yaka*] (Daeleman 1977: 192).

Nzuuzi (f/m) *[ndzh-uuh-zih]* The serval (cat): a name given to a younger twin, the older named *Tsiimba* [*Kongo*] (Daeleman 1977: 191).

Nzuzi (f/m) *[ndzh-uh-zih]* The serval (cat): name given to a younger twin, the older named *Nsiimba* [*Kongo*] (Daeleman 1977: 191); a name given to the second born of triplets [*Kongo*] (Daeleman 1977: 193); "the one that is drawn out": name given to a younger twin, the older named *Nsimba* [*Kongo*] (Ndoma 1977: 89).

-O-

Obam (m) *[oh-bahm]* Crippled; not straight [*Luo*].

Obambo (m) *[oh-bahm-boh]* The dissected fish [*Luo*].

Obare (m) *[oh-bah-reh]* "Failed to take place" [*Luo*].

Obat (m) *[oh-baht]* Arm [*Luo*].

Obel (m) *[oh-behl]* Millet [*Luo*].

Obeto (m) *[oh-beh-toh]* "He has slashed" [*Luo*].

Obia (f/m) *[oh-bih-yah]* "In the beer pot": a name such as given to one born to a father who is a drunkard [*Lugbara*] (Middleton 1961: 35).

Obiero (m) *[oh-bjeh-roh]* Placenta [*Luo*].

Obilo (m) *[oh-bih-loh]* That of charms [*Luo*].

Obota (m) *[oh-boh-tah]* "He neglected me"; "he threw me away"; "he abandoned me" [*Luo*].

Obote (m) *[oh-boh-teh]* "Neglected" [*Luo*].

Obudho (m) *[oh-buh-tdh-oh]* Pumpkin; delayed [*Luo*].

Obundo (m) *[oh-buhn-doh]* "Bald"; plateau [*Luo*].

Obura (m) *[oh-buh-rah]* "Overwhelmed me"; "too much on me" [*Luo*].

Oburu (m) *[oh-buh-ruh]* Dust [*Luo*].

Obuya (m) *[oh-buh-yah]* A kind of fruit such as that of the calabash plant [*Luo*].

Obwon (m) *[oh-bwohn]* Discriminated against; prejudiced; not liked [*Luo*].

Ochan (m) *[oh-tch-ahn]* Harvest; eaten [*Luo*].

Ochanda (m) *[oh-tch-ahn-dah]* "He/ she disturbs me" [*Luo*].

Ochido (m) *[oh-tch-ih-doh]* Dirty; wiped with the finger [*Luo*].

Ochiel (m) *[oh-tch-yehl]* "Freed"; "unleashed"; "shot" [*Luo*].

Ochieng (m) *[oh-tch-yeh-ndgh]* Sunshine [*Luo*].

Ochiodho (m) *[oh-tch-yoh-dhoh]* Muddy [*Luo*].

Ochola (m) *[oh-tch-oh-lah]* A name given to the child born first following the mother remarrying [*Luyia* and several other ethnics of eastern and central Africa] (Wako 1985: 36).

Ochomo (m) *[oh-tch-oh-moh]* "Direct"; to cool [*Luo*].

Ochoro (m) *[oh-tch-oh-roh]* "He/ she has pushed" [*Luo*].

Ochuka (m) *[oh-tch-uh-kah]* "He/ she delivered me" [*Luo*].

Ochuka (m) *[oh-tch-uh-kah]* "He/ she has caught up with me" [*Luo*].

Ochungo (f/m) *[oh-tch-uhn-goh]* "He/ she has raised"; resurrected [*Luo*].

Ochura (m) *[oh-tch-uh-rah]* The one who groans; groaner [*Luo*].

Ocuiti (m) *[oh-tch-uuhy-tih]* "Thrown" [*Luo*].

Ode (f/m) *[oh-deh]* "Many people fall (dead)": a name such as given to one whose father is reputed to be a wizard that causes death [The *Lugbara*] (Middleton 1961: 36).

Odek (m) *[oh-dekh]* Plant vegetable [*Luo*].

Odemba (m) *[oh-dehm-bah]* "One that caresses me"; "one who handles me with care" [*Luo*].

Odendo (m) *[oh-dehn-doh]* "Taking care"; "tender" [*Luo*].

Odhialo (f/m) *[oh-djah-loh]* "He/ she pampers" [*Luo*].

Odhiambo (m) *[oh-djahm-boh]* A name given to one born in the evening [*Luo*].

Odhuno (m) *[oh-tdh-uh-noh]* "He has pinched" [*Luo*].

Odiera (m) *[oh-dih-yeh-rah]* Truthful [*Luo*].

Odiero (m) *[oh-dih-yeh-roh]* The pink one; the white man [*Luo*].

Odinga (m) *[oh-dihn-gah]* Cheek bone [*Luo*].

Odipo (m) *[oh-dih-poh]* Kitchen [*Luo*].

Odira (m) *[oh-dih-rah]* "I have been tossed"; "I have been thrown" [*Luo*].

Odiye (m) *[oh-dih-yeh]* "It has squeezed (or squashed) him" [*Luo*].

Odiyo (m) *[oh-dih-yoh]* "He has squeezed" [*Luo*].

Odoki (m) *[oh-doh-kih]* A name given to a child born to a mother that is threatening to leave her husband and go back to her parents [The *Acholi*] (Nzita 1995: 92).

Odondo (m) *[oh-dohn-doh]* "Pecking" [*Luo*].

Odongo (m) *[oh-dohn-goh]* A name given to a second born of twins [*Iteso, Langi, Luyia,* and several other ethnics of eastern and central Africa] (Wako 1985: 38).

Odua (f/m) *[oh-duh-wah]* "As an omen": a name such as given to one whose birth, it is alleged, will cause someone to die [The *Lugbara*] (Middleton 1961: 35).

Odundo (m) *[oh-duhn-doh]* "The short one" [*Luo*].

Odunga (m) *[oh-duhn-gah]* Walking stick [*Luo*].

Oduol (m) *[ohd-wohl]* Animals' shed [*Luo*].

Oduor (m) *[ohd-wohr]* Dawn [*Luo*].

Odur (m) *[oh-durh]* A name given to a child whose mother experienced difficult and painful birth labor pains that involved administration of herbs and divination; consequently, the child's umbilical cord became buried under a rubbish heap [*Acholi*] (Nzita 1995: 92).

Oduwo (m) *[oh-duh-woh]* "Destroyed"; "disorganized" [*Luo*].

Odwar (m) *[ohd-wahr]* "Looked for"; "searched for"; "hunted for" [*Luo*].

Odwong (m) *[ohd-woh-ndgh]* A name given to a child whose mother experienced difficult and painful birth labor pains that involved administration of herbs and divination; consequently, the child's umbilical cord became buried under an *odwong* tree [The *Acholi*] (Nzita 1995: 92).

Ofwono (m) *[ohf-woh-nah]* To be against me [*Luo*].

Ogada (m) *[oh-gah-dah]* Bamboo [*Luo*].

Oganda (m) *[oh-gahn-dah]* Beans [*Luo*].

Ogawo (m) *[oh-gah-woh]* Watches [*Luo*].

Ogeto (m) *[oh-geh-toh]* "Admiring" [*Luo*].

Ogolla (m) *[oh-gohl-lah]* Pavement; "removed me" [*Luo*].

Ogomba (m) *[oh-gohm-boh]* "Desiring"; "wishing" [*Luo*].

Ogony (m) *[oh-goh-ndjh]* "Unloosen"; "unchain"; "untether"; "released"; "set free" [*Luo*].

Oguok (m) *[ohg-wohk]* Dog [*Luo*].

Ogwallo (m) *[oh-gwahl-loh]* The one with large biceps [*Luo*].

Ogwang (m) *[ohg-wah-ndgh]* Wolf [*Luo*].

Ogwel (m) *[oh-gwehl]* Bow legged [*Luo*].

Ogweno (m) *[oh-gweh-noh]* Chewed [*Luo*].

Oile (m) *[oh-yih-leh]* One who is caused to itch [*Luo*].

Oinotet (m) *[ohy-noh-teht]* God; "the spirit" [*Sapei*] (Huntingford 1930: 103).

Oiro (m) *[oh-yih-roh]* That of smoke; bewitched [*Luo*].

Ojiambo (m) *[ohj-yahm-boh]* A name given to one born in the evening [*Samia, Luo*].

Ojukaa (m) *[oh-djuh-kaah]* "He has caught up with me"; "he has found me" [*Luo*].

Ojwando (m) *[oh-djh-wahn-doh]* "Left carelessly" [*Luo*].

Ojwanga (m) *[oh-djh-wah-ndgh-ah]* The one that has been neglected [*Luo*].

Okal (m) *[oh-kahl]* Millet [*Luo*].

Okal (m) *[oh-kahl]* "Pass him" [*Luo*].

Okatch (m) *[ohk-atch]* "Not empty" [*Luo*].

Okawo (m) *[oh-kah-woh]* "He has escorted me" [*Luo*].

Okendo (m) *[oh-kehn-doh]* "He/ she has married" [*Luo*].

Okera (m) *[oh-keh-rah]* "Spread me"; "cause me to be wide apart" [*Luo*].

Oketch (m) *[ohk-eh-tch]* "The hungry one"; hunger": a name such as given to one born during a period of famine [*Luo*].

Okeya (m) *[oh-keh-yah]* "He has bitten me"; the last born [*Luo*].

Okeyo (m) *[oh-keh-yoh]* Scattered [*Luo*].

Okinda (m) *[oh-kihn-dah]* "Diligent" [*Luo*].

Okinyo (m) *[oh-kih-ndjh-oh]* A name given to one born in the morning just before the sun has emerged [*Luo*].

Okite (m) *[oh-kih-teh]* Stones; characters; moods [*Luo*].

Okiya (m) *[oh-kih-yah]* "He/ she does not know"; "he/ she does not know me"; "unaware" [*Luo*].

Okoko (m) *[oh-koh-koh]* The noise maker [*Luo*].

Okola (f) *[oh-koh-lah]* A name given to a woman whose husband has died, but he does not as yet have an heir [*Luo*].

Okongo (m) *[oh-koh-ndgh-oh]* Alcohol; liquor [*Luo*].

Okoro (m) *[oh-koh-roh]* "Now"; "predicted" [*Luo*].

Okot (m) *[oh-koht]* Bell [*Luo*].

Okoth (m) *[oh-koh-sth]* Rain [*Luo*].

Okudo (m) *[oh-kuh-doh]* "Gurgle" [*Luo*].

Okul (m) *[oh-kuhl]* Cow shed [*Luo*].

Okullo (m) *[oh-kuhl-loh]* Of the stream; of the river [*Luo*].

Okulu (m) *[oh-kuh-luh]* The one whose shoulders are bent and sagging [*Luo*].

Okumba (m) *[oh-kuhm-bah]* Elbow [*Luo*].

Okumu (m) *[oh-kuh-muh]* A name given to one conceived soon after (within a period of a month) the preceding sibling is born [*Luyia*].

Okumu (m) *[oh-kuh-muh]* "Punished" [*Luo*].

Okune (m) *[oh-kuh-neh]* "He has been rejected" [*Luo*].

Okuthe (m) *[oh-kuh-sth-eh]* Thorns [*Luo*].

Okwach (m) *[oh-kwah-tch]* Leopard [*Luo*].

Okwanyo (m) *[oh-kwah-ndjh-oh]* "He picked" [*Luo*].

Okwom (m) *[ohk-wohm]* Hunchback [*Luo*].

Okwisia (f/m) *[oh-kwiih-sjah]* "Concluding": name given to one fond of bringing an end to his speech with the expression *"nakwisia"* i.e. "I have concluded" [*Luyia*].

Olago (m) *[oh-lah-goh]* One who sleeps with the widow [*Luo*].

Olal (m) *[oh-lahl]* "He/ she is lost" [*Luo*].

Olanana (m) *[oh-lah-nah-nah]* The one whose body is soft (or tender) [*Maasai*].

Olang (m) *[oh-lah-ndgh]* Bell [*Luo*].

Olanya (m) *[oh-lah-ndjh-ah]* A name given to a child born to a mother who feels abandoned [*Acholi*] (Nzita 1995: 92).

Olawo (m) *[oh-lah-woh]* Saliva; "he chased"; "run after" [*Luo*].

Olayo (m) *[oh-lah-yoh]* Beans; urinated [*Luo*].

Olemo (m) *[oh-leh-moh]* Fruit [*Luo*].

Olenaeku (m) *[oh-leh-nah-yeh-kuuh]* The one that comes early [The *Maasai*].

Olenyo (m) *[oh-leh-ndjh-oh]* Liquefied [*Luo*].

Olero (m) *[oh-leh-roh]* "He has lightened"; "he has brightened" [*Luo*].

Oliech (m) *[oh-lih-yehk]* Elephant [*Luo*].

Olilo (m) *[oh-lih-loh]* "Has caused to be dirty" [*Luo*].
Olima (m) *[oh-lih-mah]* "He/ she visited me"; one who visits [*Luo*].
Olipeere (m) *[oh-lih-peh-eh-reh]* The one of the spear [*Maasai*].
Oloimutie (m) *[oh-lohy-muh-tjeh]* The one that has come late [The *Maasai*].
Oloitiptip (m) *[oh-lohy-tihp-tihp]* The one that showers [*Maasai*].
Oloitu (m) *[oh-lohy-tuh]* The one that comes back [*Maasai*].
Ololepisho (m) *[oh-loh-leh-pih-tsh-oh]* The one that milks [*Maasai*].
Ololngojine (m) *[oh-lohl-ngoh-jih-neh]* The son of a limping one; the one of the hyena [*Maasai*].
Ololo (m) *[oh-loh-loh]* Eye movers [*Luo*].
Ololojukar (m) *[oh-loh-loh-juh-kahr]* The one with a bushy (or hairy) chest [*Maasai*].
Ololpisia (m) *[oh-lohl-pih-sih-yah]* The one with chains of beads [The *Maasai*].
Ololshorua (m) *[oh-lohl-tsh-oh-ruh-wah]* The one that gives [*Maasai*].
Oloodo (m) *[oh-loh-oh-doh]* The tall one [*Maasai*].
Olowe (m) *[oh-loh-weh]* Tongue, nausea, nagging tendencies [*Luo*].
Oludhe (m) *[oh-luh-tdh-eh]* Stick [*Luo*].
Oluoch (m) *[ohl-woh-tch]* Cold; chill; mist [*Luo*].
Oluru (m) *[oh-luh-ruh]* Grass [*Luo*].
Olwande (m) *[oh-lwahn-deh]* Rock [*Luo*].
Olwenda (m) *[oh-lwehn-dah]* Cockroach [*Luo*].
Olweny (m) *[oh-lweh-ndjh]* Fight [*Luo*].
Omach (m) *[oh-mah-tch]* "Fire" [*Luo*].
Omaya (m) *[oh-mah-yah]* "Disposed me" [*Luo*].
Omba (f/m) *[ohm-bah]* A name given to a twin or a triplet [The *Tetela*] (Daeleman 1977: 192).
Ombaka (m) *[ohm-bah-kah]* One who loves to engage in conversation; one who loves telling tales [*Luo*].
Ombiga (f/m) *[ohm-bih-gah]* "Locust collecting": a name such as given to one born to a mother while she has gone out to gather edible locusts [*Lugbara*] (Middleton 1961: 35).
Omenya (m) *[oh-meh-ndjh-ah]* "He has lighted me" [*Luo*].
Omil (m) *[oh-mihl]* Sugary [*Luo*].
Omino (m) *[oh-mih-noh]* "Strewn"; "consulted" [*Luo*].
Omogi (m) *[oh-moh-gih]* "They have been dried"; air [*Luo*].
Omogo (m) *[oh-moh-goh]* Floor [*Luo*].
Omondi (m) *[oh-mohn-dih]* Very early; "the early one" [*Luo*].
Omore (m) *[oh-moh-reh]* Oaf; one that is naive [*Luo*].
Omoro (m) *[oh-moh-roh]* As of the eyes wide open [*Luo*].
Omoto (m) *[oh-moh-toh]* "Gathering firewood" [*Luo*].
Omudho (m) *[oh-muh-tdh-oh]* Darkness [*Luo*].
Omuge (m) *[oh-muh-geh]* Rhinoceros [*Luo*].
Omulo (m) *[oh-muh-loh]* "He/ she touched" [*Luo*].

Omuya (m) *[oh-muh-yah]* Of the air [*Luo*].

Omwa (m) *[oh-mwah]* "Bring us" [*Luo*].

Omwono (m) *[oh-mwoh-noh]* Plastered (as with a house) [*Luo*].

Omwony (m) *[oh-mwoh-ndjh]* Swallow [*Luo*].

Ondia (m) *[ohn-dih-yah]/* **Ondirua** (f) *[ohn-dih-ruh-wah]* Name given to one born to a mother previously thought to be barren [*Lugbara*] (Middleton 1961: 35).

Ondiek (m) *[ohnd-yekh]* Hyena [*Luo*].

Ondigie (m) *[ohn-dih-gjeh]* Hyenas [*Luo*].

Ondo (m) *[ohn-doh]* One associated with a person that has a passion for eating pumpkin [*Luyia*].

Onduru (m) *[ohn-duh-ruh]* "Scream" [*Luo*].

Oneiso (m) *[oh-nehy-soh]* "Has has told a lie" [*Luo*].

Oneko (m) *[oh-neh-koh]* "Has killed"; madness [*Luo*].

Oneso (m) *[oh-neh-soh]* "Has saved" [*Luo*].

Ongai (f/m) *[oh-ndgh-ahy]* "Thank the Lord" [*Shona*] (Jackson 1957: 121).

Ongole (m) *[oh-ndgh-oh-leh]* "He has cut it" [*Luo*].

Ongongo (m) *[oh-ndgh-oh-ndgh-oh]* One who makes faces; cheeky [*Luo*].

Ongoro (m) *[oh-ndgh-oh-roh]* Big eyes [*Luo*].

Ongute (m) *[oh-ndgh-uh-teh]* The one with a characteristic of the neck [*Luo*].

Oniko (m) *[oh-nih-koh]* Hurried [*Luo*].

Onindo (m) *[oh-nihn-doh]* "He is sleeping" [*Luo*].

Onyango (m) *[oh-ndjh-ahn-goh]* Dawn [*Luo*].

Onyinyo (m) *[oh-ndjh-ih-ndjh-oh]* "Broken into pieces"; interest from savings [*Luo*].

Onyiso (m) *[oh-ndjh-ih-soh]* "Has shown" [*Luo*].

Onyuka (m) *[oh-ndjh-uh-kah]* Porridge [*Luo*].

Onyurubia (f/m) *[oh-ndjh-uh-ruh-bih-yah]* "At the throwing of good things": a name such as given to one whose parents have been so poor that they have had to eat other people's leftovers [The *Lugbara*] (Middleton 1961: 36).

Ooko (m) *[oh-woh-koh]* Outside [*Luo*].

Ooro (m) *[oh-woh-roh]* Cow dung; "he sent" [*Luo*].

Opande (m) *[oh-pahn-deh]* "He/ she has hidden it" [*Luo*].

Opanga (m) *[oh-pahn-gah]* Arranged; adamant [*Luo*].

Opany (m) *[oh-pah-ndjh]* "Grinding stone"; "grinding pot" [*Luo*].

Opar (m) *[oh-pahr]* "Remembered" [*Luo*].

Opara (m) *[oh-pah-rah]* "He has remembered me" [*Luo*].

Openda (m) *[oh-pehn-dah]* Placenta [*Luo*].

Opeth (m) *[oh-peh-sth]* Spread as a bed [*Luo*].

Opicho (m) *[oh-pih-tch-oh]* A name given to one who is fast at running; a name given to one of athletic qualities [*Luyia*].

Opii (m) *[oh-piih]* "Of water" [*Luo*].

Opimo (m) *[oh-pih-moh]* Measured [*Luo*].

Opio/ Opiyo (m) *[oh-pih-yoh]* Name given to a first born of twins [*Alur, Iteso, Jopadhola, Langi, Luyia*, and several other ethnics of eastern and central Africa] (Wako 1985: 38).

Opondo (m) *[oh-pohn-doh]* "He is kidding" [*Luo*].

Opuk (m) *[oh-puhk]* Tortoise [*Luo*].

Opuka (m) *[oh-puh-kah]* "I have been poured" [*Luo*].

Oramat (m) *[oh-rah-maht]* The one that tenders (or gives) [*Maasai*].

Orege (m) *[oh-reh-geh]* "He has grinded it" [*Luo*].

Oremo (m) *[oh-reh-moh]* Bloody [*Luo*].

Orenge (m) *[oh-reh-ndgh-eh]* The legs of a chicken [*Luo*].

Orengo (m) *[oh-reh-ndgh-oh]* Fly whisk [*Luo*].

Oricho (m) *[oh-rih-tch-oh]* Evil; sin [*Luo*].

Oriku (m) *[oh-rih-kuh]* The one that leads [*Maasai*].

Orimba (m) *[oh-rihm-bah]* Trawler fishing nets [*Luo*].

Orinda (m) *[oh-rihn-dah]* "Ties"; "He has tightened me"; one who tightens [*Luo*].

Orito (m) *[oh-rih-toh]* "He/ she has waited"; "he/ she is waiting" [*Luo*].

Oriwo (m) *[oh-rih-woh]* "Added"; "walks aimlessly" [*Luo*].

Orogo (m) *[oh-roh-goh]* This is a manifestation of a supernatural power said to have come from the neighboring *Bunyoro* territory and is said to have fallen on the *Alur* ethnics and possessed them [The *Alur*] (Southall 1951: 187).

Oruko (m) *[oh-ruh-koh]* Chaotic; that causes confusion [*Luo*].

Orwa (m) *[oh-rwah]* "Our in-law"; "massaged" [*Luo*].

Orwenyo (m) *[oh-rweh-ndjh-oh]* "He has become confused"; "lost" [*Luo*].

Oseki (m) *[oh-tseh-kih]* The traditional drinking straw [*Luo*].

Osieno (m) *[oh-tsjeh-eh-noh]* "Pointed at" [*Luo*].

Osimbo (m) *[oh-tsih-mboh]* Shield [*Luo*].

Osogo (m) *[oh-tsoh-goh]* A species of bird [*Luo*].

Osoro (m) *[oh-tsoh-roh]* Trotter; one who trots [*Luo*].

Osuga (m) *[oh-tsuh-gah]* The name of a species of vegetable [*Luo*].

Osur (m) *[oh-surh]* Scythe [*Luo*].

Oswayo (m) *[oh-tswah-yoh]* One who is malicious; one who habitually tells on others [*Luo*].

Otama (m) *[oh-tah-mah]* "He has denied me"; "he has refused to let me"; "I do not understand him/ her" [*Luo*].

Otas (m) *[oh-tahs]* Paper [*Luo*].

Otek (m) *[oh-tekh]* Strong [*Luo*].

Otengo (m) *[oh-teh-ndgh-oh]* That is shaken so as to clean or dry [*Luo*].

Othim (m) *[oh-sth-ihm]* Forest [*Luo*].

Otiende (m) *[oh-tjehn-deh]* That of the legs [*Luo*].

Otieno (m) *[oh-tjeh-noh]* Night [*Luo*].

Otigo (m) *[oh-tih-goh]* Beads [*Luo*].

Otin (m) *[oh-tihn]* Small [*Luo*].

Otina (m) *[oh-tih-nah]* "He/ she works for me" [*Luo*].

Otinda (m) *[oh-tihn-dah]* "Amen"; the end [*Luo*].

Otok (m) *[oh-tohk]* "Served"; "hatched" [*Luo*].

Otonde (m) *[oh-tohn-deh]* Skinny, ropy [*Luo*].

Ottite (m) *[oht-tih-teh]* Moustache [*Luo*].

Otuke (m) *[oh-tuh-keh]* Playful [*Luo*].

Otula (m) *[oh-tuh-lah]* Owl [*Luo*].

Otundo (m) *[oh-tuhn-doh]* "He has arrived" [*Luo*].

Otuoma (m) *[oh-twoh-mah]* "He/ she knocked me" [*Luo*].

Otura (m) *[oh-tuh-rah]* "Broken me"; "burdened me" [*Luo*].

Ouko (m) *[oh-wuh-koh]* Pocket [*Luo*].

Oupa (m) *[ohw-pah]* "Grandfather": a name commonly given by the named child's grandparent in honor of an ancestor or a late husband [*Zulu*] (Suzman 1994: 268, 270).

Ousa (m) *[oh-wuh-sah]* "Sold me"; "betrayed me" [*Luo*].

Ovoa (f/m) *[oh-voh-wah]* "In laziness": a name such as given to one born to parents who are lazy [*Lugbara*] (Middleton 1961: 35).

Ovurueir (m) *[oh-vuh-rweh-irh]* God; "the friendly one" [The *Syan*] (Huntingford 1930: 103).

Owabunoha (m) *[oh-waah-buh-noh-hah]* "With whom is their (i.e. people) place?": a name given to child born into a family that is poor, the name carrying the same meaning as "whose house does he belong to?" and implying that the family is so poor and undistinguished that the child does not have a household to which it can refer to with pride [*Nyoro*] (Beattie 1957: 103).

Owaele (m) *[oh-wah-yeh-leh]* The one who is friendly, especially to kin [*Luo*].

Oweggi (m) *[oh-wehg-gih]* "They have been abandoned/ left" [*Luo*].

Oweya (m) *[oh-weh-yah]* "Left one" [*Luo*].

Owila (m) *[oh-wih-lah]* "Has changed me" [*Luo*].

Owino (m) *[oh-wih-noh]* Fishing hook [*Luo*].

Owiny (m) *[oh-wih-ndjh]* Bird [*Luo*].

Owiro (m) *[oh-wih-roh]* Painted [*Luo*].

Owiye (m) *[oh-wih-yeh]* Big head [*Luo*].

Owoko (m) *[oh-woh-koh]* "He has washed" [*Luo*].

Owuor (m) *[oh-wuh-ohr]* "He is greedy" [*Luo*].

Oyamo (m) *[oh-yah-moh]* "Wind" [*Luo*].

Oyat (m) *[oh-yaht]* A name given to one whose mother experienced difficult and painful birth labor pains that involved administration of herbs [*Acholi*] (Nzita 1995: 91).

Oyet (m) *[oh-yeht]* God; "the spirit" [*Aramanik*] (Huntingford 1930: 103).

Oyieke (m) *[ohy-yeh-keh]* Scatters (as with grains) *[Luo]*.
Oyieng (m) *[ohy-yeh-ndgh]* "Satisfied"; "sated" *[Luo]*.
Oyier (m) *[ohy-yehr]* "The hairy one" *[Luo]*.
Oyiera (m) *[ohy-yeh-rah]* "I have been chosen" *[Luo]*.
Oyieyo (m) *[ohy-yeh-yoh]* Rat *[Luo]*.
Oyinge (m) *[oh-yihn-geh]* Name *[Luo]*.
Oyoo (m) *[oh-yoh-oh]* "Of the path": a name such as given to one born along the path (or road) *[Luo]*.
Oyugi (m) *[oh-yuh-gih]* Rubbish: a name such as given to one born in rubbish conditions *[Luo]*.
Ozo/ Ozoo (m) *[oh-zoh-oh]* Chief *[Lugbara]*.

-P-

Paamba (f) *[paahm-bah]* The name of the first woman said to have given birth to twins; a name given to a parent of twins [The *Luba*] (Daeleman 1977: 194).
Paendombela (f) *[pah-yehn-dohm-beh-lah]* "There goes the rain": this name is commonly associated with the proverb "There goes the rain, there looks the crowd; there goes a beauty, there looks one" implying that there are items and necessities that are either in the public domain and/ or are essentially appreciated by all (such as adequate rainfall, good air, good leadership, peace), whereas there are aspects and interests that are appreciated by just one person or by just a small population [*Ovimbundu*] (Ennis 1945: 4).
Pala (f/m) *[pah-lah]* Knife *[Luo]*.
Palala (m) *[pah-lah-lah]* Ox, bull, or any large animal in a herd: a name such as given to one who is powerful and strong [*Kaguru*] (Beidelman 1974: 288).
Palesa (f) *[pah-leh-sah]* Flower [*Sotho*] (Mohome 1972: 178).
Pamba (f/m) *[pahm-bah]* Cotton *[Luo]*.
Pamidzai (f) *[pah-mihd-zahy]* "Do it again": a name such as given to a child born to a long married mother, the child's birth is tremendously welcomed, and there is a prevailing desire for another child to be born soon [*Zezuru*] (Marapara 1954: 8).
Pandasala (f) *[pahn-dah-sah-lah]* "You search": this name is commonly associated with the proverb "You search your heart, but there is a heart at another village" implying that 'the heart knows its own bitterness, but it cannot know that of another,' the name given to a child whose parents are perplexed at the attitudes of kin or neighbors towards the family [*Ovimbundu*] (Ennis 1945: 3).
Parintuku (m) *[pah-rihn-tuh-kuh]* The one that washes [*Maasai*].
Paseka (m) *[pah-seh-kah]* Passover/ Easter: a name such as given to one born during Passover or Easter [*Sotho*] (Thipa 1986: 289).
Pasi-Hapazari (f/m) *[pah-tsih-hah-pah-zah-rih]* "The ground is never fi-

lled": a name given to a child born into a family that has lost many of its members to death, the name metaphorically implying that despite the numerous numbers of deaths, the earth indefinitely continues to provide burial ground and never declares that it is too full for more people to die [*Shona*] (Jackson 1957: 118).

Pasika (m) *[pah-sih-kah]* Passover/ Easter: a name such as given to one born during Passover or Easter [*Zulu*] (Suzman 1994: 270; Thipa 1986: 289).

Pazvichaenda (f/m) *[pahtz-vih-teh-ah-yehn-dah]* "We have no idea of where these matters will end"/ "we have no idea of what will put an end to all this trouble": a name such as given to one born during an endless family dispute with kin, or one born during a family dispute with neighbors that does not seem to end [*Shona*] (Jackson 1957: 117).

Pesa (f/m) *[peh-sah]* Money [*Luo*].

Pfutila (f/m) *[pfuh-tih-lah]* "Ransom"/ "the act of ransoming": a name given to one whose birth follows that of his or her twin siblings, the name implying that the birth of this child reinstates the mother into the normal course of giving birth that is no longer marked by the sacredness of the birth of twins [*Yaka*] (Daeleman 1977: 191); a name given to a triplet [*Yaka*] (Daeleman 1977: 192).

Phamehlo (m) *[pah-meh-eh-loh]* "Give an eye": a name such as given to a child born with only one eye [*Zulu*] (Koopman 1979: 68).

Phehello (m) *[peh-ehl-loh]* Persistence: name such as given to a child born during times of hardship/ or to a first-born whose father struggled hard to win over the love of the mother [*Sotho*] (Mohome 1972: 176).

Phepheng (f) *[peh-peh-ndgh]* Scorpion: an unpleasant name given to one whose previous born sibling was stillborn or died before weaning, this attributed to sorcery--the name is a means to safeguard this child "by making a show of neglecting it in the hope of lulling the sorcerer's vigilance" [*Sotho*] (Ashton 1952: 33).

Phepheng (m) *[peh-peh-ndgh]* Scorpion: an unpleasant girl's name that can be given to a boy born after a long succession of female siblings who have survived though the boy's earlier born male siblings died as children [*Sotho*] (Ashton 1952: 33).

Phethwengani (m) *[uh-peh-sth-wehn-gah-nih]* "How was I treated?": a name such as given to a child whose mother is further bringing to notice that she is severely mistreated by her in-laws [*Zulu*] (Suzman 1994: 267).

Philisani (f) *[pih-lih-sah-nih]* "Give forth health" [The *Zulu*] (Koopman 1979: 158).

Phindle (m) *[pihn-dih-leh]* "Repeated" [*Zulu*] (Suzman 1994: 268).

Phumasilwe (m) *[puh-mah-sih-lweh]* "He comes out and we fight"; "come outside and let us fight" [*Zulu*] (Koopman 1979: 161).

Phumzile (m) *[uh-puhm-zih-leh]* "Rested": a name such as given to a

child born to parents whose family relationship has markedly improved from the deteriorated state it was in [The *Zulu*] (Suzman 1994:
267).

Phuthuma (m) *[puh-tuh-mah]* "Hasten" [*Zulu*] (Koopman 1979: 158).

Piepie (m) *[pih-yeh-pih-yeh]* A name given to one of harsh mannerism
[*Luyia*].

Polo (m) *[poh-loh]* Alligator: this derogatory/ non-human name given to
a child whose preceding sibling or siblings died, there being pessimism that this one will survive, is however intended to effectuate the
opposite of its literal meaning [*Sotho*] (Mohome 1972: 176).

Polo (m) *[poh-loh]* Sky [*Luo*].

Potlako (m) *[poht-lah-koh]* A hurry: a name such as given to a child
who is the product of a premature birth [*Sotho*] (Mohome 1972: 177).

Pulane (f) *[puh-lah-neh]* "Little rain": a name such as given to one
born on a rainy day [*Sotho*] (Mohome 1972: 173-174).

Pulane (f) *[puh-lah-neh]*/ **Pule** (m) *[puh-leh]*/ **Puleng** (f) *[puh-leh-
ndgh]* Rain: names such as given to ones born during periods of
rainfall [*Sotho*] (Thipa 1986: 289).

Pule (m) *[puh-leh]* **Puleng** (f) *[puh-leh-ndgh]* (Born) in rain: names
such as given to ones born on a rainy days [*Sotho*] (Mohome 1972:
173-174, 179).

Punyua (m) *[puh-ndjh-wah]* The one of dust [*Maasai*].

Pururai (f/m) *[puh-ruh-rahy]* "Strip off (i.e. as leaves from a branch)": a
name given to a child born into a family that has lost many of its members to death, the name implying that the members have easily be-
en stripped away, just like leaves off a branch [The *Shona*] (Jackson
1957: 118).

Puseletso (f) *[puh-seh-leht-soh]* Compensation: name such as given
to one born following the death of a preceding sibling [The *Sotho*]
(Mohome 1972: 174).

Puseletso (m) *[puh-seh-leh-tsoh]* Reward/ compensation/ recompense
: a name given to one who has lost two or more preceding siblings to
death, the name implying that this child serves as welcome restitution, by the action of God or the ancestors, for the deceased [*Sotho*]
(Thipa 1986: 290).

Pushati (m) *[puh-tsh-ah-tih]* The one that is aggressive [*Maasai*].

-Q-

Qhikiza (f) *[tch-ih-kih-zah]* "Full-grown girl" [*Zulu*] (Koopman 1979:
154).

Qinisela (m) *[kwih-nih-seh-lah]* "Persevere": a name such as given to
a child whose mother is acknowledged to be having to put up with a
lot from her husband's family, the name encouraging her to be strong
and hold on until the problems dissipate [*Zulu*] (Suzman 1994: 269).

Rabanga (m) *[rah-bahn-gah]* Name of the supreme being and creator also regarded as a spirit, referred to as "Mother Earth," and the one responsible for human births: this name is commonly given to a younger twin *[Madi]* (Nzita 1995: 143).

Rabuor (m) *[rah-buh-wohr]* The brown one *[Luo]*.

Raburu (m) *[rah-buh-ruh]* Dusty; of the dust *[Luo]*.

Rachier (m) *[rah-tch-ih-yehr]* A poisonous snake; one who resurrects *[Luo]*.

Radier (m) *[rah-dih-yehr]* Brown *[Luo]*.

Rading (m) *[rah-dih-ndgh]* Protruding cheeks; swollen cheeks *[Luo]*.

Raila (m) *[rahy-lah]* "That itches me" *[Luo]*.

Ralak (m) *[rah-lahk]* Of the teeth *[Luo]*.

Ralebelo (f) *[rah-leh-beh-loh]* "The one of speed": an initiation name *[Sotho]* (Mohome 1972: 184).

Ramatjato (f) *[rah-maht-jah-toh]* "The one of agility": an initiation name *[Sotho]* (Mohome 1972: 184).

Ramatla (f) *[rah-maht-lah]* "The one of strength": an initiation name *[Sotho]* (Mohome 1972: 184).

Ramona (f) *[rah-moh-nah]* "The one of selfishness": an initiation name *[Sotho]* (Mohome 1972: 184).

Randiga (m) *[rahn-dih-gah]* One like a bicycle *[Luo]*.

Rantsho (m) *[rahn-tsh-oh]* "The father (or the one) that is black" [The *Sotho*] (Mohome 1972: 182).

Rantwa (m) *[rahn-twah]* "The father (or the one) that is of the war" *[Sotho]* (Mohome 1972: 183).

Rao (m) *[rah-woh]* Hippopotamus; brief visit *[Luo]*.

Rapule (m) *[rah-puh-leh]* "The father of *Pule*"; "the father (or the one) that is (born) in rain": a name such as given to one born on a rainy day *[Sotho]* (Mohome 1972: 181-183).

Rateng (m) *[rah-teh-ndgh]* Black *[Luo]*.

Ratsebo (f) *[rah-tseh-boh]* The one of knowledge: an initiation name *[Sotho]* (Mohome 1972: 184).

Raviro (f/m) *[rah-vih-roh]* Promise *[Shona]* (Jackson 1957: 121).

Rendepes (m) *[rehn-deh-pehs]* Rinderpest (as adapted from the European word) *[Sotho]* (Thipa 1986: 288).

Resa (m) *[reh-sah]* "Save me" *[Luo]*.

Retshedisitswe (m) *[reh-tsh-eh-dih-siht-sweh]* "We have been consoled"/ "we have been made to cross": a name given to one who has lost two or more preceding siblings to death, the name implying that this child serves as welcome solace, by the action of God or the ancestors, for the family of the deceased *[Sotho]* (Thipa 1986: 290).

Rewo (m) *[reh-woh]* Burning; roasting; heating *[Luo]*.

Rieko (m) *[rjeh-koh]* Intelligence *[Luo]*.

Rirhandzu (f/m) *[rih-rahn-dzuh]* Love: a name such as given by the mother and expresses high opinion of and good relations with her co-wife who sent her clothes for this baby the mother was pregnant with [*Zulu*] (Herbert 1995: 4).

Ritshuni (f/m) *[riht-shuh-nih]* Dust: a derogatory-protective-pessimism related name such as given to a child whose previously born sibling died, and the name implies that this newborn is as fragile and vulnerable as dust [*Zulu*] (Herbert 1995: 4).

Riwa (m) *[rih-wah]* Idiot; imbecile [*Luo*].

Rombo (m) *[rohm-boh]* Sheep [*Luo*].

Rubanga (m) *[ruh-bahn-gah]* This is a manifestation of a supernatural power said to have come from the neighboring *Bunyoro* territory and is said to have fallen on the *Alur* ethnics and possessed them [*Alur*] (Southall 1951: 187).

Ruboija (m) *[ruh-bohy-jah]* "It (i.e. death) pecks (as a fowl does)": a name given to a child born during a period of widespread death--the fowl will peck up a handful of scattered grain on the ground, though no one would know which grains it will select and strike straight and hard at--likewise, no one would know which persons would next be struck down by death [*Nyoro*] (Beattie 1957: 101).

Rudo (f/m) *[ruh-doh]* Love [*Shona*] (Jackson 1957: 121).

Rufu (f/m) *[ruh-fuh]* Death: a name given to a child born into a family that has lost many of its members to death [*Shona*] (Jackson 1957: 118).

Rugongeza (m) *[ruh-gohn-geh-zah]* "It (i.e. death) causes anger": a name such as given to a child whose earlier born siblings died, or to one born during a period of bereavement, or to an alarmingly sick child not expected to survive [*Nyoro*] (Beattie 1957: 101).

Rukagyaha (m) *[ruh-kah-jaah-hah]* "Where has it (i.e. death) gone off to?": a name such as given to a child that is alarmingly sick and is not expected to survive, or to one born into a family that has had several deaths, or to one born during a period of many deaths [*Nyoro*] (Beattie 1957: 102).

Rukambuza (m) *[ruh-kahm-buh-zah]* "It (i.e. death) still causes me to lose myself": a name given to child born into a family that has had several deaths, and the name implies that the family has had to move house several times to circumvent the cause suspected of being either the neighbors involved in (witchcraft) malice, or the forces of Fate, or the ancestral spirits [*Nyoro*] (Beattie 1957: 102).

Rukasisa (m) *[ruh-kah-sih-sah]* "It (i.e. death) has spoiled/ destroyed": a name such as given to a child whose earlier born sibling died [The *Nyoro*] (Beattie 1957: 101).

Rukiriyo (m) *[ruh-kiih-rih-yoh]* "It (i.e. death) is still present/ there": a name such as given to a child born into a family that has had several deaths, or one born during a period of many deaths [*Nyoro*] (Beattie 1957: 102).

Rukyalekere (m) *[ruh-tch-ah-leh-keh-reh]* "It (i.e. death) is still leaving (or putting) off": a name given to child born into a family that has had several deaths, or one born during a period of many deaths, and the name implies that the phenomenon of death does "mark down" its victims before actually manifesting itself in surprisingly taking them away [*Nyoro*] (Beattie 1957: 102).

Rulani (f) *[ruh-lah-nih]* "Comfort": a name such as implying that the parent expresses so much ease at the birth of this girl who tradition-ally symbolizes a bride dowry source of cattle/ *lobolo* [*Zulu*] (Herbert 1995: 3).

Ruvengo (f/m) *[ruh-vehn-goh]* Hatred: name given to one born during a family dispute with kin or with neighbors, the parent so appalled at the hatred displayed [*Shona*] (Jackson 1957: 117).

Rwahuire (m) *[rwah-hwiih-reh]* "It (i.e. death) has put aside for itself": name given to child born into a family that has had several deaths, or one born during a period of many deaths, and the name implies that the phenomenon of death "marks down" its victim without necessarily taking him away at once [*Nyoro*] (Beattie 1957: 102).

Rwesemereza (m) *[rweh-seh-meh-reh-zah]* "It (i.e. death) pleases its-elf": the name implies that death is at liberty to take away or let live whenever it pleases, so it may wait to victimize this child after it has grown older and more attractive before it strikes; the name also imp-lies that impending death prepares the victim, or that the potential victim improves himself prior to the mishap [*Nyoro*] (Beattie 1957: 102).

-S-

Saabaddu/ Ssaabaddu (f/m) *[ssaah-bahd-duh]* The name-title of the head of the servants of a chief, but who are not living in his comp-ound; the name-title of the chief that is third in rank; one that is prom-inent among servants [*Ganda*].

Saabagabo/ Ssaabagabo (m) *[ssaah-bah-gah-boh]* The name-title of the chief that is fourth in rank; one that is prominent among those who are manly (or brave) [*Ganda*].

Saabaganda/ Ssaabaganda (f/m) *[ssaah-bah-gahn-dah]* One that is prominent among the *Ganda* ethnics.

Saabakaaki/ Ssaabakaaki (m) *[ssaah-bah-kaah-tch-ih]* One that is pr-ominent among those who crack (or strain, or stretch); name-title of a chief mainly entrusted to supervising the pages and the boys in the royal enclosure [*Ganda*].

Saabakulungo/ Ssaabakulungo (m) *[ssaah-bah-kuh-luhn-goh]* One that is prominent among those who mould (or knead, or circle around, or make round, or roll along, or rub along, or roll over); that of the cir-cle (or the globe, or the sphere, or the environs) [*Ganda*].

Saabalangira/ Ssaabalangira (m) *[ssaah-bah-lahn-gih-rah]* One that is prominent among those who are princes [*Ganda*].

Saabata/ Ssaabata (m) *[ssaah-bah-tah]* One that is prominent among those that free (or let go of, or release) [*Ganda*].

Saabatakula/ Ssaabatakula (m) *[ssaah-bah-tah-kuh-lah]* One that is prominent among those who scratch [*Ganda*].

Saabawaali/ Ssaabawaali (m) *[ssaah-bah-waah-lih]* The name-title of the chief that is fifth in rank [*Ganda*].

Saabwe/ Ssaabwe (m) *[ssaah-bweh]* Smearing (such as of oil or butter on the body); dung; excrement [*Ganda*].

Saagalambule (f) *[ssaah-gah-laahm-buh-leh]* "I do not want the person to disappear from me (or to become lost from me, or to go astray from me)"; "I do not want to have to miss him/ her" [*Ganda*].

Saaka/ Ssaaka (m) *[ssaah-kah]* Mallet used in the beating of barkcloth in its first stage processing; one who moves around to obtain food for purchase or in exchange for services; one that forages for food; digging up (or ferreting) information [*Ganda*].

Saalinge (f) *[ssaah-lihn-geh]* "I do not spy out" [*Ganda*].

Saani (m) *[saah-nih]* Eating plate [*Luyia*].

Saanya/ Ssaanya (m) *[ssaah-ndjh-ah]* To make fitting (or suitable); to merit [*Ganda*].

Saayi (f) *[saah-yih]* Blood; one who clears by cutting (such as of grass, or the head by shaving) [*Ganda*].

Sabaganzi/ Ssaabaganzi (m) *[ssaah-bah-gahn-zih]* "Lord (or the best) of the favorites"; name-title of the oldest brother of the king's mother [*Ganda*].

Sabata (f/m) *[sah-bah-tah]* Sabbath (as adapted from the European word): a name given to one born on Saturday [*Sotho*] (Thipa 1986: 289).

Sabavuuma/ Ssabavuuma (m) *[ssaah-bah-vuuh-maah]* One that is prominent among those that make hissing (or rumbling, or whizzing) noises [*Ganda*].

Sabazira/ Ssaabazira (m) *[ssaah-bah-zih-rah]* An extremely brave person; (one prominent amongst) heroes [*Ganda*].

Saidimu (m) *[sahy-dih-muh]* The one who is able [*Maasai*].

Sairowua (m) *[sahy-roh-wuh-wah]* "One who not in action" [*Maasai*].

Saitabau (m) *[sahy-tah-bahw]* The one who ensures that it has been delivered [*Maasai*].

Saitoti (m) *[sahy-toh-tih]* The one who feeds [*Maasai*].

Sajjakkambwe/ Ssajjakkambwe (m) *[ssahj-jahk-kaahm-bweh]* "Fierce man" [*Ganda*].

Sajjalyabeene/ Ssajjalyabeene (m) *[ssahj-jah-ljaah-beh-eh-neh]* "The man that belongs to superiors (or to others)" [*Ganda*].

Saka (m) *[ssah-kah]* Thicket or bush [*Ganda*].

Sakhayedwa (m) *[sahk-hah-yehd-wah]* "Build all on his own" [*Zulu*] (Koopman 1979: 79).

Salamuka (m) *[ssah-lah-muh-kah]* "Become a muslim" [*Ganda*].

Samanya (f/m) *[sah-mah-ndjh-ah]* "The unknown one": a name such as given to one whose mother did not expect to become pregnant/ or had not known that she was pregnant [The *Kaguru*] (Beidelman 1974: 288).

Samba/ Ssamba (m) *[ssahm-bah]* To kick; peddle; that kicks (such as a soccer player); shackles; fetters; irons; plantation; farm; large garden; plot of cultivated land [*Ganda*].

Sambwa/ Ssambwa (m) *[ssahm-bwaah]* A ghostly Spirit believed to frequent natural phenomena such as trees or brooks but which can appear in various forms such as through a woman as the medium [*Ganda*].

Sammula (m) *[ssahm-muh-lah]* "Sprinkle"; "splash"; "scatter"; "shake off"; "reject"; "repudiate" [*Ganda*].

Samula (m) *[sah-muh-lah]* Scattered; splashed; sprinkled; rejected; repudiated [*Ganda*].

Samya (m) *[saah-mjah]* One who talks excessively and carelessly and in the process divulges secrets [*Ganda, Soga*].

Sancha-Molu (m) *[sahn-tch-ah-moh-luh]* A name given to one whose nose is big and has an oily shine [*Luyia*].

Sandanezwe (m) *[sahn-dah-neh-zweh]* "We are increasing with the country" [*Zulu*] (Koopman 1979: 161).

Sandile (m) *[sahn-dih-leh]* "Increase": name such as given to express that is a very welcome child that will ensure that the family line continues [*Zulu*] (Suzman 1994: 267).

Sandla (m) *[sahn-dlah]* "(He has) beautiful hands" [*Zulu*] (Koopman 1979: 71).

Sanga/ Ssanga (m) *[ssahn-gah]* Elephant tusk; ivory [*Ganda*].

Sango/ Ssango (m) *[ssahn-goh]* A kind of fine and red barkcloth [The *Ganda*].

Sangura (m) *[sahn-guh-rah]* A name bestowed on one given birth to under a *musangura* tree [*Luyia*].

Sanjula (m) *[ssahn-juh-lah]* "I do not introduce (or present, or announce)" [*Ganda*].

Sansa (m) *[ssahn-sah]* To scatter or to sow [*Ganda, Soga*].

Sanyu (f) *[ssah-ndjh-uh]* Happiness; pleasure [*Ganda*].

Sarai (f/m) *[tsah-rahy]* "Good-bye": a name given to a child born after the father dies [*Shona*] (Jackson 1957: 118).

Sarua (f/m) *[sah-ruh-wah]* "In wandering": name such as given to one born to parents who are so poor that they have had to wander from kin to kin to beg for food [*Lugbara*] (Middleton 1961: 35).

Savuni (m) *[sah-vuh-nih]* The one that saves [*Maasai*].

Sebabenga/ Ssebabenga (m) *[sseh-bah-behn-gaah]* One that is prominent among those who sharpen tools (such as knives or spears) [*Ganda*].

Sebaddidde/ Ssebaddidde (m) *[sseh-bahd-dihd-deh]* "They have come back (or come, or gone back, or gone) for/ to"; "they have done again" [*Ganda*].

Sebadduka/ Ssebadduka (m) *[sseh-bahd-duh-kah]* One who urges others to run or hurry up; "they run (or run away, or flee)" [*Ganda*].

Sebagenzi (m) *[sseh-bah-gehn-zih]* Departed ones (or travelers) [The *Ganda*].

Sebagereka/ Ssebagereka (m) *[sseh-bah-geh-reh-kah]* One that is prominent among those who assess (or apportion, or distribute, or assign) [*Ganda*].

Sebageya/ Ssebageya (m) *[sseh-bah-geh-yah]* Slanderer; a backbiter; this name is commonly associated with the proverb "those who make slanderous statements are (like) birds, with the (quietly listening) wagtail on the (rooftop openings of the) house" meaning that backbiters are always in danger of their talk getting heard by listening sources they are not aware of [*Ganda*].

Sebaggala/ Ssebaggala (m) *[sseh-bahg-gah-lah]* "those (i.e. people) who shut (or enclose, or bring to an end, or discontinue)"; "those (i.e. people) who close"; this name is commonly associated with the proverb "those who close the doors forget that there are still spaces between the door and the wall" implying that there is a tendency for people to dwell on one source of trouble and evil, though they ought to consider the multiple sources [*Ganda*].

Sebakiggya/ Ssebakiggya (m) *[sseh-bah-tch-ihj-jah]* "They take it away/ off/ out (such as a food crop)"; "they take it" [*Ganda*].

Sebakiggye/ Ssebakiggye (m) *[sseh-bah-tch-ihj-jeh]* "May they take it away/ off/ or out (such as a food crop)"; "may they take it" [*Ganda*].

Sebakiinyanga/ Ssebakiinyanga (m) *[sseh-bah-kiih-ndjh-ahn-gah]* Those that deride (or sneer at, or taunt, or are sarcastic towards) [*Ganda*].

Sebalabye/ Ssebalabye (m) *[sseh-bah-lah-bjeh]* (One prominent among) those who have experienced (or suffered) a lot [*Ganda*].

Sebalijja/ Ssebalijja (m) *[sseh-bah-lihj-jah]* Chief herdsman; the official in charge of the king's cattle; "they will come (or arrive)" [The *Ganda*].

Sebalu/ Ssebalu (m) *[sseh-bah-luh]* That is associated with flogging (or spanking); that is associated with crackling (or flaring up, or giving off sparks, or exploding, or bursting, or throbbing, or tingling); that is associated with the breaking out of (such as war or sickness); that is associated with intense sunshine; that is associated with coming out of (such as a small path or road) [*Ganda*].

Sebamulidde (m) *[sseh-bah-muh-lihd-deh]* "They have eaten (or consumed) him/ her" [*Ganda*].

Sebanakitta/ Ssebanakitta (m) *[sseh-bah-naah-tch-iht-taah]* Those that will kill (or destroy, or abolish, or ruin, or cancel) it [*Ganda*].

Sebandabawa (f/m) *[sseh-bahn-dah-bah-wah]* "Where do they see me (or perceive me)?" [*Ganda*].

Sebandidde (m) *[sseh-bahn-dihd-deh]* "They have consumed (or finished) me"; "they are about to consume (or finish) me up" [*Ganda*].

Sebanga/ Ssebanga (m) *[sseh-bahn-gah]* That establish; those who found [*Ganda*].

Sebanyiiga/ Ssebanyiiga (m) *[sseh-bah-ndjh-iih-gah]* Those who complain greatly; those who get very angry [*Ganda*].

Sebasalire/ Ssebasalire (m) *[sseh-bah-sah-lih-reh]* That are cut up for (or on behalf of); that are decided for (or cut for, or slaughtered for); that are apportioned for (or allotted for); name-title of the chief herdsman [*Ganda*].

Sebata/ Ssebata (m) *[sseh-bah-tah]* Those that set free (or release, or let go of) [*Ganda*].

Sebatindira/ Ssebatindira (m) *[sseh-bah-tihn-dih-rah]* "They (i.e. people) erect a surrounding framework of trellis protection"; this name is commonly associated with the proverb "they (i.e. people) erect a surrounding framework of trellis protection to just the one (i.e. tree) that has ripened with fruit" which implies that ingratitude is commonplace, that "friends" often desert the one that has become impoverished, and that people tend to not support those they do not hope to profit from [*Ganda*].

Sebatta/ Ssebatta (m) *[sseh-baht-tah]* Those who kill (or destroy, or abolish, or ruin, or cancel); name-title of the Police Chief [*Ganda*].

Sebawubi/ Ssebawubi (m) *[sseh-bah-wuh-bih]* That cause to overlook (or miss); "they cause to (unintentionally) slip by"; "they cause to lose color"; "they cause to change beyond recognition" [*Ganda*].

Sebawuubi/ Ssebawuubi (m) *[sseh-bah-wuuh-bih]* "They cause to wave (or swing about)"; that cause to be bothered; "they cause to keep on the go"; "they cause to move about" [*Ganda*].

Sebawuunye (f/m) *[sseh-bah-wuuh-ndjh-eh]* Those that are wonderful or marvelous; of those that look astonished; those that make indistinct sounds; those that moan (or groan); those that reply with a grunt [*Ganda*].

Sebawuuta/ Ssebawuuta (m) *[sseh-bah-wuuh-tah]* Those that sup (or sip); (those prominent among/ or those associated with) the chief cooks of the king [*Ganda*].

Sebayeeye/ Ssebayeeye (m) *[sseh-bah-yeh-eh-yeh]* "Those who repeat over and over again"; "those who, (in a ridiculing or taunting way that involves hostility or vexation,) are incessantly talked about"; a long line-up of people [*Ganda*].

Sebayigga/ Ssebayigga (m) *[sseh-bah-yihg-gah]* That hunt [*Ganda*].

Sebayizzi/ Ssebayizzi (m) *[sseh-bah-yihz-zih]* That are hunters [The *Ganda*].

Sebazinga/ Ssebazinga (m) *[sseh-bah-zihn-gah]* That encircle (or surround/ or wrap up) [*Ganda*].

Sebbaale (m) *[ssehb-baah-leh]* Deity; native God; heavens; the sky

[*Ganda*].

Sebbale (m) *[ssehb-bah-leh]* Few; counted [*Ganda*].

Sebbanja (m) *[ssehb-bahn-jah]* One that is owed a lot; one that persistently demands debt payments (or reparations) [*Ganda*].

Sebbika/ Ssebbika (m) *[ssehb-bih-kah]* That dips (or immerses, or dives); that is or looks unhappy (or distraught); that is easy to steal (or to rob); that is liable to be stolen; that is easy to cheat [*Ganda*].

Sebbowa/ Ssebbowa (m) *[ssehb-boh-waah]* One that confiscates/ appropriates/ seizes (e.g. as security for the payment of a debt) [The *Ganda*].

Sebbunga/ Ssebbunga (m) *[ssehb-buhn-gah]* One who rambles (or wanders around aimlessly) [*Ganda*].

Sebbunza (m) *[ssehb-buhn-zah]* That causes to wander (or ramble); that hawks for sale; that offers for sale [*Ganda*].

Sebbuzi (m) *[ssehb-buh-zih]* Large goat; one who causes to lose (or disappear, or lack) [*Ganda*].

Sebide/ Ssebide (m) *[sseh-bih-deh]* Bells.

Sebigwo/ Ssebigwo (m) *[sseh-bih-gwoh]* Wrestling matches; throws in wrestling; trips; falls; wrestler [*Ganda*].

Sebijeerwe/ Ssebijeerwe (m) *[sseh-bih-jeh-eh-rweh]* One among those rendered miserable, wretched, or destitute [*Ganda*].

Sebikka (m) *[sseh-bihk-kah]* That of going down (or descending).

Sebili (m) *[seh-bih-lih]* That one of two: a name given to the older of a set of twins [*Sotho*] (Ashton 1952: 33).

Sebilinyana (m) *[seh-bih-lih-ndjh-ah-nah]* The younger one of two: a name given to the younger of a set of twins [*Sotho*] (Ashton 1952: 33).

Sebina/ Ssebina (m) *[sseh-bih-nah]* Bend; curve [*Ganda*].

Sebinene/ Ssebinene (m) *[sseh-bih-neh-neh]* That are big (or large) [*Ganda*].

Sebintu/ Ssebintu (m) *[sseh-bihn-tuh]* Things; possessions; belongings; wealth [*Ganda*].

Sebinyansi/ Ssebinyansi (m) *[sseh-bih-ndjh-ahn-sih]* That is indigenous; that of the world/ earth; that of the country [*Ganda*].

Sebiranda/ Ssebiranda (m) *[sseh-bih-rahn-dah]* "That flourish"; "that wanderingly travel around"; "that creep (or spread, or climb)" [The *Ganda*].

Sebirumbi/ Ssebirumbi (m) *[sseh-bih-ruhm-bih]* That attack (or assault, or provoke); that assail verbally [*Ganda*].

Sebiso/ Ssebiso (m) *[sseh-bih-soh]* Knives [*Ganda*].

Sebisubi/ Ssebisubi (m) *[sseh-bih-suh-bih]* Grass [*Ganda*].

Sebitengero/ Ssebitengero (m) *[sseh-bih-tehn-geh-roh]* Fearfulness; terrors; nervousness; shakiness [*Ganda*].

Sebitoogo/ Ssebitoogo (m) *[sseh-bih-toh-oh-goh]* Stalks of papyrus; areas of papyrus [*Ganda*].

Sebitosi/ Ssebitosi (m) *[sseh-bih-toh-sih]* Mud; wet clay [*Ganda*].

Sebiyembe/ Ssebiyembe (m) *[sseh-bih-yehm-beh]* The horns (of an animal); fetishes; spirits associated with fetishes; spells; hexes [The *Ganda*].

Sebiyombya/ Ssebiyombya *[sseh-bih-yohm-bjaah]* That cause to quarrel (or makes lose one's temper) [*Ganda*].

Sebiyubu/ Ssebiyubu (m) *[sseh-bih-yuh-buh]* Peelings off (from the skin); sloughings of the skin (of a snake); getting out of tough spots [*Ganda*].

Sebudde/ Ssebudde (m) *[sseh-buhd-deh]* Of the time (or weather, or occasion); "may they return" [*Ganda*].

Sebuganda/ Ssebuganda (f/m) *[sseh-buh-gahn-dah]* (One prominent in) the territory/ kingdom/ environment of *Buganda*; (one prominent among) the "small" *Ganda* ethnics [*Ganda*].

Sebuggala/ Ssebuggala (m) *[sseh-buhg-gah-lah]* (That do) the closing (of the entrances) [*Ganda*].

Sebuggwawo/ Ssebuggwaawo (m) *[sseh-buhg-gwaah-woh]* That run out (or get completely used up, or diminish) [*Ganda*].

Sebujja/ Ssebujja (m) *[sseh-buhj-jaah]* Overlord; landlord; a territorial master [*Ganda*].

Sebukanja/ Ssebukanja (m) *[sseh-buh-kahn-jaah]* Small malt grains; small strains (or dregs, or residuum) of beer, tea, coffee, or something squeezed or strained [*Ganda*].

Sebukoleere/ Ssebukolere (m) *[sseh-buh-koh-leh-eh-reh]* That is lit (or lighted, or ignited) [*Ganda*].

Sebukoolera/ Ssebukolera (m) *[sseh-buh-koh-oh-leh-rah]* An uprooting; weeding out; that uproots (or weeds out) [*Ganda*].

Sebukule/ Ssebukule (m) *[sseh-buh-kuh-leh]* "May they grow (or mature)" [*Ganda*].

Sebukyu/ Ssebukyu (m) *[sseh-buh-tch-uh]* Dregs in beer [*Ganda*].

Sebuliba/ Ssebuliba (m) *[sseh-buh-lih-bah]* Small skins (or hides) [*Ganda*].

Sebulime/ Ssebulime (m) *[sseh-buh-lih-meh]* Freshly tilled land (not sown) [*Ganda*].

Sebuloolo/ Ssebuloolo (m) *[sseh-buh-loh-oh-loh]* That looks shyly (or with interest, or with concern); glazed (or dull) stares; flabbergast; a species of tiny insects [*Ganda*].

Sebuta/ Ssebuta (m) *[sseh-buh-tah]* An aimless stagger around; being at loss; being in confusion; being exhausted; being at the end of one's wits; small calabashes (or gourds) [*Ganda*].

Sebutinde/ Ssebutinde (m) *[sseh-buh-tihn-deh]* That are made a bridge over (or bridged, or erected a framework/ ceiling over); that are provided with a trellis [*Ganda*].

Sebuyengo/ Ssebuyengo (m) *[sseh-buh-yehn-goh]* Small water waves; that are stirred and dissolved (or diluted, or mixed) [*Ganda*].

Sebuyiira/ Ssebuyiira (m) *[sseh-buh-yiih-raah]* (One associated with) a pouring or spreading out [*Ganda*].

Sebuyira/ Ssebuyira (m) *[sseh-buh-yih-rah]* Small rippling noises/ gurglings (such as of water); small rumbles/ roars (such as of water-falls, the sea, or an airplane); small snorts; small purrs; small whee-zes; small snores [*Ganda*].

Sebwaalibuggya/ Ssebwaalibuggya (m) *[sseh-bwaah-lih-buhj-jah]* "It was (or had to do with) envy/ jealousy"; "it was (or had to do with) newness"; "they were (small) newcomers/ recruits"; "it was (or had to do with) the (small) newcomers/ recruits" [*Ganda*].

Sebwaalibugya/ Ssebwaalibugya (m) *[sseh-bwaah-lih-buh-jah]* "It was (or had to do with) being fitting/ suitable/ appropriate"; "it was (or had to do with) fitting in/ having room/ corresponding to/ being equi-valent" [*Ganda*].

Sebwaalunnyo/ Ssebwaalunnyo (m) *[sseh-bwaah-luhn-ndjh-oh]* Th-ose (or that) associated with a stretch of barren soil; those (or that) associated with a drying rack (such as for coffee or cotton); those (or that) associated with a long tooth (or a jagged edge); those (or that) associated with a stretcher (or a bier) [*Ganda*].

Sebwaana/ Ssebwana (m) *[sseh-bwaah-nah]* (One associated with) small children [*Ganda*].

Sebwami (m) *[sseh-bwaah-mih]* Chief; master; power; authority [The *Ganda*].

Sebwampeke/ Ssebwampeke (m) *[sseh-bwaahm-peh-keh]* Those (or that) associated with grains (or seeds, or pills) [*Ganda*].

Sebwayo/ Ssebwaayo (m) *[sseh-bwaah-yoh]* Of the place (there) [*Ganda*].

Sebyala/ Ssebyala (m) *[sseh-bjaah-lah]* (With a peculiarity of large) nails (talons, or claws); "they increase (or become abundant, or multi-ply, or spread)" [*Ganda*].

Sebyayi/ Ssebyayi (m) *[sseh-bjaah-yih]* Dried plantain fibers [*Ganda*].

Sebyondya/ Ssebyondya (m) *[sseh-bjohn-djah]* That is used to plait (or twine, or twist) [*Ganda*].

Sebyoto/ Ssebyoto (m) *[sseh-bjoh-oh-toh]* Fire places; hearths [The *Ganda*].

Sebyuma (m) *[sseh-bjuuh-mah]* Machines; metals [*Ganda*].

Seddagala/ Sseddagala (m) *[ssehd-dah-gah-lah]* (The one associated with) medicinal drugs (or herbs, or chemicals); name-title of the royal potter [*Ganda*].

Seddume (m) *[ssehd-duh-meh]* Masculine; manly [*Ganda*].

Seddyabanne/ Sseddyabanne (m) *[ssehd-djah-bahn-neh]* "The marri-age of his companions (or associates, or colleagues, or friends)" [The *Ganda*].

Sedogo (m) *[sseh-doh-oh-goh]* One who walks slowly [*Ganda*].

Seduumi/ Sseduumi (m) *[sseh-duuh-mih]* One that grows rapidly (such as a child or a young adolescent); that springs up rapidly [*Ganda*].

Sedyeko/ Ssedyeko (m) *[sseh-djeh-koh]* That involves lying to (or making a dupe of, or fooling, or deceiving); that involves cajoling (or humoring, or flattering) [*Ganda*].

Sedyuuko (m) *[sseh-djuuh-koh]* That involves abrasiveness (or reverberation) in tone; rage [*Ganda*].

Seebabiri (m) *[seh-eh-bah-bih-rih]* "The father of two/ twins": a name given to a parent of twins [*Hutu, Tutsi, Twa*] (Daeleman 1977: 194).

Seebushuri (m) *[seh-eh-buh-shuh-rih]* "Father of bull-calves (i.e. of triplets)": a name given to a parent of triplets [The *Hutu, Tutsi, Twa*] (Daeleman 1977: 194).

Seekambuza (m) *[sseh-eh-kahm-buh-zah]* "I do not speak angrily and rudely (to superiors)"; "I do not bluster" [*Ganda*].

Seerabidde (f) *[sseh-eh-rah-bihd-deh]* "I have not forgotten" [*Ganda*].

Seetebosigo (m) *[seh-eh-teh-boh-sih-goh]* "Do not visit by night" [The *Sotho*] (Moloto 1986: 215).

Seezi/ Ssezi (m) *[sseh-eh-zih]* That overcharges (or sells at undue costs) [*Ganda*].

Sefako (m) *[seh-fah-koh]* Hail: name such as given to one whose birth coincides with a period of hailstorm activity [*Sotho*] (Mohome 1972: 175).

Sega/ Ssega (f/m) *[sseh-gah]* A bald patch running back from both sides of the forehead [*Ganda*].

Segaali/ Ssegaali (m) *[sseh-gaah-lih]* That was [*Ganda*].

Segaba/ Ssegaba (m) *[sseh-gah-bah]* That gives away (or gives as a present, or distributes, or designates) [*Ganda*].

Segambaani/ Ssegambaani (m) *[sseh-gahm-baah-nih]* "Who should be told?"; "who should I tell?" [*Ganda*].

Segamwenge/ Ssegamwenge (m) *[sseh-gah-mwehn-geh]* That is associated with a species of small mushroom that often grows where beer (*mwenge*) has been brewed; (that is associated with) beer [The *Ganda*].

Segawa/ Ssegawa (m) *[sseh-gah-wah]* The patas monkey [*Ganda*].

Segembe/ Ssegembe (m) *[sseh-gehm-beh]* A trap for large animals [*Ganda*].

Seggaali/ Ssegaali (m) *[ssehg-gaah-lih]* A wheeled vehicle; car; cart; bicycle; wheelbarrow [*Ganda*].

Segganja (m) *[ssehg-gahn-jah]* The favorite; the beloved; the popular [*Ganda*].

Seggendo (m) *[ssehg-gehn-doh]* Long voyage; trip [*Ganda*].

Seggirinya/ Sseggirinya (m) *[ssehg-gih-rih-ndjh-ah]* "They go up (or ascend, or mount, or tread on, or step on)"; "they rise (in price)" [The *Ganda*].

Seggoma/ Sseggoma (m) *[ssehg-goh-mah]* One who moves about, to and fro; one who stampedes or rampages [*Ganda*].

Seggombe (m) *[ssehg-gohm-beh]* Associated with the place of the dead (or the other world) *[Ganda]*.

Seggombya/ Ssegombya (m) *[ssehg-gohm-bjaah]* One who plaits (or ties crosswise); one who entangles; one who complicates; to cause to plait or tie crosswise *[Ganda]*.

Seggonzi (m) *[ssehg-gohn-zih]* One who flatters (or soothes) *[Ganda]*.

Seggugu (m) *[ssehg-guh-guh]* One who has a large load; species of water grass *[Ganda]*.

Seggujja (m) *[ssehg-guhj-jah]* "It comes (or arrives, or happens)" [The *Ganda*].

Seggulu/ Sseggulu (m) *[ssehg-guh-luh]* The heaven; the sky; lightning; one that is filthy; one that is unrefined; (with the peculiarity of) large legs; the name-title of a chief *[Ganda]*.

Seggumba (m) *[ssehg-guhm-bah]* Large bone *[Ganda]*.

Seggwaanyi/ Sseggwaanyi (m) *[ssehg-gwaah-ndjh-ih]* Large coffee berry; that is judge worthy of; that is wished for; that makes suitable (or seemly, or fitting); that makes worthy of *[Ganda]*.

Seggwaawo (m) *[ssehg-gwaah-woh]* That falls (or happens, or occurs there); "fall there"; "happen there"; "occur there" *[Ganda]*.

Seggwaaya (m) *[ssehg-gwaah-yah]* Large scale pillaging; large scale plunderer; a large scale forager/ forage (for food); that became burnt (or cooked, or fermented); that became exhausted (or tired out) [The *Ganda*].

Seggwanyi/ Sseggwanyi (m) *[ssehg-gwah-ndjh-ih]* Holding up (or supporting, or sustaining); holding out; making an effort *[Ganda]*.

Segonja/ Ssegonja (m) *[sseh-gohn-jah]* Large sweet banana that is either baked or boiled *[Ganda]*.

Seguku/ Sseguku (m) *[sseh-guh-kuh]* Large piece of firewood [The *Ganda*].

Seguluma/ Sseguluma (m) *[sseh-guh-luh-mah]* That assumes an air of self importance; that overrates oneself; that bites (or pinches, or hurts, or pains, or aches); that accuses (or charges with a fault) [The *Ganda*].

Sehloho (m) *[seh-loh-hoh]* Cruelty: name such as given to one whose mother died when giving birth to him *[Sotho]* (Ashton 1952: 32).

Sehloho (m) *[seh-loh-hoh]* Disaster: name such as given to one whose birth coincides with a period of calamity *[Sotho]* (Mohome 1972: 175).

Sehlulekile (m) *[seh-luh-leh-kih-leh]* "We have failed" *[Zulu]* (Koopman 1979: 79).

Sejjaaka (m) *[ssehj-jaah-kah]* One who flatters *[Ganda]*.

Sejjala (m) *[ssehj-jah-lah]* Large-scale famine (or hunger); a large nail; large talon; large claw *[Ganda]*.

Sejjemba (m) *[sehj-jehm-bah]* That talks in a noisy and foolish manner; that talks nonsense; that rants *[Ganda]*.

Sejjengo (m) *[sehj-jehn-goh]* Large water wave.

Sejjulu/ Ssejjulu (m) *[ssehj-juh-luh]* That is in torrents; that is in a rage (or temper); that is associated with madness; that becomes altered in form or structure; that moves to a different location; that becomes unraveled [*Ganda*].

Sejjuuko (m) *[ssehj-juuh-koh]* That is abrasive (or reverberating) in tone; rage [*Ganda*].

Sejophofu (m) *[seh-joh-poh-fuh]* "Like an eland": this name is associated with the proverb "like an eland, food is a rarity," implying that a good son is a rarity [*Sotho*] (Moloto 1986: 215).

Seka (f) *[sseh-kah]* Laugh [*Ganda*].

Sekaana/ Ssekaana (m) *[sseh-kaah-nah]* Father of a small child.

Sekaayanirwa/ Ssekayanirwa (m) *[sseh-kah-yah-nih-rwah]* That is disputed over (or argued about) [*Ganda*].

Sekaayi/ Ssekaayi (m) *[sseh-kaah-yih]* Bitterness; unpleasantness to the taste; quarrelsomeness; bitterness towards [*Ganda*].

Sekabanjwa/ Ssekabanjwa (m) *[sseh-kah-bahn-jwah]* That is asked to pay a debt [*Ganda*].

Sekabazzi/ Ssekabazzi (m) *[sseh-kah-bahz-zih]* A small ax; small carpenter [*Ganda*].

Sela (f) *[seh-lah]* The name of the first woman (as synonymous with the biblical Eve) [*Luyia*].

Sello (m) *[tsehl-loh]* "Cry of bereavement": name such as given to one born at a time a relation dies [*Sotho*] (Thipa 1986: 290).

Sello (m) *[sehl-loh]* The act of crying: a name such as given to one whose birth coincides with a period of mourning/ or with a calamity [*Sotho*] (Mohome 1972: 175).

Sellwane (f) *[sehl-lwah-neh]* Small crying; small cries: name such as given to one whose birth coincides with a period of mourning/ or with a calamity [*Sotho*] (Mohome 1972: 175).

Sembuli (m) *[sehm-buh-lih]* Litigation: a name such as given to one associated with a dispute involving himself, or with a dispute involving his parents at the time he was born [The *Kaguru*] (Beidelman 1974: 288).

Semvua (m) *[sehm-vuh-wah]* Name given to a child born during the rainy season [*Pare*] (Omari 1970: 71).

Sengezakhe (m) *[sehn-geh-zaah-keh]* "He milks his own (cattle)" [The *Zulu*] (Koopman 1979: 161).

Senko (m) *[sehn-koh]* A name given to a child associated with a period in which there were lots of monkeys in the area [*Pare*] (Omari 1970: 71).

Senkondo (m) *[sehn-kohn-doh]* Name given to a child conceived or born during a time of war [*Pare*] (Omari 1970: 71).

Senyagwa (m) *[sseh-ndjh-ah-gwah]* "Eloquent": a name such as given to an orator/ or a mediator [*Kaguru*] (Beidelman 1974: 288).

Senzangakhona (m) *[sehn-zahn-gah-koh-nah]* "Rightful doer" [*Zulu*]

(Lugg 1968: 13).

Senzighe (m) *[sehn-zih-geh]* "Locusts": name such as given to a child conceived or born during a period of invasion by locusts [The *Pare*] (Omari 1970: 71).

Senzota (m) *[sehn-zoh-tah]* A name given to a child conceived or born during a period of large-scale famine [*Pare*] (Omari 1970: 71).

Seponono (f) *[seh-poh-noh-noh]* "The pretty one" [*Sotho*] (Mohome 1972: 178).

Seqacaca (m) *[seh-eh-kwah-tch-ah-tch-ah]* One who owns (or is associated with) *caca* plants [*Hutu, Tutsi, Twa*].

Serame (m) *[seh-rah-meh]* Cold: a name such as given to one whose birth coincides with a weather period of coldness [*Sotho*] (Mohome 1972: 175).

Sesa (f/m) *[seh-sah]* A broom: a "non-human" and usually temporary name given to a newborn [*Kongo*] (Ndoma 1977: 89).

Sevengwani (m) *[tseh-vehn-gwah-nih]* Flat piece of wood tied around the neck and employed to rub off perspiration: a name given to a child who is (or is expected to be) work help relief for his mother [The *Shona*] (Jackson 1957: 120).

Sevuri (m) *[seh-vuh-rih]* A name given to a child conceived or born during a short season of rain [*Pare*] (Omari 1970: 71).

Sewela (f) *[tseh-weh-lah]* "The one who fell amidst boys": a name given to a first born girl among several older male siblings [*Tlokwa-Sotho*] (Kruger 1937: 109).

Shako (f/m) *[tsh-aah-koh]* A name given to a twin or a triplet [*Tetela*] (Daeleman 1977: 192).

Shambadzirai (f/m) *[tsh-ahm-bah-dzih-rahy]* "Barter me to the witches": a name such as given to one born during a family dispute with kin or neighbors, whereby there is suspicion that the antagonists are engaged in malicious acts of witchcraft against the parent [*Shona*] (Jackson 1957: 117).

Shambise (m) *[tsh-ahm-bih-seh]* (That of) wandering about [The *Zulu*] (Koopman 1979: 156).

Shangase (m) *[tsh-ah-ndgh-aah-seh]/* **Soshangane** (m) *[soh-tsh-ah-ndgh-aah-neh]* (The one associated with) wandering about [The *Zulu*] (Koopman 1979: 73).

Shani (m) *[tsh-ah-nih]* The one of the tree [*Maasai*].

Shisia (f/m) *[tsh-ih-sih-yah]* A name given to one whose birth follows that of his or her twin siblings [*Luyia*] (Wako 1985: 38).

Shiyinduku (m) *[tsh-ih-yihn-duh-kuh]* "Leave the stick behind" [*Zulu*] (Koopman 1979: 75, 79).

Shumirai (f/m) *[tsh-uh-mih-rahy]* "Serve the Lord" [*Shona*] (Jackson 1957: 121).

Sibongakonke (m) *[sih-bohn-gah-kohn-keh]* "We are grateful for everything" [*Zulu*] (Koopman 1979: 161).

Sibongile (f) *[sih-bohn-gih-leh]* "We are grateful" [*Zulu*] (Koopman 1979: 162).

Sibusiswe (m) *[sih-buh-sih-sweh]* Blessed [*Zulu*] (Suzman 1994: 268).

Sibusiswe (f) *[sih-buh-sih-sih-weh]* "We are blessed" [The *Zulu*] (Koopman 1979: 162).

Sichangi (m) *[sih-tch-ahn-gih]* A name given to one associated with an artist [*Luyia*].

Sichenje (m) *[sih-tch-ehn-jeh]* One named after his grandfather who is renowned for his excellent dancing skills [*Luyia*].

Siendilavo (f) *[tsih-yehn-dih-lah-voh]* "I shall not go with them": this name is associated with the expression "Whom shall I go with? I shall not go with them" which is metaphorically the lamentation of an oppressed or mistreated woman who does not have many blood relatives around (or of a child of one in such a situation), or of a child who is an orphan, or of a slave (in past times) who does not see any alternative refuge to her present situation [*Ovimbundu*] (Ennis 1945: 6).

Sifuna (m) *[sih-fuh-nah]* A name given to one who is of a breech birth i.e. one born feet first (other than the conventional head first) [*Luyia*].

Sihlangusakhe (m) *[sih-lahn-guh-sah-keh]* "His shields" [The *Zulu*] (Koopman 1979: 80).

Sikhonkwane (m) *[uh-sih-kohn-kwah-neh]* "Nail": name such as given by the named child's mother (in a polygamous unit) to signal that by bearing a boy, she has hit the nail on the head [*Zulu*] (Suzman 1994: 259).

Sikilavo (f) *[tsih-kih-lah-voh]* "I am not of them (or of their locale)": this name is commonly associated with the expression "I am not accustomed to them"/ "I do not feel at home with them" which is metaphorically the lamentation of an oppressed or mistreated woman who does not have many blood relatives around or does not get along with her husband's kin (or of a child of one in either situation), or of one who is (or feels) so alienated from home while in the unfamiliar surroundings (or of a child of one in such a situation) [The *Ovimbundu*] (Ennis 1945: 6).

Sikuku (m) *[sih-kuh-kuh]* A name given to one born on Christmas [The *Luyia*].

Silima (f) *[sih-lih-mah]* A name given to one born at night [*Luyia*].

Simali (m) *[sih-mah-lih]* A name given to a very dark complexioned child [*Luyia*].

Simatua (f/m) *[sih-mah-tuh-wah]* A name given to a first born twin [*Nandi*] (Hollis 1969: 68).

Simba (m) *[sihm-bah]* Lion [*Embu*].

Simbovala (f) *[tsihm-boh-vah-lah]* "While you mark out a planting field": this name is commonly associated with the proverb "While you mark out a planting field, death marks you out in life" and is given to a child some of whose previously born siblings died, or to one born into a family that has recently had deaths [*Ovimbundu*] (Ennis 1945: 3).

Simiyu (m) *[sih-mih-yuh]* A name given to one born during a dry season [*Luyia*].

Simo (f) *[sih-moh]* Legend/ or story: name such as given to one good at reciting stories [*Kaguru*] (Beidelman 1974: 289).

Sindani (m) *[sihn-dah-nih]* A name given to a very intelligent and determined child [*Luyia*].

Sindawonye (m) *[sihn-dah-woh-ndjh-eh]* "We are together" [*Sotho*] (Moloto 1986: 215).

Sipatala (f) *[tsih-pah-tah-lah]* "I do not dispute": this name is commonly associated with the proverb "That which God says, I do not dispute" and is given to a child some of whose previously born siblings died, or to one born into a family that has recently had deaths [The *Ovimbundu*] (Ennis 1945: 3).

Siphipho (m) *[uh-sih-pih-poh]* "Cause for divorce": a name such as given to a child born to parents that are not on good terms [The *Zulu*] (Suzman 1994: 267).

Sipho (m) *[siih-poh]* "Gift" [*Zulu*] (Koopman 1979: 154).

Sipho (m) *[uh-siih-poh]* "Gift": a name such as given by the named child's poverty stricken mother who expresses gratitude for the kindness of the child's grandmother who tended to her needs after she gave birth [*Zulu*] (Suzman 1994: 261, 268); a name such as implying that the parents consider this child a generous gift from God since, given the birth of three girls in a row, they have so much longed for a boy [*Zulu*] (Suzman 1994: 263).

Sipopi (f) *[tsih-poh-pih]* "It do not speak": this name is commonly associated with the expression "I do not speak, I am a slave and not a noble" which is the lamentation (in former times) of a woman who is a slave or concubine, the name commonly given to one who is oppressed and mistreated (or to a child of one who is treated so) [The *Ovimbundu*] (Ennis 1945: 6).

Siro (m) *[tsih-roh]* "Support"; market [*Luo*].

Sirtoy (m) *[sihr-tohy]* "The jumper": (usually) a post-childhood nickname [*Nandi*] (Hollis 1969: 67).

Sitawa (f) *[sih-tah-wah]* A name given to one born in an environment of anthills [*Luyia*].

Sithole (m) *[sih-toh-leh]* Heifer [*Zulu*] (Koopman 1990: 334).

Situkali (f) *[sih-tuh-kah-lih]* "The meat that you eat": this name is commonly associated with the proverb "The meat that you eat reddens you with blood" implying that there is a lot of telltale evidence of what one possesses, and what one apparently has and can share with others should not be kept all to oneself [*Ovimbundu*] (Ennis 1945: 5).

Siyabonga (f/m) *[uh-sih-yah-bohn-gah]* "We thank": a name such as given to express gratitude to God for the return of the named child's uncle who had disappeared away from the family for several years, and whose reappearance coincides with the birth of his nephew [*Zulu*] (Suzman 1994: 260); a name such as given by the parents of the named to express thankfulness to God for providing them with a good and large family--the parents are now glad to rest from having any more children, upon the birth of this sixth child [*Zulu*] (Suzman 1994: 261).

Siyabonga (m) *[sih-yah-bohn-gah]* "We are grateful" [*Zulu*] (Koopman 1979: 79).

Siyamtusa (m) *[sih-yahm-tuh-sah]* "We praise Him" [*Zulu*] (Koopman 1979: 161).

Sizakele (f) *[sih-zah-keh-leh]* "She is helpful" [*Zulu*] (Koopman 1979: 162).

Sizwe (m) *[sih-zweh]* "Clan": a name such as given to a child born to parents whose family relationship has markedly improved from the deteriorated state it was in, and they are working towards building a strong family that will strengthen the clan [*Zulu*] (Suzman 1994: 267).

Sobantu (m) *[soh-bahn-tuh]* "Father of the People" [*Zulu*] (Koopman 1979: 71).

Sokulunga (m) *[soh-kuh-luhn-gah]* "(God) the righteous one" [*Zulu*] (Koopman 1979: 71).

Somandla (m) *[soh-mahn-dlah]* "(God) the Almighty" [*Zulu*] (Koopman 1979: 71).

Somfana (m) *[sohm-fah-nah]* "Boy" [*Zulu*] (Koopman 1979: 155).

Sonkomose (m) *[sohn-koh-moh-seh]* (One associated with a) cow [*Zulu*] (Koopman 1979: 73).

Sonwabu (m) *[sohn-wah-buh]* Chameleon [The *Zulu*] (Koopman 1979: 155).

Sopia (m) *[soh-pih-yah]* The one that is brownish in complexion [The *Maasai*].

Ssubi (m) *[suh-bih]* Grass; this name is sometimes associated with the proverbs "men are (like) grass: they (are used to) tie up themselves" and "men are (like harvested) grass: one stalk ties up the rest" which is in reference to the hardy grass used for thatching or squeezing out juice from bananas, the name implying that men (such as the powerful and the influential) can be so unreasonably domineering and oppressive of their fellow men; this name is also sometimes associated with the proverb "even the bananas that will not eventually materialize into banana-beer, are still catered to, starting with the harvesting of grass to squeeze out their juice for brewing" implying that whatever the circumstances, nothing or no one is to be easily dismissed as being of limited use or hope [*Ganda*].

Stophi (m) *[uhs-toh-pih]* "Stoplight": this name adapted from the European word "light" is such as given to a child born at a stoplight [*Zulu*] (Suzman 1994: 262, 270).

Sukuakuece (m) *[suh-kuh-wah-kweh-tch-eh]* "May God free you": this name is commonly associated with a proverb that implies that though doctors may boast of doing the healing, their work would come to na-ught without the hand of God [*Ovimbundu*] (Ennis 1945: 2).

Sukuapanga (m) *[suh-kuh-wah-pahn-gah]* "God willed": this name is commonly associated with the proverb "God willed, but Death (or Fa-te, or 'the abode of the dead') unwilled" and is given to a child some of whose previously born siblings died, or to one born into a family that has recently had deaths [*Ovimbundu*] (Ennis 1945: 3).

Sukuohembi (m) *[suh-kwoh-hehm-bih]* "God is a liar": this name is commonly associated with the proverb "God is a liar: he has lied to us about life" and is given to a child some of whose previously born siblings died [*Ovimbundu*] (Ennis 1945: 2).

Sukuonjali (m) *[suh-kwohn-jah-lih]* "God is a kind and helpful parent": this name is commonly associated with the proverb "God is a parent: he does not spill, he only tips over" [*Ovimbundu*] (Ennis 1945: 2).

Sumari (f) *[suh-mah-rih]* One of (or one associated with) *Somali* ethnics (as adapted from the word) [*Embu*].

Sungai (f/m) *[tsuhn-gahy]* "Tie up!"/ "fasten!": a name given to a child born out of infidelity and symbolizes the ritual cry of a mother who after the delivery is traditionally hand tied and then willingly confess-es the name of her collaborator so the life of the child and herself may be spared [*Shona*] (Jackson 1957: 119).

Sungano (f/m) *[tsuhn-gah-noh]* Covenant [The *Shona*] (Jackson 1957: 121).

Svondo (f/m) *[ts-vohn-doh]* Sunday: a name such as given to one born on Sunday [*Shona*] (Jackson 1957: 120).

Swelabatsheli (m) *[uh-sweh-lah-bah-tsh-eh-lih]* "No one to tell them (i.e. the children)": name such as given by the named child's poverty stricken mother who is left to raise the children alone since her hus-band has disappeared, the name implying that now there is no father to guide and instruct the children [*Zulu*] (Suzman 1994: 261).

Sweleni (f) *[sweh-leh-nih]* "What does she lack?" [*Zulu*] (Koopman 1979: 162).

Swohemba (f/m) *[swoh-hehm-bah]* "False": disharmony related name such as given by this newborn's mother and expresses her dissatis-faction with her treatment in the homestead and her mother-in-law's demeanor towards her [*Zulu*] (Herbert 1995: 6).

-T-

Taabu (f/m) *[taah-buh]* "Trouble": a name given to one conceived at a time the parents were having many problems [*Luyia*].

Tabu (f/m) *[taah-buh]* "Difficulty": a name such as given to one born during troubling times [*Kaguru, Swahili,* and several other eastern and central African ethnics] (Beidelman 1974: 288).

Tadi (f/m) *[tah-dih]* Stone: a "non-human" and usually temporary name given to a newborn [*Kongo*] (Ndoma 1977: 89).

Tafireyi (m) *[tah-fih-reh-yih]* "What are we dying for?": a name such as given to a child born to a family where the husband often mistreats his wife who happens to have many children by him, and in which family the husband refuses to pay the bride price arrears [The *Zezuru*] (Marapara 1954: 8).

Tahleho (m) *[tah-leh-hoh]* "The state of being neglected" [The *Sotho*] (Mohome 1972: 177).

Tajeu (m) *[tah-jehw]* "Be safe" [*Maasai*].

Takaendisa (f/m) *[tah-kah-yehn-dih-sah]* "We went too far away--had we married closer to home, there would not have been that much trouble": a name such as given to a child whose maternal kin are involved in a dispute with the paternal kin, more so the maternal grandmother regretting one of their's having married so far away from home as to create such a considerable social distance between the child's mother and maternal grandmother [*Shona*] (Jackson 1957: 117).

Takagarisa (f/m) *[tah-kah-gah-rih-sah]* "We have been around too long --we should have left this husband a long time ago": a name such as given to a child whose maternal kin are involved in a dispute with the paternal kin, the maternal kin regretting one of their's having married such a man [*Shona*] (Jackson 1957: 117).

Takawira (m) *[tah-kah-wih-rah]* "We fell into it": a name such as given to a child born at a time his parents are in trouble [*Zezuru*] (Marapara 1954: 8).

Takundwa (m) *[tah-kuhn-dwah]* "We have been defeated": name such as given to a child born into a small family i.e. which family's fertility rate is considered relatively low [*Zezuru*] (Marapara 1954: 8).

Talia (f/m) *[tah-lih-yah]* "In a rage": name such as given to one whose mother is angrily told by her husband's kin to work harder [*Lugbara*] (Middleton 1961: 36).

Tamnyole (f) *[tahm-ndjh-oh-leh]* "The well dressed one": (usually) a post-childhood nickname [*Nandi*] (Hollis 1969: 67).

Tangbo (f) *[taah-ndgh-boh]* "The mother of twins": a name given to a parent of twins [*Ngbandi*] (Daeleman 1977: 194).

Tanzi (f/m) *[tahn-zih]* Machete: a "non-human" and usually temporary name given to a newborn [*Kongo*] (Ndoma 1977: 89).

Taonga (f/m) *[tah-wohn-gah]* "We say 'thank you'" [*Shona*] (Jackson 1957: 121).

Taparusei (f) *[tah-pah-ruh-sehy]* "The owner of the blue (or black) bullock": (usually) a post-childhood nickname [*Nandi*] (Hollis 1969: 67).

Tapera (m) *[tah-peh-rah]* "We are finished": a name such as given to a child born at a time his parents are in fear of death [The *Zezuru*] (Marapara 1954: 8).

Tapkiken (f) *[tahp-kih-kehn]* "She who waits": (usually) a post-childhood nickname [*Nandi*] (Hollis 1969: 67).

Taprapkoi (f) *[tahp-rahp-kohy]* "The wealthy one": (usually) a post-childhood nickname [*Nandi*] (Hollis 1969: 67).

Tariro (f/m) *[tah-rih-roh]* Hope [*Shona*] (Jackson 1957: 121).

Taru (f/m) *[tah-ruh]* An abbreviation of names like *Taruberekera*, *Taru-sarira*, *Taruona*, and *Tarusenga* [*Shona*] (Jackson 1957: 119).

Taruberekera (f/m) *[tah-ruh-beh-reh-keh-rah]* "We have given birth for the sake of it (i.e. death)": a name given to a child born into a family that has lost many of its members to death and whereby there is pessimism as to whether this one will survive, the name metaphorically implying that the going to so much trouble to give birth is in vain [*Shona*] (Jackson 1957: 119).

Taruona (f/m) *[tah-ruh-woh-nah]* "We have have seen death": a name given to a child born into a family that has lost many of its members to death and whereby there is pessimism as to whether this one will survive, the name metaphorically implying that those of the family have witnessed so many deaths in the unit and become so drained that as a result death now manifests itself as a commonplace phenomenon [*Shona*] (Jackson 1957: 119).

Tarusarira (f/m) *[tah-ruh-sah-rih-rah]* "We are left behind only to be used by death": a name given to a child born into a family that has lost many of its members to death and whereby there is pessimism as to whether this one will survive, the name metaphorically implying that those of the household that are still living are expecting to soon be consumed by death as did happen to the deceased [*Shona*] (Jackson 1957: 119).

Tarusenga (f/m) *[tah-ruh-sehn-gah]* "We have carried it (i.e. death)": a name given to a child born into a family that has lost many of its members to death and whereby there is pessimism as to whether this one will survive, the name metaphorically implying that the family is carrying around with it the phenomenon of death which is easily exerting its toll [*Shona*] (Jackson 1957: 119).

Tatello (m) *[tah-tehl-loh]* Insistence: a name such as given to a child born during times of hardship/ or to a first-born whose father struggled hard to win over the love of the mother [*Sotho*] (Mohome 1972: 176).

Tauni (m) *[tahw-nih]* "Town": a name adapted from the European word and given to a child associated with one who bore the name and was born during the beginnings of urbanization in the vicinity [*Luyia*].

Tebello (f/m) *[teh-behl-loh]* Expectation: a name such as given to a child who is the product of an unduly long pregnancy period with the birthdate long overdue [*Sotho*] (Mohome 1972: 177).

Teboho (m) *[teh-boh-hoh]* Gratitude; a name given to the younger of a set of fraternal twins [*Sotho*] (Mohome 1972: 174, 179).

Techteget (m) *[teh-tch-teh-geht]* "He who shields his chest": (usually) a post childhood nickname [*Nandi*] (Hollis 1969: 68).

Tefelo (m) *[teh-feh-loh]* A name given to the younger of a set of fraternal twins; "payment on behalf of another" [*Sotho*] (Mohome 1972:

179).

Tefo (m) *[teh-foh]* "(Compensatory) payment"; name given to the older of a set of fraternal twins; a name given to one born following the death of a preceding sibling [*Sotho*] (Mohome 1972: 174, 179).

Tefo (m) *[teh-foh]* Payment: a name given to one who has lost two or more preceding siblings to death, the name implying that this child serves as restitution, by the action of God or the ancestors, for the deceased [*Sotho*] (Thipa 1986: 290).

Teko (m) *[teh-koh]* Temptation [*Sotho*] (Mohome 1972: 177).

Tenamwenye (m) *[teh-nah-mweh-ndjh-eh]* "The one that does not have his own"; "the fatherless child": a name such as given to a child whose father died before it was born [*Pare*] (Omari 1970: 71).

Teyai (f/m) *[teh-yahy]* "Set traps so that I shall be bewitched": a name given to one born during a family dispute with kin or neighbors, whereby there is suspicion that the antagonists are engaged in malicious acts of witchcraft against the parent [*Shona*] (Jackson 1957: 117).

Thabang (f) *[tah-bah-ndgh]* "Rejoice"; "be happy"; a name given to the younger of a set of twins; a name given to the younger of a set of twins, one of which is a boy (named *Thabo*) [*Sotho*] (Mohome 1972: 174, 179).

Thabiso (m) *[tah-bih-soh]* "That which causes to be gratified"; a name given to the older of a set of twins, one of which is a girl (named *Nthabiseng*) [*Sotho*] (Mohome 1972: 179).

Thabo (m) *[tah-boh]* Joy: name given to the older of a set of fraternal twins; a name given to the older of a set of twins, the other of which is a girl (named *Thabang*) [*Sotho*] (Mohome 1972: 174, 179).

Thandaza (f) *[tahn-dah-zah]* "Pray" [*Zulu*] (Koopman 1979: 158, 164).

Thandekile (f) *[tahn-deh-kih-leh]* "She is likable (or lovable)" [*Zulu*] (Koopman 1979: 162).

Thandi (f) *[tahn-dih]* A pet name and abbreviation of *Thandekile*: "She is likable/ lovable" [*Zulu*] (Koopman 1979: 162).

Thandiwe (f) *[tahn-dih-weh]* "She is loved"; "the loved one" [*Zulu*] (Koopman 1979: 162).

Thandiwe (m) *[tahn-dih-weh]* "Love" [*Zulu*] (Suzman 1994: 270).

Thandukwazi (m) *[tahn-duh-kwaah-zih]* "Love knowledge" [The *Zulu*] (Koopman 1979: 68).

Thanduyise (m) *[tahn-duh-yih-seh]* "He loves his father" [The *Zulu*] (Koopman 1979: 160).

Thandwawubani (m) *[tahn-dwah-wuh-bah-nih]* "Who is he loved by?" [*Zulu*] (Koopman 1979: 161).

Thathani (f) *[tah-tah-nih]* "Take" [*Zulu*] (Koopman 1979: 158).

Thathazonke (m) *[tah-tah-zohn-keh]* "He takes everything" [The *Zulu*] (Koopman 1979: 161).

Themba (f) *[tehm-bah]*/ **Thembani** (f) *[tehm-bah-nih]* "Trust"; "hope"

[*Zulu*] (Koopman 1979: 158).

Themba (f/m) *[tehm-bah]* Trust: a name such as given by the mother and expresses high opinion of and good relations with her trusted mother-in-law, as she hopes that this new born and all her other children will grow up to be like her in-law [*Zulu*] (Herbert 1995: 4); "hope": name such as given to express that is a very welcome child who, it is hoped, will ensure that the family line continues [*Zulu*] (Suzman 1994: 267).

Thembani (m) *[tehm-bah-nih]* "Hope" [*Zulu*] (Suzman 1994: 268).

Thembani (m) *[uh-sth-ehm-beh-nih]* "What can you trust?": a name such as given by the named child's mother (who is a second wife in a polygamous unit) to express that it is difficult to trust anyone [*Zulu*] (Suzman 1994: 259); "who were you trusting?": name such as given to a child born to parents that are not on good terms [*Zulu*] (Suzman 1994: 267).

Thembekile (f) *[tehm-beh-kih-leh]* "She is trustworthy" [The *Zulu*] (Koopman 1979: 162).

Thembeni (f) *[tehm-beh-nih]* "What does she hope for?" [The *Zulu*] (Koopman 1979: 162).

Thembi (f) *[tehm-bih]* A pet name and abbreviation of *Thembekile*: "She is trustworthy" [*Zulu*] (Koopman 1979: 162).

Thembisile (f) *[tehm-bih-sih-leh]* "She has caused there to be hope" [*Zulu*] (Koopman 1979: 162).

Theuri (m) *[sth-ehw-rih]* The revealer [*Kikuyu*].

Thieri (m) *[sth-yeh-rih]* One who goes on behalf of another [*Kikuyu*].

Thigo (m) *[sth-ih-goh]* Door [*Luo*].

Thikiza (f) *[tih-kih-zah]* "Be trusted" [*Zulu*] (Koopman 1979: 158).

Thoko (f) *[toh-koh]* A pet name and abbreviation of *Thokozile*: "She has rejoiced"/ "she is happy" [*Zulu*] (Koopman 1979: 162).

Thokozani (f) *[toh-koh-zaah-nih]* "Be happy" [*Zulu*] (Koopman 1979: 158, 164).

Thokozile (f) *[toh-koh-zih-leh]* "She has rejoiced"; "she is happy" [*Zulu*] (Koopman 1979: 162).

Tholakele (f) *[toh-lah-keh-leh]* "She is available" [*Zulu*] (Koopman 1979: 162).

Thota (m) *[toh-tah]* Plain: a name such as given to a child delivered in countryside plain/ or one born when the father or a close kin was in the plain [*Sotho*] (Mohome 1972: 176).

Thotobolo (m) *[sth-oh-toh-boh-loh]* Place for dumping rubbish (or refuse): a derogatory name given to one who has lost two or more preceding siblings to death, the name (paradoxically) intended to devalue and hence serve as protection for this child through dissuading the forces of evil and death from taking such a "useless" child away [*Sotho*] (Thipa 1986: 290).

Thukayizwe (m) *[tuh-kah-yih-zweh]* "Insulted by the people": a name such as given to a child both whose father and himself were insulted by people in the vicinity [*Zulu*] (Suzman 1994: 262).

Thulani (f/m) *[tuh-lah-nih]* "Be quiet" [*Zulu*] (Koopman 1979: 158).

Thulani (m) *[uh-sth-uh-lah-nih]* "(Be) quiet": a name such as given by this child's mother who is telling her dissatisfied and whining mother-in-law to quieten down [*Zulu*] (Suzman 1994: 259, 268).

Thulasizwe (m) *[tuh-lah-sih-zweh]* "He is quiet that we might hear"; "be quiet and let us hear" [*Zulu*] (Koopman 1979: 161).

Thuo (m) *[sth-uh-woh]* One who limps [*Kikuyu*].

Tiang (m) *[tjah-ndgh]* Sugarcane [*Luo*].

Tibaijuka (m) *[tih-bahy-juh-kah]* "They (i.e. the neighbors) do not re-member": the parents of a child given this name are heralding the message that they are displeased at neighbors for not remembering, reciprocating, or acknowledging the help that the parents rendered th-em in the past [*Nyoro*] (Beattie 1957: 104).

Tibaiseka (m) *[tih-bahy-seh-kah]* "They (i.e. people) are not to laugh (i.e. at poverty)": a name such as given to a child born into a family that is poor, the name implying that being in a situation of poverty is so draining i.e. that poverty is not something that deserves to be la-ughed at [*Nyoro*] (Beattie 1957: 103).

Tibakunirwa (m) *[tih-bah-kuh-nih-rwah]* "It is difficult (or impossible) to be polite to them (i.e. the neighbors)"/ "they (i.e. the neighbors) can-not be expressed politeness to": the name implies that the father of the child named so, is at loss since his dedicated efforts to appease and reconcile with antagonistic neighbors through treating them civil-ly and considerately, have not yielded the desired results [The *Nyoro*] (Beattie 1957: 104).

Tibamwenda (m) *[tih-bah-mwehn-dah]* "They (i.e. the neighbors) do not like him/ her": the parents of a child given this name are herald-ing the message that the neighbors do not like either the child or one of the parents [*Nyoro*] (Beattie 1957: 104).

Tibanagwa (m) *[tih-bah-nah-gwah]* "(Despite the circumstances) they (i.e. children) are not thrown away": a name such as given to an alar-mingly sick child not expected to survive, or to one whose previously born siblings died [*Nyoro*] (Beattie 1957: 101).

Tibananuka (m) *[tih-bah-naah-nuh-kah]* "They (i.e. the neighbors) do not trust": the name implies that the father of the child named so, vividly recalls in reminding neighbors that they have in the past false-ly accused him or unjustly doubted his word [*Nyoro*] (Beattie 1957: 103-104).

Tibeita (m) *[tih-behy-tah]* "They (i.e. people) do not kill themselves (i.e. on account of poverty)": a name given to child born into a family that is poor, the name implying that being in a situation of abject po-verty, though so draining and laden with the potential to lead one to want to kill oneself, is accompanied by aspects to be thankful for and the possibility that the situation will improve [*Nyoro*] (Beattie 1957:

103).

Tibuhoire (m) *[tih-buh-hohy-reh]* "It (i.e. sorrow) has not as yet come to an end": a name such as given to a child born during a period of misfortune [*Nyoro*] (Beattie 1957: 100).

Tichivangani (f/m) *[tih-tch-ih-vahn-gah-nih]* "How many of us are left?": a name such as given to a child born into a family that has lost many of its members to death and whereby there is pessimism as to whether this one will survive, the name metaphorically implying that the family has lost count of how many have died [*Shona*] (Jackson 1957: 119).

Tieho (m) *[tih-yeh-hoh]* Delay: a name such as given to a child who is the product of an unduly long pregnancy period with the birthdate long overdue [*Sotho*] (Mohome 1972: 177).

Tigalyoma (m) *[tih-gah-ljoh-mah]* "They (i.e. the tears) will not dry up": a name such as given to an alarmingly sick child not expected to survive, to one whose previously born siblings died, or to one born during a time of sorrow whereby the pessimism lingers on [The *Nyoro*] (Beattie 1957: 101).

Tigulyera (m) *[tih-guh-ljeh-rah]* "It (i.e. the heart of the parents) does not become pleased": a name such as given to a child whose previously born siblings died [*Nyoro*] (Beattie 1957: 101).

Tiisetso (m) *[tiih-seht-soh]* Endurance: a name such as given to a child born during times of hardship/ or to a first-born whose father struggled hard to win over the love of the mother [The *Sotho*] (Mohome 1972: 176).

Tindyebwa (m) *[tihn-djeh-eh-bwah]* "I do not forget (i.e. the injuries people have inflicted on me)": the parent of a child given this name is heralding the message that he/ she is still hurt by what was done to him/ her (by neighbors) in the past [*Nyoro*] (Beattie 1957: 104).

Tinga (m) *[tihn-gah]* Tractor [*Luo*].

Tingbo (f/m) *[tih-ndgh-boh]* "Twin's arm": a name given to the second child born after twin siblings [*Ngbandi*] (Daeleman 1977: 192).

Tipo (m) *[tih-poh]* Shadow [*Luo*].

Titi (f) *[tih-tih]* A pet name [*Kongo*] (Ndoma 1977: 98).

Tladi (m) *[tlah-dih]* Lightning: a name such as given to one whose birth coincides with a period of lightning [*Sotho*] (Mohome 1972: 175).

Tlala (m) *[tlah-lah]/* **Tlaleng** (f) *[tlah-leh-ndgh]* Hunger: a name such as given to one born during a period of food shortages [*Sotho*] (Thipa 1986: 289).

Tlalane (f) *[tlah-lah-neh]* **Tlale** (m) *[tlah-leh]* **Tlaleng** (f) *[tlah-leh-ndgh]* Famine; hunger: a name such as given to one whose birth coincides with a period of famine/ or hunger [*Sotho*] (Mohome 1972: 175).

Tlangelani (f) *[tlahn-geh-lah-nih]* "Fortunate": name such as implying that the parent for whom this birth, which registers a consecutive female gender birth, symbolizes good fortune [*Zulu*] (Herbert 1995:

4).

Tobiko (m) *[toh-bih-koh]* The one that delays [*Maasai*].

Toloki (m) *[toh-loh-kih]* Interpreter: a name such as given to a newborn whose father's skill at explaining stories is compared to that of an interpreter [*Zulu*] (Herbert 1995: 5).

Tongbo (m) *[toh-oh-ndgh-boh]* "The father of twins": a name given to a parent of twins [*Ngbandi*] (Daeleman 1977: 194).

Tongesayi (m) *[tohn-geh-saah-yih]* "Take us before the courts". name such as given to a child born at a time his parents are involved in a legal dispute [*Zezuru*] (Marapara 1954: 8).

Tororeta (m) *[toh-roh-reh-tah]* God; the sky; "that which is above" [The *Mosiro*] (Huntingford 1930: 102-103).

Tororut (m) *[toh-roh-ruht]* God; the sky; "that which is above" [*Endo, Nandi, Suk*] (Huntingford 1930: 102-103).

Tozivaripi (f/m) *[toh-zih-vah-rih-pih]* "Death has silenced us--we are thoroughly dumfounded"/ "what word is there that we know?": a name such as given to a child born into a family that has lost many of its members to death and whereby there is pessimism as to whether this one will survive, the name metaphorically implying that the toll of death has been so severe as to be beyond words or description [*Shona*] (Jackson 1957: 119).

Tsakani (f/m) *[tsah-kah-nih]* "Happy": a name such as implying that the named child's paternal grandmother is so delighted that her son has a newborn [*Zulu*] (Herbert 1995: 4).

Tsameleni (f) *[tsah-meh-leh-nih]* "Why are you staying?": name such as implying that there is perplexion as to why a woman whose husband dies before she conceives a child (and therefore her establishment in the husband's family is not firm) still hangs in and around her late husband's kraal and homestead instead of taking another step such as going out and attempting to remarry [*Zulu*] (Herbert 1995: 4).

Tsebetsabaloi (m) *[tseh-beh-tsah-bah-lohy]* Sorcerer's ears: a name such as given to one whose birth coincided with a mysterious incident [*Sotho*] (Ashton 1952: 32).

Tsebo (f) *[tseh-boh]* Knowledge [*Sotho*] (Mohome 1972: 178).

Tseko (m) *[tseh-koh]* A dispute: a name such as given to a child born during a time of social discord within the family or with neighbors [*Sotho*] (Mohome 1972: 177).

Tselane (f) *[tseh-lah-neh]* Path; small road: a name such as given to a child delivered along a road [*Sotho*] (Mohome 1972: 176, 179).

Tseleng (f) *[tseh-leh-ndgh]* "In/ at the road": a name such as given to a child delivered along a road [*Sotho*] (Mohome 1972: 176).

Tshanibezwe (m) *[tsh-ah-nih-beh-zweh]* "Grass of the land" [The *Zulu*] (Koopman 1979: 156).

Tshediso (m) *[tsh-eh-dih-soh]* "Consolation": a name such as given to one born following the death of a preceding sibling [*Sotho*] (Mohome 1972: 174).

Tshediso (m) *[tsh-eh-dih-soh]* "The one who has consoled us"/ "the one who has made us cross": a name given to one who has lost two or more preceding siblings to death, the name implying that this child serves as solace, by the action of God or the ancestors, for the family of the deceased [*Sotho*] (Thipa 1986: 290).

Tshepiso (f) *[tsh-eh-pih-soh]* "Promise"; a name given to the younger of a set of twins, one of which is a boy (named *Tshepo*) [The *Sotho*] (Mohome 1972: 174, 179, 181).

Tshepo (m) *[tsh-eh-poh]* "Hope"; "trust"; a name given to the older of a set of twins, one of which is a girl (named *Tshepiso*) [The *Sotho*] (Mohome 1972: 174, 179, 181).

Tshitshi (f) *[uh-tsh-ih-tsh-ih]* "The sound of milk coming forth": name such as given by the named child's mother to express happiness that she has borne a girl who will consequently be a source of bride dowry wealth (*lobolo*) [*Zulu*] (Suzman 1994: 261).

Tsie (m) *[tsih-yeh]* Locust: a name such as given to one whose birth coincides with a locust invasion [*Sotho*] (Mohome 1972: 175).

Tsietsi (m) *[tsih-yeht-sih]* Accident: name such as given to one whose birth coincides with a misfortune in the family [*Sotho*] (Mohome 1972: 173).

Tsiimba (f/m) *[tsiihm-bah]* Wild cat: a name given to an older twin, the younger named *Nzuuzi* [*Kongo*] (Daeleman 1977: 191); wild cat: the older of twin girls, the younger named *Nzusi* [*Yaka*] (Daeleman 1977: 191); a name given to a female triplet [*Yaka*] (Daeleman 1977: 192).

Tsoene (f) *[tsoh-weh-neh]* Monkey: an unpleasant name given to one whose previous born sibling was stillborn or died before weaning, this attributed to sorcery--the name is a means to safeguard this child "by making a show of neglecting it in the hope of lulling the sorcerer's vigilance" [*Sotho*] (Ashton 1952: 33).

Tsungai (f/m) *[tsuhn-gahy]* "Be brave" [*Shona*] (Jackson 1957: 121).

Tuayunge (f) *[tuh-wah-yuhn-geh]* "We picked": this name is commonly associated with the expression "When we picked (crops) they ate plenty, but with hard times they did not come" which is metaphorically the lamentation of one who had plenty of friends when she was rich, but they desert her and do not help her when she becomes poor (or of a child of one of such a situation) [*Ovimbundu*] (Ennis 1945: 6).

Tufila (f/m) *[tuuh-fih-lah]* "Accompany us (i.e. the twins)": name given to one whose birth precedes that of his or her twin siblings [*Yaka*] (Daeleman 1977: 193).

Tumelo (m) *[tuh-meh-loh]* Belief: a name such as given to a child born during times of hardship during which there is still hope for a situation of success and normalcy/ or a name given to a first-born whose father struggled hard to win over the love of the mother [The *Sotho*] (Mohome 1972: 176).

Tumo (m) *[tuh-moh]* Fame [*Sotho*] (Mohome 1972: 174).

Tungamirai (f/m) *[tuhn-gah-mih-rahy]* "Lead the way, oh Lord" [*Shona*]

(Jackson 1957: 121).

Turumanya (m) *[tuh-ruh-mah-ndjh-ah]* "It (i.e. death) would not (or does not) understand": the name implies that in taking away those so young while leaving alone those that are old, the phenomenon of death is pitilessly unreasonable; the name is given to a child born into a family in which some young have died, or to a child who is alarmingly sick and is not expected to survive [*Nyoro*] (Beattie 1957: 102).

Turuni (m) *[tuh-ruh-nih]* The one that is dug out [*Maasai*].

-U-

Udude (m) *[uh-duh-deh]/* **Ukwing** (m) *[uh-kwih-ndgh]* This is a manifestation of a supernatural power said to have come from the neighboring *Bunyoro* territory and is said to have descended on the *Alur* ethnics and possessed them [*Alur*] (Southall 1951: 187).

Ummango (m) *[uhm-mahn-goh]* "The long and steep (hill) incline": a name such as given to one of determination, one prepared to face and overcome any difficulty [*Zulu*] (Lugg 1968: 12).

Umuweiri (m) *[uhm-wehy-rih]* God; "the friendly one" [The *Luyia*] (Huntingford 1930: 103).

Unsokosonkwana (m) *[uhn-soh-koh-sohn-kwaah-nah]* "The thin, tall, and stately one" [*Zulu*] (Lugg 1968: 12).

Usenge (m) *[uh-sehn-geh]* Bush: a name such as given to one born in the field or in the woods [*Ovimbundu*] (Ennis 1945: 7).

-V-

Valala (m) *[vah-lah-lah]* Enemies: a name such as given to a newborn to imply that boys act like enemies since they continuously want to fight [*Zulu*] (Herbert 1995: 5).

Vasuvuka (f) *[vah-suh-vuh-kah]* "They hate me": this expression is directed to neighbors or kin by a parent of the child so named, and the implication is that the accused agency is suspected of gossiping as well as the ill-will that involves manipulating forces of evil and witchcraft to cause sickness and death in the family [*Ovimbundu*] (Ennis 1945: 6).

Vatalele (f) *[vah-tah-leh-leh]* "They have seen": this name is commonly associated with the expression "They have seen an elephant, but a warthog does not cause the rain to fall on me" which metaphorically portrays the determination of a widow who does not intend to remarry (and she bestows the name on herself) [*Ovimbundu*] (Ennis 1945: 5).

Vatenala (f) *[vah-teh-nah-lah]* "They are gone": this name is commonly associated with the expression "They are gone, though my mother bore a crowd" and relates to one who has lost several of her siblings to death [*Ovimbundu*] (Ennis 1945: 5).

Vatukemba (f) *[vah-tuh-kehm-bah]* "They lie to us": this name is commonly associated with the proverb "They lie to us: God has lied to us about life" and is given to a child some of whose previously born siblings died [*Ovimbundu*] (Ennis 1945: 3).

Vatusia (f) *[vah-tuh-sih-yah]* "They leave us behind": the expression relates to a child born into a family that has had several deaths, and implies that "the dead are gone and have left us behind" [*Ovimbundu*] (Ennis 1945: 5).

Vela (m) *[veh-lah]* "Appear" [*Zulu*] (Koopman 1979: 74).

Velaphi (m) *[uh-veh-lah-pih]* "Where does he come from?": name such as given to one born out of wedlock, out of infidelity, or one whose paternity is uncertain [*Zulu*] (Suzman 1994: 259).

Velongoye (m) *[veh-lohn-goh-yeh]* "Appear at *Ngoye*" [The *Zulu*] (Koopman 1979: 79).

Vengai (f/m) *[vehn-gahy]* "Hate ye": a name such as given to one born during a hatred loaded family dispute with kin or with neighbors [The *Shona*] (Jackson 1957: 117).

Vengesai (f/m) *[vehn-geh-sahy]* "Hate me much": name such as given to one born during a family dispute with kin or with neighbors, the parent so appalled at the hatred displayed [*Shona*] (Jackson 1957: 117).

Vengwa (f/m) *[vehn-gwah]* The hated one: a name such as given to one born during a family dispute with kin or with neighbors, the parent so appalled at the hatred displayed [*Shona*] (Jackson 1957: 117).

Vihemba (f) *[vih-hehm-bah]* Medicine/ charms: a name such as given to one who is the product of a difficult birth (or pregnancy) whereby native remedies were applied [*Ovimbundu*] (Ennis 1945: 7).

Vika (m) *[uh-vih-kah]* "Parry (blows)": a name such as given to a child born to parents that are not on good terms [The *Zulu*] (Suzman 1994: 267).

Vikamatshe (m) *[vih-kah-maht-sheh]* "Warding off stones": name such as given to a child born at a time of discord in the family [The *Zulu*] (Koopman 1979: 68).

Visolela (f) *[vih-soh-leh-lah]* "Those that you long for": this name is commonly associated with the proverb "Those that are longings are of waterfalls, those that you just pick over are of the drying trays" implying that a lot of things that we desire (such as a utopia) seem to be almost impossible to achieve (this exemplified by the gush of waterfalls which we have little control over), but the ordinary things of life (like sorting out grains) we can use our judgment on and control); the proverb also implies that the desires of the heart are (like waterfalls) difficult to control, whereas there are many mundane things that we can control at our discretion [*Ovimbundu*] (Ennis 1945: 5).

Vonani (f/m) *[voh-nah-nih]* "Look!": name such as given to a newborn whose father is pointedly referring to the unbelievable act of the headman who sold his cows while the father was away and engaged in migratory employment [*Zulu*] (Herbert 1995: 7).

Vondila (f) *[vohn-dih-lah]* "They borrow": this name is commonly associated with the expression "They borrow a basket and sieve, but a
face you cannot borrow" which is the lamentation of a woman who
has lost a child (who unlike many ordinary things or even the subsequent birth of additional children, cannot be borrowed or replaced
after dying) and relates to a child who has lost a sibling (or mother
who has lost a child) [*Ovimbundu*] (Ennis 1945: 5).

Vu (m) *[vuh]* "Of a sudden drop" [*Zulu*] (Koopman 1979: 163).

Vukayibambe (m) *[vuh-kah-yih-bahm-beh]* "Rouse yourself and catch
it" [*Zulu*] (Koopman 1979: 79).

Vusi (m) *[vuh-sih]* A pet name and abbreviation of *Vusumuzi*: "he revives (or awakens) the family"/ "wake up the household" (i.e. "start a
new family") [*Zulu*] (Koopman 1979: 163).

Vusindaba (m) *[vuh-sihn-dah-bah]* "Revive the matter" [The *Zulu*]
(Koopman 1979: 79).

Vusumuzi (m) *[vuh-suh-muh-zih]* "He revives (or awakens) the family"/
"wake up the household" (i.e. "start a new family"): a name convent-
ionally given to a first born son [The *Zulu*] (Koopman 1979: 160, 163,
164).

Vusumuzi (m) *[vuh-suh-muh-zih]* "Revive the home": a name such as
given to a firstborn to express that is a very welcome child that will
ensure that the family line continues [*Zulu*] (Suzman 1994: 263, 267,
268).

Vutomi (f/m) *[vuh-toh-mih]* Life: name such as implying that this child
is a product of the mother having been too lax and liberal with life
whereby she left school then became pregnant [*Zulu*] (Herbert 1995:
4).

-W-

Wabomba (m) *[wah-bohm-bah]* A name given to one whose weight, as
a baby, is below normal [*Luyia*].

Wabwile (m) *[wah-bwih-leh]* "The one of the night": a name such as given to one born in the depth of night [*Luyia*].

Wabwire (m) *[wah-bwih-reh]* "The one of the night": a name such as
given to one born in the night [*Samia*] (Nzita 1995: 73).

Wabwoba (m) *[wah-bwoh-bah]* "The one of mushrooms": a name such
as given to one born during a season of mushroom abundance [The
Luyia].

Waceera (f) *[wah-tch-eh-rah]* One who loves visiting [*Kikuyu*].

Waceke (f) *[wah-tch-eh-keh]* One who is thin [*Kikuyu*].

Wacuira (m) *[wah-kuhy-rah]* One who loves to engage in disputes [The
Kikuyu].

Wafula (m) *[wah-fuh-lah]* A name given to one born during a rainy season [*Luyia*].

Wahome (m) *[wah-hoh-meh]* Of the weak [*Kikuyu*].

Waigera (m) *[wahy-geh-rah]* Blacksmith [*Kikuyu*].

Waihenya (m) *[wahy-heh-ndjh-ah]* One who is always in a hurry [The *Kikuyu*].

Wainza (f) *[wah-yihn-zah]* One who likes to work in the food crop garden [*Kikuyu*].

Waititu (m) *[wahy-tih-tuh]* One born in a forest [*Kikuyu*].

Wakhisi (m) *[wah-kih-sih]* "Of the antelope": a name given to one born during the hunting of *chikhisi* antelopes [*Luyia*].

Wakhungu (m) *[wah-kuhn-guh]* A name given to one born during an invasion by army worms [*Luyia*].

Wakungila (m) *[wahn-kuhn-gih-lah]* "Of a road/ path": a name given to one born at a time the mother was on a journey; a name given to one born on a wayside [*Luyia*].

Walekhwa (f/m) *[wah-leh-kwah]* "That is left": a name such as given to a child whose twin sibling dies [*Luyia*] (Wako 1985: 38).

Walekhwa (m) *[wah-leh-kwah]* "The one left/ abandoned": name given to one whose mother dies soon after giving birth to him, or to one whose parent (or parents) died when he was very young [*Luyia*].

Waliaula (m) *[wah-ljah-wuh-lah]* A name given to a child born when family domestic animals, for fulfilling bride dowry obligations, are in the process of being taken away [*Luyia*].

Walukhu (m) *[wah-luh-kuh]* "Of a log": a name given to one born after several of his preceding siblings died [*Luyia*].

Walumbe (m) *[wah-luhm-beh]* "Of a scourge/ illness": a name given to one born during an epidemic [*Luyia*].

Wamai (m) *[wah-mahy]* The one of the water [*Embu*].

Wamakonjo (m) *[wah-mah-kohn-joh]* A name given to a child prone to wounds; a name given to a child associated with a person that was susceptible to wounds [*Luyia*].

Wamalabe (f/m) *[wah-mah-lah-beh]* Name given to a child associated with a person that lost all of his or her children to death [*Luyia*].

Wamalwa (m) *[wah-mah-lwah]* "Of beer": a name given to one born at a time of a beer drinking festival [*Luyia*].

Wambiro (f) *[wahm-bih-roh]* One who loves to cook; one who loves to deal with soot [*Embu*].

Wamoni (m) *[wah-moh-nih]* A name given to one with characteristically large eyes [*Luyia*].

Wambuga (m) *[wahm-buh-gah]* Fortune teller; medicine man [*Embu*].

Wambui (f) *[wahm-buhy]/* **Wamboi** (f) *[wahm-bohy]* Singer [The *Kikuyu*] (Stewart 1993: 138).

Wambura (f) *[wahm-buh-rah]* A name given to one born during a rainy season [*Embu, Kikuyu*].

Wamiti (f) *[wah-mih-tih]* "Of the trees": name given to one born close to a forest [*Embu*].

Wamocha (m) *[wah-moh-tch-ah]* "The one that is never satisfied" [The *Luyia*] (Stewart 1993: 140).

Wamukota (m) *[wah-muh-koh-tah]* "The one with the left": name given to one that is left handed [*Gisu, Luyia*].

Wanambuko (m) *[wah-nahm-buh-koh]* A name given to a child born during an abundance of tsetse flies [*Luyia*].

Wandemu (m) *[wahn-deh-muh]* A name given to a child whose parents are, just like the snake, ferocious and venerated; a name given to one whose parents rear snakes [*Luyia*].

Wandiri (f) *[wahn-dih-rih]* One who loves to pound on a mortar [The *Embu*].

Wangari (f) *[wah-ndgh-ah-rih]* One who is mean [*Kikuyu*].

Wangila (m) *[wah-ndgh-ih-lah]* "Of a road/ path": a name given to one born at a time the mother was on a journey; name given to one born on a wayside [*Luyia*].

Wang'ombe (m) *[wah-ndgh-ohm-beh]* One who loves cattle; one who owns a lot of cattle [*Kikuyu*].

Wangombe (m) *[wah-ndgh-ohm-beh]* "The one of many cows" [The *Kikuyu*] (Stewart 1993: 140).

Wangwe (m) *[wah-ndgh-weh]* A name given to one born after several of his preceding siblings died [*Luyia*].

Wanhija (f) *[wahn-hih-jah]* "They run off": name such as given to one given birth to without help from the midwives, such as one born to a mother in the fields or on a journey [*Kaguru*] (Beidelman 1974: 288).

Wanja (f) *[wahn-djah]* Outside [*Kikuyu*].

Wanja (f) *[wahn-djah]* The one who owns the immediate compound; "paternal grandfather" [*Embu*].

Wanjala (m) *[wahn-jah-lah]* "Of hunger": a name given to one born during a period of famine [*Gisu, Luyia*].

Wanjera (f) *[wahn-jeh-rah]* "The one of the road": a name such as given to one whose preceding siblings died, this child consequently subjected to a ritual to cleanse away death [*Kikuyu*] (Cagnolo 1933: 66).

Wanjira (f) *[wahn-djih-rah]* "Of a road/ path": name given to one born along a road or a wayside; a name given to one who loves to travel [*Embu, Kikuyu*].

Wanjiru (f) *[wahn-jih-ruh]* Of black [*Kikuyu*].

Wanjohi (m) *[wahn-joh-hih]* Brewer [*Kikuyu*].

Wanyama (m) *[wah-ndjh-ah-mah]* "Of meat": name given to one born at a time there is plenty of meat to eat [*Luyia*].

Wanyonyi (m) *[wah-ndjh-oh-ndjh-ih]* "Of a weed": a name given to one born during a weeding season [*Luyia*].

Warigia (f) *[wah-rih-gih-yah]* One who always comes in last when she participates in a group activity [*Kikuyu*].

Wariitui (m) *[wah-riih-tuhy]* One who looks after livestock [*Kikuyu*].

Waruguru (f) *[wah-ruh-guh-ruh]* The one from the northside [*Kikuyu*].

Wasansua (m) *[wah-sahn-suh-wah]* "He has been well taught" [*Kongo*] (Ndoma 1977: 96).

Wasike (m) *[wah-sih-keh]* A name given to one born during a locust invasion (or season) [*Luyia*].

Wasolo (m) *[wah-soh-loh]* A name given to one born after all of his preceding siblings died [*Luyia*].

Wasuna (m) *[wah-suh-nah]* Mosquito [*Luo*].

Waswa (m) *[wah-swah]* A name given to one born during a season when there is an abundance of edible white ants [*Luyia*].

Watenya (m) *[wah-teh-ndjh-ah]* A name given to one whose weight, as a baby, is below normal [*Luyia*].

Watoya (f/m) *[wah-toh-yah]* A name given to a mongoloid child [The *Luyia*].

Waweru (m) *[wah-weh-ruh]* One that is from the desert [*Kikuyu*].

Wawira (f) *[wah-wih-rah]* The hardworking one [*Embu*].

Webale (m) *[weh-bah-leh]* A name given to one who is difficult and uncompromising [*Luyia*].

Wechabubi (m) *[weh-tch-ah-buh-bih]* "The one who came in a bad way": a name given to one who is of a breech birth i.e. one born feet first (as opposed to the conventional head first) [*Luyia*].

Wefwafwa (m) *[weh-fwah-fwah]* A name given to a child whose parents are fond of eating *lifwafwa* vegetables [*Luyia*].

Wekesa (m) *[weh-keh-sah]* A name given to one born during a period of harvesting [*Luyia*].

Wekhanya (m) *[weh-kah-ndjh-ah]* One associated with a person who had the habit of grabbing things [*Luyia*].

Wekhwela (m) *[weh-kweh-lah]* "The one who pays for himself": name given to one who pays the dowry for his bride on his own [*Luyia*].

Wele (f/m) *[weh-leh]* A name given to a child that is quite mysterious [*Luyia*].

Weloba (m) *[weh-loh-bah]* A name given to one born after several of his preceding siblings died [*Luyia*].

Wendo (m) *[wehn-doh]* Visitor [*Luo*].

Weng'ua (m) *[weh-ndgh-wah]* A name given to one who consistently has a running nose [*Luyia*].

Weninga (m) *[weh-nihn-gah]* A name given to one born after several of his preceding siblings died [*Luyia*].

Wenwa (m) *[wehn-wah]* A plea; "leave it to us" [*Luo*].

Wepukhulu (m) *[weh-puh-kuh-luh]* A name given to a child who has survived though several of his siblings died [*Luyia*].

Were (m) *[weh-reh]* God; "the friendly one"; "father of grace" [*Gisu, Kikuyu, Luyia*] (Huntingford 1930: 103; Stewart 1993: 104).

Were (m) *[weh-reh]* "Sing for him/ her" [*Luo*].

Wetaya (f/m) *[weh-tah-yah]* A name given to one whose parents are drunkards [*Luyia*].

Weyusia (f/m) *[weh-yuh-sjah]* "The one who turns about": name given to one who often kicked and turned while in the womb [*Luyia*].

Wotuni (m) *[woh-tuh-nih]* The one that is fetched [*Maasai*].

-X-

Xifununu (f/m) *[ksih-fuh-nuh-nuh]* Dung beetle: derogatory-protective-pessimism related name such as given to a child whose previously born siblings died, and whereby this newborn is relegated to the level of an insect of a filthy environment [*Zulu*] (Herbert 1995: 4).

Xihlamaniso (f) *[ksih-lah-mah-nih-soh]* "Surprised": a name such as implying that the father was so surprised at the news that his wife had given birth to this girl [*Zulu*] (Herbert 1995: 4).

Xihoxo (f/m) *[ksih-hoh-ksoh]* "Mistake": a disharmony related name such as given by this newborn's mother and expresses her dissatisf-action over the demeanor of her husband whereby she believes she made a mistake in marrying the man that she consistently fights with and who is apparently of a beer-drink indulging family [*Zulu*] (Herbert 1995: 6).

Xihundla (f/m) *[ksih-huhn-dlah]* "Secret": a disharmony related name such as given by this newborn's mother and expresses her dissatisf-action over her treatment in the homestead and her mother-in-law's demeanor towards her [*Zulu*] (Herbert 1995: 6).

Xolani (f/m) *[ksoh-lah-nih]* "Sorry" [*Zulu*] (Suzman 1994: 268).

-Y-

Yamwaka (m) *[yah-mwaah-kah]* A name given to a child born of an unduly long pregnancy period [*Pare*] (Omari 1970: 71).

Yanga (f/m) *[yahn-gah]* "The long dry season": a name given to a twin, the other named *Mobanda* [*Gombe*] (Daeleman 1977: 190).

Yendelela (f) *[yehn-deh-leh-lah]* "It keeps going": this name is comm-only associated with the proverb "'It keeps going' does not remain fat on the hoof" which can imply that "a rolling stone gathers no moss" and "out of sight, out of mind," and that one who frequently travels away from home forfeits building on his reputation and influence, and instead is often among strangers who have little regard for him--this name appears to relate to a child whose father is a seasonally migra-ting worker [*Ovimbundu*] (Ennis 1945: 3).

Yigga (m) *[yihg-gah]* "Hunt"; to hunt; this name is sometimes ass-ociated with the proverb "the beautiful are like the dog with big, beau-tiful, and startling eyes: it will turn out to either be a thieving dog or a good hunter" which depicts that there is a general tendency to believe that those of exceptional esthetic appearance will exploit the advantage to effect good or evil in either extreme [*Ganda*].

Yuaya (m) *[ywah-yah]* "Pull me" [*Luo*].

Yugi (m) *[yuh-gih]* Rubbish [*Luo*].

Yuku (f/m) *[yuh-kuh]* "Kite": a name such as given to one whose father wandered away from his wife and into the countryside like a kite or an eagle i.e. to look for other women [*Lugbara*] (Middleton 1961: 36).

-Z-

Zakhelani (m) *[uh-zah-keh-lah-nih]* "Who will build for them (i.e. the children)?": a name such as given by the named child's mother's parents who in angry response to her bearing this child out of wedlock, given the absence of a providing father for the children asked, "Who will build their house?" [*Zulu*] (Suzman 1994: 261).

Zamakunda (f/m) *[zah-mah-kuhn-dah]* That are of love; that are associated with love [*Hutu, Kiga, Nyankore, Nyoro, Toro, Tutsi, Twa*].

Zamayedwa (m) *[zah-mah-yeh-dwah]* "Try all on his own" [The *Zulu*] (Koopman 1979: 79).

Zamekile (f) *[zah-meh-kih-leh]* "She has been tried for" [The *Zulu*] (Koopman 1979: 162).

Zandile (f) *[zahn-dih-leh]* "They have increased" [*Zulu*] (Koopman 1979: 162).

Zanele (f) *[zah-neh-leh]* "They are enough" [*Zulu*] (Koopman 1979: 162).

Zayoru (f/m) *[zah-yoh-ruh]* "No meat": name such as given to one born at a time the parents were too poor to even afford meat [*Lugbara*] (Middleton 1961: 35).

Zibhebhu (m) *[zih-beh-buh]* "The thick set and broad shouldered one" [*Zulu*] (Lugg 1968: 13).

Zikhali (m) *[zih-kah-lih]* Weapons; weapon [*Zulu*] (Koopman 1990: 335; Koopman 1979: 154).

Ziningi (f/m) *[zih-nihn-gih]* "They (i.e. the girls) are many" [The *Zulu*] (Koopman 1979: 163).

Zinkawini (m) *[zihn-kah-wih-nih]* "Amongst the monkeys" [The *Zulu*] (Koopman 1979: 71).

Zinti (f/m) *[zihn-tih]* "Thin sticks": a name such as given to a child of small size [*Zulu*] (Suzman 1994: 269).

Ziqubu (m) *[zih-kwuh-buh]* Speed; haste [*Zulu*] (Koopman 1990: 335).

Zodwa (f) *[zoh-dwah]* A pet name and abbreviation of *Ntombizodwa*: "Only girls" [*Zulu*] (Koopman 1979: 162).

Zola (f/m) *[zoh-lah]* "Love" [*Kongo*] (Ndoma 1977: 96).

Zondinhliziyo (m) *[zohn-dihn-lih-zih-yoh]* "Hate the heart": name such as given to a child born at a time of discord in the family [The *Zulu*] (Koopman 1979: 68).

Zonke (f) *[zohn-keh]* A pet name and abbreviation of *Ntombizonke*:

"All girls" [*Zulu*] (Koopman 1979: 162).

Zorodzai (f/m) *[zoh-roh-dz-ahy]* "Cleanse me" [*Shona*] (Jackson 1957: 121).

Zvakona (f/m) *[zvah-koh-nah]* "They (i.e. your attempts to bewitch me) have failed": name given to one born during a family dispute with kin or neighbors, whereby there is suspicion that the antagonists have engaged in malicious acts of witchcraft against the parent, but these acts have not met with success [*Shona*] (Jackson 1957: 117).

Zvandakaitirwa (f) *[zvahn-dah-kahy-tih-rwah]* "That which has been done unto me"; "that which God has done for me" [*Shona*] (Jackson 1957: 122).

Zwelabantu (m) *[zweh-lah-bahn-tuh]* "Country of the people/ or blacks" [*Zulu*] (Koopman 1979: 157).

Zwelabelungu (m) *[zweh-lah-beh-luhn-guh]* "Country of the whites" [*Zulu*] (Koopman 1979: 156).

Zwirimumoyo (m) *[zwih-rih-muh-moh-yoh]* "It is in the heart": a name such as given to a child born to a mother nursing a grievance [The *Zezuru*] (Marapara 1954: 8).

REFERENCES

Asante, Molefi K. *The Book of African Names*. Trenton, NJ: Africa World, 1991.

Ashton, Hugh. *The Basuto*. New York, NY: Oxford, 1952.

Beattie, John H.M. "Nyoro Personal Names." *Uganda Journal* 21, no. 1 (1957): 99-106.

Beidelman, J.H.M. "Kaguru Names and Naming." *Journal of Anthropological Research* 30, no. 4 (1974): 281-293.

Butt, Audrey. *The Nilotes of the Sudan and Uganda*. London, England: International African Institute, 1952.

Cagnolo, R.J. *The Akikuyu*. Nyeri, Kenya: Catholic Mission Printing School, 1933.

Chuks-Orji, O. *Names from Africa*. Chicago, IL: Johnson, 1972.

Churchill, Winston S.L. *My African Journey*. London, England: Hodder and Stoughton, 1908.

Cohen, David W. *Towards a Reconstructed Past: Historical Texts from Busoga, Uganda*. London, England: Oxford, 1986.

_____. *The Historical Tradition of Busoga: Mukama and Kintu*. London, England: Oxford, 1972.

Crane, L. *African Names: People and Places*. Urbana, IL: University of Illinois, 1982.

Daeleman, Jan. "Proper Names used with 'Twins' and Children succeeding them in Sub-Saharan Languages." *Onoma* 21, (1977): 189-195.

Davis, M.B. *A Lunyoro-Lunyankole-English and English-Lunyoro-Lunyankole Dictionary*. London, England: Macmillan, 1952.

Diagram Group. *Peoples of Africa: Peoples of Central Africa*. New York, NY: Facts on File, 1997.

_____. *Peoples of Africa: Peoples of East Africa*. New York, NY: Facts on File, 1997.

_____. *Peoples of Africa: Peoples of Southern Africa*. New York, NY: Facts on File, 1997.

Edel, May M. *The Chiga of Western Uganda*. New York, NY: Oxford, 1957.

Ennis, Elisabeth L. "Women's Names among the Ovimbundu of Angola." *African Studies* 4, no. 1 (March 1945): 1-8.

Fallers, Lloyd A. *Law Without Precedent: Legal Ideas in Action in the Courts of Colonial Busoga*. Chicago, IL: University of Chicago, 1969.

Gulliver, P. and P.H. Gulliver. *The Central Nilo-Hamites*. London, England: International African Institute, 1953.

Gulliver, P.H. "Bell-oxen and Ox-names among the Jie." *Uganda Journal* 16, no. 1 (1952): 72-75.

Hemans, T.J. "A Note on Amandebele Names." *NADA* 9, no. 5 (1968): 74.

Herbert, R.K. "The Sociolinguistics of Personal Names: Two South African Case Studies." *South African Journal of African Languages* 15, no. 1 (1995): 1-8.

Hollis, A.C. *The Nandi: their Language and Folk-lore.* Oxford, England: Clarendon, 1969.

Huntingford, G.W.B. "Further Notes on some names for God." *Man* 30, no.79 (June 1930): 102-103.

Isabirye, Stephen B. *The Dynamics of Social Conflict in Uganda.* Flagstaff, AZ: Northern Arizona-University, 1990 (Thesis).

Jackson, S.K. "The Names of the Vashona." *NADA* 34 (1957): 116-122.

Kagwa, Apolo. *Ekitabo kye Mpisa za Baganda.* London, England: Macmillan, 1952.

_____. *The Customs of the Baganda.* New York: Columbia, 1934.

Kasirye, Joseph S. *Abateregga ku Nnamulondo ya Buganda.* London, England: Macmillan, 1959.

Kimambo, Isaria N. *A Political History of the Pare of Tanzania.* Nairobi, Kenya: EAPH. 1969.

Kimenyi, A. *Kinyarwanda and Kirundi Names: a Semiolinguistic Analysis of Bantu Onomastics.* Lewiston, NY: Edwin Mellen, 1989.

Kiwanuka, M.S.M.S. *A History of Buganda.* New York, NY: African Publishing, 1972.

Knappert, Jan. *East Africa: Kenya, Uganda & Tanzania.* New Delhi, India: Vikas, 1987.

Koopman, Adrian. "Some Notes on the Morphology of Zulu Clan Names." *South African Journal of African Languages* 10, no. 4 (1990): 333-337.

_____. "Male and female names in Zulu." *African Studies* 38, no.2 (1979): 153-166.

_____. "The Linguistic Difference between Nouns and Names in Zulu." *African Studies* 38, no.1 (1979): 67-80.

Kruger, F. "Tlokwa Traditions." *Bantu Studies* 9, no. 2 (June 1937): 85-116.

Lubogo, Y.K. *A History of Busoga.* Kampala, Uganda: East Africa Literature Bureau, 1923.

Lugg, H.C. *Zulu Place Names in Natal.* Durban, South Africa: Daily News, 1968.

Malandra, A. *A New Acholi Grammar.* Kampala, Uganda: Eagle, 1955.

Mamdani, Mahmood. *Politics and Class Formation in Uganda.* New York, NY: Africa World, 1976.

Marapara, Malakia. "Wazezuru Names and their Meanings." *NADA* 31 (1954): 7-9.

McKinzie, H. and I. Tindimwebwa. *Names from East Africa.* Nairobi, Kenya: McKinzie, 1980.

Middleton, John. "The Social Significance of Lugbara Personal

Names." *Uganda Journal* 25 (1961): 34-42.

Mohome, Paulus M. "Naming in Sesotho: Its Sociocultural and Linguistic Basis." *Names* 20 (1972): 171-185.

Moloto, E.S. "The Subtleties of Naming." In *Names 1983*, ed. P.E. Raper. Pretoria, South Africa: HSRC, 1986.

Murphy, John D. *Luganda-English Dictionary.* Washington, DC: Consortium, 1972.

Musere, J. and S.C. Byakutaga. *African Names and Naming.* Los Angeles, CA: Ariko Publications, 1998.

Musere, Jonthan. *African Proverbs and Proverbial Names.* Los Angeles, CA: Ariko Publications, 1999.

_____. "Proverbial Names of the Baganda." *Names* 46, no. 1 (March 1998): 73-79.

_____. "Proverbial Names in Buganda." *Onoma* 33 (1997): 89-97.

_____. *African Sleeping Sickness: Political Ecology, Colonialism, and Control in Uganda.* Lewiston, NY: Edwin Mellen, 1990.

Ndoma, Ungina. "Kongo Personal Names Today: a Sketch." *Names* 25, no. 2 (June 1977): 88-96.

Nsimbi, Michael B. *Luganda Names, Clans, and Totems.* Pasadena, CA: Munger Africana, 1980.

_____. *Olulimi Oluganda.* London, England: Longmans, 1962.

_____. *Amannya Amaganda n'Ennono zaago.* Kampala, Uganda: East African Literature Bureau, 1956.

_____. "Baganda Traditional Personal Names." *Uganda Journal* 14, no. 2 (September 1950): 204-214.

_____. "African Surnames." *Makerere* 3, no. 2 (1949): 17-20.

_____. *Siwa Muto Lugero.* Kampala, Uganda: BCS, 1948.

Nzita, R. and Mbaga-Niwampa. *Peoples and Cultures of Uganda.* Kampala, Uganda: Fountain, 1995.

Okeke, Chika. *Kongo.* New York, NY: Rosen, 1997.

Omari, C.K. "Personal Names in Socio-cultural Context." *Kiswahili* 40, no. 2 (September 1970): 65-71.

Osei, G.K. *Your Lost African Name.* London, England: African Publication Society, 1975.

Roscoe, John. *The Baganda: A Study of their Native Customs and Beliefs.* London, England: Macmillan, 1911.

Sanyika, Bekitemba. *Know and Claim your African Name.* Dayton, OH: Rucker, 1975.

Southall, Aidan. "The Alur Legend of Sir Samuel Baker and the Mukama Kabarega." *Uganda Journal* 15, no.2 (September 1951): 187-192.

Ssaalongo, Y.S. and Y. Semugoma. *Ndi-Mugezi: Kitabo kya Ngero za*

Luganda. London, England: Macmillan, 1952.

Steinhart, E.I. *Conflict and Collaboration.* Princeton, NJ: Princeton, 1977.

Stewart, Julia. *African Names.* New York, NY: Citadel, 1993.

Suzman, Susan M. "Names as Pointers: Zulu Personal Naming Practices." *Language in Society* 23, no. 2 (1994): 253-272.

Taylor, Stephen. *Shaka's Children: A History of the Zulu People.* London, England: HarperCollins, 1994.

Thipa, H.M. "By their Names you shall know them." In *Names 1983*, ed. P.E. Raper. Pretoria, South Africa: HSRC, 1986.

Tosh, John. *Clan Leaders and Colonial Chiefs in Lango: the Political History of an East African Stateless Society c. 1800-1939.* Oxford, England: Clarendon, 1978.

Vansina, Jan. *Paths in the Rainforests.* Madison, WI: University of Wisconsin, 1990.

_____. *Kingdoms of the Savanna.* Madison, WI: University of Wisconsin, 1968.

Wako, Daniel M. *The Western Abaluyia and their Proverbs.* Nairobi, Kenya: Kenya Literature Bureau, 1985.

Walser, Ferdinand. *Luganda Proverbs.* Berlin, Germany: Reimer, 1982.